VERDUN

BOOKS BY JOHN MOSIER

Institutional Research

Men and Women Together

The Artist Under Socialism

The Myth of the Great War:
A New Military History of World War I

The Blitzkrieg Myth: How Hitler and the Allies
Misread the Strategic Realities of World War II

Cross of Iron: The Rise and Fall of the
German War Machine, 1918–1945

Grant: A Biography

Deathride: Hitler Versus Stalin—
The Eastern Front, 1941–1945

JOHN MOSIER

VERDUN

THE LOST HISTORY
OF THE MOST
IMPORTANT BATTLE
OF WORLD WAR I,
1914–1918

NAL
CALIBER

NAL Caliber
Published by the Penguin Group
Penguin Group (USA) LLC, 375 Hudson Street,
New York, New York 10014

USA | Canada | UK | Ireland | Australia | New Zealand | India | South Africa | China
penguin.com
A Penguin Random House Company

First published by NAL Caliber, an imprint of New American Library,
a division of Penguin Group (USA) LLC

First Printing, October 2013

LIBRARY OF CONGRESS CATALOGING-IN-PUBLICATION DATA:
Mosier, John, 1944–
Verdun: the lost history of the most important battle of
World War I, 1914–1918/John Mosier.
p. cm.
Includes bibliographical references and index.
ISBN 978-0-451-41462-5
1. Verdun, Battle of, Verdun, France, 1916. 2. Verdun (France)—
History, Military—20th century. I. Title.
D545.V3M68 2013
940.4'272—dc23   2013016460

Printed in the United States of America
1   3   5   7   9   10   8   6   4   2

Set in Sabon
Designed by Spring Hoteling

OCT 1 4 2013

History, it has been said, does not repeat itself.
The historians repeat one another.

—Sir Max Beerbohm

CONTENTS

CONTENTS

MAPS

VERDUN

1

Battles Known and Unknown

If I were to be tied down to one word for my
impression of this war, I should say this war is *Queer*.
It is not like anything in a really waking world, but
like something in a dream.

—H. G. Wells[1]

Verdun is one of the great battles of the modern era. It is also one
of the most complex, and probably the most misunderstood part of
a war only imperfectly grasped, even today.

To begin with, it is a serious mistake to think that there was
only one battle for Verdun, that battle being the 1916 struggle described so eloquently and misleadingly by Alistair Horne in his
classic study, *The Price of Glory*.

The original Michelin guides spoke, quite correctly, of multiple
battles, and recent French accounts have done the same. A. J. P.
Taylor once quipped that the difficulty about the Second World
War was trying to decide when it began, and when it comes to Verdun we have an analogous problem. The first battles took place in
August of 1914. The German stranglehold was not removed until
late September 1918. The difficulty arises when trying to compute
exactly how many battles there were.

Although for readers who grew up believing that Alistair Horne's account was the definitive tale, the notion of multiple Verduns is surprising, perhaps incredible, the idea of several battles for the same piece of ground, and with the same name, is hardly unique. There were two battles of the Bull Run in the Civil War. The Italians and the Austrians fought no fewer than twelve battles of the Isonzo between 1915 and 1917. Although the American reader would never know it, the 1916 Battle of the Somme was not the first battle of the Great War that was fought there. It was the second battle, and it was the first one that stimulated Jean Bernier to his memorable description.

> Joffre, comfortably installed, snored: "I gnaw at them," and threw or let throw on the barbed wire and the German machine guns the purest French blood.
>
> There followed the inexplicable offensives of the first winter, the first battle of the Somme in December 1914, of which one never breathes a word, during which, from Mametz and Carnoy to la Boisselle, the regiments rushed every day the enemy lines, without a cannon-shot fired.[2]

The admission that this battle was unknown even in France makes us aware of the real—as opposed to the mythic or propagandistic—war that was fought between the French and the Germans.

The presence of rotting logs deep in the forest primeval testifies that they do indeed crash to the earth even if no one's around to hear them. The fact that a battle is unknown, was passed over in silence, does not by any means justify the notion that it was not fought. Or, more precisely, that in some way it was an insignificant struggle, a mere skirmish. That few people outside of France have heard of the first Battle of the Somme, that the battles of the Isonzo usually run together in the reader's mind, does not mean they didn't happen, or that they are devoid of importance.

Indeed, as we shall see, the Allies had most excellent reason for glossing over these battles. In every case they failed to come any-where near achieving their stated objectives. The failure of subse-quent generations of historians to correct the record is less excusable, but understandable. The nearly impenetrable secrecy with which the French army cloaked all their operations, the ob-scurity of the places named (and of French geography in general), the genuine geographical ignorance of foreigners for whom France was as alien as Manchuria or Paraguay, all converged to create a perfect storm of delusional complacency.

THREE SIMPLE ERRORS

But before enumerating these unknown or misplaced battles for Verdun, there are three errors, areas of confusion, to be clarified.

The first is a simple error indeed. The battles fought there were not like the battle for Stalingrad or Berlin, or the 1870 siege of Paris or the 1863 siege of Vicksburg. As we shall see in chapter two, the actual city of that name had no strategic value whatso-ever. Verdun was simply a convenient shorthand for a series of rather awkward French military terms that shifted over time: the *camp retranchée de Verdun*, the *place fortifiée Verdun*, the *region fortifiée Verdun*.

The French terms are doubly inconvenient, as over the years they shifted from one to another. So for the sake of simplicity, when the word *Verdun* appears, it almost invariably means the area encompassed by the field of fire from the forts. In the few cases where there might be some confusion as to whether the city or the fortified region is meant, the text makes clear which is which.

However, it is a mistake to assume that Verdun was in some way analogous to Vicksburg in the American Civil War or Stalingrad in the Second World War. This observation may seem a truism, but the casual reader can easily come away with this impression, because early on, the 1916 battle was characterized as just such an attempt. As is the case with many of the misrepresentations and distortions of the Great War, the idea is accomplished subtly. One of the first and by no means the least authoritative French accounts of the struggle does just that, beginning with an account of the history of the town, by showing photographs and drawings of its buildings, leaving the reader with the impression that the German objective was the historic city with its ancient citadel, and American accounts often reinforce this idea.[3]

But Verdun was a very small town, the smallest of the frontier towns. A frontier town—in 1914 it was only forty kilometers from the German border—was the first town of any size a traveler would encounter going west from Germany to Paris. Its population of 12,780 was dwarfed by that of Nancy (83,648), of Reims (99,000), and of Lille (120,570); it was little more than half the size of Belfort.[4] There were very few people living there, no industry, and no town of even half the size of Verdun anywhere in the vicinity. The surrounding area was mostly forest. The town, ringed on three sides by commanding heights, had no military value whatsoever. An invading army could easily bypass it, crossing the Meuse river on either side.

But the suggestion, the inference, that the town was an important military objective allowed Allied propagandists to create a straw man, to claim that they had won an important victory because they had kept the Germans from getting into the town itself.

Such suggestions, skillfully planted, in turn led to another important area of confusion: a failure to grasp the sheer size of the battlefield. The forts were not physically connected, but rather were emplaced so as to provide (hopefully) overlapping fields of fire, both from their own guns and from heavy weapons in batteries located behind them. If we establish an imaginary line connecting the forts we get one measurement. If we construct an even more imaginary line connecting the limits of the fields of fire, we get a second. If we measure the forward positions held by the infantry, we get a third, and so on.

Compounding the difficulty is that the French military analysts and historians, many of them veterans of the war, tended to rely on rather elastic geographical concepts as they talked about the various battles. City dwellers do the same thing. They know that there is a legally defined entity called the city, which is contiguous to other legal entities, but that all taken together form the metropolitan area. The difficulty is that although New Yorkers and New Orleanians know all these distinctions, other people do not. So it is when the word *Verdun* is mentioned, a confusion that has led to a great many more as foreign historians have tried to write accounts of the fighting there.

However, no matter what measurement we use, the sheer breadth and depth of Verdun is impressive. Jules Poirier, a distinguished military historian who wrote the first account of the main battle, gives a figure at the start of the 1916 German offensive of 166 kilometers.[5] A simple comparison: in January 1916, that is, before the start of the February German offensive, the British section of the Western Front was 63 kilometers.[6] Verdun was larger than the entire British and Belgian sectors combined, larger than all the other sectors of the Western Front west of the Moselle river: Champagne, Artois, Picardy, the Somme.

The third error, then, stems both from an erroneous understanding of the objective and a failure to grasp the size of the battlefield. It is the error of supposing that operations at Verdun were all of a piece, that they can be treated like Gettysburg or Waterloo or even the Somme.

Given the river, and the size of the front, both the Germans and the French tended to treat operations on the two sides of the river as being entirely separate affairs. The Meuse river was not a trivial obstacle. The forces engaged on one side could not be diverted easily to the other (nor were they, in practice), and the outcome of an engagement on the right bank of the river did not automatically have some dramatic impact on what was happening on the left bank. There was certainly leverage, and once the fighting began in August 1914, both the French and the Germans tried to effect that pressure in various ways. However, in terms of actual operations, the forces on either side of the river largely conducted themselves independently of each other.

THE 1916 BATTLES

A brief and basic correction of some of these, the more obvious difficulties, paves the way for an enumeration of the various battles of Verdun, beginning with the most famous one, as it provides a perfect illustration of the various confusions and errors.

Now, the idea of numerous battles is not some recent notion, an attempt to make a novel claim. One of the names proposed for what the French high command decided—purely for propaganda purposes—to call the Battle of the Marne was the Battle of Paris-Verdun. Gabriel Bichet explains, and goes on to establish the linkage.

> In 1914, during the historic Battle of the Marne, French dispositions were articulated on two pivots, constituted, as foreseen by Séré de Rivière, by Paris and Verdun. . . . In 1915 the French seized the initiative with an operation on the wings, attempting to retake the observation buttes of the Vauquois and Les Éparges. In 1916 it was the German attack of 21 February. . . . In 1917 the French gained the initiative and rejected the enemy from the positions they held at the start on 1916. In 1918, the Allies maintained that initiative. The position of Verdun was the base for the final Franco-American offensive to the north and east.[7]

As we shall see, Bichet omits several important details, and skirts around others, but he establishes a very precise framework that allows us to understand the importance of Verdun, and, as well, to make sense out of much about the First World War that otherwise is simply a senseless slogging match.

Breaking any prolonged struggle down into separate installments, or battles, is often something of an arbitrary decision, and this is particularly the case given the enormous size of the Verdun battlefield. So, for example, the German attack of February and March 1916 was exclusively concerned with the right bank. But at the end of March, the Germans launched an entirely separate offensive against the left bank, and then, in May, a joint offensive against both—although the main effort was, once again, on the right bank. We might liken this to the classical one-two-three knockout sequence.

Now, given the sequence of these attacks, with one merging into the other without any real pause, it is perfectly reasonable to lump them together as one continuous battle that began in February and wound down in early July.

That is exactly how the Germans themselves saw it. In July, the staff of their Fifth Army, charged with conducting the offensives on both banks, called off their offensive, went over entirely to the defense, and shifted their resources elsewhere. For the German army, the 1916 battle began in February and lasted until early July.

The French licked their wounds. Nearly three months passed before the fighting on any serious level was resumed. But in October 1916, the French launched their own attack, aimed at regaining the ground lost on the right bank. This offensive occurred in two installments, one in October and one in December, but the French army, reasonably enough, lumped them together. The French high command, the famous (or, in the view of many veterans of the war, infamous) Grand Quartier Général, or GQG, blandly merged the two together.

This sleight of hand was characteristic of how both the Allied high commands operated. The GQG wanted everyone to believe that the fighting had gone on continuously for nearly an entire year. Equally, they wanted the government to believe that they had forced the Germans all the way back to their January 1916 positions.

As we shall see, this kind of misrepresentation and sleight of hand was typical of the GQG, and before proceeding any further, it is useful to understand how skillfully the Allied high commands manipulated the news. They managed it so excellently that successive generations of historians have rarely been able (or willing) to divine what actually happened. Hardly any claim made can withstand a close investigation, and the realization that the two entirely separate battles for Verdun in 1916 were deliberately conflated—and that historians accepted the conflation—is simply the tip of the iceberg.

THE ART AND SCIENCE OF MISREPRESENTATION

But the conflation was skillfully done. The presumable warrant for this claim was that all through the war, offensives by one side were more often than not met by counterattacks. That was particularly the case when the Allies attacked the Germans, who, in the majority of cases, promptly launched local offensives, most of them meeting with success. But the amount of time that elapsed before the return stroke was measured in hours, not weeks.

So the notion that the 1916 fighting was all one battle that lasted for eleven months is a complete misrepresentation. Bichet, for instance, is unwilling to confront the issue head-on. Instead, he speaks of the 1916 struggle as lasting for nine months, a rather sly way of telling the truth without appearing to say directly that the official story is incorrect.

Welcome to the official histories of the Great War. As the man in charge of the French army's archives observed after the war was over,

> Here is how one will write history in fifty years, when, the witnesses having died, conscientious historians, anxious to go to good sources, will read the archives of the headquarters. Immediately shout at them: "Beware! Danger!" Let's put them on guard against this vast enterprise of attenuation of the truth that I myself saw accomplished, day by

day, right before my eyes. And if they do not keep this in mind, they will make us question the history entire.[8]

When the man who is keeping the official records tells you to be wary of depending on them, there is indeed a problem. And even the most cursory glance at how the Allied high commands massaged reality shows a fascinating pattern.

The one unquestioned success of the war for the French high command, the Grand Quartier Général, was its success in spinning events. A comparison of what actually happened with the official claim results in mixed feelings: anger at the outrageousness of the claim, tempered with a certain professional admiration for how brilliant the deception was.

Ingeniously, the French spoke of assaults on ridges or hilltops as though the only objective were to plant the flag on the highest point, as though their infantry were playing a football game in which it was only necessary to get the ball over the goal line. That in fact they never were able to stay on the crest, or that, militarily speaking, the highest point was irrelevant, was blandly ignored. When the French spoke of German attacks, they employed the same device in reverse. The chapters that follow will provide fascinating and horrifying examples of how this was done, and, as was the case above with the brief remarks of Jean Bernier, it is difficult to convey, in translation, the choking and bitter anger with which those who were there speak of the real war.

The skeptical reader is entitled to ask how is it that we can be so sure that all this was done. Generally speaking, the evidence is archaeological. When, for example, one hikes up the Hartmannswillerkopf in the Vosges, and stands on the plateau, the ludicrousness of the GQG's claim that the army had gained a great victory by getting to the crest is painfully apparent. All that can be seen is a sort of misshapen battleship in concrete, a forest of German blockhouses and pillboxes, all of them still intact—as they were during the war.

The clusters of dates on grave markers in cemeteries, the existence of monuments, the remnants of entrenchments still visible in the dense woods, the perspectives to be seen from certain elevations, all provide a valuable corrective to the bland assertions of the high commands.

And in the case of the French, there are numerous accounts by privileged witnesses, as well as intensive and highly critical analyses by men who were experts as well as veterans. Like the massive fortifications of all different sizes and shapes, everything is still there. Buried somewhere, but a matter of the record.

But the official stories have all been duly enshrined, and have the considerable virtue of simplifying complex and unpleasant events into satisfying tales. In the course of this book, the reader will find numerous examples, each one of which is explained in detail, but here is an excellent summary of the whole scheme of misrepresentation.

> The reports passed on to the ministers were, as we all realized much later, grossly misleading. Victories were much overstated. Virtual defeats were represented as victories, however limited their scope. Our casualties were understated. Enemy losses became pyramidal. That was the way the military authorities presented the situation to Ministers—that was their active propaganda in the Press. All disconcerting and discouraging facts were suppressed in the reports received from the front by the War Cabinet— every bright feather of success was waved and flourished in our faces.[9]

The man who wrote those lines was neither a journalist nor a historian; nor was he writing a private note. He was David Lloyd George, the prime minister of Great Britain from November 1916 on, and the passage is taken from his memoirs.

The prime minister was not the only person in authority to be deceived in this fashion. Figuring out what really happened in this war, as opposed to what the army commands claimed had happened and succeeded in having transferred into the histories of the war, is an exceedingly difficult task.

In fact, this issue of misrepresentation surfaces almost immediately, even when we restrict ourselves to the famous battle of 1916. Not only was it actually two separate battles, but the results announced by the GQG were simply untrue.

One would assume that Lloyd George, as the British prime minister, and moreover one determined to assume control over his country's war effort, would know the truth. On the contrary, here is his appreciation of the results of the second battle, in which he summarizes what he was told: "In barely fifteen days the French Army completely wiped out the results of the grim and costly German attacks [at Verdun] which have gone on for eight months."[10]

This bland statement is a minefield of mistakes, starting with the glaring one that the German offensive began at the end of February and was shut down in early July. But let us not split hairs over the matter of a few months. The real problem is more fundamental. It is absolutely not true that by the end of December the French drove the Germans back to their starting positions, and the fact that the claim was duly picked up and inserted into the historical record does not make it so.

Aha! The skeptical reader (or devotee of Alistair Horne) is likely to exclaim: where's the proof they were lying?

As the quote from Bichet suggests, and as a later chapter will discuss in detail, we have all sorts of evidence, from cemeteries to maps, as well as an account of the battle by a French historian. Nor is it all that difficult to explain why this 1917 offensive was swept under the rug. Having loudly proclaimed that they had driven the Germans back to their starting lines at the end of December 1916, the GQG grasped the obvious point that they could hardly now claim to have launched a second offensive to retake exactly the same ground.

Of course, the fall of 1916's French offensive had been directed against the German positions on the right bank; so some sort of justification could have been made. But the army had excellent reasons for not wanting to call attention to Verdun in 1917. Anyone who bothered to look closely would realize that the French offensive of fall 1916 was not nearly as successful as the army claimed at the time. That, despite what was claimed, the Germans still had Verdun in a chokehold.

So, although it was arguably the first completely successful French offensive of the war, the fall of 1917 battle disappeared into the proverbial memory hole. The army, having made the claim that Lloyd George accepted as true, could not very well now reveal that, actually, they hadn't done what they had claimed. The British army command, assuming it even knew about the battle, had its own reasons for not bringing it up: the notion that the French were capable of successful offensive operations so soon after the famous mutiny of spring 1917 undercut their claim that they had been forced to shoulder the burden of the war almost entirely, owing to the collapse of the French.

The first question the researcher who begins to dig into the realities of the Western Front ponders is how it is that the army was able to hide what was happening so easily. There were three reasons why they managed to conceal the realities of the war as effectively as they did, befuddling their own government, their allies, the general population, and generations of foreign historians: a genuine geographical obscurity, absolute control over the flow of information, and wishful thinking.

THE CONFUSIONS OF GEOGRAPHY

Geographical obscurity is the simplest and also the most embarrassing, but foreigners have always had great difficulty in untangling the often bewildering names the French use to categorize their country, as the names are a mixture of the legal, the historic, and the local, so that some places have multiple names, just as a good many French towns have names that are pronounced one way by the locals, another way by their fellow countrymen, and still a third by educated foreigners.

During the war, the French high command was greatly aided by the obscurities of French geography, just as in the present day the French wine exporting industry is greatly hampered by it. Few American wine lovers know that chablis, Pouilly-Fuissée, and Mâcon-Lugny are all wines from a place called Burgundy, and that by definition they're all made from chardonnay grapes. The first three places named are legal entities, but Burgundy is a historic name derived from the Middle Ages, when it was a separate state—called Bourguignon.

One supposes that all French wine drinkers know this, or anyway claim to know it if asked, but the truth is that French geography is confusing.

Although French army spokesmen were certainly not lying when they spoke of fighting in Lorraine or the Argonne or Champagne, such identifications were hardly helpful. By 1914 France was divided into *départements*, the legal administrative unit. So none of those three historic names actually existed, in the formal, or legal, sense. Lorraine, like Bourguignon, was a separate statelet, one moreover that had only been incorporated into France rather late, by Louis XIV. The Argonne, like Champagne, or the Riviera (which in French would be the Côte d'Azur), were simply traditional place names, had never existed at all—except as constructs in the minds of the people who lived there.

So if the various names had different origins, different significations, what they all had in common was that none of them could be found on any map of France done since the French Revolution of 1789.

There was no *département* named Lorraine, for instance, which was divided among no less than four separate administrative entities. The historic boundaries were vague, and required wading through a mass of ancient maps to uncover.

Other geographical terms were so elastic as to be meaningless. Most of the left bank of the Meuse above Saint-Mihiel was called the Argonne, which was simply the southern extension of the Ardennes, a great forest that covered (and still covers) Belgium east of the Meuse, together with much of Luxembourg.

Confusingly, however, the northernmost part of the Argonne forest in France is actually known as the Ardennes, which also happens to be the name of the *département*. The result, befuddling even to the natives, is bewildering to foreigners. The fact that one of Great Britain's leading military historians has a major French river flowing west to east when the greater part of it flows south to north—and that another, almost equally respected one, seems to believe that an observer could see what was happening on the reverse slope of a ridge that was actually higher than his vantage point—suggests the nature of the problem.[11]

The battles of Verdun were all technically fought in Lorraine, a part of France that was hardly ever visited by Frenchmen, and, except for its historic capital of Nancy, virtually unknown. Lorraine was thus a relatively recent acquisition, and a good many of its inhabitants—perhaps as many as four out of five—didn't even speak French.[12]

In 1879, the celebrated popular novelist Jules Verne wrote a multivolume series of books recounting the voyages of discovery of the great explorers. In speaking of the French ornithologist Le Vaillant, he makes the interesting observation that although he was born in Dutch Guinea, his parents were French, and he "visited Europe with them as a mere child, and traversed Holland, Germany, Lorraine, and the Vosges, on his way to Paris."[13]

Lorraine was a distant and unfamiliar corner of the country: its chief cities of Metz and Nancy were over three hundred kilometers from Paris. By contrast, the German lines in Champagne and Artois were close to the French capital: Soissons was barely a third of that distance from the capital.

Moreover, there was nothing much there. Of the two historic areas that together comprised most of Lorraine, one was nothing but forest (a part of the Argonne forest, on the left bank), and the other was a vast plain, whose name (the Woëvre) was derived from a word that basically means "wet." And indeed a good bit of it was. Aside from a string of small towns on the Meuse, there were no settlements of any real size, no reason for anyone to go there.

Although the numerous small towns are as old and established as any in France (Provence excepted), Lorraine lacks the great cathedrals and monasteries that are the infallible signs of historic significance. Indeed, there is no tourism there even to this day, and the French themselves are poorly informed about the area.[14]

Now the French army, always precise and legalistic, was quite aware of these historic designations. They called the part of the front on the left bank immediately adjacent to Verdun the Argonne, the parallel area on the right bank the Woëvre. The same precision extended all along the 80 percent of the Western Front under French army control, with army group commands being assigned to each section, the entire front being legally designated as the Zone of the Armies, and controlled by the military.

By referring to each theater of operations by its historic and also rather vague name, the army obscured matters wonderfully. So to the historian dependent on documents, even French documents, these sections of the front immediately adjacent to Verdun are as separate, as far away, as Champagne or Artois—or the Somme.

But here's the error, or the difficulty: these places are all intimately related.

From tip of the butte of the Vauquois in the Argonne, the great tower of the ossuary of Douaumont—the central point of the battle for the right bank—can easily be seen with the naked eye. In point of fact it is only 26 kilometers from the Vauquois to the fort of Douaumont, and only 13 kilometers from the butte to the westernmost fortification of the RFV, the ancient Poste à Bruyères.

Now, very few students of military history have heard of the Vauquois, but as chapter four explains, the German possession of it in 1914 cut off the main east–west rail line into Verdun, and the French were never able to wrest control of it until the Americans smashed through the German lines in September 1918.

American readers may well be familiar with the butte of Montfaucon, as there is a great American monument there. The largest American military cemetery in Europe, Romagne-sur-Montfaucon, is 5,250 meters to the north, and the butte itself is the next hill to the north of the Vauquois, only 8,700 meters to the northeast of the butte.[15]

But as the names of a good many villages testify, this section of the left bank below Verdun is still, historically, part of the Argonne. In fact, the region known as the Argonne simply wraps around the left-bank forts. But it does so literally: the Verdun positions on the left bank are basically in the Argonne.

To extend these remarks further: in spring 1916, when the Germans attacked the French positions on the left bank, they were technically fighting their way through the Argonne itself: The famous struggles for Côte 304 and the ridge of Mort Homme, were not in fact parts of Verdun, but were positions in the Argonne, about 5,200 meters north of the left-bank forts.

A similar situation prevailed on the right bank. From Point X, a famous observation site on the butte of Les Éparges, the Verdun forts of the southeastern quadrant could likewise be seen. Or they would be except that one of them has been destroyed and replaced by a waste site, and the other is a ruin deep in the forest, as are the smaller supplementary fortifications. But anyone who studies the guide on the stone pedestal at Point X can see quite easily that the fate of Les Éparges is intimately tied up with the fate of Verdun: Point X is only 12 kilometers from the *ouvrage de Déramé*, and only nine from the *ouvrage de Jaulny*. Ominously (for the French) the butte is actually to the southeast of those positions.

The area known as the Woëvre is analogous to the Argonne on the left bank: Both wrap around Verdun. As our quote from Gabriel Bichet makes clear, the fighting there was an integral part of the battles in which the Germans attempted to surround Verdun and pinch it off, and the French attempted to throw them back.

Now, these geographical designations are perfectly logical, and based on the historical names given both regions, but in using them, the army, whether deliberately or not, created a great deal of confusion. The Woëvre is a large area that stretches from the Meuse to the Moselle rivers and from Luxembourg far to the south. The Argonne, slightly smaller, was still enormous.

Nor does it help that both areas were divided among no less than five French administrative units, or *départements*. A communiqué that mentioned fighting in either one was thus about as helpful as a Civil War dispatch that spoke of fighting in the Mississippi River valley.

TRUE LIES

The American or English reader may well be surprised at the idea that four-fifths of the Western Front was controlled by the French, and that our knowledge of the war there is derived almost entirely from the small piece held by the British.[16] But that is indeed the case, as a correspondent for the *New York Times* remarked in 1915.

> France has been so silent about her army and her Generals, and so indifferent to the use of journalism in the war it is scarcely realized even in France that 450 of the 500 miles of fighting front are held by the French and only the remaining 50 by the British and Belgians.[17]

What the correspondent for the *Times* failed to mention was that the secrecy and the silence were part of a deliberate policy on the part of the army. To the genuine obscurity that prevailed with regard to this part of France must be added the deliberate and highly successful attempts of the army high command to throw a veil of secrecy over everything within the zone of the armies.

When the war began in August 1914, the French and British governments—or, more precisely, the military bureaucracies of those countries—were determined that there would be no repeat of the embarrassing revelations that had characterized their earlier conflicts. There would be no independent journalists or interested civilians poking around the battlefields and drawing their own conclusions.

There would be no Florence Nightingale to expose the complacent bungling of the British War Office. The dispatches alleging great French victories over the North German Confederation in September 1870 would not be contradicted by impartial observers.

Nor would there be independent journalists or even educated witnesses around to point out the contrast between what was actually happening and what the government claimed was happening. There would be no counterparts to Archibald Forbes or Alfred Vizetelly or Elizabeth Latimer, recording government lies and government ineptitude.

In the Franco-Prussian War, the government had distinguished itself by fabrications, as Elizabeth Latimer, who was there, reports.

> The very day of the Battle of Wörth . . . the Parisians were made the victims of an extraordinary deception. A great battle was reported, in which the Crown Prince had been made prisoner. . . . A dispatch was published, and universally accepted with confidence and enthusiasm, announcing that three German army corps had been overthrown at the Quarries of Jaumont. There are no quarries at Jaumont, there were no Prussians anywhere near the spot, and none had been defeated; but the Parisians were well satisfied.[18]

Alfred Vizetelly's more general summary was as true in 1914 as it had been in 1870, when this experienced journalist and translator was on the scene. The government foisted off all sorts of deceptions on its citizens.

> Most of our war-news, or, at least, the earliest intelligence of any important engagement, came to us in the fashion I have indicated, townsfolk constantly assembling outside the prefectures, subprefectures, and municipal buildings in order to read the day's news. At times it was entirely false, at others some slight success of the French arms was magnified into a victory, and a petty engagement became a pitched battle.[19]

The difference this time was the controls the government announced right at the start of the war, guaranteeing that no one would be in a position to contest their claims. Whatever else the army might or might not have learned from 1870, they had absolutely learned how to control the news.

The French regulations promulgated for journalists were severe. Their draconian nature is not sufficiently understood, so the relevant portions are worth quoting in detail. On Saturday, August 15, the fourteenth day of what was called the mobilization, the American correspondent Charles Inman Barnard, an enthusiastic Francophile, recorded in his diary what had been announced. "The official regulations for war correspondents are much more severe, however, than those enforced during the Japanese and Turkish wars," he writes.[20] "In the first place, only Frenchmen and correspondents of one of the belligerent nationalities, that is to say French, British, Russian, Belgian, or Serbian, are allowed to act as war correspondents. Frenchmen may represent foreign papers."

So until America entered the war, we were totally dependent on journalists from the Allied side. Then Barnard records the practical problems everyone faced: "All dispatches must be written in the French language and must be sent by the military post, and only after having been formally approved by the military censor" (79). There were certainly a few English journalists who spoke French, the military correspondent for the *Times* being an outstanding example. But very few Englishmen or Americans did, and writing a foreign language is a far different matter from speaking it well enough to get around.

But that was simply the tip of the censorship iceberg. "No dispatches can be sent by wire or by wireless telegraphy," Barnard notes. So the military censors could hold up troublesome news items indefinitely. There were not going to be any scoops by enterprising reporters.

Nor were they going to be allowed to poke around on their own. "No correspondent can circulate in the zone of operations unless accompanied by an officer especially designated for that purpose." The entire front—together with the areas immediately behind it—was off-limits, and this decree was rigidly enforced right up until the end of the war. When, at the war's end, one resourceful American journalist drove through the zone and into Germany, where he was able to get an interview with Paul von Hindenburg und Beinecke, the German chief of staff, he was reprimanded, and the interview—one of the more significant documents to come out of the war—wasn't published for ten years.[21]

Now comes the most draconian provision of the regulations: "All private as well as professional correspondence must pass through the hands of the censor. War correspondents of whatever nationality will, during their sojourn with the army, be subject to martial law, and if they infringe regulations by trying to communicate news not especially authorized by the official censors, will be dealt with by the laws of espionage in war time" (80).

Given that at this point in the war, the government was energetically rounding up "spies" and shooting them, this threat was hardly to be taken lightly. Nor was this all. Barnard ends his summary by writing, "These are merely a few among the many rigid prescriptions governing war correspondents" (80).

As a firm believer in the cause, Barnard adds optimistically that his French contacts "All expressed the opinion that that war correspondents would enjoy exceptional opportunities, enabling them to get mental snap-shots and to acquire valuable first-hand information for writing magazine articles and books," but they were forced to admit that "from a newspaper standpoint there would be insurmountable difficulties preventing them from getting their 'news to market.'" (80)

The former proved a fantasy, the latter an absolute reality. By late August 1914, the Allies controlled the front in the most absolute sense, choosing what to say and what not to say, and preventing correspondents from even talking to anyone who'd been there.

The Allied control was not simply negative. At the same time as they quashed any sort of independent reportage, the Allies published, through surrogates, an enormous flood of purportedly objective news and new analysis that spun the official government positions in convincing fashion. The British and the French governments realized, correctly, that educated men and women would view official government bulletins with a certain skepticism.

So they fostered, or created, a parallel campaign of disinformation, in which supposedly independent writers generated convincingly objective accounts that just happened to support the Allied position. The authors of one study of the subject characterize it as a deliberate attempt to "strive for the appearance of objectivity. . . . It was . . . essential to ensure a measure of credibility even for the incredible."[22]

This clever strategy began early on in the war, creating an almost impenetrable barrier to any accurate understanding of what was really happening. And, unlike the propaganda used by the Bolsheviks after they came to power, the Allied efforts were skillful exercises, often resting on actual facts. They were perfect illustrations of what the great British historian Thomas Babington Macaulay had encapsulated in a memorable quip: that it was possible to write a history in which all the details were true, but the history itself was a falsehood.

Colonel Charles Repington, the war correspondent for the *Times*, gives us a fine picture of the result.

> The ignorance of the people concerning the war, owing to the Censorship, is unbelievable. Lunching at the Hautboy [where] . . . the proprietor—a good-class intelligent looking man—told me that the Serbians were going to beat the Germans; that there was nothing in front of our Army in France; and that we were going to be in Constantinople in ten days time. These are the kind of beliefs into which the country has been chloroformed by the Censorship.[23]

The difficulty, of course, is that Colonel Repington, like Lloyd George and a host of other intelligent and highly privileged men, themselves had an inordinate amount of difficulty in figuring out what was true and what was part of the chloroform.

Pesky journalists were not the only people shut off from the zone. When the president of France wanted to visit his soldier constituents, he had to ask the army high command for permission. They laid on a carefully guided tour, buttressed by wonderfully optimistic reports of their progress. It was not until 1916 that carefully selected men of some reputation, such as Arthur Conan Doyle and Herbert George Wells, were given tours of the actual front.

BUREAUCRACY AND SELF-DECEPTION

Let us not, however, fall into the error of concluding that there was nothing but a cynical cover-up, that the army high command deliberately lied about the situation. Indeed, one of the keys to understanding the decisions made by the high commands is to realize the extent to which they had deceived themselves, or were being deceived.

The French historian and combat veteran (of Verdun) Jean Norton Cru provides a perfect example of how this process worked.

> The combatants bring away a multitude of facts that prove the ignorance of the general staff even til this day concerning the situation on the front. . . . On 10 January 1917. The 133rd division where I was a sergeant and chief of a section took a sector of Verdun between Bezonvaux and the Chambrettes farm, ground conquered 25 days earlier. My section found itself on the extreme left, in liaison with the neighboring division, but I was not able to occupy the position because the trench, that existed on the plan at Corps, had only been traced with a pick. Our predecessors had received an imperative command to finish the trench in the week succeeding the 15 December attack.[24]

Given the frozen ground, the lack of decent equipment, the incidence of frostbite, it is hardly surprising that the trench hadn't been dug—or that it wouldn't be for some time.

In fact, as Norton Cru records, as a result, for three months there was a two-hundred-meter gap in the French line, with absolutely nothing there for a defensive position. As he was well aware from his research, this example is a telling one. Over the course of this book, we will see numerous examples of catastrophic failures caused by the ignorance of the various levels of command as to what was actually taking place at the front.

Norton Cru uses this example to support a larger point, the same one made by Jean de Pierrefeu, the army's archivist. We should be extremely wary of official documents. True, they were based on reports from the front, but as they passed upward, they were subjected to four or five "redactions," in which the basic observations were transformed to suit the views of those in command.

Raymond Poincaré, president of France, puts it rather elegantly. Speaking of how the war was going in the Argonne, he enunciates a syllogism: "At headquarters they say that everything is fine, we're having great success. At army group headquarters, they say, yes, there's progress, but it's slow. Down at the corps level, where they're actually fighting the Germans, the commanding general tells me 'we're losing a hundred meters a month; the Germans are devouring us, the letters from the soldiers are deeply discouraged.'"[25]

As these two examples make clear, decisions were being made based on an alternative reality where losing was transformed into winning, and lines traced by picks became defended trenches. Notice as well that we have now moved from what the army would like the general public to believe was happening to what they believed was happening: self-deception with a vengeance.

In fact, there was a synergism at work here. The army high command, fed by reports that became progressively more optimistic as they made their way up from the front, fortified by wonderfully precise and detailed intelligence reports—whose only fault was that they were completely wrong—really believed that they could win the war with only one more additional increment. One more offense, one more ally, one more division, one more month, would see victory.

This idea, deeply held by the army commands, created another sort of self-perpetuating cycle. Early on in the war, by December 1914 in fact, the hapless civilians in both governments, resigned to what they perceived as a stalemate in the west, began arguing for an expansion of the war effort to other theaters. The Anglo-French landing on the Turkish coast is for most American readers the most notorious, and it certainly encapsulates the futility of much of what the Allies did. However, it is not an isolated example. In terms of diversion of resources, the French adventure in Greece is probably more significant.

The point here, however, is that as the two governments pried resources away from their respective army high commands, sending them off to the Balkans, to Africa, and finally to Italy, they unwittingly provided both the British and the French military leadership with the perfect alibi, allowing them to adopt a classic passive-aggressive behavior.

At the same time, the army chiefs, knowing their horrible losses, may be forgiven for clinging to slender reeds, or for even going completely into absolute denial. Colonel Repington provides a perfect example of how the denial worked. On August 4, 1916, he met with General William Robertson, who had been going over the casualty reports. The general told him that

> We had had about 150,000 casualties in France, which were certainly very heavy, but that 60,000 of these had happened on the first day [of the Battle of the Somme], and that we now had not lost lately more than 20,000 a week. . . . The enemy had suffered 750,000 casualties in the course of the past two months on all fronts. We went into these figures, which included the 382,000 mainly Austrian prisoners. . . . (1.298)

Given that the first day on the Somme saw more British soldiers killed than in all the country's previous wars put together, Robertson can be forgiven for taking refuge in the idea that German losses were much worse. As a caring, compassionate human being, that is; as a member of the high command, however, he should have been able to see what the numbers were saying, as Colonel Repington was gently trying to remind him.

When he spoke of the "last two months," Robertson could only be referring to June and either May or July. Given the date of August 4, it is difficult to believe he already had the German data for July, but even if he did, since his figures were, as he admitted, for "all fronts," and hence included German losses at Verdun during the heaviest period of the 1916 fighting, as well as on the eastern front and in the Balkans, simple arithmetic suggested the distinct possibility that German losses were equal to or lower than British losses, and that in the worst possible case, he had no German data for the Somme at all.

Moreover, although British writers sometimes fail to make this clear, the Somme was a joint offensive. By early August the French were winding down their part of it, General Émile Fayolle, one of the few competent French commanders, having come to the conclusion that a further continuation would be futile. Now Robertson surely had to know that this was a joint offensive. Even if he had not been given any French casualty figures for their part of the Somme, the reasonable assumption would have been that their losses were about the same as the British losses.

So: 150,000 times 2 is 300,000; and 750,000 minus 382,000 is 368,000, a simple conclusion that is far from reassuring—especially since we're comparing German losses on all fronts with Allied losses on one section of the front.

Put that way, the error seems blindingly obvious. But in order to understand how the Allies fought the war, they must be allowed exactly this error, because they made it over and over again. At the peak of the 1916 battle for Verdun, André Maginot did an even more basic arithmetic for his colleagues in the Chamber of Deputies: the total of German losses on all fronts was either the same as or less than French losses on the Western front.[26] His announcement caused an uproar, as well it might.

THE UNKNOWN BATTLES FOR VERDUN

Now that the extent to which information about the war was manipulated, distorted, or simply suppressed entirely is known, it is easy to see why minor embarrassments like the 1917 battle for Verdun were simply omitted from the record.

But that is only the beginning. There was a whole series of battles for Verdun, all of them completely hidden from view. The 1916 German offensive was the exception, but, as we shall see, that was through no fault of the French high command: They did everything possible to manipulate the situation—everything possible except defeating their opponents.

Now comes the more complicated part of our enumeration. During the war, it was widely remarked that the preferred German tactic was envelopment. This was hardly news: the German army had incorporated the idea of the flank attack, the *aufrollen*, into its doctrines back in 1888.[27] That is to say that whenever possible, they tried to work around the front of their opponents, delivering their main thrust either to one flank, or, ideally, to both flanks (a double envelopment). If perfectly executed, the enemy would find himself completely surrounded, could then be destroyed at a relatively low cost to the attackers. In theory, an enemy so surrounded might simply quit.

As the eminent British military theorist and historian Basil Liddell Hart points out, this was, on a grand scale, what the Germans attempted in August 1914.[28] More precisely, they attempted two double envelopments, one around Verdun, the other aiming to surround the bulk of the French forces farther to the west.

The idea of envelopment, like its close relation the flank attack, was hardly a novel idea. Hannibal had done it to the Romans, Napoleon had done it to the Mamluks in Egypt, and if the recent study of Gettysburg is correct, Lee was attempting it against Meade. This latter example suggests the difficulty: even a single envelopment or flank attack is difficult to execute successfully, much less the classical double envelopment attributed to Hannibal.

As we shall see in chapter three, Verdun was not the sort of position that an army would wish to attack head-on if it could be helped (the question of why the Germans did just that in 1916 is another complicated affair that is explained in chapter seven). So it is hardly surprising that the Germans first tried this alternative rather than attacking the forts directly.

In August–September 1914, they did exactly that: Two separate German armies tried to envelop Verdun, pinch it off at the base. They came extremely close, were probably only thwarted by the general retreat that was ordered on 12 September 1914.

But the Germans retreated to positions on the left bank that still left them in place to stop the flow of supplies into Verdun, as they could interdict the main rail line into what was now a slight bulge or salient projecting into the German lines.

So, not surprisingly, on 23 September 1914, they launched a major offensive on the right bank, and succeeded in cutting off the main supply lines from the south. At that point, defending Verdun became an extremely difficult proposition. So properly speaking, there were two battles for Verdun in the first months of the war. Those battles, Verdun 1 (September 6–12) and Verdun 2 (September 23–October 4), are described in chapter four.

The French understood their peril, and launched two separate offensives, one on each bank. The right-bank offensive lasted roughly from January 1915 to early April, when it was finally called off. The left-bank offensive consisted of a series of intermittent offensives, the first being in midwinter (1914–1915). The two offensives were supposed to be coordinated, and there was supposed to be a final offensive in the summer of 1915, but the Germans attacked first, aborting what was to have been a major French effort.

So, to sort through a complicated and confusing situation, we can therefore speak of Verdun 1 (the coordinated German offensives of August 1914), Verdun 2 (the right-bank German offensive of September 1914), Verdun 3 (the French left-bank offensives of 1914–1915), and Verdun 4 (the French right-bank offensives of spring 1915).

So the most famous Verdun battle, February–July 1916, is actually Verdun 5. The French right-bank offensive on the right bank in fall 1916 is Verdun 6, and the fall 1917 left-bank offensive is Verdun 7. The two Franco-American offensives in August and September 1918 are thus Verdun 8 and Verdun 9.

Verdun 5 is the most famous. Except for the last two—whose purpose is generally misunderstood—the others hardly appear in the standard English histories of the war, and get short shrift even in France. So there's an understandable tendency to assume they were little more than minor skirmishes, footnotes in a war that pale to insignificance beside Flanders and the Somme and Champagne.

A MATTER OF SCALE

To the American reader nurtured on those battles, the scale of the Verdun fighting is startling. So too for the French reader whose knowledge is derived from one of the standard histories the war. As the English-language reader may not be aware of the more well-known battles the French army fought during 1915, here is a brief list of them taken from an authoritative and really excellent history.

During 1915 there were four *grandes offensives*.[29] The first, Champagne I, which began on 15 March, involved the Third Army Corps (two divisions and supporting elements). That offensive was followed on 25 September by a second attempt, involving the Fourth and the Tenth Army Corps—four divisions. There were two offensives in Artois, the section of the front to the northeast of Champagne. Artois I began on 9 March, and was carried out by the Sixth Army Corps. Artois II was coordinated with Champagne II, and relied on the Third and the Sixth Army Corps.

In theory, a French army corps had a strength of 45,000 men: two divisions of 16,000, with the rest being made of cavalry and artillery personnel. As the war progressed, the sizes of the units shrank, and gradually enumerations were of divisions and even brigades. But as a rough rule of thumb then, for the French and the Germans, initially a division was about 20,000 men, and a brigade about half that.

Very early on in the war, the whole issue of counting heads became extremely complex. The counting, or rather the miscounting, by the Allies was one of the major intelligence failures of the war, the implications of which emerged in spring 1915. But a simple enumeration of the sizes of the forces engaged in the battles for Verdun is illuminating.

In Verdun 1, the French deployed no less than five separate army corps and four independent divisions to counter a German threat comprised of four army corps and elements of the Fourth Army Group. The battle lasted for nearly a week on a front of nearly 50 kilometers—an area almost the size of the Champagne and Artois fronts taken together, and hardly insignificant by any standard of measurement.

For Verdun 4, known in France as the Battle of the Woëvre, the French unleashed six army corps, two independent divisions, and a brigade drawn from the Verdun garrison, all directed against the German positions on the right bank. Coincidentally, in numbers, the French force was basically the same as the German deployment at Verdun for the February 1916 attack.

As the numbers involved grew, so did the casualties. In absolute numbers, French losses in Verdun 4 were about the same as British losses on the Somme, with even less to show for it.

Not all the Verdun battles were to this same scale. In Verdun 2, the Germans only deployed two army corps and some detached heavy artillery units. But although this was a small offensive by Franco-German standards, it represented a considerably larger force than the British had in France at that point in 1914, as they had already suffered 56,056 casualties, were hard-pressed to put

35,000 men into action. By comparison, the German offensive of Verdun 2 was gargantuan.[30]

Verdun 2 was also one of the major victories of the war for the Germans. They caught the French still regrouping from Verdun 1, broke through all the way down the right flank of Verdun. In a war where the Allies measured their gains in one or two kilometers, if that, the Bavarians advanced over 20 on a broad front of roughly 25 kilometers. They crossed the Meuse at the town of Saint-Mihiel, physically cutting the only main rail and road link remaining into Verdun, and forced the main French fort below the city to capitulate.

As measured by the death toll, the fighting was intense. The French 75th Division was simply erased, to use the French word, to such a degree that the army didn't even attempt to reconstitute it— one of the few instances in the entire war.

The success of the German offensive on the right bank, and the complete failure of the French to reverse those gains, go a long way toward explaining why these engagements quickly disappeared into the memory hole.

Nor were the French ever able to reverse the totality of the German gains. Even by the end of 1917, the French offensives had still not relieved the pressure on Verdun. The Germans had lost territory, but they still had Verdun in a stranglehold.

So in August 1918, there was a joint Franco-American offensive on the right bank that pushed the Germans all the way back to where they had been in August 1914, followed by an offensive in September that did the same thing for the left bank, and freed Verdun completely, and thus the importance of the great American offensives of 1918, Verdun 8 and Verdun 9.

In one of the more interesting passages in his account of the war, Winston Churchill notes how many battles were fought by relatively small forces. It's an intriguing argument of the sort that specialists find fascinating, and one that makes the scale of these unknown battles all the more impressive.[31] Make no mistake: the French threw enormous numbers of men into these battles, and their losses were appalling.

Jean Bernier sums up these disasters perfectly. Significantly, the obscure places he names in this passage were all German strongpoints on the right and left banks.

> Then there came, in the mud, in the rain, in a veritable confiture of cadavers, The Argonne, les Éparges, le bois d'Ailly, le bois Le Prêtre, about which France knows only lies. Despite the stupefying percentage of losses, the generals never admitted the regularity of their checks (46–47).

As is the case with many of the most searing passages describing this war, the words are not simply overheated rhetoric, but point to what can only be described as a massacre.

In the attempts to relieve the German grip on the Verdun salient during the first half of 1915, an official but highly secret French government report admitted that the army sustained casualties of 215,000 men, or about a third of all French casualties for the period. By comparison, official British losses for the entire year were 296,583 (as contrasted with French figures of 1,256,000).

It is interesting to compare the actual historical record with the assertion that begins Alistair Horne's account of Verdun.

> Three and a half years elapsed between the First Battle of the Marne, when the Kaiser's armies reached the gates of Paris, and Ludendorff's last-gasp offensive that so nearly succeeded in the spring of 1918. During this time the Germans remained on the defensive. . . . Only once did the Germans deviate from this strategy that paid off so handsomely. In February 1916, they attacked in the Verdun sector. . . .[32]

Indeed, the smooth eloquence of this opening paragraph is exceeded only by its errors. Like much that has been written about this war—and particularly about Verdun—the level of inaccuracy, of ignorance, and of downright falsehood calls to mind the pithy remark usually attributed to the physicist Wolfgang Pauli: so wrong it's not even wrong.

As everyone knows, the motto of the French republics was "Liberty, Equality, and Fraternity." During the First World War, that noble slogan became something else entirely: Mistakes, Misrepresentations, and Myths.

2

How Political Geography Dictated Strategy

Verdun, c'est la boulevard moral de la France.

—Pétain[1]

When, in 1871, Otto von Bismarck prevailed on Helmuth von Moltke the Elder and Wilhelm I of Prussia to support his demand that the French cede Alsace and northern Lorraine, he set off a chain of unforeseen consequences that would determine the shape of the Western Front from August 1914 right through to the end of the war.

At first glance, considered from a strategic point of view, Bismarck's idea seems sound enough. The historic border between Alsace and Lorraine was formed by the crest of the Vosges mountains. Seize the relatively few passes that led through this surprisingly rugged mountain chain, and a French offensive would have the devil's own time getting into the flat and fertile Alsatian plain.

Germany proper—which is to say, the Germany of July 1870—would be forever out of reach. The old common border that stretched from the Rhine over to Luxembourg was gone. All that territory was now part of what the Germans called Elsaß-Lothringen—a sly reminder that the primary language of over 90 percent of the inhabitants was Elsassitch, a dialect of German, along with their architecture and their cuisine.

This notion may come as a surprise to anyone brought up on the ferocious propaganda of the First World War, with its impassioned plea to free the enslaved peoples of the area, so here are the census figures. In the last census done before the 1870 war, there were 1,097,000 people living in the Alsace, and 1,291,000 living in Lorraine, for a total of 2,388,000 people, of which 1,359,158 claimed German as their primary language. After 1918 census data was collected differently, but as late as 1936, of the 1,219,381 inhabitants of Bas-Rhin and Haut-Rhin (the two administrative parts of the Alsace), 1,149,251 still listed German as their primary language, and their Germanic roots are amply attested to by significant cultural indicators as well.[2] So Bismarck's idea had a certain basis for it.

The Vosges are a formidable obstacle, but at their northern and southern extremities, they become tamer, easier to cross. With an anxious eye to the extremities, Bismarck wanted northern Lorraine, as the rolling country there was not much of an obstacle to a French invasion.

The key to the north was the town of Metz, perched on a series of bluffs overlooking the Moselle river valley. Unlike the other towns of the two provinces—Haguenau, Verdun, Strasbourg, Pont à Mousson, Mulhouse—the heights of Metz made it a natural fortress.

Initially, Bismarck had wanted Belfort, at the other end of the Vosges, as well. There was a *trouée*, a natural break in the mountains, that separated the Vosges from its cousins the Alps. In theory this opening afforded an army easy passage northward to the Alsatian plain. But Bismarck compromised, probably because Belfort was too far to the south and east of Paris. Like Germany and Italy and Austria-Hungary, France only had so many men to make up an army. Deployment of a force of any size through the *trouée de Belfort* would fatally weaken the armies to the north.

Once the war began in August 1914, Germany's desire to conquer Europe became the obsession of Allied propagandists and their fellow travelers amongst Anglo-American intellectuals, second only to characterizations of the hapless German emperor as a mentally deranged warlord. Germanophobia began as a minor derangement, but quickly metastasized into a mental complex. "I hate Germany, which has thrust this experience upon mankind, as I hate some horrible, infectious disease," H. G. Wells announced, putting aside his pacifism and expansive humanism.[3] At least he was honest enough to tell everyone, didn't hide behind a mask of scholarly pretense. But the hatred is nevertheless painfully on display, and it rapidly became a sort of religion, whose basic assumptions were not to be questioned.

There was no limit to the perfidies of the ferocious Hun, and the absorption of Alsace and northern Lorraine became exhibit A in the indictment. It was but one tiny step from this cruel annexation to Hitler's dismemberment of Czechoslovakia.

However, Bismarck's aims, as revealed both by his private conversations and the accounts of Adolphe Thiers, the representative of the French government who did most of the negotiating with him in 1870–1871, were purely defensive, and we know from a confidential letter that he wrote to the British ambassador to France in November 1870 that William Ewart Gladstone, the British prime minister at the time, regarded the French position as "quite untenable in the case of a country which has made recent annexations."[4]

Bismarck regarded France as an aggressive and expansionist power whose eastward impulses he wanted to check. Thiers, who was a good and honest man, insisted that the new, republican France was no longer the France of the two Napoleons. Insofar as the future president of the Third Republic was concerned, this claim was absolutely true. However, the recent history of France made his claim a difficult one to swallow. Napoleon III had considered the acquisition of Belgium, had installed a foreign regime in Mexico, had ruthlessly pushed the ambitions of Cavour and his adherents toward the creation of modern Italy—and those are simply the high points of a wildly reckless career. Whether reckless adventurism or not, right up until the disasters of August and September 1870, Napoleon III had the enthusiastic support of his subjects.

It requires a great deal of mental gymnastics to suppress such details, but the propagandists of 1914 were certainly equal to the task. Suddenly France was a peaceful and harmless nation, while the perfidious Huns, now invested with all the ambitions any objective observer would have assigned to France prior to September 1870, were capable of any sort of wickedness. Why, Bismarck even tricked the French Chamber of Deputies into declaring war on the North German Confederation in a unanimous and enthusiastic vote! Clearly there were no limits either to German perfidy or ingenuity.

So it is well to recall the words of the great British historian A. J. P. Taylor about the European situation before the war: "Every statesman in Europe regarded France and Russia as the two dynamic, restless powers, who would turn the continent upside down."[5]

The point of bringing up these inconvenient details of Franco-German history is, however, not to vindicate Bismarck. The point is that in his anxieties to protect the newly created German empire from a French invasion, he posed successive generations of military thinkers severe difficulties—probably the main reason why von Moltke the Elder was dubious about the whole affair of annexations.

This decision, made for defensive reasons, became a classic example of Merton's Law of Unintended Consequences. In order to solve one problem, Bismarck created a whole set of others.

THE PROBLEM

Helmuth von Moltke the Elder was, after Frederick the Great, the greatest of German commanders. He had led Prussia to startling victories in three successive wars (against Denmark, Austria-Hungary, and France). He subscribed to the sensible idea that generals should exhibit a certain reticence, and not wander around expatiating on the weaknesses of their adversaries—or their civilian colleagues.

He was hardly the sort of fellow to engage in table talk. But it is easy to imagine his objections. The best way to fight an enemy was to fight them on their own ground, to go on the attack—precisely what he had done in all three wars—and what he understandably felt the Prussian army did best.

Indeed, given the extent to which historically Prussia had been surrounded by countries that in theory could put substantially larger armies into the field, even in a one-to-one fight, the best strategy was the one perfected by Frederick the Great: to attack your enemy in detail, defeating his forces one by one before he could combine them and overwhelm you. Moreover, the most likely threat in the future, as in Frederick's time, was a combination of enemies, an anti-German alliance.

Napoleon III had attempted to enlist all of Bismarck's neighbors in his projected war with Prussia. Once the war began, Thiers ran from capital to capital, trying to persuade the other powers to intervene on France's side. That the Italians, the Austrians, the Russians, and even the Bavarians stayed on the sidelines was through no fault of the emperor's before the war, or the future president's after it began.

The chief object of both French leaders was Russia, the other great European military power, and, not by coincidence one bordering Prussia's eastern frontier. Thiers was either blind, desperate, or extremely naive. Because Prince Gorchakov, the czar's chancellor, and the first man to exercise any real power in that position, had a long and amiable history with Bismarck, whom he knew intimately. The prince quite failed to see why he should bring about a sea change in Russian foreign policy to bail out France from a self-imposed disaster.

So long as he was chancellor, the Russians would waffle on the notion of an alliance with France, but the career of an imperial chancellor was precarious and uncertain. The alliance that Napoleon III had pursued might well happen now that he was gone.

And when von Moltke considered the new Franco-German frontier, he didn't much care for what he saw. Bismarck was absolutely correct: the Vosges is a surprisingly formidable mountain chain. There are passes through it, but few of them are amenable to the deployment of large armies.

The problem is that the mountain passes that run from Lorraine into Alsace also go from Alsace into Lorraine. In the event of a future war, the Germans would have precisely the same difficulty in attacking the French as would have existed the other way around.

The amateur strategist may sneer at the obviousness of this deduction, but, as von Moltke famously remarked, strategy is basically common sense—a quality notoriously lacking in theorists as well as sometimes in amateurs.[6] Indeed, as we shall see, one sadly visible strand that runs through the Anglo-French direction of the war is the triumph of abstruse theory over von Moltke's notion of common sense.

So Bismarck had saddled von Moltke and his successors with a pretty problem. The great battles of annihilation that had characterized 1870 had all been fought within spitting distance of the frontier. Wissembourg, where the first major battle had been fought, was in fact a frontier town. So was Sarreguemines. Wörth, Froeschwiller, Spicheren had all been won by German armies that were just across the frontier, and had short and uninterrupted lines of supply.

But the battles to the west of Metz—Saint Privat, Gravelotte, Mars-la-Tour—had been stiffer affairs, and the final engagements, fought to the south and northwest of Paris, had been even worse.

Von Moltke, no more than any other sensible commander, disliked the idea of fighting a major battle hundreds of kilometers from his home country. You might win at first, but finally, you'd end up in the same predicament as Hannibal—and that was if you won. If you lost, well, the lamentations of several Roman emperors were eloquent proof of the problematic nature of battles fought deep in enemy territory.

But in effect, Bismarck's new frontier had guaranteed that in the event of a future war with France, the only easy route for a German offensive would be along the roughly 50-kilometer frontier between Metz and Luxembourg. Geography therefore precluded both surprise and the double-envelopment offensive that von Moltke's students were dutifully made to learn.

Now, it's distinctly possible that Bismarck knew what he was doing, that he wanted peace, and thought this was the way to ensure it. This is, after all, the man who observed contemptuously that all the colonies were not worth the bones of a single Pomeranian musketeer, and that, "Anyone who has ever looked into the glazed eyes of a soldier dying on the battlefield will think hard before starting a war."[7]

But not even A. J. P. Taylor could rehabilitate Bismarck, given the Church of Germanophobia, which sees him as being simply a wicked and evil predecessor of Adolf Hitler. However, it's worth noting that Bismarck's peace lasted for forty years, and that it took the combined efforts of a whole phalanx of European statesmen—most of whom preened themselves on being vastly superior to the grouchy Prussian Junkers—to overturn it. Again, Taylor's sarcastic summary gets right to the point. "Most statesmen seek to show that they have acted from high-minded motives, but have failed to live up to them. They do not plan wars; they drift into war and think it an adequate excuse to plead that this was unintentional. . . . Bismarck's planned wars killed thousands; the just wars of the twentieth century have killed millions" (79).

Whatever von Moltke thought, in the 1870s the German army devoted most of its efforts to internal improvements and the construction of fortifications designed to keep the French out.

Metz, already in a commanding position overlooking the Moselle and the Woëvre, was girdled with forts. Another set of forts guarded the main passes through the Vosges that led to Strasbourg. In the Vosges itself, building an actual fort was unnecessary, but the Germans constructed some very formidable defensive positions in key places, most notably at the key positions of the Lingekopf and the Hartmannswillerkopf.

THE CHALLENGE

The idea of planning offensive operations is inherent in the mind of the professional staff officer, or anyway the German ones who were raised in the traditions of von Moltke the Elder, and the very difficulty of coming up with a workable solution made the idea only all the more attractive. Not that there's any reason to restrict this line of thought to the Germans. Their opposite numbers in France and Austria and Russia all had similar hobbies, and before we dismiss them as warmongering militarists, perhaps we should remember the hoary Roman adage that the best way to ensure peace is to prepare for war. That is what professional soldiers are supposed to be doing.

But professionals have genuine differences of opinion, and peacetime armies have the luxury of entertaining them without any real resolution. The French, with their usual knack for nomenclature, termed these divisions *chapels*. Not a bad way to get at the true nature of the divisions, as they were held with religious conviction.

As we shall see in our accounts of the war itself, the chapels in the French military were responsible for a great deal of mischief, not to mention the slaughter of a good many French soldiers.

The Germans were hardly immune to this disorder, the chief difference being that instead of half a dozen different groups, there were basically only two of any importance. One group, looking at what Bismarck had done, and what the French were likely to do (and capable of doing), decided that in the event of a two-front war—the most likely possibility—the best solution was to stand on the defensive in the west, and mount offensive operations in the east.

For want of a better word, we can call these people the Easterners, and those who felt the other way, the Westerners. As everyone knows, when the war began, the German army went on the offensive in the west, but the Easterners by and large still felt they were right, and when the war in the west degenerated into the stalemate of the trenches, they took that as confirmation of the rightness of their views. So the war, far from settling the debate, only exacerbated it.

As we shall see, this internal division had serious repercussions for Verdun. As with the French chapels, it sometimes appears that on both sides the adherents of the opposing ideas were more interested in proving they were correct than in defeating a common enemy. Of course, every war sees the emergence of differing views about the best way to win it (or how not to lose it), but it would appear that in this particular war the divisions ran much deeper, and had much more serious repercussions than in others.

Certainly more so than in previous conflicts, one of the more important reasons being that this was the first major conflict of any duration—and almost the first conflict, period—in which the functions of the general staff were being exercised by all the combatants. Although it is generally agreed that this phenomenon, which began with the Prussians, transformed the nature of warfare, organizationally speaking, what is often left unsaid is the extent to which it created what we might think of as a professorial military class.

That is, professional officers who, not being burdened with having actual command responsibilities, were free to speculate, to dictate—and to interfere. That freedom naturally encouraged them to think abstractly, was the natural concomitant not only of the rise of the staff as an institution, but an integral part of the increasing acceptance of a good education being the sine qua non for a successful officer. Educated men and women are always intrigued by theory.

Although, like the emergence of the chapels (the logical outgrowth of the emphasis on education and the rise of the general staff), theory would play an important role in shaping the way the war was fought; it also explains the basic, underlying attraction of an offensive in the west.

In a word, the notion had a much greater intellectual fascination, simply because it was so challenging. A plan of offensive operations in the east was simple to the point of being tiresome—for Russia and Austria-Hungary as well as Germany. The open spaces meant a war of maneuver, or, to be candid, a classic war in which you went out into the field and engaged your opponent in a great battle à la Borodino, Austerlitz, or Waterloo. It was a test of courage, of steadfastness, of discipline—of all the traditional military virtues.

THE WALL AND THE FORT

But a future war in the west was an entirely different matter. Before 1871, the projected, or anticipated, theater of operations in a Franco-German war was the relatively small area that stretched from Wissembourg (and the Rhine) over to Luxembourg, about 100 kilometers. Not only was there not much uncertainty as to where the enemy would attack, but a defending army would be able to move easily to counter any thrust. In consequence, the combatants knew where to move to engage their opponent. There were no negative consequences for being out of position. In August 1870, the French knew the Prussians were going to come across the border at Wissembourg and Sarreguemines and were ready to engage them.

The Bismarck border meant that in the event of war, both sides would be dealing with a landlocked border of over 300 kilometers. Possible areas of attack were spread out from one end to the other. Guess wrong about your opponent's intentions, and he'd be deep inside your country before you could relocate your forces and engage him in battle.

Historically, the solution to this problem had been to construct walls and forts, the exact mix depending on the geography. There once was an idea that gunpowder meant the end of masonry, that cannons meant castles were no longer relevant. Not so; time and time again the armies of the Thirty Years' War found themselves frustrated by ordinary city walls built many years earlier: La Rochelle, Stralsund, Magdeburg, Dunkirk—a very long list. Artillery simply changed the architecture; the concept remained the same.

In one way, however, there was a conceptual shift. Artillery meant that the wall, instead of being literal, as was the case with the Romans, the Chinese, and the Danes, could be what might be thought of as virtual: a barrier created by the field of fire directed by the guns mounted in forts. Properly sited, taking advantage of the terrain, forts could be used to prevent invasions, block potential avenues of attack. At the very least, they would delay the attacks, allowing the defense time to move its armies to the threatened areas.

Nowadays, in the age of airpower, this last point is overlooked, but right up through the end of the Second World War, properly built fortifications were almost completely invulnerable to aerial attacks. In May 1940 German bombers were unable to do any damage whatsoever to the French fort of Schoenenbourg in northeastern Alsace, and in fall 1944 the Franco-German fortifications at Metz proved equally resistant to Patton's attacking units.[8]

So the idea of blocking potential invasion routes with fortifications that would hold out long enough to allow the defenders to deploy their armies was a perfectly sound idea. Ideally, the defenses might be so formidable that the invasion route was abandoned entirely, thus channeling lines of advance into predictable areas. Given the length of the new border, this idea had a particular appeal to both sides.

Now this brief explanation may seem gratuitous, but over the years there has been a great deal of nonsense written about fortifications, the abysmally misunderstood Maginot Line being the prime exhibit in this regard. Historians have gone off on highly entertaining disquisitions about the Maginot Line mentality this revealed in France, about the uselessness of the whole project, about in fact almost everything under the sun except what actually happened.

The misunderstanding of the concept, the genuine ignorance of how it actually worked in the Second World War, thus leads to ideas about the previous war that take us even farther from reality. As a result, the reader is inclined to throw in the intellectual towel at the mere mention of fortifications and defensive lines. But as we shall see, when armed and garrisoned by determined men, even the oldest and most vulnerable forts were more than a match for their attackers.

Instead of reading the past from some refracted vision of the present, it is more profitable to consider the actual problem the French and the Germans faced, and how they attempted to deal with it. An understanding of the specific problem the French army faced after 1871 allows us to see the logic of the initial decisions they made, and then, as the decades passed, to see how they strayed from their own logic.

Their experiences in 1870 had given them—temporarily, as it

turned out—a certain healthy dose of realism. First and foremost was the enormous difficulty France faced in mobilizing its army and getting it into the presumed theater of war. The 1870 conflict brought this home with a vengeance, as it was in great measure Europe's first railroad war. The armies of Richelieu, Louis XIV, and Napoleon I had walked toward the frontier, but then so had their adversaries. War was in some respects a leisurely affair, and the armies in those days were smaller.

It is sometimes forgotten that although it was France who declared war on Prussia, the reason von Moltke's armies moved across the border first was because the Germans had mobilized more quickly, in large measure owing to their advanced rail network.

So the French rather belatedly realized that Germany had a great advantage when it came to mobilization. Not only did they have a better rail network, but they had a smaller and more densely populated country. France was, at that time, the largest country in Europe proper, with a population scattered to the edges of its borders, and with a rugged terrain that made the sort of rail network the Germans had well-nigh impossible.

There was no way they could ever hope to match Germany's speed in mobilization: geography was against them. At the same time, the new and revolutionary way in which the European armies were assembled for war gave an enormous advantage to the side that was ready to go into action first.

This revolution in military affairs might more properly be called an evolution; whichever term we use, it denotes a new approach to manpower, beginning with the idea that in theory, every able-bodied male would either complete a fixed term of service in the army or would be currently serving in it.

In France this was particularly true, as a good 80 percent of the male eligibles had done their service. But as no country could afford to maintain a standing army comprising even a significant minority of the male population, each army consisted of three components.

There was a core of what we might term professional soldiers, enlisted men, officers, and noncommissioned officers, who formed the cadres of each unit. Then there was a much larger group, consisting of those men currently doing their military service. Each year a portion of them left, were replaced by a new cohort. So in the French army, the regular units were all maintained at some fraction of their wartime strength. Mobilization meant that their numbers would be completed by adding men who had recently completed their military obligation.

It should be said in passing that this rather basic fact is often not fully understood by military historians. With the exception of certain elite units, the European armies of 1914 were composed of a majority of men who had been recalled from their civilian life, as the general proportion of these units was about one currently enlisted soldier to two recalled ones. There were very few units that went into action in August 1914 composed of what in the American army of 1840 or 1860 would have been called "regulars."

The only appreciable difference was a function of how recently the men recalled had completed their service. The so-called "reserve" divisions were simply topped off with men who had last been in uniform six or ten years before. In this way the combatants hoped to move from a peacetime army of roughly a million men, to a wartime army of four or five million.

Clearly the mere act of mobilization would be an enormous logistical task, and the stakes would be high. There was no way the French could match the Germans at this game. The basic geography and demography of France was against them. No matter how good they were at the process, they'd never be able to beat the Germans at mobilization. Making the problem even worse was that Germany could put more men into the field than France could, simply because they had a larger population.

Size was not the only hindrance. The rail system, such as it was, went from the provinces to Paris, hardly beneficial if you wanted to mobilize troops from the west and south and get them to the northeast.

There was another factor that complicated French troop deployments considerably. The German and Austro-Hungarian armies were all concentrated inside their respective national borders. In consequence, their professional core was distributed more or less evenly among the units of their armies, with the best units adjacent to their frontiers.

But France, like Great Britain, was a colonial power. Moreover, its most important possessions had come into its grasp very late. In consequence, the French maintained significant forces abroad, most of them in North Africa. British troops were scattered all over the globe, but then Great Britain, an island power with a formidable navy, didn't have to worry about being invaded by its neighbors. And by continental standards, the British army was insignificant. The French forces in North Africa alone were about the same size as the entire British army.

The nature of these forces has always been poorly understood, largely owing to the name. The single largest block was the *infanterie coloniale*, a name that suggests native troops. France certainly had army units composed of men from its African and Asian colonies, but the *infanterie coloniale* was composed of Frenchmen, just as the *Legion étrangère* was composed of Europeans of various nationalities.

Basically the *infanterie coloniale* was the equivalent of the marines in the United States: elite units maintained at closer to their establishment strength, since they actually saw combat. Any sensible general would want them in the forefront of his army in the event of a European war, but getting them into position to repel an invasion would take time. In that sense France's colonial empire worked against it, just as did Great Britain's.

In fact, one of the difficulties the French faced in a future war was the high percentage of their experienced soldiers who had been culled out and were in these elite units. Every army has that problem, even today. One school argues that it's better to distribute the more experienced and able soldiers all through the army, and that elite units dilute that, deprive the regular units of responsible leaders. The other school argues that these elite units have a combat capability out of all proportion to their numbers. In most armies there is generally a compromise, with only a small number of elite units.

But the French had a substantially higher percentage of men in elite units. In addition to the *infanterie coloniale*, they had 30 battalions of *chasseurs* and *chasseurs alpins*. Although technically battalions, and oftentimes treated by military historians as "light" infantry or "riflemen," in France the *chasseurs* were more heavily armed than regular infantry units, and operated at a much higher peacetime strength. As a group, they were the best soldiers France had.

The difficulty was that almost all of them were south of Paris, and, not surprisingly, the twelve battalions of mountain troops (the *chasseurs alpins*) were all in the Alps, that is to say, southwest of Switzerland.

Once again, geography defined crucial elements of national defense policy. Given all these factors, no matter how efficient the mobilization scheme was, it would take weeks to deploy the French army to the frontier. What was required was a way to keep the invaders from penetrating deep into France while the armies were assembled and moved into action.

THE FRENCH SOLUTION

In June 1872, less than a year after the triumph of the Third Republic over the Communards, the government began deliberating on how this problem could be solved. Adolphe Thiers created a Committee of Defense to consider how best to guard the country against a future invasion, and in June 1873, one of France's outstanding military engineers, Adolfe Séré de Rivières, was appointed secretary to the committee.[9]

After due deliberation, this body decided that the best solution to the problem was the construction of fortifications at key places on the frontiers, everywhere from Dunkirk to Nice. The system would fulfill two functions (at least): It would block the key invasion routes into France, and it would give the country time to mobilize and deploy its enormous conscript armies.

Born in 1815, Colonel Séré de Rivières had spent his professional career working with fortifications; indeed, in 1868 he had been charged with developing forts around Metz. With his prodding, the council formally renounced the complex geometrical shapes that had been a common feature of forts from the time of Vauban on, laying down the general plan for a much simpler and sturdier design.

Never a nation to pull back from great engineering projects, the council decided not only to protect the three land frontiers, but to protect most of the major cities as well. There was a certain logic to this latter move. The reason Paris had held for months and months in 1870 was owing to the forts that surrounded it. In consequence, cities comfortably distant from the frontier were girded by forts: Nice, Besançon, Lille, Lyons. The double-pronged approach is probably why so many people were confused about Verdun: knowing that other cities in France were protected by forts, it was easy to conclude that the battles for Verdun were for possession of the town.

This was an engineering project on a grand scale indeed. Over the next 35 years the French constructed 504 forts of various sizes, and an additional 278 prepared artillery emplacements.[10] No less than 32 forts guarded the gateway of the Meuse.

Given the vast scale of the project, and the widely differing conditions, a description is difficult. The engineers called the forts polygons, and most of them, seen from above, resembled nothing so much as the outline of a small house. There was one feature that was a carryover from the original structures of Vauban and his descendants, Marc-René de Montalembert and François-Nicolas Haxo: the idea of a dry moat and sharply angled walls to render an infantry assault extremely difficult.

However, the new system of forts used a greatly simplified plan, and in the northeast in particular, the forts were largely dug into the reverse slopes of ridges. As might be expected, the designs evolved over the decades, largely in response to the increasing effi-cacy of artillery, as we shall see in the next chapter.

The French word for *fort* is the same as the English word, but, like everything else in France, there were specific subclassifica-tions, so the grand total of 504 structures included three separate categories, the basic distinction simply being size: 306 forts (the largest structures), 31 *redoutes*, and 167 *ouvrages*. Practically speaking, however, the only distinction was a matter of moder-nity and size; that is to say, most of the forts were constructed before 1885 (196) and most of the *ouvrages* were constructed af-ter that point (114).

So technically, nine of the 34 Verdun structures were actually *ouvrages*, but we can call them all forts without doing violence to the basic idea, since the only real difference was size.

The prepared artillery positions, called batteries, deserve some explanation. Although the forts possessed some artillery, the basic idea, poorly understood, was that the real firepower would reside in the guns emplaced in prepared positions behind the fort itself. So one of the chief tactical functions of the fort was to provide a pro-tective barrier for the gunners, and a shielded observation post from which observers could direct artillery fire.

In the 1870s—and for decades afterward—heavy artillery was not particularly mobile. So the idea was to have the guns already in position, permanently mounted on stable stone and concrete platforms, with the ammunition stored in secure magazines that would minimize catastrophic accidents or lucky hits from enemy gunners.

THE MEUSE AND VERDUN

Before 1871, the quickest route into France for the Germans was the one they took in July 1870. They massed their armies on the 100-kilometer stretch of the border between the two countries, crossed it, and then spread out.

With the new frontier, the German stronghold of Metz was now less than 40 kilometers from what was potentially the most vulnerable point in French territory: the Meuse river valley. When Pétain spoke of Verdun as being the boulevard into France, he was speaking symbolically—in terms of that distinct French term *moral*—but he was also speaking very literally. The valley is the highway into France.

From the very first days of its meetings, the defense committee realized the importance of blocking the Meuse valley, as it was a logical path of entry into France, and, given the new German frontier, by far the most logical route. The other convenient entry point that led into France, the *trouée des Charmes*, was a good 100 kilometers farther down, and German armies using it would have to work their way through the Vosges mountains and around the plateau dominated by the city of Nancy. But the stretch of the river above the city of Verdun, all the way up to Stenay (about 45 kilometers), is ideal.

The course of the Meuse is serpentine. It winds its way up from Toul, past Saint-Mihiel, Verdun, Stenay, makes a sharp northwesterly turn around Charleville-Mezières, then curves back to the north, flows through Givet, and then up into Belgium. It goes past Dinant and Namur, now taking a northeasterly course, finally emerging north of Liége as the Maas, where it makes another shift, this time back to the northwest, and flows through the Netherlands to the sea.

Unlike the Rhine, the Meuse is not very wide—although it was a reasonable obstacle for nineteenth-century armies. The land on each side of it, the valley, is surprisingly broad and flat, the average width being about nine kilometers. The chief problem, militarily speaking, is that for most of its course, and particularly from the point at which it curves back to the northwest and up to Sedan, the valley terminates abruptly in steep, forested ridges, the beginnings of the great forest of the Ardennes that sprawls across Luxembourg and southeastern Belgium.

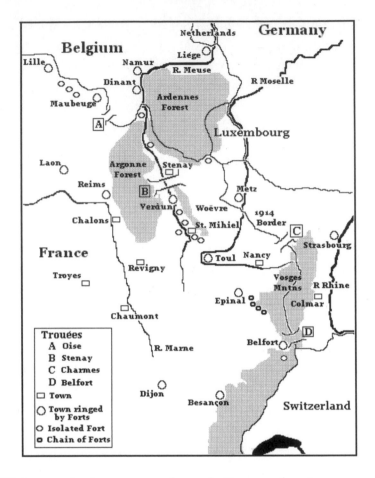

Belgium — Netherlands — Germany — Lille — Liége — Namur — R. Meuse — Dinant — R Moselle — Maubeuge — Ardennes Forest — Luxembourg — A — Laon — Argonne Forest — Stenay — Metz — Reims — B — Verdun — Woëvre — St. Mihiel — 1914 Border — C — Chalons — Strasbourg — France — Toul — Nancy — Troyes — Revigny — Vosges Mntns — R Rhine — Epinal — Colmar — Chaumont — D — R. Marne — Belfort — Dijon — Besançon — Switzerland

Trouées
A Oise
B Stenay
C Charmes
D Belfort
□ Town
◯ Town ringed by Forts
⊙ Isolated Fort
◼ Chain of Forts

However, in its passage through France, the river resembles nothing so much as a furrow in the ground, as though a giant plow had thrown all the dirt it excavated for the actual channel up onto the banks.

The term *forest* in this instance is accurate insofar as the trees go, but misleading in that a forest can be on a relatively flat stretch of land. The Ardennes, like its southern continuation the Argonne, is extremely rough territory: bluffs and steep ridges running off at sharp angles. There had been paths through it since time immemorial, and the Romans had built roads, so it was not impassable. But the relatively few passages through it were simply insufficient to support an army of any size.

From the German point of view, the terrain was unfortunate, because the valley of the Meuse was a perfect superhighway into France and Belgium. In that latter country, the left bank of the river was comparatively flat, the beginnings of a large coastal plain that stretched out to the English Channel. The difficulty was how to get into the valley. So far as Belgium went, there was only one practical entry point: Liège.

The Belgians were quite aware of this. Their army had a great engineer as well, and under the leadership of Henri-Alexis Brialmont, the Belgians surrounded Liège with twelve forts and Namur, 60 kilometers to the southwest, with nine. Brialmont reasoned, correctly enough, that once an invader crossed the Meuse between those two cities, Belgium would be impossible to defend. So the military solution was to make the crossing well-nigh impossible.

The French weakness was more serious. Below Stenay, the terrain flattens out for a 30-kilometer stretch, providing easy access to the valley in both directions. Given the proximity of what in France was known as the *trouée de Stenay* to the new frontier, the logical move by the Germans would be to get there as quickly as possible and drive south.

The next town upriver from Stenay is Verdun. A short distance north of the town, the landscape changes. On the right bank (the side facing Germany), there is a series of rough, forested ridges stretching all the way down to just south of Saint-Mihiel, about 60 kilometers. This stretch of rugged terrain was called the heights of the Meuse. True enough, but since the same term could be applied to about three-quarters of the right bank (and several stretches of the left bank as well), it is easy to get confused.

However, the point is that the heights of the Meuse, like the Ardennes, was a serious obstacle. Given any choice in the matter, the Germans would head directly for the *trouée de Stenay* and move south. Because just to the south of Verdun, the countryside opens up, becomes more agricultural, and there are no natural obstacles to stop an advancing army aiming to strike deep into the heart of France.

What made the Meuse so tempting as well as puzzling was that the ground forming the actual valley was generally a plain of decent width, so there were rail lines and highways running alongside the river itself. Anyone who looked at the Meuse could see that it was a wonderful highway bisecting Belgium and running deep into France.

Moreover, there were sizable stretches along the left bank that provided easy access to the interior. Specifically, there was one from just below Stenay that went all the way to Charleville-Mézières, and a second one below Verdun that went all the way down past Saint-Mihiel to Toul.

So basically, if you were the German general staff, you would simply mass a large army north of Metz, tell them to head east, turn south at the river, go upstream for 50 kilometers, then turn west and head for Paris.

There was a reason for the dogleg. The left bank of the Meuse, running all the way down from Belgium and Luxembourg to below Verdun, was a rugged forested area, the southern extension of the Ardennes forest, the Argonne. It was a natural barrier. Although the Romans had cut a road through it, very little had been done since. It was not the sort of area that an army would find easy to pass through, formed a natural barrier.

So an invader would have to move due south once he reached the river.

Their advance through the valley would be further channeled, because the most vulnerable part of the Meuse—from just below Stenay all the way down below Saint-Mihiel—is protected by another natural barrier, known as the *côtes de Meuse*. Another peculiar French word, *côte* can mean anything from *coast* to *slope* to *side*, but in this case, the best English word is *height*. Because the heights of the Meuse were very much that: a series of abrupt ridges and bluffs, occurring at irregular angles to each other and the river itself.

Generally speaking, the area between the Meuse river and its neighbor to the east, the Moselle, is rolling country, ideal for maneuvering. But as one moves west, the *côtes* are an impressive obstacle. Heavily forested, with irregular buttes rising up to over 350 meters, the ridges flank the right bank of the river to a depth of ten kilometers and sometimes more.

The Heights of the Meuse really have to be seen to be appreciated as obstacles. They lack the dramatic verticals of the Southwestern United States, for instance, but they more than make up for it by their density. Seen from a good vantage point—say, the Autoroute de l'Est just before exit 32 (about twenty kilometers east of Verdun)—they literally stretch all the way across the horizon, a wall of green that gives the impression of being one impenetrable mass. The impression is not an illusion.

Similarly, the *trouée de Stenay* is an equally dramatic sight, clearly visible after leaving the village of Pillon and heading toward Mangiennes (about 25 kilometers north by northeast of Verdun). Although there is an impressive mass directly ahead, over on the horizon to the right the mass of green simply ends. There's an opening.

The best way to think of this natural obstacle on the right bank above and below the city of Verdun is to envision it as a miniature Vosges mountain range: not so high, not so wide, not so steep. But as far as armies were concerned, quite steep, and impenetrable enough. Moreover, this 60-kilometer mini–mountain range was in exactly the wrong place, so far as the Germans were concerned. Draw an imaginary line from Saint-Mihiel to Metz. The terrain above the line is wonderful country for mass deployment: nothing but endless rolling fields.

So the solution (von Moltke's common sense again) would be to come storming out of Lothringen through the *trouée de Stenay*, head straight down the valley and break out into the interior. Because basically, if you draw another imaginary line, this one from Verdun to Reims, the terrain to the south of it is by and large more of the same rolling country, ideally designed for mass armies.

Now, the French could see this as plainly as the Germans, and indeed one of the first priorities of the defense committee was to block the Meuse. The ideal place for this was at that point where the heights on the right bank and the rugged terrain of the Argonne on the left come closest to the river itself, forming a natural bottleneck.

Now Séré de Rivières was hardly the first Frenchmen to notice this fine natural feature. In fact, there had been a castle there for centuries, and gradually, around the castle, a town: Verdun. But cannon had transformed warfare in one significant way: A castle overlooked by ridges and hills was hardly a defensible proposition, and Verdun, straddling the river itself, was the classic case. Gunpowder made it indefensible, but then again, no one was interested in defending it.

It simply happened to be the closest town to the choke point, because, fortuitously (if you were a French engineer), right above the town, the ridges of the Argonne are more or less perpendicular to the river. The topography simply speaks for itself, and the French began building forts. In 1875 they built five on the right bank, on the heights of the Meuse, and four on the left, on the Argonne ridges closest to the river.

The heights were too good a natural defensive position to ignore, so the engineers laid out a series of forts along the heights to the south. The term used to denote this group of forts was *les forts de rideau*, *rideau* being another all-purpose French word that literally means *line*, but in the sense of a line of trees. A line of obstacles impeding our view, and the forts of the *rideau* formed a defensive line blocking access to the valley all along the heights.

From Verdun to Toul there were seven of these, six on the right bank, and one on the left, and five of them were located on the 30 kilometer odd stretch of the river between the towns of Verdun and Saint-Mihiel. In consequence, they played a key role in the first battles for Verdun. So, even though they were not, for administrative purposes, part of Verdun, were not part of the *camp retranché de Verdun*, French accounts of the fighting tend to treat them as though they were. Thus Gabriel Bichet, in writing a monograph entitled "The Role of the Forts in the Battle of Verdun" (and quoted in the opening chapter), begins by describing the bitter fight for the Fort de Troyon in September 1914, even though Troyon was actually one of the *rideau* forts and not part of Verdun at all.

The distinction may ludicrously legalistic, but what it speaks to is the point made in the opening chapter of this book: these areas are all closely related, are all part of the same strategic objective, so the battles there are all of one piece.

The forts of the *rideau* were all completed before 1877, at which point the engineers added two more forts to Verdun.

The easiest way to conceptualize what was going on is to envision a circle, with the town of Verdun at the center. The twelve-o'clock position would be due north, and since the shape is a circle, we can measure it off in degrees, with twelve o'clock being zero degrees.

The first set of forts on the right bank had formed a rough arc from about 10 degrees to about 70, with Belleville being at 10, Tavannes being at 70, the other three forts in between. The next two forts, constructed in 1877, extended the arc to about 160 degrees, the approximate position occupied by Fort Houdainville, to the southeast.

In 1881, three more were added. Vaux, on the right bank, part of a plan to fill in the enormous arc to the northeast, was at about 45 degrees, about nine kilometers to the northeast of the city. The other two were on the left bank.

The 1875 forts on the left bank had all been put to the southwest of the city; that is, they formed a rough arc from about 190 to 250 degrees. There was one exception: Marre, at about 310 degrees, located on one of the Argonne ridges to the northeast of the city. Now the engineers added one fort to the northwest, at about 300 degrees, and seven kilometers from the city. Called the fort Bois Bourrus, it was located on a ridge in the Argonne of the same name.

At the same time, a smaller fort, technically an *ouvrage*, was

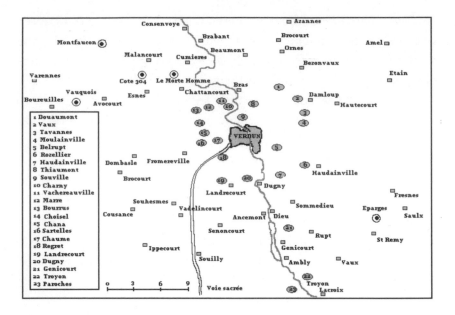

added in the southwest, fleshing out the defensive position there. The reason for building forts in the southern half of the circle was to bock the passage of troops to the flanks, keep them from getting into the valley below the main defensive line.

In 1883, five more forts were added. Moulainville was built on the right bank, at the 90-degree position, between Tavannes and Rozelier. The other four were all on the left bank. One, the *ouvrage* of Belle Epine, was located on the eastern edge of the ridge of Bois Bourrus, and the other three were all in the south-western quadrant.

Essentially what the engineers were doing was to fill in the gaps systematically, now that they had sketched out in concrete and masonry the general outline of the position.

But in 1885, they started a process of expansion; that is to say, they moved the defensive perimeter out farther. First, they constructed a formidable anchor point for the right bank, the fort of Douaumont, about 10 kilometers to the northeast, in the 15-degree position, so it was the northernmost fort. It also happened to be the largest of the forts.

Two years later, seven forts were added, six on the right bank and one on the left. The *ouvrage* on the left bank, Charny, was the closest position to the river itself, and across from it were two important positions: Froidterre and Thiaumont. The other structures were slotted in to flesh out the right-bank arc.

At that point construction of new forts basically stopped, as the engineers had to start upgrading the existing structures, owing to advances in artillery explained in the next chapter. However, other forts were planned. The engineers wanted to extend the southwestern quadrant of the left bank considerably, and planned to build a fort at Sivry-la-Perche, four kilometers to the west of Sartelles, which was the westernmost of the forts.

One new fort was actually built. In 1910, Vacherauville was added on the left bank, slightly above Charny so that there were now no less than three forts on the ridge: Bois Bourrus, Vacherauville, and Marre, in addition to two fortified blockhouses, one at either end.

Although Verdun received the most attention, the forts along the Meuse were not the only ones the French constructed. Other key locations were protected as well, most notably Toul and Belfort. But again, although the forts are identified with the adjacent cities, they weren't built to protect the towns; they were built to guard the logical invasion routes. In the case of Toul, the *trouée de Charmes*, and in the case of Belfort, the *trouée de Belfort*.

Generally speaking, the names of the forts were parceled out according to the nearest village or hamlet. Thus, for example, the fort of Moulainville, on the right bank, got its name because of its proximity to the village of the same name, as was the case with Fromeréville on the left bank. If there was no village around, the name was taken from some local topographical feature or historical association, as with the fort of Bois Bourrus on the right bank, and the Fort du Camp des Romains upstream from Saint-Mihiel.

Meanwhile, in Belgium, Brialmont applied the same lessons to the same problem. The key places where the Meuse could be crossed in Belgium were Dinant, Namur, and Liège. The Belgians built forts to protect all three, together with the port of Antwerp and the vulnerable area around Maubeuge.

At some point toward the end of the century, the Meuse had been locked up tight. There was no way to get into it, and not much point in trying to cross its southern reaches. There was a second *trouée* down there, the *trouée de Charmes*. But all the earlier objections still held: A German army would have to deploy through the Vosges, a tricky prospect even if the French didn't oppose them. And when they got through, they'd be too far to the south, while in their forward thrust they'd be vulnerable on both flanks.

Nor was there much chance of getting help from an army coming out of Lothringen and moving south. Historically, the land between the two rivers (the Meuse and the Moselle) had been called the Woëvre, an archaic French word that means, simply, *wet*. Over the centuries generations of enterprising farmers had dried out the northern portion—the part above our imaginary line from Verdun to Metz—turning it into excellent farmland, and, not coincidentally, good ground for maneuver.

But the southern portion still justified the original appellation. It was a curious combination of lakes, swamps, low-lying ground, and isolated outcroppings looking for all the world like they were cattle that had wandered off from the herd constituted by the *côtes de Meuse*. The French called these isolated outcroppings *buttes*, a word that means pretty much the same as it does in English; that is to say, it denotes an isolated mountain with a flattish top.

Several generations of French officers had surveyed this part of the Woëvre and decided it was completely unsuitable for military operations, just as was the core of the Argonne on the other side of the river. In his excellent study of U. S. Grant's generalship, Marshal-Cornwell observes that the American Civil War was mostly fought on terrain that no European army would have gone anywhere near.[11] Looking at the two areas that would become the flanks for Verdun, one can see his point, and certainly the professionals of the French general staff did. They considered the area "impracticable in all its routes."[12]

So there was a period in the immediate aftermath of the Franco-Prussian War when it appeared that there might be a lasting peace after all, if for no other reason than that the two principal combatants couldn't figure out a way to have at each other. But, of course, that was to overlook human ingenuity.

3

The War of the Engineers

Why the forts?

—Gabriel Bichet[1]

The French engineers who designed the forts were well aware that the rifled, breech-loading guns that were increasingly coming into use in the 1870s were far superior to the cannon that Vauban and his followers had in mind when they designed and built their forts. The difficulty men like Séré de Rivières faced was unprecedented, however. In the decades between 1871 and 1914, there were three successive revolutions in gunnery.

These dramatic and sweeping changes transformed the nature of warfare in a fundamental way. This shift can be seen quite clearly, because, starting with the wars of the 1860s and 1870s, the medical services of many of the combatants began to keep records of their woundeds' cases. As most of us would expect, the vast majority of wounds were caused by standard infantry weapons: rifles and sidearms. The only surprise revealed by these reports is the extremely low incidence of wounds caused by edged weapons—bayonets, knives, and swords. As the American summary of the Civil War data points out, there was very little hand-to-hand combat: "The bayonet and saber were military weapons of little significance," is how the United States surgeon general put it.[2] The contrary idea is a myth. But then, as Jean-North Cru pretty much established, a great many battlefield accounts are fictional.

The point is germane, suggests a certain healthy skepticism about stories of intense hand-to-hand fighting in the trenches. That is particularly the case given the dramatic shift in the causes of wounds that occurred in the First World War. Abruptly, the vast majority of wounds now came from artillery shells of various kinds. And this was true despite all the attention given to the power of the machine gun. In studying the data recorded by the medical services of the combatants, one comes to the conclusion that very few soldiers fell victim to rifle fire.

Another way of looking at what happened is to see it as a paradigm shift, as indeed it was. The successive revolutions in artillery transformed the nature of warfare. Some armies adapted to it much more quickly than others, which is why they were more successful in combat. As with armies, so with their chroniclers: A good many military historians continued to write about this war as though it were of a piece with the wars of Napoleon, with the Crimea, or South Africa. Nor is it fair to blame them. Stories of marksmanship and man-to-man combat are inherently more satisfying than Bernier's image of human bodies being transformed into a ghastly confiture.

Moreover, just as gunners and engineers were always better educated than their counterparts in the cavalry and infantry, understanding their concerns, like mastering understanding their craft, requires delving into technical areas. But without a certain understanding of those areas, it is basically impossible to understand grasp both the battlefield successes of the Germans during the war, and the complicated sequence of events that led to the battles for Verdun. Besides, the story of these revolutions is intrinsically interesting.

THE FIRST TRANSFORMATION

As Séré de Rivières and his colleagues at the defense committee worked out their plans in the 1870s, they were well aware of how recent developments in the weaponry available both to the infantry and the artillery had impacted the battlefield. But to their way of thinking, the most recent advances would work to the advantages of the forts, with their prepositioned heavy artillery, safely shielded from view.

Up until the 1860s, or about the time of the American Civil War, the standard infantry weapon was a smoothbore musket. Although sturdy and durable, these weapons were highly inaccurate, and with a very short range. Forty meters was about the optimal, and even then the chances were pretty good that musket fire would miss.

In consequence, gunners who were one or two hundred meters back were basically invulnerable, could fire directly at their targets. So rifling, the practice of grooving the insides of the barrel of the gun tube, was a rude shock. A projectile fired from a rifled gun tube was vastly more accurate, and over a much longer range, particularly if it was a breech- as opposed to a muzzle-loading weapon.

Muzzle-loaded rifled muskets had been around for more than a century. But soldiers using rifles (as opposed to smoothbores) were specialists. Their weapons were finicky and fragile, and reloading them was a laborious process. The rifled weapon only became truly practicable on the battlefield when the technology improved to the point that a breech-loading weapon firing a metallic cartridge became cheap and reliable. By the mid-1860s, both the French and the Germans were equipping infantry with such rifles. These early weapons were a far cry from the rifles of 1914, but they were also a long way from the muskets of 1815.

Suddenly gunners realized that their traditional positions during battle turned them into so many targets. A volley of decently aimed rifle fire from a platoon of ordinary infantry could wipe out a whole battery of gunners, so the sensible response was to move out of range.

But that led to a problem: the gunners could no longer see their targets. So artillery fire became a much more complicated affair. The gunners needed observers to watch the fall of the shells and relay back corrections. This relatively new idea of not being able to see your target was called indirect fire.

Now it seemed to the committee, logically enough, that when it came to indirect fire, fortifications would give the defenders a great advantage. The observers were protected by the forts, would be looking out of small observation slits, or be in armored cupolas. The guns would mostly be well behind, but the beauty of the idea was that since both observers and guns were fixed in place, it would be an easy matter to dial in the exact location where you wanted to land your shells.

By contrast, the attackers would have to get into position to figure out what to do, and all the while they'd be under fire from the defense. Trying to attack a fort would be tantamount to suicide.

Producing infantry rifles was a much simpler process than producing rifled artillery, because the forces expended when the projectile was fired were so much less. Of course, the breech-loaded projectile fit much more snugly than the old muzzle-loaded one, so in consequence the forces generated were much greater, as there was hardly any leakage. But still, in order to make this principle workable for the ordinary soldier, the bullets themselves became lighter, even as their velocity increased.

Now the difficulty for artillery designers lay in scaling up the weapons. The forces required to propel a 75-millimeter-diameter shell were not simply ten times greater than what was required to propel a 7.6-millimeter shell, because the artillery shell weighed numerous multiples more than the bullet. And this was made all the more difficult if the gun was a breech-loader, since all rearward force was directed against this end of the barrel, which, in order to operate properly, had to have a mechanism that allowed it to open and close—otherwise the shell couldn't be loaded into the rear.

But by the mid-1870s, about the time that fort building was well launched all over France (and Germany and Belgium and Austria and Russia), European gun designers began to close in on the problem. In Germany and Austria, this was done by private firms working on their own: Krupp and Skoda. In France the situation was slightly more complex, with individuals working for both government and private arsenals.

The key breakthrough for the French was made by a military officer, Charles Ragon de Bange, who figured out how to design a breech mechanism that would handle the forces involved. By 1878 his guns were in production, and in recognition of his abilities, French gunners referred to almost all the guns designed during this period by his name, even though some were actually designed by someone else. But *De Bange* became the generic designation for all French artillery designed right up until 1897.

Thus far—by, say, 1881—the engineers weren't worried, because although the De Bange guns had more hitting power and longer range, they had factored all that into their designs. Even a direct hit from one of the new De Bange guns wouldn't do any serious damage to their forts.

That was because there was a trade-off involved with these new guns. Since the expanding gases were so much more powerful, the gun tube and its mount had to be considerably sturdier. And although advances in metallurgy meant that immensely stronger metal could be employed, a certain mass was still necessary, and that mass meant weight.

Practically speaking, then, if an artillery piece was going to be mobile, able to accompany troops in the field, its weight was restricted to what could be pulled by a team of six horses. That worked out to a sort of constant; that is to say, everybody's standard field gun turned out to be a weapon that fired a shell of around 80 millimeters over a relatively flat trajectory, with a usable range of about 6,000 meters at most. The shells fired by these guns could do horrible damage to infantry, but their explosive payload was too feeble to do anything much against fortifications, and indeed gunners mostly carried only shrapnel shells—effective only against masses of troops in the open.

Heavier weapons were thus not simply those firing larger (heavier) shells, but guns that weighed considerably more. To the extent that the armies all divided their artillery into two categories: field artillery, described above, and siege artillery. The latter was not really designed to be transported into the field and sent into action immediately. So the fort builders, eyeing their hundreds of batteries of heavy weapons, already in place, their magazines securely protected, naturally felt that the advantages were all on their side. The guns directed by the forts could destroy any enemy artillery before they could even get set up to fire.

Besides, there was no need for the fort to be invulnerable. It had to do its duty for only a week to ten days, by which time the armies would have been deployed, the battle joined.

THE GUNNERS STRIKE BACK

Unfortunately for the engineers, their great project was only just winding down when they received some truly frightening news. Between 11 August and 25 October 1886, French gunners conducted a series of experiments on the fort of Malmaison, outside of Laon. Malmaison was a 36,000-square-meter rectangle, and had been selected because of its relatively exposed position. While a delegation of delighted gunners and apprehensive engineers watched, the fort was bombarded.

The gunners fired 167 155-millimeter shells and 75 shells from 220-millimeter mortars, all system De Bange guns dating from 1878.

The results were very bad news for the engineers. To their consternation, the shells, particularly those from the mortars, smashed in the carapace of the fort, pretty much destroying it completely.

The guns hadn't changed, but the explosives used in the shells had. The new explosive was substantially more powerful than what everyone had been using before. The forts had been designed to withstand the older version, but the new shells were devastating.

Now, by the 1870s, everyone involved understood the chemistry of high explosives. There was a whole family of trinitrates, including trinitrophenol (TNP) and trinitrotoluene (TNT), and any competent chemist could make them in a school chemistry lab—provided he had the raw materials. Assuming he didn't blow himself to glory, since TNT in its pure state is an extremely volatile compound, and TNP is even worse—or better, in terms of explosive energy.

The difficulty is that the trinitrates are extremely volatile: any sort of shock will set them off, such as heat or vibration. Firing an artillery shell involves both of these factors, so the difficulty was figuring out how to adulterate the explosives so they could be used in shells. In modern parlance, this is called weaponizing, and by the mid-1880s the French succeeded in weaponizing trinitrophenol, which they called melinite, in a rather feeble attempt to disguise what it actually was.

A kilogram of this new material contained three or four times as much energy as what gunners had been using. So much so that the new melinite shells were promptly dubbed *les obus torpilles*, or torpedo shells, since, compared to the older shells, the new ones were more like naval torpedoes.

De Bange was no fool: His weapons, particularly the 120- and 155-millimeter guns, were massively overbuilt, could easily fire the new shells. Prudently, the defense committee realized that the Germans probably weren't far behind, and that in consequence everything built before 1885—which was basically everything—was now obsolete.

For the engineers who had been beavering away with fortifications, the system of De Bange weapons firing melinite shells was a horrifying development. As they saw with the Malmaison, the new shells were capable of destroying the masonry of their forts. Gloomily, they reckoned that everyone else would soon be filling their shells with some version of melinite, and they were right. Within a few years all the major powers were using some local variant of one of the trinitrates. The Germans, prudently, went for weaponized trinitrotoluene, which was less nasty to handle, but the end result was pretty much the same.

The 220-millimeter mortar shell was a particularly obnoxious development. Historically, siege artillery aimed to blow holes in the walls of a fort or castle. There were several practical reasons why gunners confined themselves to that function, the most significant being that, generally speaking, fortifications tended to be on higher ground, so the besiegers had to contend with steep angles of fire if they were going to get a shell over the wall. Before the advent of melinite, the actual explosive force of a typical shell was such that there wasn't much damage to be done by one that simply flew over the walls and landed . . . somewhere.

Mortars were guns with very short barrels, capable of near-vertical fire over short ranges (one being a function of the other). They had been around for a long time, but, aside from naval uses, they weren't very effective, precisely for that reason: the shells didn't have enough explosive force to be worth the difficulties of aiming and firing, and, of course, gunners preferred to be able to see their targets.

But a 220-millimeter melinite shell was a different matter entirely. The relatively short range of the mortar meant less stress, because less explosive was needed to force it out of the barrel. Since the shell was less stressed, it could have a higher explosive payload. Drop one of these shells onto the roof of some part of the fort, and it would do enormous damage.

What made the situation truly distressing was that both of these new guns were, comparatively speaking, portable. Not in the sense that the standard field guns used by all the major powers were, but the weight and size of the shorter version of the 155-millimeter gun meant that it could be pulled along the same roads as its smaller brethren, albeit at slower speeds and with more effort. But it was light enough that you could mount it on a regular wheeled gun carriage, which meant that it could be pulled up and brought into action just like a field gun.

Now, the engineers had never claimed their fortifications were invulnerable, only that they could withstand the artillery that an army was likely to bring up during its advance. By the time it got its siege guns into place, mobilization and deployment would have been completed, and the traditional battles would begin.

So the Malmaison demonstration was the complete reversal of the basic suppositions that had led to the forts. The keystone of the national defense policy that Séré de Rivières had lobbied for was now dangerously obsolete.

THE RIPOSTE

On the other hand, now that the engineers knew what the new shells could do, coming up with a way to counter them was not all that difficult, at least in theory. Basically, the material that formed the carapace of the fort simply had to be made stronger. As with the development of melinite, the trick was figuring out the way to put the theory into practice.

The *polygon* basically had three components. The walls and the dry moat were simply there to protect the garrison and its weapons and supplies. Inside the walls, therefore, were various storage facilities. Then there were the positions for the guns and for observers to direct the fire, as well as positions enabling the defenders to beat off an infantry assault.

In the original design, hardly any attention had been paid to the structures that were inside the fort. The only exception was where the ammunition for the guns was housed, since an explosion there could be catastrophic. But now, faced with the possibility of highly destructive shells landing inside the fort itself, the engineers were forced into some serious rethinking.

Actually, they were faced with a whole set of problems. On the one hand, they had to figure out what to do with the hundreds of forts that had already been constructed, while on the other they had to make fundamental design changes in the new ones that the defensive scheme called for.

Moreover, each of the three components required a different approach. Without going into even more tedious technical details, the engineers employed a mix of three basic techniques. They developed a sturdier and more resistant concrete, generically referred to as reinforced concrete, that they could test to see that it was proof against the new shells.

Wherever possible, however, they used a much cheaper and even more effective technique: either digging down into the ground or sandwiching earth and masonry. Although the most visible sign of this was thicker walls, what was really going on was that more and more of the structure was subterranean, as that was the easier and most efficient way to protect the interior structures of the fort.

Gradually, therefore, the polygon became simply an enormous hulking mound whose most visible feature was the entrance (at the rear), and the dry moat and wall configuration marking the perimeter.

So far, so good, but there still remained the rather more difficult matter of protecting the guns and their observers. Simply making the walls thicker was not a solution, since the thickness would severely limit the mobility of the gun. So gradually, over the next twenty years, the engineers began to rely more and more on thick iron plates.

In fact, as time passed, the visible surface of one of the newer forts (or one that had been extensively renovated) was beginning to look more like some sort of bizarre naval vessel, with round humps scattered over its surface, some of them looking like squat iron chimneys, others simply bulges.

But upgrading a fort was an expensive proposition, and there was only so much money available for national defense. The parties of the left were more amenable to spending money on fortifications than on arming a professional military, but as the years rolled by, and the modernization of the forts consumed more and more money, the competition increased, with a growing cadre of officers questioning whether the money couldn't be better spent on weapons, and members of the government wondering whether it was necessary to spend anything at all on national defense.

Given the horrific nature of the war, we sometimes forget the extent to which the elected representatives who formed the governments of the major powers were increasingly of the opinion that wars were obsolete, or impossible, or anyway to be avoided at all costs. And as is usually the case with parliamentary democracies, the result was generally a patched-together compromise that didn't satisfy anyone. The engineers got enough money to upgrade some forts, and the gunners got enough money to develop a new gun—a compromise that left both groups at odds with each other, and with the government.

THE RECOIL REVOLUTION

As if the widespread adoption of TNP as the preferred explosive material for shells was not enough of a challenge for the beleaguered engineers, by 1897, they were faced with yet another innovation, one that fundamentally transformed the nature of artillery, and had an impact on the battlefield that was even more dramatic.

Although Sir Isaac Newton didn't work it out as a law until 1687, every gunner realized that when he fired his cannon, the expanding gases generated by the explosion did much more than hurl the cannonball at the enemy. The gases, confined by the cannon barrel, also pushed back. This was a practical example of Newton's third law, that for every action, there is an equal and opposite reaction. Gunners called it recoil. Fire the gun and it moved backward, shifted position.

Over the centuries the recoil phenomenon got worse, first as the fit of the projectile in the barrel became tighter, and then, with the advent of rifling, breech loading, and TNP, a serious problem.

At first, navies largely were immune, because their guns were mounted directly to the ship itself. Most of us have at least a passing familiarity with the squat four-wheeled gun carriages of sailing vessels. When one of them was fired, it rolled back, was slowed down by its own weight, by the friction of the wheels on the deck, and by cables attached to the carriage.

Much the same principle applied to cannon mounted in forts. The gun mounts connected the carriage directly to a mass of stonework embedded in the earth, and the sheer disproportion of the mass absorbed the energy of the recoil. Provided the gun mount was sturdy enough to take the stress, the gun would remain firmly in place.

But gunners who were required to move their weapons from battle to battle had a bit of a problem. The most practical way to transport a cannon was to mount the gun carriage on wheels and pull it behind a team of horses. But then, when you fired it, those same wheels worked against you, as the gun would move backward, or jump wildly.

As the problem became more acute, gunners came to depend more and more on mechanical devices to keep the gun from moving around each time it was fired. Not only was the movement dangerous to the gunners, but it meant that they had to manhandle it back into position after each round, and aim all over again. The more potent the gun, the worse the problem.

To dampen the recoil, gunners used mechanical wedges, ramps, and dirt—anything and everything that would absorb the energy. But as the range of the guns increased, as indirect fire became the norm, the inherent weakness of mechanical recoil devices became more noticeable. As long as the gunners were aiming directly at the target, simply sighting the gun as if it were a giant musket, the fact that it moved after each round was fired was not much of a problem.

But in indirect fire it was. Even at a relatively short range of, say, 5,000 meters, a one-degree shift in the position of the gun tube from one round to the next would mean that the second round would land nearly 100 meters from the first—and that was assuming the gunners could reposition the gun to within one degree of the initial position. So in actual practice, the margin of error was significant.

So the gunners in a fort had a terrific advantage. They had a fixed field of fire, and could figure out the precise aim necessary to hit any given target well in advance. Or, in other words, they could, through practice, master the terrain, while their opponents couldn't. Besides, getting a heavy siege gun in position would take a great deal of time. The potency of an explosive like melinite meant that although there had been serious advances in metallurgy over the course of the nineteenth century, gun carriages still had to be extremely heavy, so they could withstand the shock of being fired and absorb some of the recoil. It would hardly do to block the wheels of the gun carriage so it couldn't move, only to have the barrel fly off when it was fired. Nor would the gunners be enthusiastic about firing such a weapon.

But by 1897, French artillery designers had come up with a truly elegant solution to the problem. The gun tube was resting on a trough, attached to the gun mount by hydraulic cylinders. When the gun was fired, the barrel moved back, the cylinders absorbed the forces generated, and then recoiled, moving the barrel back to exactly the same position.

There were all sorts of advantages to this scheme. The gun tube remained in exactly the same position, indispensable for indirect fire. The gun mount and carriage could be much lighter, since the hydraulic rams absorbed the shock of firing. And since nothing moved, the rate of fire increased dramatically. The new French field gun, the justly legendary 75, could in theory fire 15 rounds per minute, whereas the gun replaced could only manage three.[3]

Suddenly, everybody's artillery was obsolete. The new French gun, on account of the size of the shell, was the best field gun in the world. And the French army had it: it was lighter and hence more mobile, it had a much higher rate of fire, and its explosive shells had a significantly higher payload of high explosive.

The 75 really was the perfect gun of its type, and neither the Germans nor the Austrians were able to match it. Although by

1914 their standard field gun used the same principle, their weapons were markedly inferior. The 75 is really a fascinating piece of machinery, because generally speaking, devices relying on new technology always have teething problems, and rarely deliver immediately on the claims of their inventors, one reason being a failure on the part of the user to understand what he has.

But here, almost uniquely, was a weapon that sprang forth in perfection, more or less like Athena from the forehead of Zeus. So by 1900, the attitude of French artillery officers, basically, was that they had the perfect weapon, and there was no need to develop more.

The superiority of the 75 was not mythical. It was better than its German counterpart, the 7.7-centimeter field gun, in two key respects: It had a 1,400-meter range advantage firing shrapnel shells, and although the range was the same for both guns when firing high-explosive shells, the French shells contained five times as much explosive as did the German ones (0.650 kilograms as opposed to 0.160 kilograms).[4] The first advantage evaporated fairly quickly, as both sides discovered that high-explosive shells were more effective, but this only emphasized the advantage of the French gun in firing explosive shells, owing to the considerably greater amount of explosive carried.

Had the armies of 1914 and after relied exclusively on field-pieces of less than 80 millimeters, the French would have had a tremendous superiority, and a good many analysts seem to believe that this was the case, writing as though these guns were the mainstays of German and French divisional artillery.[5] Unfortunately for the French, the battlefields of 1914–1918 would be controlled by a combination of heavy artillery, field howitzers, and infantry guns, principally mortars.

But the French put all their faith in the 75. In 1914, a French army corps had 120 of them. A German army corps had only 108 7.7-centimeter field guns. But in addition it deployed 36 10.5- and 16 15.0-centimeter howitzers. When the American army began doing tests, they found that at distances from two to three thousand meters, the howitzer was two and a half times as accurate as the 75-millimeter field gun, and that over the practical range of both weapons, the howitzer would always do significantly more damage than the field gun.[6] Multiplying out the values obtained by the American experiments suggests that each German infantry division had as much killing power in its 105-millimeter howitzers as did all the artillery of a French division. Given that enormous advantage, a German army corps simply outgunned its French (or British) counterpart.

THE INTERNAL DEBATE

In order to understand how that came to happen, and why it continued for the first part of the war, it is unfortunately necessary to peer into the labyrinth of the Third Republic, where basically, the army was run by a committee called the Conseil Supérieure de la Guerre. Although at first glance this seems a tedious detour, it helps to explain much of what was going on once the war began, and why the army was so woefully unprepared to fight it.

The CSG was composed of the five or six officers who would become army commanders if a war broke out. The chair, or president, was the minister of war. If there was an actual war, the vice chair would then become commander in chief of the general staff.

Given the revolving door at the ministry, this was a most unsatisfactory solution, one made all the worse by the fact that the vice chairmanship was almost as unstable as the ministry itself, as a brief account of the changes in 1910–1911 makes clear. In June 1911, Adolphe Messimy became minister of war, replacing François Louis Goiran (and not, as is sometimes said, Jean Brun).

The vice chair of the CSG was General Trémeau. But Trémeau was succeeded by General Michel, who was also president of the Haute-commission des Places Fortes, and thus presumably more interested in the continuous renovation and modernization of the forts than in dealing with the army's many problems.

A month after becoming minister of war, Messimy tried to re-

organize the command structure, although it was in such a bureau-
cratic muddle that it would be more correct to say he tried to create
a command structure. He realized, correctly, that in order for the
army to function properly, it needed an actual head, a chief of staff,
not a rotating committee head. So Messimy was proposing the
same model that existed in Germany and Austria-Hungary (and
elsewhere). The chief of staff would be an actual position, held by
a senior officer on a quasi-permanent basis. If there was a war, that
man would become the overall commander in chief of the army.

Better late than never, one might say; at least Messimy was
trying to create a coherent system of command and control for the
army. Given the distrust and even fear that the parties of the left
had for the army, this was a major step. The difficulty was finding
a senior officer who would take the job, because the government
was adamant that whoever this man was, he would not have the
authority to recommend officers for promotions at the higher levels, that is, from colonel to general and thence on up the ranks to
the level of the army commanders.

This demand was a considerable sticking point. The parties of
the left had controlled the government since 1871, and they had
never been enthusiastic about the army, an institution that in their
view was controlled by generals whose politics were an anathema.
Professional officers were monarchists, Roman Catholics, fundamentally opposed to the values of the Third Republic. The army
had been the instrument that raised the two Napoleons to power,
had massacred the Communards.

The somewhat mythical and certainly grossly exaggerated rise
of General Georges-Ernest Boulanger in the 1880s had turned their
fears into a sort of obsession. The idea of *Boulangerisme*, a military coup, haunted them, and, as a logical result, the government
had insisted on making a political orientation the litmus test for
promotion. Under Louis André, minister of war from 1900 to
1904, there was a real inquisition mounted to root out practicing
Roman Catholics, as it was felt that those were the most politically
unreliable.

Unfortunately, the four years of the André ministry was the most long lived of the group. From the end of the André ministry in November 1904 until the war began in August 1914, France had no less than fourteen ministers of war. André's successors had hardly located their desks before they were out, so his policies had a much longer life than is suggested even by his comparatively long tenure: Of his 40 predecessors between 1871 and 1900(!), only one, Charle de Freycinet, had a longer tenure (nearly five years).

The politicization of promotion would have catastrophic consequences for the army, and for the country, once the fighting started. The process of promotion in peacetime armies is always suspect, because it tends to favor skills that have nothing much to do with fighting and winning wars. But demanding that only officers with certain political beliefs be put into leadership positions stacks the deck still further, not to mention destroying morale.

And in fact, Messimy had difficulty finding a senior officer who would take the job, given those conditions. The logical choice was General Paul Marie Pau, who, since he was born in 1848, was a safe choice, since at the age of 63, he'd be headed for retirement shortly, and wouldn't cause any difficulties politically.

But Pau wasn't about to accept the conditions imposed by the government, and turned the offer down. So Joffre, who was amenable, was given the post instead. The Third Republic wanted a politically aware general as chief, and they got one with a vengeance, as once the war began the one talent Joffre unquestionably had was in knowing how to get rid of possible rivals. It's interesting how many of the senior generals whom Joffre sacked also happened to be men who in the normal course of things would have been in the group of possible replacements. Those who were too politically connected to sack, like Maurice Sarrail, Joffre managed to dispose of rather cleverly: Sarrail, who was the poster general for the left, was shipped off to command the Anglo-French expedition to the Balkans. A better dumping ground could hardly be imagined.[7]

As a result, it took a very long time to force Joffre out, even after the unmitigated chain of setbacks and disasters of 1915. But at the same time, the generals who emerged, the few really successful men, like Pétain and Fayolle and even Foch, had all spent years watching helplessly as the government meddled and interfered in the army. As a result, they had no great love for their civilian overlords. One can imagine, for instance, how Ferdinand Foch, whose brother was a Jesuit, felt about André's anti-Catholic inquisition. And when the time came, he repaid the favor with interest.

As chief of the general staff, Joffre would also serve as vice chair of the CSG, while General Auguste Dubail would continue his job as chief of the army staff, a confusing distinction. But Dubail was basically Joffre's head of personnel, although without any actual authority (when the war began Dubail received an army command, and was then—according to him—made a scapegoat for one of the many failed offensives).

But Joffre soon found that his authority in peacetime was severely limited, not restricted just to promotions. He had no authority over the various bureaus overseeing the development of weapons, or for that matter any of what the ministry of war called the *directions des armes du ministère*. These were the specialists who decided what equipment the army needed. Given the revolving door at the ministry, they pretty much operated independently, as Joffre promptly discovered.

He had noticed what one would think was a rather blindingly obvious defect. On the one hand, the specialists at the artillery bureau had decided, along with a good many gunners, that the 75-millimeter gun was the only weapon the army needed. But as we have seen, geography dictated that the Germans would be forced into the Meuse valley, either above or below Verdun, or both. But in that case, the 75 was basically useless. That was because the barrel could be elevated to only 16 degrees from the horizontal, a typical design constraint for field guns of the period. But for the intended theater of operations, this was a serious drawback.

Because the defense of the heights of the Meuse posed a problem that could not be resolved by the flat trajectory of the 75: there existed, all along these steep heights, considerable numbers of dead angles that it would not be able to reach.[8]

So Joffre, sensibly enough, suggested the need for a 105- or 120-millimeter howitzer like the Germans had. But General Michel, who was at that time still the vice chairman of the CSG, thought the older 155-millimeter Rimailho gun was fine, despite its limited traverse, so the matter was buried. But once he became chief of staff, Joffre brought the matter up again, and this time he got his way.

Sort of: The specialists at the bureau managed to delay the matter indefinitely. There were plenty of good designs, but for some reason none of them met the specifications—a dodge that everyone who has worked with a bureaucracy understands. Nor was there any money available. Eventually the French firm of Schneider came up with a design that was approved. But production, such as it was, proceeded at a dilatory pace.

The 155-millimeter gun that Michel had been so keen on hardly existed in any quantity: There were only 84 of them in service in 1912, hardly enough to equip an army corps, and by 1914, the army only had 104 of them.[9]

Nor was it much of a weapon. As it weighed over 10,000 kilograms, it was hardly a mobile weapon; by contrast, its German counterpart, the 15-centimeter howitzer, weighed roughly a fifth of that, had a much greater angle of fire (43 degrees), and outranged the Rimailho by 2,500 meters.[10] All in all, not much of a weapon.

Production of the 105-millimeter howitzer was going at a glacial pace. The army was supposed to begin taking the gun into service at the rate of 16 guns a month, with deliveries slated to start in October 1914. As the official British Army handbook issued to its officers in July 1914 put it, "it is probable, however, that the artillery of an army-corps will be eventually increased by 2 batteries of 4 guns each of 105 millimeter guns."[11]

Moreover, to add insult to injury, the Schneider howitzer, like the Rimailho, was not all that successful a design. The equivalent German gun was lighter, fired its shells at a higher angle, and its range was nearly the same. It was far too heavy and bulky for the projectile it fired. The impression one gets from these two weapons is that the French designers had failed to grasp a basic point about howitzer design: that to be useful as divisional artillery, they had to be just as mobile as the field guns.

Nor was this a difficult task. Since howitzers have a shorter range, the stresses exerted on the shell are much less, so not only can it contain more explosive, but the same gun carriage used for the standard field gun can handle the howitzer. In consequence, the German 10.5- and 15-centimeter howitzers used basically the same gun carriage as the 7.7-centimeter field gun. Fitted out for the field, the 10.5-centimeter howitzer weighed only 190 kilograms more than the field gun, and its explosive shell contained roughly ten times as much high explosive.[12] So they were equally mobile, and could be deployed at the divisional level, as indeed they were.

The Schneider, however, was either deliberately designed so as not to be as mobile as the 75, or, perhaps more reasonably, was conceptualized as being a piece of heavy artillery, as the French simply refused to give the army corps anything besides the field guns; such heavy weapons as they had were all hoarded at the army group level.

General Fayolle noted in his diary how this worked out in practice, in his typically cheerful and nonjudgmental way.

> One of the great faults that is clung to obstinately is the duality of the command of the artillery. The heavy guns are under the orders of the Army group; that is to say, of a general who is some kilometers from the field of battle and knows nothing of the realities of the locale. . . . It is completely insane.[13]

Not only did the French not have the right weapons, not only did they refuse to adopt them until well along in the war, but they absolutely refused to parcel them out to the control of the combat commanders, the divisional generals who were actually conducting the fighting.

THE PENDULUM SWINGS BACK

After the two successive revolutions caused by the introduction of melinite and the creation of the long-recoil field gun, one faction in the army began to argue that technology had neutered the forts. That argument resonated with a gradual shift in the way the army was regarding its basic posture in the event of war.

Now, it is a capital error to assume that by August 1914 the army was committed to the principle of the offensive at all costs; it would be considerably more accurate to say that the professional officer corps, divided into various chapels, was unable to agree on any one doctrine.[14] The situation was exacerbated by the relative powerlessness of the new chief of staff, and the newness of his position.

What actually happened in the fifteen years preceding the war was the rise of a chapel arguing for a fundamental change: that the army should move away from its late-nineteenth-century notion of strategic defense, to the idea of strategic offense. To them, the adoption of the 75-millimeter field gun, and the successful planning for a speedy mobilization, all seemed to point toward this idea. The idea of taking the war to the enemy, rather than waiting for him to invade, became more and more practicable.

But at the same time, the engineers who had built the forts continued to grapple with the problems caused by the new high-explosive shells. The committee charged with overseeing the forts was now firmly enshrined in the military bureaucracy of the Third Republic. It will be remembered that General Michel, who was chairing that committee, had also been the vice chairman of the CSG before the Messimy reform that resulted in the creation of an actual chief of staff. So as a result, the engineers continued to get money, and they continued to grapple with the problems posed by the new high-explosive shells.

The problems boiled down to two: how to armor the forts so they were proof against the new shells, and how to protect their guns.

These were two entirely separate issues. To simplify the problem considerably: The first simply involved pouring more concrete, covering over the largely brick and stone walls with a sandwich of earth and concrete, and then enclosing what lay inside the walls. So when a fort was upgraded, or modernized, it increasingly started to look like a quadrilateral mound, with very little of it being exposed.

There was not enough money to upgrade every fort, but then the engineers realized that the new shells meant that some forts were no longer doing their job, while others would clearly be in a secondary role.

Earlier, in tracking the construction of the forts at Verdun, their positions were explained by asking the reader to envision an imaginary circle, with the ancient citadel at the center. Invoking that same imaginary circle, all the forts in the northeast quadrant (0 to 90 degrees) and those in the northwest quadrant (270 to 360 degrees) were all upgraded. And, of course, the structures built after 1885 were already constructed according to the new principles.

But the forts in the southern half were largely left alone. So too with the two initial forts that were on the right bank nearest the city: Belleville and Saint Michel. And hardly anything was done to the *forts de rideau*, the line of forts running from Verdun down to Saint-Mihiel.

The reason seems fairly obvious: Given the heights of the Meuse below Verdun, it was hardly likely that an invading army would be able to get the 220- or 270-millimeter mortars close enough to the forts for their shells to reach them. These weapons all had a range of roughly 5,000 meters, and the terrain around those forts was such that it hardly seemed likely that it would be possible to wrestle a weapon weighing six or seven thousand kilograms up the steep slopes that were the norm in the southern reach of the heights, and get it within the required range.

So the first problem was relatively easy to solve simply by throwing money at it. But the other problem was more complicated. Forts were essentially protected gun platforms. But in order for its guns to be useful, they had to be sufficiently protected from enemy shell fire. Prior to the introduction of melinite, this had hardly been much of a consideration. The forts looked quite different from their seventeenth-century ancestors, but the gun emplacements were pretty much the same: large openings in the outer walls through which the gun fired, the only addition increasingly being that the gun was protected above as well as in front.

But a high-explosive shell exploding close by the opening would probably wreck the gun, even if it was a near miss.

The theoretical solution to the problem was to mount the weapon in a steel turret. Now that the forts were all going to be largely enclosed structures, you could envision one as being analogous to a battleship, where, increasingly, the guns were mounted on the deck in turrets, as opposed to the older, slab-sided approach.

So between 1885 and 1910, the engineers went through a whole series of progressively more sophisticated designs, as they created the perfect mechanism. What emerged by the start of the century was a truly ingenious system.

The turret was basically a steel cylinder with a rounded steel hat as a roof. When the fort was under fire, the turret was retracted down into the body of the carapace, so that all that was visible was the rounded top, a sort of flattened tortoise shell made of thick steel. When you needed to fire the gun, the cylinder was elevated, so the basic principle was what the French engineers called the *tourelle à éclipse*, the disappearing turret.

The engineers experimented with various configurations, and quickly discovered that although a spherical turret was better able to withstand shells than a cylindrical one, the best solution was to retract the turret entirely.

The principle is simple, but the technology involved is anything but. First of all, the barrel of the gun has to be contained completely inside the steel cylinder. A turret that would contain the entire gun—and its crew—would be impossibly large, so enormous, so heavy, it would be impossible to retract it and then raise it up again.

The engineers got around this problem by the simple expedient of sawing off a piece of the barrel, a sort of aftermarket modification that enabled them to take the existing (at the time) 120- or 155-millimeter gun and fit it entirely inside the turret. That, of course, reduced the range of the gun considerably, but given the range of the heavy mortars, they reckoned, sensibly enough, that 5,000 meters was perfectly adequate.

But protecting the gun tube was only half the battle. Since the turret had to be raised and lowered, the recoil of the gun had to be absorbed somehow. Otherwise, the first time the gun was fired, the relatively delicate mechanism that raised and lowered the turret would be damaged.

The solution to that was simple as well: a hydraulic buffering system. So, although the 75-millimeter gun was the first field gun using this principle, it was already being employed in the guns mounted in the turrets—some ten years, roughly, before the advent of the field gun.

The gun the engineers picked was the 155-millimeter weapon from 1878. So the army could have easily converted this gun, put a wheeled carriage on it, and had reasonably modern heavy artillery. The system De Bange guns were excellent weapons, in terms of range and hitting power. Their only defect was the lack of a recoil mechanism, something that the fort engineers had already solved.

So basically, one branch of the army was developing a weapon that would have been a perfect fit for another part of the army—but the two sailed along in perfect disharmony. The artillery bureau had no interest in developing any other gun, or in modernizing any of their existing weapons, just like the army commands had no intention of giving heavy artillery to the local commanders.

This was, as Fayolle pointed out, crazy. Particularly because, as we shall see in the next chapter, the Germans did precisely that. Superiority in combat is not simply a function of having weapons that are better or the same as your enemy possesses. Using them efficiently on the battlefield is the key. To do that means decentralization, delegating command down to lower levels, which in turn requires highly trained officers farther down the chain of command. In another bitter passage, Fayolle writes why he believed the Germans were better. "They don't have as many mediocre and ignorant company officers as we do," he confided to his diary, and, much later in the war: "The great superiority of the German army is in training and instruction."[15]

But the two groups proceeded in immaculate independence and mutual disdain. Although the disappearing turrets were expensive propositions to build and mount, the French built some 60 of them, some with one 155-millimeter gun, others with two.

The chief difficulty with the turrets was that the gun was fixed. The gunners could make changes in elevation, but, by comparison with other mounts, their field of fire was extremely restricted. Think of the field of fire as being a triangle, with the apex sited at the point where the gun barrel was attached to the mount. The greater the angle of the apex, the more useful the gun. Of course, guns mounted in a fort by definition had a smaller field of fire— i.e., a narrower angle—because of the embrasure, but the disappearing turret restricted that angle enormously.

The engineers were well aware of this, and came up with various solutions. In certain angles of the forts, those where they judged the emplacement would not be susceptible to enemy artillery fire of the sort that would destroy the position, they placed pairs of guns in protected casemates, called *casements de Bourges*.

Although the new 75-millimeter gun had basically the same range as the older 155-millimeter weapon, it had a much smaller footprint. It weighed only about a third as much, had a lower profile, and was smaller all the way around, so it made these installations much more practicable. The 75 became the basis for all the fixed armaments of the forts designed after 1904 (although the older gun turrets were still being built and put in place right up until the start of the war).

The smaller size meant that the guns could sit comfortably back inside the protecting wall, shielded to a certain extent by an overhang, and their position made the openings extremely hard to hit. But the embrasure was such that the guns had a wide field of fire.

So the next logical step was to design a turret that not only could be raised and lowered, but also be rotated on its mount. In theory, this turret was the ideal solution, and the lighter 75-millimeter gun, coupled with its more compact shape, made the notion of a rotating turret much more practical. The smaller the weapon, the smaller the turret; the smaller the turret, the less weight, and that in turn reduced the motive power required to move it. In the years before 1914, motive power was a major issue, as the idea of diesel-powered generators was still simply an idea.

The idea was even more practicable if machine guns were used instead of field guns, so those were built as well. So now the engineers felt they had devised a set of complete solutions to their original problem. The upgraded forts were basically shellproof. The new turrets and casemates gave them integral firepower that would largely be immune to enemy bombardment. Meanwhile, the emplaced batteries that were shielded by the forts would be able to shatter the attacking forces.

Now, since almost everyone who has any familiarity with the opening of the First World War knows that the Germans overpowered the Belgian forts rather quickly, an account of these expensive engineering efforts seems pointless. And indeed, as we noticed earlier, at the same time as the engineers were solving the problems posed by the new shells, other factions in the army were increasingly restive about the whole concept of the forts.

READING BACKWARD

To a certain extent, everyone reads history backward. In this case, there is an almost irresistible temptation to view the whole Séré de Rivières project in the light of the prevailing idea about the Maginot Line, to see it either as an exercise in folly, or as a sign of defeatism, and to come to the conclusion that it certainly didn't work.

So the whole notion about the forts—in both wars—is a great example of a complex error loop, how one basic deficiency leads to another, until the conclusion becomes almost completely the opposite of what actually happened. Erroneous conclusions are often quite seductive, and untangling them can be difficult and tedious. So it is here, although the basic facts of the case are simply stated.

The first point to note is that the French and the Belgians were not the only people building forts. The Germans fortified key parts of their new possessions on the left bank of the Rhine: Strasbourg, Thionville, and, notably, Metz. They matched the French step by step in the process we have described. Nor were they the only power to become involved in such massive construction projects. Romania did the same thing, within the limitations of its budget. In fact, the genesis of the whole notion of the disappearing turret can be found in an 1885 competition organized by the Romanian government for armaments for fortifications defending Bucharest, in which both German and French designs for steel turrets were submitted.

Second, to return to the idea of reading backward, between the wars the Germans built fortifications on both frontiers, and this continued after Hitler came to power in 1933. Hitler even interfered with the designs and insisted on the engineers using his as opposed to theirs. The Swiss and the Belgians built fortifications as well. To the best of their abilities and means, so did the Finns and the Russians.

Third, as far as France goes, the Maginot Line positions were not, as is often assumed, simply bypassed. They were subjected to heavy attacks by artillery, by dive-bombers, and even by infantry assaults. When France asked for an armistice, the garrisons of the forts were still holding out. None of them had surrendered. The idea of a Maginot Line mentality is one of those wonderful fictions that has no factual basis whatsoever. Rather it rests on an astonishing level of ignorance.

Airpower, far from rendering the forts useless, proved incapable of destroying them, or even inflicting much damage. In 1944, the aging Franco-German forts around Metz, manned by the dregs of the German army, held up Patton's American forces for months, just as the primitive structures the Finns built did with the Russians in 1939–1940.

As we have seen, there were sound reasons why the engineers spent decades upgrading the forts they had built, and creating new kinds of artillery emplacements for them. They realized that the exposed masonry structures of the 1870s were not proof against the new shells and guns being developed. But all these renovations and additions took a great deal of money. The French and the Germans spent it; the Belgians did not. In consequence, when the war began, German gunners destroyed the Belgian guns mounted in the forts right off.

In some cases, their heavy guns did substantial damage to the structures themselves, although subsequent investigations revealed that the damage was substantially less than was believed at the time. But that same level of investigation makes clear that the French forts that had been upgraded and modernized were basically invulnerable to the biggest and most powerful shells.

What runs through the analysis of both the Belgian and French forts—in both wars—is a very time-honored principle. As it happens, there is an excellent historical analogy: with the fortress island of Malta, which Napoleon captured in a bold stroke in 1798. Militarily speaking, the place was impregnable—provided the defenders had the will to fight. They did not. Malta fell without a shot being fired.

That observation is not simply a historical curiosity. It leads us to a consideration of that most excellent French word *moral*. The word is related to the usual meaning of the English word *morale*, but it encompasses a great deal more than that. When Pétain observed that Verdun was the *boulevard moral* of France, he meant that it was a physical place that summed up all of the country's spiritual and intellectual qualities, embodied all of the country's mental faculties, its intellectual state of mind (simply to parse a standard French dictionary).

Or, to put it in more concrete terms, relate it to particular circumstances: the Knights of Saint John, who held Malta, weren't willing to fight for it. The Belgians who manned their forts over a century later were willing to fight, but only up to a certain point: the point at which concerns of personal safety, coupled with a sense of futility, outweighed their duty to their country—a calculation hardly confined to the Belgians: the Confederate officers who were in command of forts Henry and Donelson in 1862, like General Pemberton at Vicksburg 18 months later, all came to the same conclusion. They quit.

In all those cases, cowardice or courage had little to do with it, as indeed it has precious little to do with combat. But great captains, from Napoleon to U. S. Grant (and those before and after) all instinctively understood the importance of this French adjective. To translate it into American situations: the Alamo was the *place moral* of Texas. Belleau Wood was *bois moral* of the American marines. To fail there was such a horrifying possibility that it was inconceivable—even if that meant fighting to the last man.

Now, this linguistic and psychological digression may seem out of place in the midst of a discussion about the concrete, about the most physical and tangible parts of war. But Pétain's little phrase, like many of his seemingly bland remarks, is the key to understanding everything that happened there. The fight was not about territory; it was about willpower, the will to power, and given the emphasis a whole phalanx of German philosophers had placed on that idea, it's hardly surprising that their country's officers, who were a highly educated group of men, would fail to grasp it. The territory seized was simply the physical manifestation of a triumph of abstractions.

The real mystery is why certain men in certain situations will fight to the death, and why, in other situations, they simply quit. That observation takes us to the heart of the fundamental mystery of the Great War. One French historian, after noting that in this war, prisoners were treated very well on both sides, addresses the question directly: "Why weren't there more prisoners?"[16]

There are no easy answers to that question, and indeed, in that sense, the remark by Wells about this being a very queer war is really a deep insight. Indeed, as we wade through page after page of horrific battles, with death tolls that are really incomprehensible, the question becomes more and more disturbing.

4

The September Wars for Verdun

One could develop a complete theory about modern
France under the heading: failure seen as success.

—Jean Dutourd[1]

The French call the fighting of August and September 1914 the
Battle of the Frontiers. Although there were certainly some serious
battles directly inside the northeastern frontier, August 1914 was
not, as the rubric suggests, a repeat of 1870. Like much else about
this war, the idea of battles on the frontier was a combination of
wishful thinking and misrepresentation.

Most of the fighting, the worst of it, was deep inside France.
The worst of it was very bad indeed. About 2.8 million men were
deployed to stop the German offensive, and by the end of the second month of the war, 329,000 of them were either dead or missing, by far the highest death toll of any equivalent period in the
entire war.[2] The medical services broke down to the extent that the
army was never able to come up with any estimates of wounded
cases for this period.

Out of this mountain of corpses, the army high command de-
creed a victory: the Battle of the Marne. The Germans had been

stopped, were in precipitous retreat. Paris was saved; the dead hand of von Schlieffen had been thwarted.

THE FIRST BATTLE FOR VERDUN: (1) REVIGNY AND THE LEFT BANK

In the French Army archives, the Marne was subdivided into four separate engagements.[3] The biggest and bloodiest of these was called Revigny, for the town that lay closest to the deepest penetration. The names given to these four engagaments are geographically misleading. The engagements that defined the Battle of the Marne occurred in a great arc sweeping from the north of Paris to the south of Verdun. Like the Battle of the Frontiers, this appellation obscures some fundamental realities

The town of Revigny was at the southern end of a 50-kilometer arc that curved to the northeast, ending at Verdun, about 200 kilometers east of Paris and well over 20 kilometers north of the Marne river. There is a river nearby: the Ornain, which runs through the town.

Students of the opening phase of this war sometimes get the impression that the chief German aim was to encircle Paris in a vast flanking movement. As we noted in chapter one, the actual strategy was aimed at a complex double envelopment of the French armies that had been deployed to the northeast of Paris. But the double envelopment was complex, because within that giant pincers was a secondary double envelopment directed at Verdun, and by 6 September, units of the German Fifth Army were well below Verdun on both sides of the Meuse river.

The advancing Fifth Army was strung out in a flattened arc from Nixéville, about five kilometers from the forts of the southwestern quadrant of Verdun through Souilly, Rembercourt, the river Cher, and Revigny.

To get an idea of just how far to the south of Verdun the Germans actually were: Souilly is a village on the road that runs from

Verdun south to Bar-le-Duc. It is about 16 kilometers south of the city of Verdun, and was Pétain's headquarters during the spring 1916 German offensive. The road itself became famous as the Voie Sacrée, the only remaining link into the forts.

So the Fifth Army was not simply trying to envelop Verdun. They had already achieved that. The French responded to the threat. General Maurice Sarrail, commanding the Third Army, had the Fifth and Sixth Army Corps attacking the advancing Germans on their right flank, with four reserve divisions holding his right flank—that is to say, their position was anchored on Verdun.

As fighting began, both sides attempted to turn the other's extended flank, with the German Fourth Army trying to break through a rough line: Andernay-Revigny-Villers-sur-Vent. At Revigny-sur-Ornain, where the French Third and Fourth Army boundary was, a sizable gap had developed as the Third Army had been pushed back. In the face of German attacks on both sides of the Argonne, Sarrail (the original commander, Ruffey, had been sacked at the end of August) was folding his front down like a swinging door, the hinge being Verdun. His troops were retreating in a southeasterly direction, in order to keep from being outflanked and cut off from the French armies locked in major battle outside of Nancy, about 90 kilometers to the east.

By September 7, there was a real possibility that units of the two German armies would break through on both sides of Revigny, as the French Fifth Army Corps had now been forced back to the outskirts of the hamlet of Bussy-la-Côte, hanging on by its toenails.

As the Germans pressed on, the French General Staff shifted a new army corps, the Fifteenth, over from Commercy. This shift was a desperation move, which would have fatal consequences very shortly. However, in the three days of desperate fighting, the French managed to hold the line.

The consequences of a failure were catastrophic. Sarrail had already committed his reserve divisions to hold the northern end of the line (above the river Aire). There was literally nothing between the battlefield and Nancy, where the French were equally desperate. If the Germans broke through on either side (around Nancy or around Revigny), the entire section of the front from Verdun to Toul would simply implode. Not only would the Germans have Verdun, but they would have either destroyed or captured an entire French army group.

But then, abruptly, to the surprise and relief of the French, the Germans disengaged from the battle and began to retreat to the north.

One of the best writers to emerge from the war was Maurice Genevoix. In September 1914, he was a very junior lieutenant (age 23). His regiment, the 106th, was part of the 12th Division, 6th Army Corps, engaged in a desperate fight south of Souilly. On the evening of the last night, he was dispatched to try to get reinforcements. He walked most of the night, finally arrived at headquarters, where he was told there were no reinforcements available. So he walked back up the front with his grim news. But by the time he arrived, the battle was over. The surviving French troops, exhausted, were jubilant. The Germans had pulled back.

"So," he asked his captain, "this is a great victory?" The answer was equivocal. But the two officers realized quickly enough that if the Germans were withdrawing, they had held.[4]

THE FIRST BATTLE FOR VERDUN: (2) FORT DE TROYON AND THE RIGHT BANK

There were six forts on the heights of the Meuse between Verdun and Toul. Génicourt was the closest, and then Troyon, about 12 kilometers south of the forts and roughly the same distance to the east of Souilly, where Genevoix was fighting off the Germans. The Fort du Camp des Romains was just below the city of Saint-Mihiel, while Liouville guarded the eastern extremities of the heights ten kilometers to the southeast of the city. The remaining two forts, Jouy and Gironville, were still farther to the south, and thus played no role in the fighting.

On the left bank below Verdun, there was one fort, Paroches, one of the most elderly. Built in 1879, it hadn't been touched since then, was basically a battery—that is to say, a fortified artillery position. Its armament consisted of four 120-millimeter guns and 12 90-millimeter guns, all the same vintage as the fort, and expected to use ammunition that predated melinite.

As a result, neither Paroches nor Genicourt was going to be able to offer much support to Troyon, if it was attacked. Given its position, Troyon was the logical candidate. If the Germans could break through there, they could move upstream to Saint-Mihiel without any obstacles, cross the river there, and attack Herr's defensive positions from the rear. At the same time, they would effectively cut off Verdun from the rest of France, because there were only two main-line sets of railroad track going into Verdun: There was the Paris-Reims-Verdun line coming in from the west, and one paralleling the Meuse river, entering Verdun from the south. Given that the advancing Germans were already far past the former, cutting the latter would mean Verdun would be completely surrounded, unable to receive supplies.

As we explained in chapter two, the southern half of the Woëvre is curious terrain. It is dominated by the heights of the Meuse, with outlying buttes scattered apparently at random. The other dominant feature is a series of lakes, and the conventional wisdom in Paris was that this land was mostly swamp. That is hardly the case, but all in all, the area is difficult for military operations on any scale. For both sides, the area was terra incognita, so the advancing Prussians, Austrians, and Bavarians moved cautiously.

The French had reckoned that military operations there were basically impracticable. They had a good point. Given the rough terrain of the heights themselves, it was difficult to see how an invader would be able to get his heavy artillery in close enough range to do any serious damage to the forts, and the various valleys that ventilated the heights, led to the river valley, could easily be blocked.

Technically, the defense of the Woëvre was left to the French Second Army under Noël-Édouard de Castelnau, but de Castelnau was spread very thin. Moreover, in order to salvage Sarrail's hard-pressed troops at Revigny, he had been forced to shift troops across the Meuse.

As a result there were precious few French troops in the part of the Woëvre between Verdun and Saint-Mihiel, so General von Strantz was able to work his way diagonally across the Woëvre and concentrate on reducing the fort. Although there were several places where the French could have put up a good fight, at this point there were simply no French troops available to man those.

Indeed, in studying the records of the fighting in the Woëvre, the impression carried away is that no one at the GQG even knew this part of Lorraine existed. After the defeats along a line stretching from Cons-la-Grandville to Mercy-le-Haut, just inside the frontier with Belgium, the Woëvre had largely been abandoned, was, temporarily, a sort of gigantic no-man's-land. So on 8 September, von Strantz began pounding Troyon with impunity.

He had at his disposal what was still, in these early days of the war, something of a secret weapon. In addition to a battery of the powerful 21-centimeter howitzers, he had a battery of the much more powerful Austrian 30.5-centimeter ones. Both of these were motorized, capable of navigating the sketchy roads that would put them within range of the fort. The Austrian guns were, in theory, capable of pounding Troyon into rubble, since it had been built to withstand only the standard 150-millimeter French gun of the 1870s.

The Austrians by now had shelled enough forts to understand the physical and psychological effects on the garrison as they huddled in their cavelike shelters, trying to figure out whether they'd suffocate for lack of air, be poisoned by fumes, be buried alive, or, perhaps more mercifully, be blown to bits. So the next day, the Germans thoughtfully asked the garrison whether they were ready to surrender.

Now, the commander of Troyon, a lowly captain named Heym, was well aware of the consequences of the surrender of the fort. He refused the offer, the shelling began again, and that evening, the

Germans tried an actual assault. They moved cautiously, unwilling to risk heavy losses, and retired when they realized the defenders were not about to quit without a fight.

So the next day the shelling resumed, with Paroches and Genicourt firing in the general direction of Troyon and hoping to hit something. Although the French 120-millimeter gun had a decent range, it suffered from the defect common to any mechanical recoil weapon that was being fired over any distance: The movement of the gun as it recoiled when fired made it impossible to land successive rounds with any accuracy.

Heym was determined to hold out, as General Michel Coutanceau, the commander of Verdun, was scraping together troops from the garrison to come to Heym's relief. The Austrians kept on shelling, and by 12 September, the fort recorded ten separate barrages. But by this time, the relief column was arriving. Their approach coincided with the general order to retreat. But Heym was still holding out in the rubble.

It is not much of an exaggeration to say that this obscure officer played the role of the proverbial Dutch boy who put his finger in the dike. If Troyon had fallen, most of the French defenders on the left bank would have been trapped, and it is quite possible that this, the first battle for Verdun, would have then become the last and only. Sadly, Heym, a true hero of the first weeks of the war, did not live long enough to see his feat recognized. He was killed a few weeks later, in the desperate French attempts to defend Marchéville, in the Woëvre, and few remember his name, even among specialists.

His death was to prove doubly unfortunate for the French. As one of the few historians to recognize Heym's feat remarks, "As goes the chief, so goes the fort."[5] And if Heym had lived he could have spoken out against the delusions of the French high command regarding the weakness of the forts. Troyon was old, had never been upgraded. But Heym held out.

To elaborate on this notion from the other side: it is anyone's guess whether or not the crown prince, commander of the German

Fifth Army, or his Bavarian counterpart, in command of the Sixth, would have retreated so obediently to the north in response to the general retreat ordered by von Moltke if they had maintained their stranglehold on Verdun.

This idea may seem peculiar to the reader who has been given the somewhat distorted idea that the German army operated on principles of robotic obedience. To a certain extent that was true for ordinary soldiers—as in theory it is in any army. But it was hardly true for field-grade commanders. In 1870, von Moltke the Elder had been frequently frustrated by the actions of his subordinate generals. More than once he found himself in the same position as Lee or Grant, scrambling to try to figure out what they were actually doing, his only certitude being that they definitely weren't doing what he had told them to do. Von Moltke the Younger had ejected Kaiser Wilhelm from army maneuvers because he was disruptive, and as we shall see, his successor, Erich von Falkenhayn, had the devil's own time with Paul von Hindenburg. And this despite the fact that von Falkenhayn was his superior and in theory the supreme commander of the German army.

The commanders of the two German armies involved followed their orders not because they were blindly obedient, but because by 12 September, the battlefield situation was a stalemate. Moreover, since their colleagues were retreating, they faced the prospect of having to continue a battle against an enemy whose strength was growing.

There is no question that eventually Troyon would have been neutralized. Either the garrison would have surrendered, or the fort wrecked to the point that, like the hapless Belgians at Liège, they were powerless to stop the Germans from flowing around them.

But Séré de Rivières had never intended his scheme to result in impregnable fortifications. The whole design was predicated on buying time, and that was exactly what Troyon had done. It had held out long enough for a relief column to be approaching, which was all that could be asked of it. In fact, given its condition, it had done much more than that.

There had always been questions about the extent to which the Malmaison trials of 1888 had been a fair test. The engineers had always felt that the artillery had been allowed to operate much closer to the fort than would have actually been the case in a real-world situation. And, as we have seen, when, in 1908, there was a repeat test, at Fort Antoine, that structure proved considerably more resistant.

Troyon had received 200 direct hits from Austrian guns, and 2,800 from smaller ones. The damage to the fort was severe, but Heym had only five men killed and 23 wounded. The system definitely worked. Unfortunately, as we shall see, no one at headquarters was paying any attention to what was happening on the heights of the Meuse.

THE SECOND BATTLE FOR VERDUN: (1) THE ARGONNE

The order for the general retreat was Helmuth von Moltke's last order as German chief of staff. In the German system, the man at the top paid for the failure of his plans, a sensible approach that the Allies would have done well to follow. A. J. P. Taylor's caustic remark speaks to the central paradox: "The French had lost most of their coal supplies, all their iron fields, and much of their heavy industry. Joffre, strangely, came out with an enhanced reputation which kept him in supreme command for two more years."[6] Even more strangely, over the next decades, British military historians used von Moltke the Younger for rhetorical target practice, probably to deflect attention away from the inadequacies of their own generals.

Meanwhile, back in the real world of early September 1914, von Moltke's successor was Erich von Falkenhayn. As minister of war, he had been following events carefully, and he lost no time in redirecting German strategy in the west. On 18 September, he ordered a new envelopment of Verdun. The main effort would be on the right bank, but Fifth Army would also see what it could do in the Argonne, where the French Third Army was still licking its wounds from Revigny.

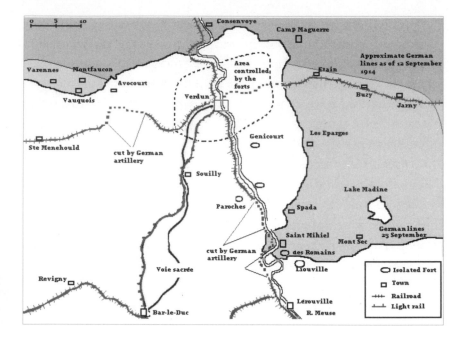

The French were caught off guard by the idea of an offensive on this side of the Meuse. The heavily forested, tough terrain of the Argonne was the kind of landscape that European armies liked to avoid. Nor was the section of the front a small piece of it. The Argonne front by itself was approximately the same size as the section held by the BEF in 1915.[7]

Trees posed unique problems for the armies of 1914. Wherever possible, of course, gunners liked to set their batteries up so that the position was screened by trees. Given the rather primitive nature of aerial reconnaissance, a small wooded area could provide excellent cover, even during the winter, and the guns could be aimed up through the branches. Provided, of course, that we are talking about guns with a high enough angle of fire, which the majority of French weapons were not. Then a site on the edge of a forest, so the guns were firing out across an open field, was the best choice.

The real problem began, however, when the shell tried to descend through the tree canopy at the other end, and its descent was obstructed—temporarily—by branches and trunks. The result was minimal accuracy. Shells went off course, plunged deep into the wet ground, or burst too high in the air. The ideal ending for a shell was to explode either right on contact with the target, or directly above it. In the former case, it would destroy the target itself, while in the latter, the blast would destroy the people beneath.

Then too it was difficult to observe where the shell actually fell. Indirect fire was totally dependent on gunner-observer coordination, the observers providing continuous feedback on the initial shots. The realistic objective was one long, one short, and then a rapid-fire barrage right on the target. But when the shell exploded beneath the tree canopy, it was next to impossible to spot it accurately. And even if the impact was observed, it was quite possible that the fall had been deflected, and the observer's correction would walk the gunners away from, rather than into, their target.

Heavily wooded areas were problematic for machine gunners as well. For their weapons to be effective, they needed large, unimpeded spaces for the weapon to traverse with its fire. So the Argonne appeared to be an area where the German advantages in matériel, especially in artillery, would be largely offset by the terrain.

It should be pointed out that the barren landscapes that immediately come to mind when we think of this war are all derived from photographs taken after the fighting had been raging in that area for months, sometimes years. But it took a surprisingly long time for all the trees of a forest to be destroyed, a fact that was true from the Argonne all the way down through the Vosges.[8]

There were stretches in Lorraine with open fields, but the heavily forested, rugged landscape of the Argonne was duplicated on the right bank of the RFV, while the ridges that led from the Argonne to the Meuse were also heavily forested, as were most elevations of the Vosges.

And it was true that initially the Germans had tough going. In their initial offensive of 23 September, the Germans had taken a reasonable piece of the forest.[9] But by the twenty-eighth, French resistance had stiffened, and then, on 2 October 1914, the French began their own attacks, the success of which created a kind of salient into the German line, centered around Bagatelle and Saint-Hubert.

The Argonne was handed over to General Karl Bruno Julius von Mudra, a spry sexagenarian with handlebar mustaches, who had been the military governor of Metz, and the head of the German combat engineers, the Pioniere. Like von Falkenhayn, von Mudra's approach was to take incremental steps, carefully planned, and certain of results. Under his leadership, the Pioniere became not merely a combat force, but one equipped with weaponry that no other army possessed.

The most famous of these was the Minenwerfer, what in Anglo-American infantry parlance would be called mortars. In the early days of the recoil revolution, the French and the Germans categorized artillery pieces according to a ratio between the length of the barrel and its diameter. Below 10, the weapon was a mortar; if it was longer than 20, it was a gun, while anything between the two was called a howitzer.[10] This was a practical distinction with all sorts of implications, obvious to anyone with a knowledge of Newtonian mechanics, or gunners, but somewhat confusing to everyone else. Short barrels not only meant short ranges, but allowed for a nearly vertical angle of fire.

Think of the shell as going almost straight up and then coming down at the near vertical. By contrast, guns (to use the definition above) fired their shells in much flatter trajectories. A simple example: If soldiers were sheltering behind a building or a ridge, shells fired from guns would pass harmlessly overhead, or crash into the solid barrier they were behind. But a shell fired from a mortar would land directly on them, and in many instances, depending on the nature of the obstacle, so would a howitzer shell.

There was a final twist to all this, which again was a function of basic physics. A shorter range meant less stress on the shell as well as the weapon. In consequence, a mortar shell could have a much greater explosive payload, and that, in accordance with another basic physical law, meant that its blast radius was substantially more lethal. It was like having a satchel of dynamite thrown at you.

Under von Mudra's guidance, the Pioniere were equipped with mortars in two sizes: 17 and 25 centimeters. The relatively low stresses involved, when coupled with the high angle of fire, made for a much flimsier mechanism, so these weapons could be man-handled into position. Get close enough, and a 17-centimeter mortar shell would wreak havoc almost unimaginable.

The idea was simple enough, and after a few years of combat, everyone had infantry mortars. The French soldiers even had a slang term for them, *les crapouillots*. But in August 1914, only the Pioniere had these weapons. Nor was that all. They also had rather primitive inflammable projectors, which by 1916 had become the infamous flamethrower.

Perhaps more important than the existence of such practical infantry weapons was that German doctrine, with its emphasis on pure firepower, meant that Pioniere, like machine gunners, were deployed along with riflemen.

Given von Mudra's background, one would expect him to be an advocate of a war in which explosives replaced men, and this was exactly his approach to fighting in the Argonne. On 21 September, his Sixteenth Army Corps, supported by a huge inventory of artillery, attacked the French Third Army units on a relatively narrow front of about 15 kilometers. At that point in time, the German position was anchored on the butte of Montfaucon and Varennes.

The German offensive can best be thought of as a slowly closing door, the hinge, or pivot, being the Meuse itself. The end result would be to force the defenders back, opening up a gap, and ultimately collapsing them back toward the Meuse itself. An ambitious plan, but it was hardly necessary to achieve it in its entirety. The sort of step-by-step increments that von Mudra preferred would work perfectly.

The main west–east railroad into Verdun was only a few thousand meters to the south of the German lines. Once the Germans got to a certain point in their advance, they could interdict the railroad line without going any farther. Most of the railroad was about twenty kilometers to the south, but there was a curve, or loop, known as the Aubreville curve, because at the village of that name, the line jogged north.

Now, only a short distance away, due north, was a large butte called the Vauquois. Observers on the crest of this hill could easily call down artillery fire on the railroad. There was a small village on the butte, so it was a fine defensive position.

Unfortunately, the French failed to grasp this basic point. Their fear, which was quite understandable, was that the Germans would break through the Argonne forest entirely. So when the German attack began, Maurice Sarrail, the French general commanding the Third Army, directed all his efforts to staving off the leading edge of the door, which was through a densely forested part of the Argonne called the Bois de la Gruerie.

Sarrail is a controversial figure, about whom more later, but at this point it is enough to say, in his defense, that he had figured out the German predilection for flanking attacks, understood that if they broke through the Gruerie and got around his left flank, it would be Revigny all over again, only worse, because by September 21, most French units under his command were still recovering from their losses, were short of ammunition—particularly artillery shells— and were desperately short of men.

Von Mudra's approach was simple. Although he was only an army corps commander, he probably had more heavy artillery at his disposal than the entire French army. In September 1914, the only long-recoil weapon the French had in service was the 75-millimeter gun. Their heavy artillery consisted exclusively of the 120- and 155-millimeter guns from 1878, mechanical recoil weapons incapable of the high-angle fire that the terrain on both sides of the Meuse required.

No army had anything like the German 21-centimeter howitzer. The French firm of Schneider was developing a long-recoil 105-millimeter howitzer, which was going into service, so officially, or technically, the French army did possess a weapon that was the equivalent of the German 10.5- and 15-centimeter howitzers. But in August 1914, the French inventory of heavy guns, as listed by Joffre himself, came down to this:

The bottom line was, that at the beginning of August 1914 . . . as heavy artillery for the army we had 104 Rimailho 155 [millimeter] Shorts divided into 26 batteries, 96 Bacquet 120 [millimeter] cannons divided into 15 batteries, and 20 batteries of 120 [millimeter] Longs either pulled by motors or traction engines. On the other side, Germany aligned: 360 10 centimeter guns, 360 13 centimeter guns, 128 21 centimeter howitzers, for a total of 838 pieces.[11]

As is often the case with the memoirs of the leading participants, the actual situation was much worse than Joffre lets on. The French commander in chief neglects to mention that while French divisions had only 75-millimeter guns, their German counterparts each possessed 18 10.5-centimeter howitzers, while each army corps had at its disposal 16 additional 15-centimeter howitzers.

When it came to firepower, the French were totally outgunned. So saying that von Mudra had more heavy artillery at his disposal than the entire French army is not an exaggeration. Unfortunately for his opponent, it was the truth.

On 19 September, German shells descended precisely onto the French positions, simply erasing them. Then the infantry cautiously moved in and occupied the wreckage.

Every 24 to 36 hours, the process was repeated. By 26 September, von Mudra had advanced roughly eight kilometers on a front of roughly 20, had captured the chief town of the region, Varennes-en-Argonne. More important, his troops had occupied the Vauquois, and had a solid front that extended on both flanks of the butte. Paradoxically, given its importance, the Germans had taken it easily, mainly because the French infantry defending it had not been told how important it was.

One of the advantages of the new long-recoil high-angle-of-fire heavy guns was that truly accurate indirect fire was possible. Once the gunners hit a train, as confirmed by the observers on the butte, they could duplicate the shot almost precisely. Railroad tracks were small targets, but they suffered the disability of not being able to move out of the way. Nor could a train traveling along them.

In consequence the only way the French could get trains into Verdun from the west was at night, and even that was risky. The eventual solution was to lay down new track, safely out of range of observers and their guns. But for the moment (strangely, the moment went on for several years), the Germans had half of a stranglehold on Verdun.

To Sarrail, a native of Carcassonne, the Argonne was as much a foreign country as Bulgaria. The same can be said for his colleague to the right, since de Castelnau had spent most of his military career in Paris with the GQG. Lacking a feel for the region where they had to fight, they approached it the same way as junior staff officers back at headquarters, depending completely on maps.

Unfortunately, map reading in its fullest military sense was a subject that French officers had very little instruction in. It takes training to be able to translate the contour line on a flat map into a three-dimensional image, training as well as experience to see that what appears to be a modest elevation may be the basis for an almost impenetrable defensive position. One of the more fascinating realizations that one has when the German lines are seen on the ground, and then compared with the map, is to see how they invariably picked out the positions that would give them a natural advantage.

Contemporary observers and subsequent writers fell all over themselves to describe the frantic German retreat of early September. What they invariably fail to mention is that however panic-stricken the soldiers were, the positions they retreated to were, across the board, the perfect basis for a defensive line. This was hardly an accident, and after von Falkenhayn took over, the Germans engaged in a series of extremely aggressive offensives to consolidate their positions and make them even tougher propositions for their adversaries.

Looked at on a map, von Mudra's offensive seemed insignificant. But seen on the ground, it was quite the opposite. In five days he had bitten off a key section of the left bank, his artillery had a chokehold on the rail line into Verdun, and he was now forcing the French to fight in an area European armies traditionally stayed as far away from as possible: a heavily forested series of ridges and small hills, with steep slopes and very few roads.

Initially, he was only the commander of the Sixteenth Army Corps, which was based in Metz, where he had been the military governor. But after the first wave of operations in September, his responsibilities were expanded to include the whole of the Argonne, and the Sixteenth Corps became a sort of ad hoc task force that grew in size and firepower.

As soon as von Mudra had moved his phone lines and headquarters farther into the Argonne, he directed another attack, which began on 4 October 1914. It was notable for being the first engagement of the war in which the Germans used everything in their arsenal: In addition to the 21-centimeter howitzers already used in the September attacks, which were normally part of corps artillery, von Mudra added a new and extremely effective weapon, the Minenwerfer, known to subsequent generations simply as mortars. The infantry and the engineers used hand grenades and flamethrowers.[12] As the Allies would discover with tanks, the use of a new weapon did not automatically mean success. The Germans had tough going, and it wasn't until the thirteenth that they had taken off the first line of trenches.

Von Mudra had objected to this offensive. Despite the new weapons, it was a costly operation. So on 13 October, he was formally put in charge of the whole sector. At his disposal he had three infantry divisions: the 33rd and 34th from the Sixteenth Corps, plus the 27th Division (on loan from Fourth Army), the 5th and 6th Jäger, three regiments of Landwehr, an extra three battalions (twelve companies) of Pioniere, and eight regiments of artillery.

Von Mudra's tactics were simple. A small section of the front was selected as the target. There was a massive artillery bombardment, but one of a very short duration, conducted by very heavy weapons. The effect was like dropping one enormous shell on the enemy positions. Then a mixed force of engineers and infantry infiltrated into the pulverized position, followed by groups of infantry and machine gunners. When the new light mortar came into production, mortar crews followed along.[13]

These tactics took time to develop, and at first they were conducted on an even smaller scale. Thus on 1 December 1914, five companies of infantry from the 27th Division grabbed three lines of trenches and took 21 prisoners, at the cost of six dead and 13 wounded. In November and December, there were nine such attacks. On 7 January 1915, another attack in the Ravin des Meurissons advanced over a kilometer and captured 800 prisoners, a major achievement only when one considers that there were almost as many live French prisoners as there were German attackers.

On 29 January 1915, there was another, somewhat bigger attack toward the Ravin de Dieusson. The French lost about 3,000 men, roughly three times the casualties suffered by the attacking Germans. In the first three months of 1915, fighting mostly in the Argonne, the French Third Army lost nearly 30,000 men.

No description, however, can make clear the desperate nature of the struggle. In the December fighting, the fourth regiment of the Foreign Legion (the Garibaldiens) was essentially wiped out, and the Garibaldi brothers, nephews of the famous Italian, killed. On 7 January 1915, General Henri Gouraud, commanding the tenth division, and an officer much admired by his men, was wounded and replaced at the Fille Morte.[14] Von Mudra's men gnawed on through the forest, accumulating a string of impressive-sounding place names. On 8 January 1915, they had taken the *crête* of the Haute-Chevauchée. On the nineteenth, Saint Hubert and then the Fontaine de Madame. On 4 February, the Bagatelle. On the tenth, Marie-Thérèse, and on the sixteenth, they were at the small hamlet of Le Four de Paris. No one place was significant, perhaps, but the string was impressive, and, in fact, the ruins of Le Four de Paris mark the end of the central core of the forest. One more push and the Germans would be out into the clear. French morale fell precipitously.

These small methodical advances solved the other problems as well: there was no need to accumulate a mass of reserve troops, no need to move guns after each lunge. The area attacked was always within range. And since there was no particular reason to attack any one spot, each attack could be delivered as a surprise: It was difficult to forecast, and the preparations for it would leave no aerial intelligence footprint.

Slowly, one small step at a time, the Germans were forcing the French back. But events on the left bank had already been eclipsed by a startling German success on the right, as well as a series of French disasters.

THE SECOND BATTLE FOR VERDUN: (2) THE WOËVRE

The German commander in the Woëvre was now General Hermann von Strantz. A native of Posen (now in Poland), when the war began he was commanding the Fifth Army Corps, recruited from his hometown and environs. On 10 September, there was a major shakeup in the German order of battle. Von Strantz was now put in charge of Armeeabteilung von Strantz, responsible for the area between the Meuse and the Moselle. In addition to his old army corps, he had the Third Bavarian and the Fourteenth Army Corps (Baden), a cavalry division (Bavarian), and the Austrian artillery batteries.

In von Falkenhayn's scheme for the second envelopment of Verdun, von Strantz would attack the heights of the Meuse at the same time that von Mudra attacked out of the Argonne. Even if von Mudra had only a limited success, his offensive would prevent the French from shuttling reinforcements across the Meuse to defend the Woëvre.

In fact, by mid-September, as the French scrambled to regroup, there was a sizable hole in their front. Basically the hole, or breach, was the area between the Meuse and the Moselle rivers, as one French army was on the left bank and its partner to the east was still centered on Nancy.

To be precise, the defense of the entire southern half of the Woëvre had been entrusted to one reserve division, the 75th. That unit had been involved in the fighting on the left bank during the Battle of Revigny, and had suffered some severe blows. It is doubtful that the division had more than 8,000 men, and its artillery consisted of two batteries of 75-millimeter guns and three batteries of ancient 65-millimeter mountain guns.

But for the staff at the GQG this was perfectly logical. As the French officer who wrote the standard and authoritative account of this theater observed, they believed the Woëvre was "impracticable in all its routes."[15]

So although von Falkenhayn's plan was ambitious, von Strantz felt he could manage it. The frustrated assault on Troyon had been a learning experience, and here as elsewhere, the Germans were very quick to learn from their mistakes. It was not enough to bombard a fort and hope that the garrison would surrender. Nor could an assault by regular infantry succeed. What was required was a sort of combined arms assault using artillery, infantry, and the Pioniere, who had the training and the weaponry needed to assault forts in a systematic fashion.

So the German plan was simple: rapidly advance to the southwest in the direction of Saint-Mihiel, neutralize the fort du Camp des Romains, cross the Meuse using the thoughtfully provided bridge at Saint-Mihiel, and physically sever the rail line into Verdun.

Given the size of the front and the depth of penetration required for the offensive to succeed, this plan seems like a tall order. But von Strantz now had a good grasp on what was going on with his opponents. The only other opposition in the area was to his right, butting up on Verdun. Holding a tenuous line between Étain and Buzy, directly to the east of the city of Verdun, but outside of the range of the artillery at forts Vaux and Moulainville, were the

72nd Reserve Division, and two regular infantry units, the 55th and the 56th, together with a few soldiers from the 75th.

The problem for the commanders of those units was that their right flank was up in the air. Buzy was directly to the west of Metz, approaching German territory, and there were no French troops anywhere near. So von Strantz, holding them in place with a frontal attack, simply thrust around them with the bulk of his forces. As Buffetaut observes grimly, "The progression to the heights of the Meuse unfolded like a peacetime maneuver" (*Verdun*, 9).

That does a serious injustice to the French soldiers who had basically been left high and dry. On 20 September, the German offensive began. The villages at the foot of the heights all were fine defensive positions. The Germans basically destroyed them, along with the general commanding the 75th Division, who was killed in the fight for the town of Hattonchâtel. So were most of his men. The division was essentially wiped out. Uniquely in the history of French divisions, it was never reconstituted, its absence being the only memorial to the disaster.

Indeed, it was a disaster. By 24 September, the Bavarians were in the town of Saint-Mihiel, and promptly crossed the bridge to Chauvoncourt. That was it for the main south–north rail line into Verdun.

All that remained was Camp des Romains. Located on a bluff to the south of Saint-Mihiel, the fort could rapidly make the Chauvoncourt bridgehead untenable. The garrison of the fort had two insurmountable problems: Although the bluff the fort was located on provided splendid views of the Meuse and the town, it was an isolated disposition, easy to surround—and by 24 September, the Bavarians had surrounded it.

So the garrison was completely cut off from the outside. Moreover, on this round the Germans were making sure there would be no disrupting fire from the closest forts. The amount of firepower von Strantz was able to bring to bear was impressive. To neutralize the battery at Les Paroches, he used a battalion of 15-centimeter howitzers and a battery of 10-centimeter guns. To suppress the fire from Fort Liouville, he used a battery of 30.5-centimeter Austrian guns, and for his main objective, the Camp des Romains, he deployed another battalion of 15-centimeter howitzers, a battalion of 21-centimeter howitzers, and another battery of 10-centimeter guns, as well as the Minenwerfer of the Pioniere.

All of these weapons were modern long-recoil artillery pieces. The French had nothing like them. The Austrian heavy guns promptly reduced Liouville to rubble, preventing its garrison from supporting artillery fire, and after three days of bombardment, the garrison of Camp des Romains were reduced to the status of cave dwellers. It was the same situation that Captain Heym had faced at Troyon, only worse, because this time the assault was carefully planned and executed.

On the morning of 25 September, a mixed force of combat engineers and infantry stormed the fort from all sides. In three hours the battle was over. Camp des Romains had fallen, was in fact the only one of the Séré de Rivières forts to be taken by a direct infantry assault.

THE AFTERMATH

Clearly, the results of Second Verdun were very bad news for the French high command. The two main railroad lines into Verdun were cut, which was bad enough, but one would suppose that what was even worse was that less than three weeks after the victory of the Marne had sent the Germans fleeing north, suddenly they were smashing through the French positions like a hot knife through butter. Von Falkenhayn had definitely sent Joffre a message.

But there didn't seem to be anyone on the other end to receive it. Only Raymond Poincaré, the president of France, got the message, and he got it instantly. On Thursday, 25 September, he records the following entry in his diary: "At the end of the day, I receive a telegram from the Prefect of the Meuse that filled me with sadness: 'Germans masters of Saint-Mihiel and Camp des Romains.'"[16]

As one can imagine, the president was not happy about hearing the news of the latest disaster from a local official rather than from the army, and on Saturday, at a meeting of the cabinet, Poincaré hit the ceiling (at least according to him):

> Lately, the press communiqués are full of falsehoods and omissions. . . . They make no mention of the capitulation of Camp des Romains. It is announced that we have retaken Berry-au-Bac et Ribécourt, but we never admitted that we had lost them. I insist, once again that we tell the truth. I demand, equally that we find out immediately why it is that the forts fell so quickly. In places where the enemy is entrenched out in the open, we can't dislodge him, and on the heights of the Meuse, in a position fortified in advance, we couldn't defend ourselves for half a day (327–28).

In the actual French, instead of "falsehoods and omissions," Poincaré uses a phrase that actually compresses into two words a somewhat different concept: that of falsehoods through omissions. Perhaps the difference is subtle, but it speaks perfectly to the techniques developed by the French army right from the start of the war. What was blandly passed over in silence was just as misleading as what was said that wasn't true.

In any event, Poincaré's open distress at the very least made Joffre realize he had a problem. The stage was thus set for the Third Battle of Verdun, which ultimately would emerge as the bloodiest and most futile battle the French army fought and lost.

5

The French Riposte:
October 1914–July 1915

If this wastage continues, the day is near when the
offensive value of our army, already severely
weakened, will be destroyed.

—Abel Ferry, July 5, 1915[1]

Belatedly, the September battles for Verdun brought the Argonne
and the Woëvre to the attention of Joffre and his staff at Chantilly.
That and the irritation of the president of the republic at discovering firsthand how the army was lying about the war. Whatever the
cause, the GQG belatedly grasped the nature of the problem. Joffre
summed it up rather well.

The consequences of this German attack were serious. It
placed in the enemy's hands at Saint-Mihiel the main road,
railway and canal by which Verdun was supplied; near
Commercy, it brought the main line under the fire of German guns, and, near Aubreville, the railway running from
Châlons to Verdun. Due to this situation, Verdun was no

longer supplied except by a single railway . . . a narrow gauge line running from Bar-le-Duc.[2]

Accordingly, he ordered the army commanders on both sides of the Meuse to recapture the lost territory and free up the supply routes into Verdun.

Joffre's directive resulted in two separate offensives, one on each side of the Meuse, and each of those in turn can best be understood as consisting of two somewhat unrelated struggles.

The Third Battle of Verdun, which was basically an attempt to free up the west–east railroad line on the right bank, began in October 1914 with a series of direct attacks on the German observation post on the butte of the Vauquois. That offensive, which lasted from October through March 1915, was supplemented, or complemented, by fighting to the west of the butte, as both sides struggled to turn the other's flank. Chronologically speaking, the fighting to the immediate west, in the Argonne forest, intensified a month or so after the attempts on the Vauquois, and reached its climax in the summer of 1915. But essentially, the two parts, the Vauquois and the Argonne, were closely related. Separating the battle into distinct parts is simply an attempt to make the narrative more readerly.

By the same token, the Fourth Battle of Verdun, on the right bank, had the same aim: to relieve the German stranglehold on Saint-Mihiel. It too can be divided into two parts, simply for the sake of coherence: Les Éparges and the Woëvre. The rationale here is that the French have always made these distinctions in writing about this aspect of the war, and as we shall see, given the way the fighting spun out of control, became an end in itself without regard for the original objectives, the divisions make a good deal of sense.

Although obscure and poorly understood, these struggles were some of the bloodiest and most horrific of the war. A secret government report listed total casualties for the two areas as well over 200,000 men.[3] The intensity of the fighting, the muddling of objectives, and the overall loss of coherence on the part of the French commanders should not distract us from keeping firmly in view that the fighting on both sides of the Meuse for the twelve-month period beginning in October 1914 was supposed to be part of a coordinated French effort to break the German stranglehold on Verdun.

Without pushing the point, the two battles have certain other similarities. The most striking is that on both sides of the river the French mounted serious and sustained attempts to seize the two hills, or buttes, that were strategically important.

On the left bank, German possession of the butte of the Vauquois enabled them to interdict the main rail line at Aubreville, as we have seen, and as Joffre admitted in the passage above. The counterpart of the Vauquois, on the right bank, was the much larger butte of Les Éparges. The strategic importance there, however, was completely different from its companion on the other side of the river. In some measure it was the obverse of the Vauquois.

If the French could eject the Germans from the butte, their observers would have a commanding view of the whole plain of the Woëvre from Verdun all the way over to Buzy, and would in theory be able to keep the Germans from reinforcing their positions in the Woëvre, and thus mounting further attacks against the French positions along the heights of the Meuse.

There is, of course, a point at which the comparison breaks down. There was nothing theoretical about the German control of the Vauquois; they had the butte, had essentially stopped the rail traffic, as Joffre admits. But the advantage to the French if they could eject the Germans from Les Éparges was totally about potential. It would only confer an advantage if two distinct and entirely separate possibilities occurred.

The butte was important to the French if there was a major offensive effort across the section of the Woëvre that the butte surveyed, a large, relatively flat area that stretched from the southeastern quadrant of Verdun all the way over to Buzy. Theoretically the Germans might launch another offensive against the heights of the Meuse or even against Verdun itself. Conversely, there could be a major French offensive on the right bank that required the Germans to rush in reinforcements.

In those cases, command of the butte could be important for the French. Provided, of course, that they could amass the heavy artillery for observers to direct. Unfortunately, that was precisely what the army absolutely could not manage. Three months into the war, the army did not have the right guns. It had hardly any guns of any sort. It had hardly any shells for the few guns it possessed, and it had no easy way of making more.

THE HIGH-EXPLOSIVES SHORTAGE

The French deficiency is so appalling, so startling, that one's initial inclination is to retort that it couldn't possibly be true. Alas, it was all too true.

As explained in the previous chapter, the French army had begun the war with a very small inventory of heavy guns in service, and the number of hydraulic-recoil, high-angle-of-fire weapons in service was essentially zero.

Although the standard field gun, the famous 75, was clearly the best weapon of its class, it had an inherent design weakness: the gun tube could be elevated to a maximum of only 16 degrees. The old mechanical-recoil heavy guns of the 1870s that formed the rest of the army's artillery park suffered from this same deficiency, albeit to a lesser degree.

Whatever Joffre's faults, he was not entirely stupid. There is no reason to doubt his postwar claim that he was quite aware of the problem: "The heights of the Meuse posed a problem not resolvable by the [flat] trajectory of the 75, as there existed all along those steep hills a dead zone with considerable angles that our guns would not be able to reach," is how he put it in his memoirs.[4]

As far back as 1910, he had been lobbying for the development of howitzers and mortars like those the Germans had. His lack of success in this matter is not entirely, or perhaps mainly, his fault.

The procurement and development of weaponry for the army involved a maze of competing bureaucracies, and the situation was not helped by the fact that the various governments changed ministers of war like a cocotte putting on new stockings. In the forty years preceding the start of the war (1875–1914), there were no less than 40 men in the position—and 17 chiefs of staff.[5]

So the development of modern artillery sputtered and stalled, and when the war began, the French were pretty much in the position of a man who brings a knife to a gunfight.

France did, however, at least in theory, possess an impressive artillery park. It consisted of approximately 3,500 vintage 120- and 155-millimeter guns that dated from the late 1870s, known generically in France as system De Bange, even though not all of them used the breech mechanism that had given rise to the sobriquet. That total could be supplemented by another 3,000 90-millimeter field guns, the weapon that the 75 had replaced.

These weapons were all mechanical-recoil guns, and the larger pieces had to be modified so they would be mobile. Mounting them on a wheeled carriage was no great feat, but it took time. As a result, by January 1915, the army had fewer than 700 pieces of heavy artillery in service. Almost all of these guns were the older, mechanical-recoil weapons.

The numbers gradually increased, and by the end of 1915, there were nearly 2,000 of these guns available. However, this was a stopgap measure at best, since the improvised mount restricted the angle of the barrel, so the problem that Joffre had noted still remained. All through the war there were areas of the German lines the French could therefore never reach with their artillery.

Moreover, as the weeks passed, the original arsenal of 75s was steadily shrinking: guns were captured, disabled, or simply wore out. Gunners all know, or are supposed to know, that the barrels of their weapons gradually wear out. The greater the force of the explosion that drives the shell up the barrel, the greater the wear. Although ultimately the effect of the wear is lethal (for the gun crew), long before that time the accuracy of the gun begins to be affected, and over long distances, the error becomes considerable—just as it would be for a mechanical-recoil weapon.

The 75 was an excellent gun, but it was a complex mechanism, largely built by hand, one piece at a time. Production was barely able to keep up with the wastage, and the problem was exacerbated by the army's discovery that it needed many more guns than it had envisioned. The only way the French could manage was to rely more and more on the older field gun, the 95.

The 95 was the weapon that the 75 had replaced: a mechanical-recoil weapon with a very slow rate of fire. By the standards of 1914 it was a woefully inadequate weapon, and it created a considerable supply difficulty. Since the 75 was the standard divisional artillery, the supply chain was simplified to one artillery shell, which existed in two versions: high-explosive and shrapnel. But now the supply chain not only had to increase dramatically the rate of flow of shells to the gunners, but it had to deal with another kind of shell.

The shortage of modern heavy weapons was actually only the tip of the iceberg. Before the war, the government had refused to appropriate money to allow the army to maintain the shell inventory the gunners reckoned they needed. When Joffre had taken over at GQG, the theoretical figure was from 700 to 1,200 shells per gun (depending on the caliber of weapon). Joffre had raised it up to a higher range (1,200 to 1,500). When the staff looked at how much ammunition was being expended in the two Balkan wars, they realized that their figures were way off: The actual inventory should be around 3,000 shells per gun. But when the war began, the inventory was 1,390 shells per gun.[6]

In short, the gunners soon ran low on shells, a problem exacerbated by the inaccuracy of their ancient weapons: They had to fire many more shells to effect the same amount of damage a shell from a modern artillery piece would cause. This is not a theoretical observation. In actual field tests, it was established that at a range of between 2,000 and 3,000 meters, it took five field gun shells to reach the same level of accuracy as two howitzer shells, while at shorter or longer ranges the ratio went up still higher.[7]

These field tests were conducted using modern, long-recoil weapons. In the case of indirect fire using a mechanical-recoil gun such as the French 120-millimeter (vintage 1878), the term *accuracy* was meaningless. Shells were fired off in the general direction of the enemy, and the gunners hoped for the best.

So the French, dependent on elderly weapons of entirely the wrong type, therefore needed a great many more shells than the Germans did, but, paradoxically, they had far fewer.

The situation was made more difficult still by a rather obscure technical point. The basic explosive ingredient required for a shell was, as we have seen, TNP, trinitrophenol. To make TNP, the manufacturer needs phenol, which is derived from coal. Unlike Germany, Belgium, and England, France does not have an abundance of coal. It hardly has any at all, and by October 1914, what coal the French had was all safely behind the German lines—as was most of Belgium. In the years before the war, the French simply imported what they required from their neighbors, that is, from Belgium and Germany.[8] So now the government had to find stable, long-term sources of raw materials for its high explosives. Most of France's steel manufacturing was in the same place as the coal mines, so the French had to outsource their raw materials.

Some of the shortfall could be made up by the British, but their armaments industry was already straining to equip their own troops, so both countries looked across the Atlantic for help. Although officially neutral, the Wilson administration simply turned a blind eye to the whole affair, and a steady stream of munitions began to flow across the Atlantic. The extent of this trade was concealed at both ends, along with a good many other equally disturbing facts, and to this day it is extremely difficult to get a handle on the dimensions of the trade.

Now, as we shall see in the next chapter, France's dependency on America, its woeful shortage of artillery and artillery shells, definitely had an impact on what happened at Verdun. It was already beginning to have a disastrous effect, as the hapless French infantry, shorn of artillery support, was thrown against the German positions on both sides of the Meuse in attack after attack, and consequently massacred.

Like the first two battles for Verdun, the next two were deftly obscured by Joffre's minions, and not only because they were dismal failures. The next fifteen months of the war, from the fall of Antwerp in October 1914 to the start of the German offensive at Verdun in February 1916, are filled with dramatic events: the Allied amphibious invasion of Turkey, the entry of Italy into the war, the beginnings of submarine warfare and the sinking of the *Lusitania*, the Allied occupation of Greece, the extension of the war both at sea and into east Africa and the Middle East, and, of course, the titanic struggles raging in Russia.

London and Paris had their hands full; their censors and propagandists were busily creating an alternative history of the struggle, and everyone afterward has been picking through the wilderness, trying to construct a sensible narrative of all these events. As the war expanded to include entire nations, the bloody and inconclusive struggles of some tens of thousands of infantry in parts of France unfamiliar to most Frenchmen seem of only minor significance.

FAILURE ON THE LEFT BANK: (1) THE FUTILITY OF THE VAUQUOIS

The Vauquois is a 400-meter-long outcropping that rises up about 300 meters from its surroundings. It merited the name of a butte because it stood in relative isolation: The nearest hill of any significance was Montfaucon, about nine kilometers to the north. So the position was strategically important. The French 82nd Infantry Regiment, charged with defending the butte, had basically abandoned it in September. Although it was a naturally defensible position, no records exist to show that the regiment tried to defend it. It was a victory on the cheap for the Germans.

Probably the French infantry commanders didn't realize the importance of the position, thought it was simply another butte out in the Argonne. Because the Vauquois was important only in this new war of indirect fire, a war in which it was no longer necessary to occupy a position physically. One could simply call down artillery fire on it, the shells coming from guns the defenders couldn't see, being fired by gun crews who had no notion of their target, only its coordinates.

In the older way of thinking, then, the butte was hardly significant. To an infantry brigadier or colonel, whose military education (such as it was) had stopped in the 1880s, the six thousand meters that separated it from the main railroad going into Verdun might as well have been sixty thousand. To an artillery observer ensconced on the butte, with batteries of modern guns whose effective ranges started at eight thousand meters and went up from there, a train moving along that railroad was the proverbial sitting duck.

The fault of our anonymous infantry commander was not entirely owing to poor training. Yes, as a group, French officers were not nearly so well educated in military matters as they should have been, but the real problem here is more fundamental. Already in 1914, the very nature of warfare had changed in a fundamental way, and many people were slow to grasp it. Most French infantry commanders had never even seen field guns in action, much less the howitzers that would define the battlefields of the Western Front.

General Alexandre Percin was inspector general of artillery for France. His reports make for gloomy reading.

On 8 July 1909 I addressed the following letter to the Minister of War. "One never sees, in the autumn maneuvers, an army corps with more than 18 batteries, each of four guns. . . . In the maneuvers of the divisions or brigades, the proportion of artillery is even weaker, although the new organization foresees the employment of 30 batteries per army corps and there is some question of going to 36. . . . Commanders are completely unprepared to manage large masses of guns. In the maneuvers I directed on 12 September last, for the 13th army corps, there were only 23 batteries for the corps, each represented by one gun. . . ."[9]

That being the case, infantry officers would have no idea of the destructive power of heavy artillery, or even what properly deployed batteries of field guns could do.

The hapless infantry of the 75th Division had discovered this the hard way in September. Now it was the turn of the soldiers of the 10th Division, who had been ordered to assault the Vauquois. It is a truism that experience is the best teacher, that the burned hand dreads the fire. True enough, but there were hardly any survivors from the 75th Division around to pass on the fruit of their bitterly learned experiences, so the infantry on the left bank had to learn on their own.

Like Montfaucon, the Vauquois had a small village atop it. The width of the butte was just sufficient for there to be a church, and three rows of stone houses aligned along the length of the outcropping. The south side, facing the new French lines, was much steeper than the other three. There was a road going up to the top at each end, but unfortunately for the attacking troops, those ends were inside the German lines.

In consequence there was only one avenue of attack: right up the front—even in the best of circumstances a risky venture, and circumstances were totally against the French. Given its altitude, the reverse slope of the butte was a dead zone for French gunners, so the defenders could install themselves comfortably, and reach their positions before the attackers could get to the top, since they had to struggle up a steep slope and contend with all sorts of obstacles: barbed wire, shell holes, and exploding shells.

In that sense, the fighting for the Vauquois, which began in October 1914, established a sort of horrific pattern for the Allied attacks of the next four years. Their infantry would struggle across the area separating the lines. In some cases, they wouldn't even make it across, but as the Allies slowly acquired more artillery, the infantry would increasingly reach the first line of the German trenches.

But the defenders rarely if ever were there. Instead, they were well behind, dug in deep beneath their stone and concrete shelters, and escaped the shelling almost unscathed. When the bombardment stopped, the defenders would emerge. A basic principle: They could reach their prearranged positions much more quickly than the attacking infantry, and in consequence, the word *massacre* is appropriate.

But in the initial attacks on the Vauquois, the French lacked the resources to subject the houses to any sort of intensive bombardment. The relatively small amounts of high explosive in the shells from the French 75- and 120-millimeter guns were not going to do much damage to the stone and masonry houses of Lorraine, whose walls were generally a meter thick.

The roof was a different matter, but since the French lacked guns capable of the required steep angle of fire, only the stray shell would have much effect. We tend to forget an obvious fact: that even today, the best way to destroy a structure is to fire a shell (or a precision-guided missile or bomb) through an opening, not to try to batter the walls down. Given the height of the butte, the trees, the relatively flat trajectories of the guns, the distance at which the artillery would have to be sited, the whole affair was problematic from start to finish. In the case of the Vauquois, basic geometry was against the French.

On 28 October 1914, fourteen companies of infantry from the 46th Regiment of the 10th Division attacked straight up the steep side of the butte. The division, composed of men from Paris, may have had the highest number of writers of any combat unit that ever saw a shot fired. One of them, Georges Boucheron, described the first assault with cold objectivity.

We advance nevertheless, always progressing, as though on maneuvers, but suddenly, a muted detonation, followed by a hiss, makes itself heard: an explosion, then others, and on the slopes, big black clouds . . .[10]

Those clouds were caused by the German shells, which Boucheron refers to as *"les grosses marmites boches,"* army slang, as a *marmite* was a simply a big pot. In this case the pot was full of high explosives, and as Boucheron watched, they fell "exactly on the positions we occupied; the groups are struck and then annihilated."

Some men want to flee, they are one after another harvested by the shells, or the machine guns, that, both on the front and the flank, greet them. . . . In only a few minutes after the first shell has hit, you can't see the dark blue tunics or the red trousers or the shell holes, only the dark green grass. All is quiet.

The initial attack had been mounted without any artillery support whatsoever. Retrospectively, it was claimed that the staff hoped to surprise the defending Germans, although given the terrain in front of the hill, this idea flies in the face of any sort of reality. Several thousand men don't sneak up on a hill, not when the area in front of it is relatively flat. Moreover, when the first attack failed, a second one was ordered for the following day. That failed as well.

The French waited over another month, tried the same approach once more. On 8 December 1914, they attacked for three consecutive days, again with nothing to show for it except casualties.

Right before Christmas, the GQG suddenly noticed that both the main supply lines into Verdun had been cut. On 23 December 1914, Joffre, in his usually bland and ingenuous way, drew "General Dubail's attention to the situation created by the simultaneous advance of the Germans on the heights of the Meuse and in the

Argonne. This advance showed how important were the operations of the 1st Army in the Woëvre, and of the 3rd Army in the Vauquois district."[11]

Having written to General Dubail about what to do, a few weeks later, on 5 January, Joffre replaced him with General Pierre Roques. Dubail was now commander of the Army Group East. One of Joffre's stratagems for getting rid of generals he found lacking in offensive spirit, but couldn't sack outright, was to kick them upstairs. Roques, like Joffre, was an engineer and, relatively speaking, an intimate of his.

While General Herr, the First Army commander, hatched a plan for an offensive on the right bank, Sarrail, whose Third Army was responsible for the Argonne, decided to expand the scope of the attacks on the Vauquois. After a suitably powerful artillery barrage, the 10th Division would attack the butte, and the 9th Division, reinforced by a detached brigade (the 105th), would attack the German positions on the left flank. Undeterred by the abysmal performance of the Third Army thus far in the Argonne, Sarrail was convinced that this offensive would smash through the German positions, recapture Varennes-en-Argonne, and isolate the Vauquois.

The plan was ambitious, the means woefully inadequate. General Micheler, whose Fifth Army Corps would do the actual fighting, had precisely two batteries of heavy mortars, one of 220 millimeters and one of 270, both dating from 1878.[12] These guns had the requisite high angle of fire. Provided they could be emplaced within 5,000 meters or so of the target, given competent observers, they could do serious damage to the German positions. But given that the German lines basically looked down on the French positions, and that the smaller German howitzer vastly outranged the French antiques, their value in the coming battle was mostly symbolic.

That was one problem. The other was that by the time Sarrail worked out his plan and had it approved, it was now the end of January 1915, and the offensive was set for 17 February. So the

Germans had over four months to prepare their defenses. Part of the French plan was that Roques and Sarrail would coordinate their attacks, thus pinning the Germans in place, and, like Sarrail's plan, Roques's was for a sizable offensive operation.

For the survivors of the first assaults, the artillery barrage was impressive. But then again, it was their first experience. After two hours of what the infantry thought was a horrible pounding that surely must have destroyed the defenders completely, the assault began. Neither Boucheron nor the talented André Pézard was in the first wave—fortunately for them—and Pézard recorded fragmentary and incoherent rumors of success. By four o'clock units of two regiments were reported to have taken the hill, as well as the village of Boureuilles in the west.

At one a.m. on the eighteenth, the supposedly official news that filtered back to the reserves was that their comrades had taken the hill at eleven that morning, and had been thrown back, but had retaken it in a renewed attack, while the Germans were barely hanging on to the cemetery at Boureuilles. Pézard records that the regimental band played "La Marseillaise" in celebration.

With the dawn came a more sobering reality. The butte was roughly 200 meters across, with a noticeable rise from south to north. The village was on the north, or German side. The infantry that managed to scale the butte then had to fight their way into the village, discovering that the shelling had left the defensive positions intact. One speaks of assaults and counterattacks, but the words imply more organization, more determination than was actually the case. The next day saw a few dozen exhausted soldiers hanging on to the edge of the village—the survivors of the two regiments that had struggled to the top. The cost: 800 men dead, wounded, or missing. Given the nominal strength of the two regiments by February 1915, the casualty rate was at least 50 percent and probably higher.

Sarrail's offensive had multiple objectives: to break through the Germans lines to the west of the Vauquois and thus outflank the German positions there; then to retake Varennes and Montfaucon, the butte to the north of the Vauquois. Achieve those goals and the railroad would be secured.

None of those goals had been achieved. As French official history admits, although elements of the two regiments had "penetrated" the butte, they had been forced to evacuate it. The attack farther to the west basically got nowhere. In terms of securing an objective of high value, the attack had been a failure. Undeterred, Joffre had the GQG order Sarrail to make another attack.

On the seventeenth, the gunners had run out of ammunition, so there was a delay while they were reprovisioned. The artillery was also reinforced by an armored train mounting two 100-millimeter naval guns. Although the range of these weapons was impressive, their relatively flat trajectory limited their value considerably. André Pézard, a platoon leader in the 46th Regiment, recorded the barrage of 28 February with a certain skepticism: "With the great day commences a very feeble cannonade. Is that the 'magnificent artillery preparation' of which the colonel spoke?"[13]

Other observers were more impressed. The houses were almost entirely destroyed; improbably, the only landmark visible was a solitary tree, although the walls of the church were still intact.

The infantry attacked a little after one p.m., and within 30 minutes they were in the ruins of the village on the western side. One of the reasons for insisting on a second assault was the reasonable belief at headquarters that the Germans were stretched to the breaking point on both sides of the river, owing to Roques's offensive on the right bank. To a certain extent, this was true: The Vauquois was held by only one battalion. There was another one in reserve, but by the time they launched a counterattack, the French were firmly established on the south side of the butte, digging rudimentary trenches in the rubble. The cost: 3,000 men in two days of fighting.

Toward the end of March, as Roques's offensive sputtered to its horrifying end, the Germans made a tentative effort to throw the French off the butte. Given the fact that the positions were now almost face-to-face, their superiority in artillery was nullified, but they had a new and unpleasant weapon in its stead: early versions of the flamethrower. But the German attacks of March 23 did little more than stabilize the front, which stayed pretty much where it was in March 1915 right up until the Americans finally broke through in September 1918.

In that sense, the battle was a stalemate. Neither side could take complete possession of the butte. But given the reason for the attack, a stalemate was a German victory. If the French had gotten the north side of the butte, they could have called in counter battery fire on the German guns that kept the trains from running. In addition, their observers could have called down artillery fire onto the relatively flat plain behind the butte, thus severely impacting any attempt to shuttle troops laterally along the front to reinforce threatened positions.

By March 1915, even a gunnery officer of modest competence would have the railroad coordinates established, so at that point, if not much earlier, having an observation post on the butte was more of a luxury than a necessity. Right from the start of the war, the German gunners had relied heavily on aerial observation. In addition to fixed-wing aircraft, once the front stabilized, they made extensive use of balloons connected to the batteries by telephone wires.

Neither form was as effective for camouflaged targets as an actual ground-based observer, who could in theory keep a suspected area under continuous observation. But that is hardly the case for a train moving along the track, even at night.

That observation may sound purely theoretical. However, it happens to be true: The French were never able to make use of either railroad. When the 1916 fighting began, all the supplies and men had to come up from Bar-le-Duc. The undisputed German possession of the butte for those early months was crucial. Afterward, it was only important to keep the French from using it as an observation post.

But since the French never got to that point, there basically was no point. All they had managed to do was to run up a horrifying body count. A secret government report estimated that Sarrail had lost ten thousand men at the Vauquois, and the official history listed Third Army losses from 15 January to the end of March 1915 as 26,540 men and 486 officers, of which 4,534 were dead and another 5,770 missing.[14]

The observant reader will have noticed that in speaking of the dimensions of the butte, the figures used are somewhat vague. There's a reason why. By the end of the war, the butte was simply a sequence of enormous craters. Anyone who hikes up to the top of it sees what looks exactly like a child's sand castle that someone stepped on: The north and south sides of the butte are still there, but the middle is a series of craters. Of the village itself, all that remains are extremely small fragments of roofing tiles and stone chips, most of them about the size of a thumbnail.

Although the war on the Vauquois after March 1915 has hardly any relevance to Verdun, it forms a horrifying and melancholy postscript, since the remains of the butte are one of the seven demonic wonders of the war.

In their February offensive the French had compensated, or tried to compensate, for their lack of heavy guns by setting off mines. They had excavated no less than four separate places, hoping to blow up the defenders from below. The results were inconclusive, but after the March 1915 fighting, both sides began tunneling into the butte. On 14 May 1916, the Germans won the grand prize in this disturbing war. They set off a mine on the west end of the butte that created a crater thirty-two meters deep, and killed 800 men from the 46th Regiment. But the craters, which were simply giant shell holes, made any advance impossible. So the lines never moved until 26 September 1918, when American troops overran the whole area in a few hours.

THE RIGHT BANK: (1) LES ÉPARGES AND THE MASSACRE OF THE INFANTRY

Les Éparges, a 346-meter hillock to the southeast of Verdun, is roughly the companion butte to the Vauquois. But it is larger, higher, and more irregular. There was no village on top; nor does the butte dominate the region as does the Vauquois. The *crête de Combres*, which the Germans had also grabbed back on 22 September 1914 during the Bavarian offensive toward Saint Mihiel, was 340 meters high, and only some 700 meters distant.

The butte is (or was) an irregular kidney shape, and the Bavarians had spent the fall entrenching themselves, with a bastion at each of the three key points of the kidney. From Point X, the east-end bastion, to Point C, the west-end bastion (in the bend of the kidney), there was a double line of trenches. The steepest side of the butte—and the most important—was the one facing back toward the German positions, and the Bavarians had taken advantage of this to tunnel into the butte, building a series of shelters for their infantry, and tunneling all the way up to the trench line itself.

Worse still for the French, the butte of Les Éparges was not an isolated outcropping, as were the majority of the others in the region, from the Vauquois and Montfaucon to the west of Verdun all the way down to Montsec in the Woëvre plain. Not only was flanking fire possible from Combres, but the topography meant that the Germans could filter men and supplies back and forth with relative impunity. At the Vauquois, it was ultimately possible for French gunners to interdict the supply routes to the butte at least some of the time, because the terrain immediately behind (on the German side) was open country. Troops could shelter in the dead angle of the back side, and be safe from French guns, but at some point they had to venture out into the open, and at key points during the March attacks, the French had managed to cut the butte off temporarily with artillery fire. The corresponding approaches to Les Éparges meant that this was not going to happen.

There was also another nasty problem. The Vauquois was originally what in the American Southwest would be called a mesa. It had a surprisingly flat top, albeit one with a noticeable tilt running (unfortunately) downhill to the French side. But the twin peaks of Les Éparges and Combres were terraced slopes, rising out of an extensive 300-meter-high plateau. Once past the 300-meter line, the attackers were going to be terribly exposed as they worked their way higher along one enormous, exposed slope.

The butte was different strategically as well. The Vauquois was a commanding observation post, one the Germans put to good use. Had the French been able to seize the entire butte, they could, at least in theory, have caused the Germans a great deal of trouble, and they might have been able to secure the reopening of the rail line into Verdun. In any event, at the Vauquois the French needed to regain the butte in order to block German operations. At Les Éparges they needed the butte to secure the only practicable route for an attack into the Woëvre plain: "The possession of les Éparges and the control of its observatories is indispensable to any offensive envisioned in that sector."[15]

Writing long afterward, the few French military historians who have studied this battle are of the opinion that the whole idea was ridiculous.[16] Although there is some truth to this view, it overlooks the removed vision of the general staff planners at headquarters, who were conducting a war based exclusively on map reading. Nor was General Roques, First Army commander, the man to argue the point. He was an engineer from Provence, not an infantry commander. Most of his service had been abroad, so his knowledge of the topography of the Woëvre was understandably sketchy. And in theory, as was remarked at the beginning of this chapter, the French needed possession of the butte.

But whether possession of the butte was pointless or not, the basic situation described above definitely portended a very difficult struggle.

Hopefully, Roques's offensive would coincide with Sarrail's, pin the defenders in place, and prevent them from reinforcing each other. In that sense the plan was sound enough. The basic

German tactic in the west was to shuttle reinforcements laterally to whatever point was threatened by an Allied attack, and indeed their defensive line was carefully positioned so as to take advantage of the railroad system in that regard. So the idea that if you attacked a very large area of the front, the defenders would not be able to reinforce one another quickly (or at all) was theoretically correct.

What Roques had in mind was a two-part attack. One of his army corps, the Sixth, would attack the butte; as that attack developed—in synchronization with Sarrail's attack on the Vauquois—a much larger offensive would be launched into the plain of the Woëvre. He knew that the assault would be difficult, but in addition to its regular infantry regiments, the corps had no less than three battalions of *chasseurs*.

The word *chasseurs* is often taken to mean light infantry, and some English historians routinely mistranslate it as "rifles," which, if we were speaking of the Napoleonic wars, would be correct. But by 1914 it would be more accurate to describe the battalions of *chasseurs* (BCP) as heavy infantry: their battalions had as many machine guns as an infantry regiment, for example. As elite units, they were (still) the best troops in the army.

The initial attack was perfectly coordinated with Sarrail's 17 February assault on the Vauquois, and as was the case on the right bank, it began with the explosion of a mine. Indeed, by the time the fighting on the butte had wound down, Les Éparges was in about the same shape as the Vauquois: anyone who drives up to the top of it is surrounded by gigantic craters, and is looking down at sizable trees growing at the bottom. The view is less dramatic simply because the butte is so much bigger.

By February 1915, the defensive tactics of the Germans in this section of the front had already evolved considerably. There was no particular effort to hold the first line of trenches. The infantry strongpoints, consisting of concrete dugouts, bunkers, and pillboxes, were set well back, and generally immune to the French artillery. When the barrage lifted, the defenders could emerge, reach their defensive positions before the attacking troops could reach the first line.

So when the 106th and 132nd regiments struggled up the slope, clambered into the first trenches, they found them largely empty, took a grand total of 23 prisoners. Then, once the French were actually in the forward trenches, the German artillery zeroed in on them. The barrage was followed up by a series of infantry counterattacks. In three days of fighting, the 10th Regiment was basically destroyed: 600 men killed or missing, 1,000 more wounded. This total was half of its theoretical strength, but it is highly doubtful that by February 1915 the regiment had anything like 3,000 men, since it had suffered heavy casualties at Revigny in September 1914. Anyone reading the horrifying account of Maurice Genevoix, who was still alive and now a full lieutenant, comes away with the feeling that there were very few men left in the regiment.[17] At any rate, by the 20 February, the French had been ejected from the butte; so, just as was the case with the Vauquois, there was a second attempt.

The French added four batteries of their ancient 120- and 155-millimeter guns, stockpiled more ammunition, and planned a second assault, this one to be delivered on 18 March, a few days ahead of its left-bank complement. Of course, the weeks that passed gave the defenders time to recover. Not surprisingly, the 18 March assault did little more than recover the trenches lost at the end of the February offensive.

So on 27 March, there was a third assault. This time a few of the *chasseurs* made it to the far end of the butte, the notorious Point X, which affords a fine view of the countryside between Verdun and Jarny. The Germans promptly counterattacked, throwing the *chasseurs* back to the southern end of the butte.

Roques's timetable called for the general offensive into the Woëvre plain to begin on 5 April. Given where the French were on the butte, that offensive would not have the benefit of observation posts on Les Éparges. So if that was the strategic objective, the attacks had failed completely.

But by now the idea of taking the butte had its own life, its own rationale. The attacks intensified. On 5 April, French troops got to Point C, the westernmost bastion, only to lose it three days later. On 10 April, the French were at Point X once again. But their grip on any part of the butte was tenuous at best, and as the French offensive on the Woëvre collapsed by the end of April, so did the efforts to take Les Éparges.

Ferry observed to the secret committee that the army had lost 35,000 men trying to take Les Éparges, and the army's own official history admits that in its "aggressive" efforts at Les Éparges, First Army lost 2,754 officers and 15,546 men.[18]

The 106th regiment was basically wiped out, along with the 25th BCP, whose troops had actually gotten to Point X. Genevoix's regiment had lost at least half of its official strength during the February attacks; it was then patched back together and attacked in March and April as well. As one of the few survivors, he had a simple title for his narrative of the attack: *La Morte*. Death.

By any reasonable standard, the struggle for Les Éparges was the most horrific of the war—certainly up to that point in time, and arguably for the future as well. The description given by one survivor is so ghastly it really defies belief.

> You cannot know what man is capable of doing to his fellow man: after five days my shoes are greasy with human brains, I crush thoraxes, I encounter entrails.[19]

Undaunted by the losses of his army corps, General Frederick Herr promptly announced that the French had taken Les Éparges, the implication being that it was a major strongpoint in the German lines that had been conquered by his troops.

Herr's claim quickly passed into the ever-expanding mythic lore of the Great War. General Herr received the American Medal of Honor for his distinguished service during the war, and the conquest of the butte was duly sanctified by the Michelin Guides in 1919: "The Éparges crest, stubbornly held by the enemy since September 1914, was definitely taken on 6 April [1915] by the 12th Division after more than a month of fiercest fighting."[20]

Not really: As General Rouquerol observed in 1939, "Never did we chase the Germans off the heights of Les Éparges which they called the position of Combres" (131). And as we shall see in the account of the February 1916 fighting, if Roques's claim had been incorrect, the single largest territorial gain of the battle for the Germans would never have happened. But by April 1915 the Allies were experts at making things up. Meanwhile, as Abel Ferry had grimly forecast, the destruction of the French infantry continued.

THE RIGHT BANK: (2) THE DISASTER OF THE WOËVRE

Although the struggles for the Vauquois and Les Éparges are little known, by comparison with the 1915 French offensive in the Woëvre they are famous, mainly because of the talented brace of writers who survived the fighting there and lived to tell the tale. Maurice Genevoix and André Pézard are arguably the most well-known writers of personal-experience narratives in the war, the equivalent of Robert Graves in Great Britain and Ernst Jünger in Germany. In his magisterial study of personal-experience narratives, Jean Norton Cru classifies writers according to the extent to which they are good witnesses, that is to say, that their accounts are reliable, it having occurred to him that war is one of those experiences that impels men to lie.

Norton Cru being French, he evaluates his witnesses and puts them into categories, ranging from those whose documentary value is practically nil to those he judges to be excellent. Genevoix, Pézard, and Cazin he places in the first rank, a judgment that is hardly to be disputed by anyone who has read their accounts. However, there are other reasonably popular accounts of the two struggles that, while of lesser value, were absorbing and widely read: the works of Georges Boucheron, Jean des Vignes Rouges, Pierre Ladoué, and André Schmitz.

In consequence, the Vauquois and Les Éparges were reasonably well-known in France after the war. It should also be added that the two regiments that did most of the fighting at the Vauquois were both recruited from Paris and its environs, and that some of the men who served and died there were at least minor celebrities. For example, Henri Collignon, former secretary to the president of the republic, and an officer of the Legion of Honor, was killed in the March assault.[21]

By contrast, the battle for the Woëvre was an obscure affair, and when it concluded in April 1915, no one in the high command, or at First Army, was particularly keen on talking about it.

However, General Roques's plan was for a major offensive. The chosen theater of operations, the German positions in the Woëvre, constituted a front considerably larger than the Somme offensive of 1916 was in terms sheer frontage one of the largest fronts of the war.[22] Roques planned a pincers attack; that is to say, he aimed to break through both at the northern end of the line, to the north of Les Éparges, and, at the same time, at the extreme southeast of the front, directly below Thiaucourt.

So his plan—which Joffre was delighted to approve—had the theoretical merit of emulating the preferred German tactic of *aufrollen*, or attacking on the flanks. If successful, he would have the entire salient in the bag, totally reverse the results of the great September breakthrough engineered by General von Strantz.

The force with which Roques aimed to envelop the German lines and eliminate the Saint-Mihiel salient entirely was commensurate. He had six army corps: the First, Second, Sixth, Eighth, Twelfth, and Thirty-first, plus two reserve divisions (the 65th and the 73rd) and an oversize brigade culled from Verdun. Given his relationship with Joffre, Roques was able to coax the GQG out of a sizable portion of the army's heavy artillery. In April 1915, the army's total artillery park of heavy guns came to a little less than 700 guns, and Herr got 360 of them for his battle, plus nearly 1,000 75s.[23]

Against this impressive force was von Strantz, still in command, and still of the same two main units, the 3rd Bavarian and Fifth Prussian Army Corps, reinforced by a collection of supposedly lesser units: the 5th Landwehr, the 33rd Reserve, and the 8th, 10th, and Guards Ersatz divisions. In the confusing German order of battle, the Landwehr were the third and next-to-lowest type of unit, while Ersatz units were drawn from those men who, prior to the war, had not seen any military service. This last may seem peculiar, given that Germany, like France and Austria-Hungary, had universal conscription. But the government was never given sufficient funds to train the entire class of eligible males, so, unlike in France, where virtually everyone did military service (over 80 percent), in Germany the figure was substantially lower.

That being the case, it would seem that von Strantz was heavily outnumbered, although the exact numbers involved are difficult to assess. Most of the French units had suffered serious losses in 1914, and those losses had not yet been made good. Further complicating the situation was that by early 1915 the Germans had embarked on a major change in the organizational structure of their divisions. Like everyone else, they had begun the war with an infantry division that was based on two brigades, each consisting of two regiments. But now they had begun to eliminate brigades entirely. They reduced the number of regiments to three, and were increasingly seeing the basic tactical unit as the battalion (a regiment consisted of three battalions, each with a theoretical strength of 1,000 men).

At the same time, the firepower available was increasing dramatically. So, for instance, although in theory the German 33rd Reserve Division should have had much less artillery than a regular division, it actually had a great deal more. Essentially, the Germans were replacing riflemen with machine gunners and combat engineers equipped with mortars and now flamethrowers, as well as hand grenades. The new "smaller" divisions had 50 percent more machine guns than their predecessors, while the 7.7-centimeter field guns were reduced—but replaced with the potent 10.5-centimeter howitzer, a weapon their French counterparts by and large still did not possess.[24]

So Roques did not have much of an advantage. Unfortunately, he also lost one of the great advantages every commander wishes for: surprise. The GQG leaked like a sieve. The Germans may not have known the date of the offensive, but Parisians certainly did. When one of Herr's brigade commanders was in Paris he met a member of the senate who greeted him with the casual remark, "Good! You're preparing to reduce the Saint-Mihiel salient!"[25]

And sure enough, right before the scheduled start date, von Strantz deployed a new division, the 121st, on his left flank. That was bad news for the plan, since it meant that the defending Germans would now outnumber the attacking French. So the whole idea was off the rails even before it started.

Roques also had another enemy: the weather. Now, this was entirely predictable. The name of this region, Woëvre, is derived from a word that means "wet." The southern section is definitely that, given its lakes and marshy ground. Given that April, in this part of Europe, is proverbially rainy, mounting an offensive there was problematic.

But apparently no one, either at GQG or at Roques's headquarters, had given much thought to either the terrain or the weather. Until the start date for the offensive, at which time the rain had turned everything to mud, and the slow warming created fog—mixed with snow in some places. It would be hard to find a worse combination of circumstances: bad visibility, mud, and an enemy who knew you were coming.

As a practical consequence of the mud, it was basically impossible to bring all the heavy guns into action to support the assault, which, as a logical result in consequence, went in without any artillery support to speak of. The result was, all too predictably, a slaughter.

To the north of Les Éparges, the 43rd Regiment, attacking into the *bois de Pareid*, lost 34 officers and 511 men in a few hours. But no one else did much better. Roques, undeterred, ordered another round of attacks for April 8. There was marginally more artillery support, but the results were nil.

By 7 April, Dubail, who was technically the overall commander as head of Army Group East, stepped in and ordered a stop to the offensive. The pincers plan was dead, to be replaced by a more methodical advance, with the infantry attacking only after there had been a thorough artillery barrage. Moreover, the objectives would be extremely limited.

Having been stopped at the northern end of the line, in a curious change of direction, the French now scrapped the original plan, and attempted to take the most formidable of the positions the Germans held in the Saint-Mihiel salient, the wooded heights between Saint-Mihiel and Apremont. It was now April 22, 1915.

Officially, the French took over 700 meters of the German trenches, but a close look reveals that these were largely positions the Germans had no intention of defending. The success was more on the order of the success of Les Éparges: That is to say, propaganda, pure and simple. The German hold on the Bois d'Ailly, as the woods were known, was not shaken in the least. Anyone who hikes back into the woods today can see this easily enough, and also see the importance of the position, as it commanded the heights overlooking Saint-Mihiel and the Meuse.

Moreover, the next day the Germans launched their own attack, up at the northern end of the line, at the Tranchée de Calonne. This was not, as one might suppose, an actual entrenchment, but rather referred to a road that had been cut through the forests to connect the town of Verdun with Hattonchâtel back in 1786. It was named after Charles Alexandre de Calonne, a controversial financier and minister to Louis XVI.

In 1914 it had become, more or less by default, the baseline for the French positions on the edge of the heights of the Meuse. Unlike the French efforts, the German offensive was successful. Within 48 hours they had overrun a four-kilometer stretch of the French positions, together with what one historian laconically calls "numerous" pieces of heavy artillery.

This attack was a costly loss for the French. On 29 April, they tried to counterattack, but to no avail. In terms of territory, the French were now worse off than when they had started their grand offensive. To add insult to injury, on 4 May, the Bavarians launched an entirely unexpected a surprise attack against the new French positions in the Bois d'Ailly. This attack was a real surprise: the

French regiment holding the position simply collapsed, and only through desperate efforts were the French able to keep this whole section of the front from collapsing as well.

But the loss was more than human lives, although that was bad enough. What was beginning to bite into the soul of the infantry was the futility of the struggle. Here is the record taken from the diary of a sergeant in the 29th Regiment.

Oh, my friends, all are cadavers here: the men, and the trees, and the reddish earth with hues of clotted blood. Have I ever known anything more sinister than these hills of the Bois d'Ailly!

It was near five o'clock in the evening when we penetrated, one by one, on our knees, rifle in hand, into the communication trenches. I saw there, for the first time, the cadavers mortared into the walls. Putrefying fingers were sticking out, hurriedly sprinkled with tar; scalps covered with a hideous mousse; feet especially, feet still in boots, powdered with lime, twisted. And the abominable odor made us become pale.

Shame on him who won't believe me!

The roots of the firs had been massacred with blows of the axe; the rocks crumbled with strokes of the pick; but no one had dared to prune the cadavers. They stayed there hindering our way, we who crawled along the stones on our knees. And we advanced cursing them. Our equipment caught itself to those feet. Those who put their hand in a rotten place didn't dare mention it, and rolled their fingers quickly in the dust.

Shame on him who won't believe me![26]

All this before the actual assault itself. And it gets worse.

My company had to take a trench. We had been told it was at seventy meters: it was more than two hundred. It was necessary to crawl and keep still: all the world was up and screaming. My half platoon held the left. I had six men around me when I reached the German wire, between eight and nine o'clock in the evening.

I stepped over their bodies, the next morning, about four o'clock.

I found the first pantless, as if claws had scratched his trousers off. His buttocks exposed, cut back and forth as though by a butcher's knife. The second hung whole on a bush, his head balancing on the end of the highest branch, like the head of a dead sparrow. The others were rolled into a porridge of mud and blood. I didn't look at them. I returned on all fours, my blanket around my neck and my packs up under my chest. When I caught sight of the stones of our trenches, I straightened up and I cried out. I was pulled in by the legs and was given cold coffee and rum to drink. The slopes were covered in haze (117).

It was a dismal end to an offensive marked from start to finish by nothing but miscalculations and disasters. Abel Ferry computed the French losses at 123,000 men, and there's no reason to doubt his accounting.

THE LEFT BANK: (2) GNAWING THROUGH THE ARGONNE

In the Argonne, the fighting was continuous from late August of 1914 until late September of 1915. Boucheron, who had been in the Vauquois assaults, after enumerating the names of the places inside the forest, observes that "each of those names recalls, not a combat, but a series of combats. An arduous and incessant struggle . . . The Argonne was a true sector of the war, never at peace, always at struggle."[27]

So it is easy to get confused about the intentions of the two sides. But, as was noted in the previous chapter, the initial attacks launched in September 1914 were part of the second envelopment of Verdun, followed by a second round of fighting occasioned by the French attempts to reverse that envelopment. Unlike the German offensives, the French plans for the Argonne were not designed to occur at the same time as the offensive of the right bank, but were set for summer 1915, after the failure of the Artois offensive in May.

What makes the situation even more complicated is that in July in the Argonne the Germans repeated what they had done earlier in Artois. Knowing that the French were ready to attack them, they attacked first.

When we left von Mudra's troops in the last chapter, they were steadily advancing through the Argonne, where, despite the dense forests, the heavy weapons of his Sixteenth Army Corps gave them a considerable advantage. Von Mudra, like his counterparts to the east, generals von Strantz and Freiherr von Gebsattel, was an officer of the first order, and under his command the Sixteenth Corps had historically been lavishly equipped, and not only with artillery (as early as 1900 it had four field artillery regiments and two heavy artillery regiments). As would be expected of an engineering officer's command, the troops were well equipped with weapons that the Allies were just discovering, thought of as experimental toys of no use to real soldiers: flamethrowers, grenades, gas shells, and, of course, the transportable mortars.

Although von Mudra is conspicuous by his absence in English-language accounts of the war, it was not so in France. He was one of the few German commanders the French referred to by name. He is the only German field commander Joffre mentions in his memoirs, while Boucheron begins his recollections of the Argonne fighting by singling him out.

It was Joffre who had coined—or been credited with—the phrase *grignotage*: gnawing at them. But as we have seen, it was von Mudra who was doing the gnawing. And he was destroying the French in the process. As Lieutenant Jean-Marie Carré, attached to the staff of the 4th Division, put it, "We lost, in four months, a little over eight hundred meters on the average. But we lost the Fourth Division."[28] Joffre was beside himself. He had always had his doubts about the Third Army's commander, Sarrail, who was prodded to take control, and to assert the superiority of the French troops over their adversaries. Sarrail, duly prodded, promised a great offensive in July.

But von Mudra had prepared a nasty surprise. In May of 1915, he met with von Falkenhayn, who, as always, was concerned about unnecessary losses. The result was that von Mudra was able to put his ideas into play in earnest. The operations in January and February had been only dress rehearsals. Now the real attacks began, a whole series. For the first, launched on 20 June, the Germans had assembled an arsenal of heavy weapons. In addition to the usual 76 field guns and 26 105-millimeter howitzers, von Mudra deployed seventeen modern heavy guns in the 100- to 150-millimeter range, ten of the 210-millimeter howitzers, and another ten guns of even larger size. As infantry support, there were forty heavy and medium Minenwerfer.

This doesn't sound like much of an arsenal when compared to offensives like the Woëvre or Champagne, where the French deployed hundreds of guns. But this is misleading. The French arsenal was deployed in support of attacks of 200,000 men spread out on a wide front aiming for a breakthrough. Von Mudra's arsenal was in support of an attack conducted on the ground by a few thousand soldiers, a brigade or even less, in an attack aimed at a few thousand meters of the line outside the village of Binarville.

As usual, von Mudra was employing the newest technology he could get. Although at Ypres in April the Germans had used gas, they had released it from cylinders, hoping it would float toward the Allied lines, but the 20 June attack was the first in which gas shells were used as part of an artillery barrage.

Ten days later, another massive attack. There were fewer of the light field guns, but now there were no less than 30 of the big 210-millimeter howitzers. In addition to its Minenwerfer and flamethrowers, von Mudra's attackers were armed with 36,000 (of the then-new) hand grenades. All this for a two-kilometer front in which the attack would again consist of a brigade. By 2 July, the Germans had captured the Bagatelle.

Joffre, deeply worried about events in the Argonne, resorted to his usual idea. He ordered the French to mount a major offensive in the Argonne, and Sarrail promptly obeyed. The French offensive, scheduled for 13 July, would relieve the increasing pressure on the left bank. At this rate, by the end of the summer the Germans would have broken though the forest and would be in the clear—and in a position to drive a wedge deep into French territory. There was a certain practical realism here. Even if there was no breakthrough, if all Sarrail managed was to push the Germans back a few kilometers, that would be enough, since Joffre was planning yet another great offensive in Champagne-Artois, to be delivered in September. A breakthrough there would solve all these problems for good.

The difficulty with French plans was that they developed far too slowly. It was impossible to conceal your intentions from your opponent in this sort of warfare. Planning for an attack of any size was quickly noticed. The Germans noticed, and they moved first.

Precisely ten days after the capture of the Bagatelle, on 12 July, von Mudra delivered another hammer blow. As this attack went in the day before the French one was scheduled, it was extremely effective. The Germans lost 525 dead, and 1,838 men were wounded. In return, they captured 3,688 French soldiers and counted over two thousand dead left on the battlefield. And, of course, more territory was gained.

Incredibly, the French attack still went in on the fourteenth, and was stopped cold in the face of German gas attacks. The first colonial brigade fought its way back into the Ravin de Dieusson, only to be rejected with nearly three thousand casualties, over half of its nominal strength. Joffre promptly sacked Sarrail, a decision that won Joffre no friends either in the government, where he was extremely well connected, or in the chamber, where he was well liked.

But von Mudra's system was munitions-intensive. So far, he had been given the resources to keep hacking away in only a fairly small area. Every battle was a victory, but the French had the luxury (still) of being able to lose men in the thousands in the Argonne while planning major offensives elsewhere. And this is what happened. In September, the Germans began diverting resources back for the anticipated Allied offensives of Second Champagne.

It is customary to speak of these theaters as being entirely separate, but von Mudra's theater of operations in the Argonne was contiguous with the Champagne Front. As the French attacked there, von Mudra's efforts had to be stopped and the guns directed to his right. In late September, he was able to mount one more operation before the resources had to be switched. On 15 September, the French lost Hill 213 and the bastion of Marie-Thérèse. On the twenty-seventh, von Mudra's last attack went in and seized yet another piece of ground, the Fille Morte.

Practically speaking, the French had lost the Argonne, which doomed in advance the chances of Second Champagne. By seizing so much of the forest, von Mudra was forcing the French to attack across the rolling country on both sides of Reims, where, as on the Somme, they would be attacking uphill against prepared positions over terrain that was ideal for artillery spotters.

Not surprisingly, Second Champagne was a gloomy repeat of the Woëvre. The French General Staff persisted in the offensive, which went on through November. The failure there would hardly have any relevance to Verdun except for one thing.

Philippe Pétain, who had worked his way up from an obscure colonel slated for retirement to an army commander, protested at the continued massacre. As Colonel Serrigny, Pétain's adjutant, remarked, "Champagne had serious consequences: it caused thousands of men to be murdered and it deceived the public," who were led to believe that the few hectares of ground gouged out represented yet another French victory.[29] Pétain's unwillingness to let the men under his command be massacred confirmed the suspicions the more offensive-minded officers in the French General Staff already had: He lacked the requisite desire to win at all costs. His soldiers felt somewhat differently.

His resistance to the continued massacre confirmed both his competence and his independence.

From the German side, the lesson seemed clear enough: It was much better to control the battlefield through offensive operations than to endure these massive kamikaze attacks. So the value of the Argonne offensives went far beyond territory gained and casualties inflicted. In terms of territory, von Mudra had sliced off, at a minimal cost, more ground than any of the Champagne offensives would get. Ferry's estimate was that the French had lost about 80,000 men (his total for the killed, the wounded, and the missing in the Argonne, not counting the Vauquois), and this seems about right: the eight French cemeteries in the Argonne contain about 36,000 French soldiers.[30]

German losses were about a fourth of that.[31] Above all, von Mudra was destroying French morale. Every attack was a success. Some of them were less successful than others, but with each the Germans took and held strongpoints the French believed to be important, inflicting heavy casualties in the process. Insofar as there was a simple key to the ability of the German army's success on the battlefield, this was it. In what was basically a year of combat on both sides of the Meuse, the French were unable to take a single important position and hold on to it for more than few days, if that. On the contrary, when the Germans attacked, they were invariably successful, and at an alarmingly low cost to themselves. During 1915, about 390,000 Allied soldiers were killed in France and Flanders; the German Medical Services reported 114,000 German soldiers killed on the Western Front.[32]

6

France's Winter of Dreams and Discontent

Such an outcome can only baffle our intelligence, for
it is difficult to discover any rational cause for it.

—Polybius[1]

By any objective standard, 1915 had been a horrible year for the
British and the French. Not that fall 1914 had been much better.
Given the nearly airtight control over the news, the British and
French governments were easily able to persuade their citizens that
the war was going reasonably well. At the same time they were
amazingly successful in inciting hatred of the enemy, and on many
different levels.

Internally, however, the civilians who ran—or anyway presided
over—the governments in London and Paris were worried. From
the start of the war the French high command dexterously fed them
good news: the great victory of the Marne, the frantic German retreat, the seizure of important positions like Les Éparges, the advances in Champagne (particularly in the fall 1915 battles there).

But even the rankest tyro could see that the war in the west was
a stalemate, that the front had hardly moved after October 1914.
Take, for example, the concerns of Maurice Hankey, secretary to
the British Imperial Defense Committee before the war, and then

secretary of the war council. An educated and conscientious civil servant, a former captain in the British marines, Hankey was very much an insider in the British cabinet. Unusually for a man in his position, he was able to think outside the box: For example, he suggested the basic idea of the tank to Churchill, and this early in the war.

Hankey's diary records the shock and surprise of the government when they learned of the fall of Antwerp in October 1914, and he understood, far better than anyone in the army or navy, the catastrophic implications of the loss of the channel ports.[2] Although like everyone else in the highest circles in both capitals, he was ignorant of just how bad the war was going in France, he seized upon the idea of a stalemate very early on, by January 1915 at the latest. He was perhaps in advance of his colleagues, but not by much.

Seeing the war in France as a deadlock, the civilians began casting around for alternatives. Since they were skeptical that the war could be won in France, it would have to be won somewhere else. That belief, sensible enough, triggered a basic conflict between the army high commands and the civilians who were, at least in theory, in charge of the war effort.

Basically, the civilians had four alternatives to argue. The first involved finding some radically new technology that would break the stalemate. The tank, for instance: Hankey proposed the idea to Churchill in December 1914. The French had the idea as well, and in point of fact it was the automobile constructor Louis Renault who developed the first modern tank.[3] The point, however, is that in both London and Paris the idea of using new technologies to break the deadlock occurred early on.

The second idea involved finding allies. When the war had begun, the British and the French placed great hopes in what was popularly called the Russian Steamroller. Millions of Russians would descend on the eastern frontiers of Germany and Austria-Hungary, forcing Berlin to shift troops to the east. By December 1914 it was pretty clear that hadn't worked out very well, although the notion that the German drive to Paris had failed owing to the transfer of units out of France persisted for decades.

Undaunted by the failure of the Russians to win the war for them, the Allies cast around for someone else: first Italy, whom they persuaded—or rather bribed—to enter the war in April 1915; then Romania in August 1916; and finally the United States in April 1917—third time being lucky, as it were.

The fourth idea was closely related to the third: attacking Germany and Austria-Hungary somewhere else, opening up a new theater of operations that would overload their military capabilities. Concurrently with Italy's entry into the war, in April 1915, the Allies carried out their ill-fated Allied amphibious landings on the Turkish coast, subsequently known as Gallipoli. As everyone knows, this venture hardly brought about the desired result, although by the end of the year, it had sucked in more than half a million—mostly British—troops. Undaunted by the disaster, the civilians insisted on a second foray, this one to the Balkans, where, acting in coordination with a new ally, Greece, a potent new threat to the central powers would emerge.

Now, these forays demanded men and resources. If there was one thing that the British and French high commands could agree on, it was that they needed every single soldier, every last shell, in the west. Actually, that was about the only thing they could agree on, so, in addition to the simmering conflict between the armies and their nominal civilian leaders, there was the conflict between the British and the French. They had, after all, been enemies for hundreds of years.

Now, in this conflict with their governments, the army chiefs had two advantages. They controlled the news of what was happening on the Western Front, and since during this time period— all through 1915—most of the front was controlled by the French, London was at a considerable disadvantage. There was, as we shall see, some leakage inside the French army, but little to none of it got to London, one important reason why subsequent generations of British historians wrote in blissful ignorance.

The other advantage was that although the front might be a stalemate, the civilian ideas had all spectacularly misfired. The Greek expedition, usually referred to by the Allied landing city, Salonika, was a festering disaster; nor was Italy's entrance into the war having much of an effect.[4]

So for the GQG, it was easy to retreat behind a reserve of passive-aggressive professionalism. Bolstered by the steady stream of adroitly managed encouraging news, the high command never lost the opportunity to remind the civilians that they had no real expertise, their ideas were amateurish, that the only way to win the war was to win it in the west, and that required a concentration of national resources.

Gradually, as the months went by, it began to dawn on the civilians that perhaps there was a fourth solution, the one that Abraham Lincoln had employed in the American Civil War: keep changing commanding generals until you found one who could win the war.

But there were difficulties with this approach, since the generals could, with some justification, claim that the main drag on their success was the diversion of resources into these schemes to fight the war elsewhere.

GRAND DELUSIONS

Besides, the Allied high commands in France were taking refuge in an unimpeachable argument. Although they were forced to admit to the civilians that they had not yet broken through the German defenses, and that it was true that not much territory was changing hands, their soldiers were inflicting heavy casualties on the Germans. If the civilians would just be patient, Germany would soon run out of manpower and be forced to quit the war.

The French term, which Joffre may or may not have actually used, was a word usually restricted to descriptions of rodents: gnawing, or perhaps nibbling. And in their steady gnawing, they were killing enormous numbers of Germans. German losses were, initially, the one category of hard information that the GQG was delighted to let be published.

In June 1915, the *New York Times* printed what they claimed (truthfully) was an abstract of a French government report dated March 27, 1915: "by the middle of January [1915], the German losses on the two fronts were 1,800,000 men."[5] After subtracting 500,000 men as "the normal proportion" of wounded who were healed and then returned to service, the report established a casualty figure of 1,300,000 deaths. This section of the article is entitled, "Wastage of German Effectives," the point being that the Germans, who were supposed from their own documents to be expending men at the rate of 260,000 a month, would soon run out of soldiers, and had already started to run out of trained troops. The conclusion of the report was that the "available [German] resources for the year 1915 will not suffice to fill the gaps of a war of ten months."

Numerous articles in the *Times* spoke to the heavy German casualties. In July 1915, an article reported that

> estimates published in the English papers derived from indications given in the Prussian official lists of casualties carry the German losses to a total of 3,500,000. This figure largely exceeds the computations made by the German authorities . . . [who] admit that Germany up to the end of June had 482,000 men killed and 852,000 wounded. In regard to prisoners the German[s] admit a loss of 233,000 up to the end of last month [June? 1915], altogether a grand total of 1,567,000 killed, wounded, and missing . . . according to Teutonic computations, Great Britain had lost 116,000 killed, 229,000 wounded, and 83,000 prisoners, a total of 428,000. When there is such a discrepancy between the German claims and the British governmental statements as to British losses the possibly natural inference is that the German claims . . . are like to be exaggerated (4:1042–1043).

The newspaper articles the *Times* summarized were supplemented by analysis by various experts. Depending on the time period used, the figures ranged from a low of 1.9 million to a high of 3.7 million.[6]

On 25 January 1916, Colonel Repington, who had access to the highest circles of both governments, reported that "the Germans had a total available of 11,000,000 men to fight, and that they have lost 3,500,000," a figure that is remarkably close to what was being reported in the various newspapers and journals.[7]

Now, the interesting fact is that these figures track very closely what the high commands of the two armies actually believed. Although they were released to aid the Allied war effort, to spin the war, they do not represent propaganda, but rather reflect the actual intelligence estimates that Joffre was receiving and passing on to the civilians. We know, for example, from Marshal Fayolle's secret diary, that Ferdinand Foch believed them to be true.[8]

We also know from Lloyd George's memoirs that Lord Kitchener assured the British cabinet in February 1915 that the Germans were running out of manpower and in a "few months" would "have exhausted their reserves."[9] One therefore infers that both Kitchener and the *Times* were citing the same official French report.

The army was convinced that it was winning the war of attrition—to the point that it was telling the world about it, and releasing its intelligence estimates.

In other words, when Lord Hankey and his French counterparts looked at the map and saw a stalemate, the generals reassured them that they had nothing to worry about: They were killing the Germans off in splendid fashion. They'd soon be running out of men, and all the evidence pointed to this conclusion.

The notion that the Allies were winning the war of attrition decisively therefore became the key piece of evidence the armies of both nations had to argue their case, was why they were so dead set against these wild expeditions and problematic alliances. All Paris and London had to do was to give them the resources they needed, and the war would soon come to an end—as opposed to Salonika and Greece, which between them tied up nearly 600,000 troops—a force of about the same size as von Hindenburg's entire command on the eastern front at the time—a fact either passed over in silence by historians or blandly dismissed.

So on the one hand, this was the evidence the army commands used to counter the criticisms of the government, and the civilians— especially in London—had no choice but to believe it.

Two militarily sound conclusions could be drawn from the Allied advantage in the casualty exchange ratio, and those ideas formed the basis of Allied military strategy as it emerged in the December 1915 conferences, where the British and the French commanders planned their next move.

The first was that the Germans were on the ropes. By fall 1915 they simply lacked the manpower to pose much of a threat. In addition to what the GQG claimed were very precise estimates of heavy German losses, there were numerous other factors that supported their conclusions. The three most important are worth explaining in detail, so the reader will understand how solid the evidence appeared to be.

Already, in spring 1915, the German manpower shortage was such that they could no longer support the traditional two-brigade divisions. They had been forced to downsize their divisions, which now only had three regiments of infantry as opposed to four. Whereas at the start of the war they had used divisions and brigades, increasingly they were able only to shift regiments or even battalions.

This was how the experts explained away the observation that it appeared that the Germans had more divisions than before. At first, the Allies had claimed that what was going on was simply sleight of hand: that the German high command was shuttling divisions between the two fronts—that, in fact, one reason their initial offensive had failed was owing to that.

Like many beliefs about the war, this one was untrue, and on two different levels. When the war began, the Germans had 97 divisions on the Western Front, and 26 in the east, for a total of 123 divisions.[10] It is true that divisions were shifted to the east, and that the victorious von Hindenburg was presiding over a growing force: by December 1915, there were 46 divisions in the east. But there were now 125 in the west, for a total of 172 divisions.

But this was all explained away by the argument that the divisions were actually much smaller, that the whole thing was smoke and mirrors—a convenient assumption, but since the French high command controlled most of the front, and hence almost all the solid intelligence, no one had access to information sufficient to point out the fallacy.

Increasingly the French were finding positions held by various categories of reservists, a clear indication that their opponents were running low on manpower. Both in the Woëvre and in the Vosges, key positions such as Les Éparges and the Hartmannswillerkopf were held almost entirely by Landwehr. Germany simply lacked the regular troops to hold its defensive positions on the front.

In fact, the only way that the Germans were able to manage this three-front war was by shuttling troops from one threatened area to another. Here is how Joffre justified the failed offensive in Champagne-Artois. First, he linked what was going on in France with what was happening on the Russian front. In May 1915, von Falkenhayn put together a joint Austro-German offensive that sent the Russians reeling, and forced them to retreat all the way back to their prewar frontier. So Champagne-Artois was necessary in order to "afford moral and material aid to our Russian Allies," since in order to mount that offensive, the Germans had reduced their forces in the west: The Allies now had 1,384 French, 330 Belgian, and 80 British battalions, and the Germans had only 1,113.[11]

Joffre used the same excuse to justify the September offensives in the same area, noting that in August 1915, "Three more divisions were withdrawn from the French front and moved to Eastern Theatre" (*Memoirs*, 357).

It would be hard to find a better example of how wildly off the French estimates were. In March 1915, there were 101 German divisions on the Western Front, and 56 in Russia. In May, the month Joffre first referenced, there were 64 divisions in the east; true enough, so there were eight additional divisions in the east, all of them sent there presumably for the May offensive.

So Joffre was correct in arguing that the number of troops in the east had increased owing to the offensive. His error—which was continuous all through the war—was to assume that this increase was achieved only by shuffling and reorganizing. Yes, there were now eight more divisions in the east. But there were now five more divisions in the west, so instead of 101 divisions, the Germans now deployed 106.

True, the movement of German troops during the war was complicated. During this one three-month period in 1915, eight divisions were shifted out of the Western Front, while 20 were deployed in the east. But 21 divisions replaced the 20 that had been withdrawn. Joffre's intelligence department was simply seeing what it wanted to see, ignoring, or failing to understand, any evidence to the contrary.

Now, probably, had someone like Abel Ferry or General Fayolle had access to all this data, and questioned the generalissimo as to the soundness of his conclusions, his answer would have been (if pressed) that the Germans were simply engaging in a sleight of hand. They had more divisions because the divisions were smaller: Instead of four infantry regiments, they only had three.

In retrospect, the mistake is glaringly obvious: Instead of measuring firepower, Allied intelligence was counting manpower, riflemen instead of machine gunners, just like they were still counting field guns instead of howitzers and mortars. So one mistake reinforced the other.

J. F. C. Fuller, one of the great military theorists of the century, would later note the overwhelming importance of modern firepower on the battlefield, expressing it as an axiom, that "in all wars, and especially in modern wars—in which weapons change rapidly—no army of fifty years before any date selected would stand a 'dog's chance' against an army existing at that date."[12]

VERDUN

Although the heavy French artillery of 1915 was not—
technically, anyway—fifty years old, as it mostly dates from 1878,
the comparison is not all that far off. Allied intelligence persisted in
counting apples and claiming they were acorns, in confusing manpower with firepower, and in discounting entirely the efficacy of
the technical innovations that marked the German arsenal.[13]

Finally—and the GQG regarded this proof as conclusive—
there had been no major offensive operations on the Western Front
at all in 1915. Why? Because the Germans were grossly outnumbered, simply lacked the manpower required. All they could do was
hang on. The evidence was overwhelming. The civilians in the government had no choice but to agree, however grudgingly.

So the civilians in Paris simply accepted the figures they were
given for casualties on both sides. Indeed, they had no choice, since
the GQG controlled the sources of information.

In consequence, by the end of 1915 the idea that the Allies were
decisively winning the casualty exchange, that the Germans were
running out of men, was firmly embedded in the Allied conscious-
ness, had reached the level of a fundamental assumption not to be
challenged.

There were, of course, German casualty figures that were sur-
facing in the German newspapers (and in the Reichstag), but when
they were occasionally mentioned, it was only to be dismissed out
of hand: "like to be exaggerated" was the blandly dismissive word-
ing of the *Times*.[14]

Indeed, by the end of 1915, anti-German propaganda was such
that the most preposterous stories were routinely believed. Indeed,
the Allied propaganda was so successful that many of the fabrications have duly entered the historical record and are accepted as fact.
There was no limit to the perfidious behavior of the barbarous Huns,
led by their reckless warlord, Kaiser Wilhelm. Lying was the least of
their crimes, and certainly no one would believe anything that came
out of Berlin, not even the supposedly neutral Americans.[15]

At the same time, the government in Paris was being given
some extremely misleading data about their own losses. On 4 Feb-

ruary 1915, Alexandre Millerand, the new minister of war, gave the secret war council a brief report on French losses to date. The army admitted it had recorded 151,900 dead, 217,500 missing, and 368,500 wounded.[16]

Abel Ferry, who recorded the figures from the report data in his secret diary, accompanies it with a dry comment: "After the war, it will be interesting to verify the accuracy of these figures" (248). And indeed it is, but in 1915 the GQG controlled all the information coming out of the war. The skeptics, few in number, had nothing on which to base their arguments.

At the same time, the army was able to claim that it was getting steadily stronger. It had twice as many machine guns in service as it had at the start of the war: 11,000 as opposed to 5,000.[17] The increase in heavy artillery was even more striking. At the start of the war the French had only 300 pieces of heavy artillery, and now (now being January 1916), they had 3,916 (2:597). Modern howitzers were finally beginning to appear, to replace the antiques of 1914, and by midsummer the gunners would have plenty of ammunition, thanks to their American suppliers.

So although Joffre was not nearly so crudely dismissive of the civilians as Sir William Robertson, who at one point told Lloyd George, "It is a waste of time explaining strategy to you; to understand my explanation you would have had to have my experience," his attitude was basically the same.[18]

By autumn 1915, with the admission that the expedition to Turkey had failed and must be withdrawn, now that the Greek expedition was mired in bickering and acrimony, the army high command felt that the civilians should get out of the way and let the generals win the war the way they wanted.

And, unlike Sir William Robertson, as well as Sir Douglas Haig, the brand-new commander of the British Expeditionary Force, Joffre had a plan.

THE ALLIED PLAN

So as 1915 came to an end, Joffre unfolded his plan for the coming year. It was based on one simple idea, which he had been patiently developing for over twelve months. Everyone understood the idea of breaking through the German lines, what the French called *la percée*. The problem, Joffre realized, was that the piercing was never done on a sufficiently broad front. As a result, the Germans could move reinforcements in from both sides and snuff out the advance through counterattacks.

The solution was a *coup de belier*, or great hammer blow, delivered on such a broad front that it would simultaneously smash through the defensive lines while the scale of the blow would be such that reinforcements would not be able to stanch the hemorrhage.

Joffre was very consistent about that, from his urging Sarrail to expand the Vauquois offensive, to his approval of the Roques plan for the Woëvre. Indeed, the very notion of coordinating the February offensives on both banks speaks to that issue. The attacks ended up badly, but that was because the local commanders were never able to execute them properly, mostly because they lacked the guns and the shells. It was certainly no fault of Joffre and his staff, who were supremely confident of their strategic acumen.

So now Joffre envisioned an offensive on much greater scale, not so much as to the section of the front, but as to the forces employed. In fact, Joffre did not have enough men to manage the thing on his own, but that was hardly a problem. The British already had a million men in France. By early summer there would most likely be half a million more. The trick was getting them to fight.

When the French looked at the front, they saw a million British soldiers holding down about 100 kilometers, and 2.8 million French soldiers holding down nearly 650. Simple math suggested there was a problem. The solution, as far as Joffre was concerned, was to find something for those soldiers to do, and the great joint offensive was the answer.

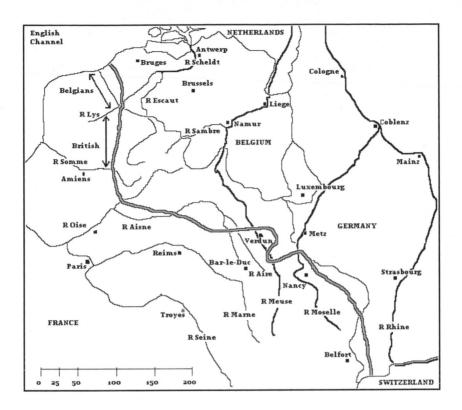

Since the only way such an offensive could be mounted was in conjunction with the British, everything reduced itself to picking a place where both armies could operate side by side in sufficient strength to break through the German lines.

A moment's reflection will suggest that this is hardly the way to choose your battlefield, and indeed, the area agreed on, the Somme, had absolutely nothing to recommend it strategically. The area was selected purely because it was the only place where the two armies could mount a joint offensive, side by side, on a broad enough scale. A. J. P. Taylor sums up the whole situation perfectly.

> Haig had always a favorite strategical idea: to attack Flanders and then "roll up" the Germans from the north. Joffre did not like this idea. He doubted whether the British would

fight hard enough unless he had them under his own hand; and for this a combined offensive was necessary. Joffre therefore pointed to the Somme, the spot where the British and French lines joined. This was a strange choice. There was no great prize to be gained, no vital center to be threatened. The Germans, if pressed, could fall back to their own advantage, with better communications and a shorter line. Joffre did not care. The great thing was to pull the British into heavy fighting.[19]

The only relevant fact that this observation omits is that Haig's idea was even more preposterous than Joffre's. In theory—and we are talking about the French here—a genuine breakthrough on the scale proposed would divide the Germans armies into two portions, allowing the French, who would be on the inside, or right flank of the offensive, to move behind the main German positions from Champagne on over, going all the way laterally across below the Belgian frontier, where the terrain favored mass maneuvers.

So although Joffre's plan was far too hypothetical, it was not in total defiance of geography. The basic problem with Haig's "strategical idea" was that it assumed Belgium was a tabletop that the infantry could walk across, once they broke through the German lines. In the real world, a formidable set of rivers ran up through Belgium to the sea, each one of them being wide enough and deep enough to be a serious obstacle. The Meuse was only the most formidable.

The idea was geographic nonsense, but Haig's conceit was no worse than the whole idea of the "soft underbelly" of Europe that led the Allies to have such high hopes for the impact the Italians would have on the course of the war. Apparently the Alps that formed the border between Italy and Austria were simply a few insignificant ridges that the Italian infantry could walk over in a few days.

However, as 1915 came to a close, Joffre was convinced that he had to do something to get the British to fight, and if the Somme was hardly the answer to the problem of ending the war, it was definitely the answer to the problem that was increasingly nagging at both the government in Paris and the GQG out in Chantilly: how to get the British to bestir themselves from their fraction of the front and used their rapidly growing army to fight the Germans.

Although the British, both then and forever afterward, bristle at the very idea, it must be said that the French felt this imbalance very strongly. When, in June 1916, Arthur Conan Doyle visited the French front, he made the following observation.

> Our guide is a Commandant of the Staff, a tall, thin man with hard, gray eyes and a severe face. It is the more severe towards us as I gather that he has been deluded into the belief that about one out of six of our soldiers goes to the trenches.[20]

On the face of it, the French officer had a fair point, and although generations of British historians have made all sorts of arguments proving—in their minds, anyway—why Haig required an army as large as France's to hold down a fraction of the front the French were holding, the numbers are really against them.

Indeed, one of the more fascinating things about the war is the extent to which, both then and afterward, it was so completely a war against arithmetic, with mostly but not entirely English historians denying the basic numbers, just as, during the war, the GQG kept insisting that the German army was shrinking, and would run out of men any minute now.

But at least Joffre and Haig had an excuse: their intelligence (which was mostly French) insisted that they were winning the war of attrition. So all they had to do was speed it up, and so Joffre's plan of expanding the actual frontage for an offense was both sensible and logical, and was supported by the facts, one of the more important being that since the Germans were so greatly weakened by their losses, time was against them. Joffre was content to wait until the summer, when the British troops would be more numerous and better trained.

In addition, meeting the objections, or needs, of his civilian overlords, the idea was that the great summer offensive in the west would be coordinated with other offensives in Italy, the Balkans, and Russia.

The Allies were dickering with Romania, trying to bribe it to enter the war, and felt they had a good chance of success, so there would be a joint Russian and Romanian offensive that would drive directly into eastern Hungary, possibly even coordinated with a thrust across the southern Carpathians into Transylvania. At the same time, the Allied expeditionary force in Greece, operating in conjunction with the Greek army, would thrust up into the southern part of Hungary, while the Italians would attack (yet again) on their front.

The basic plan was simple—which is a virtue in military matters. Nor did it particularly require some careful coordination, as far as time went. The pressure applied would be like tightening a vise. So long as the offensives occurred within a two- or three-month window, they would have the desired effect. Given all this pressure, whether simultaneous or in a series of repetitive blows, Austria-Hungary would collapse, and Germany would be unable to prop them up.

In fact, ideally, the best sequence would be for the other offensives to precede the one in the west, so the Germans would already be desperate, and would have drained their forces in France to prop up their allies in the east.

A FEW DIFFICULTIES

The problem with Joffre's scheme was that he lacked the resources to carry it out, even waiting for the summer to roll around, hoping that the Germans would occupy themselves in the east. Basing your plans on the assumption that your opponent will allow them to ripen is always a bad idea, although it seems strangely typical of a good deal of strategic planning.[21]

Then too, Joffre and his British colleagues, and their subordi-

nate staffers, seem not to have seriously considered the consequences of failure. What if the Germans spoiled their plans? What
if the breakthrough failed to occur? There doesn't seem to have
been a plan B, in other words.

That was not the only difficulty. Regardless of contingencies,
Joffre simply lacked the resources to succeed. He lacked the men,
and he lacked the firepower. So when the Germans attacked in
February, the French were simply unable to match the overwhelming firepower the Germans brought to bear. For that matter, they
hardly had the manpower to hold the section of the front that was
under attack.

Both of these deficiencies are critical to an understanding of
what actually happened when the Germans attacked at Verdun in
February 1916. Although the artillery problem is, once again,
rather technical, it is also crucial. So too with the manpower situation: the German attack set off a series of chain reactions, one
event having a dramatic influence on the next. The attacks of spring
1916 crippled Joffre's plans for the Somme. The divisions he had
intended for the French share of the offensive had largely been used
up by June 1916, one of the main reasons why the July offensive
there failed so signally. From that point on, a whole string of dom-
inoes fell, so that by August 1918, it was left to the Americans to
force the Germans back from their positions around Verdun. The
French no longer had the ability to conduct offensive operations on
that scale.

The artillery problem is particularly relevant. When the German bombardment began, nothing like it had been seen in warfare.
Nowadays, accustomed, perhaps even hardened, to photographs of
blasted cities, to enormous vistas of carnage caused by missiles and
bombs, it is difficult to grasp the magnitude of the barrage with
which the Germans began their offensive.

And given the technical nature of the subject, and how systematically the French misrepresented it, it is natural to assume that
there was some sort of equivalence between the two sides, when in
actuality they were asymmetrical.

THE ARTILLERY PROBLEM

As we have seen, when the war broke out, France's artillery park consisted of approximately 4,000 of the new 75-millimeter guns, and a few hundred antique heavy guns from the 1870s. Despite what outsiders believed, and were told, when the war began the gunners had none of the modern 105-millimeter Schneider howitzers in service, and only about 100 of the 155-millimeter weapons.[22]

But if the army was to be believed, after the first months, the situation steadily improved. By July 1915, in addition to the 4,000-odd field guns, the army had no less than 2,470 heavy weapons in service. That was the claim, and when Joffre penned his memoirs, he repeated it.

But on 11 July 1915, the cabinet was given an entirely different accounting. It turned out that actually, there were only 2,800 field guns in service. The Germans had captured 500, and another 1,200 had in one way or another been destroyed. In response to a pertinent question, it was revealed that the factories were not able to produce guns fast enough so that the losses could be made good.

It should be pointed out that in the normal course of use, artillery pieces wear out. So, leaving aside captures and weapons destroyed by the enemy, there has to be a steady flow of replacement guns into the units to replace those worn out through use. But, like the enormous expenditure of ammunition modern war required, this had not been foreseen. Although the exact production figures for the 75 are not readily available (or available at all), we can, by a rough rule of thumb, see that only a few hundred a year were being produced for the army in the years before the war, so it is hardly a surprise that the factories were having difficulties.

That was particularly the case since most of the raw materials for the gun had to be imported from abroad. Moreover, the 75, like the 155, was an extremely complicated mechanism, and was basically built by hand. It was hoped to increase production dramatically, up to what looked like over 200 a month or more, but here it was nearly a year into the war, and promises are cheap.

The situation with regard to heavy artillery was dreadful. The 2,740 figure was basically a sleight of hand. The army was counting the field guns that the 75 had replaced in 1898 as heavy weapons, since technically they had bigger barrels. So 1,230 of those guns consisted of the 90- and 95-millimeter weapons of the 1890s that the 75 had supposedly rendered obsolete.

That hardly passed muster with the cabinet, but the numbers were horrifying. There were 75 of the new Schneider howitzers, and 104 of the older 155-millimeter weapons. So if the French were going to equip their divisions to the same scale as the Germans, they had enough field guns to equip 26 divisions, enough 105-millimeter howitzers to equip four, and enough of the heavier howitzers to equip 10.

As for the truly heavy weapons, the army had exactly 312 155-millimeter guns in service. There were enormous stocks of weapons in the forts: between 2,500 and 3,000 guns. Of course, all of them dated from the 1870s, and gun mounts would have to be fabricated if they were to be used in the field at all, so the situation was grim.

The horrifying part of this report was the total absence of the two categories of weapons that the Germans possessed in quantity: the hundreds of portable trench mortars used by the combat engineers, and the large arsenal of heavy weapons of 21, 30.5, 38, and 42 centimeters that they had brought into action at the start of the war.

At one point someone in the cabinet, observing that the Germans were shelling Dunkirk, wanted to know why the army wasn't shelling Baden, since the distance from the French positions to the duchy was about the same as from the German lines to the town on the channel. Embarrassed silence: The French simply didn't possess guns with that range.

But the charade continued on, unchecked. Officially, there were no less than 828 pieces of artillery located at Verdun in this same time period, a figure that to the layman would seem more than sufficient. But of that number, 468 were field guns whose restricted angle of fire made them highly impractical, and only 255 of those were the modern 75-millimeter weapons. Except for 49 155-millimeter guns, the balance consisted of antique mechanical-recoil pieces from the 1870s.

Just as the British, in their section of the front, kept their cavalry horses at the ready so as to exploit the breakthrough that their generals were convinced would eventually take place, their French colleagues kept on counting the antiques in their arsenal as though they were actually pieces of heavy artillery. A queer war indeed, as H. G. Wells had remarked.

So in other words, the French still were grossly outnumbered by the Germans when it came to heavy guns. The great increase in numbers was achieved by counting all the mechanical-recoil weapons produced half a century earlier and pressed into service because that was all the army had.

Looking back, what is really striking is the lack of any sense of urgency about the situation. There were worries about supplying the gunners with enough shells, but there's nothing about supplying them with weapons to match the German artillery park. Instead, the people responsible for artillery design, and the headquarters in Chantilly, took refuge in two arguments.

First, they observed, correctly, that French shells contained a much higher explosive payload than German shells did. This rather obscure technical point was true across the entire range of weaponry. The French 120-millimeter gun fired a 20-kilogram shell that contained 4.2 kilograms of explosive, while the German 13-centimeter gun fired a 40-kilogram shell that contained only 2.5 kilograms of explosive. The 75-millimeter gun delivered 0.650 kilograms, as opposed to the German 7.7 centimeter's 0.160-kilogram payload.[23]

Then there was the argument that the 75 completely outclassed its German and British equivalents. Not only did it fire shells with considerably more high explosive, but it fired more of them per minute. It was also lighter, more accurate, and had a longer range. And that was that.

True enough, but the argument was seriously flawed, because it overlooked the importance of weapons firing shells at a very high trajectory, so they would descend at the near vertical, what French gunnery experts called *tir courbe*.

> The consequences of the lack of modern artillery with a high angle of fire . . . were the following: 1, the lack of effects against German fortifications. . . . French artillery, almost completely composed of guns firing shells over a flat trajectory, with very rare 155 millimeter howitzers and 220 millimeter mortars having a slow rate of fire, were seriously lacking the means to destroy the German fortifications.[24]

In an extremely important note appended to this argument, General Gascouin makes the following observation.

> German artillery had light howitzers disposing a great number of shells, sufficiently powerful for all our fortifications, capable of rapid fire with precision. They had, in addition, a great number of heavy howitzers and trench mortars capable not just of a high trajectory of fire, but of vertical fire. Hardly any part of our line was immune to their shells. On the contrary, there existed until 1917 and even 1918, many dead angles, in the greater part of our sectors, where a shell never fell, owing to the generally flat trajectory of our weapons as described above. The study of aerial photographs of certain sectors shows that clearly (116).

Obstinately, the experts stuck to their position. On 22 January 1919, well after the end of the war, General Fayolle had dinner with Émile Rimailho and General Sainte-Claire Deville. Rimalho, it will be recalled, was the man who had invented, or rather developed, the 155-millimeter gun the French used. The two men showed Fayolle photographs of new guns and mounts for the 75 that enabled it to have a much higher angle of fire. Why weren't these adopted during the war? Fayolle asked. "The rivalries of the chapels," the men replied.[25]

Chapel was the word used in the army to characterize officers who adhered to certain beliefs with the obstinacy of members of a religious cult. They resisted the conclusions reached by inductive reasoning based on evidence, no matter how strong those conclusions would seem to be in retrospect. Or, to put it another way, they had come to certain ideas, and those ideas had become assumptions, beliefs, that they clung to regardless of the evidence.

Given the dramatic changes in warfare that the Great War ushered in, and particularly in artillery, it is not surprising to see such a phenomenon among gunners. The refusal to accept that the field gun of 1914, basically the lineal descendant of the cannon of earlier centuries, was not the right weapon for the modern battlefield, was one of those notions, even though in the decades after the end of the war, every army in the world replaced those guns with howitzers of the same configuration and size as the Germans had been using from the start.

It is easy to identify other examples of beliefs that were held in complete defiance of reality. In the years before the war, field guns like the French 75 had two different types of shells. There were shells whose payload consisted of nothing but high-explosive, adulterated TNP, in the case of the French, TNT, in the case of the Germans. Then there were shells whose payload consisted mostly of bits of metal. Those shells, generically called shrapnel shells, were designed to be used against troops, preferably against troops caught in the open.

When the war began, French and German field gunners therefore carried a mix of high-explosive and shrapnel shells. Now, when soldiers were entrenched, or simply hiding behind a barrier of some sort, clearly only high-explosive shells were of any use. That was particularly the case as the typical entrenched position began to emerge: soldiers sheltered in dugouts or blockhouses, with barbed wire preventing access to their positions.

For that reason, when General Gascouin wrote the treatise on artillery we have quoted from above, he omitted any discussion of shrapnel shells: the conditions of the war made them useless—except to British artillery experts, who persisted in the notion that shrapnel shells could be used to cut barbed wire. Two years into the war and British gunners were still firing more shrapnel shells than high-explosive, just as the French were still relying on their antique mechanical-recoil weapons from the 1870s.

In both cases we have a keen observer who noticed the telling details, and recorded them. "We appeared to be using more shrapnel and the Germans more high explosives, but that may have been just the chance of the day," Sir Arthur Conan Doyle wrote when he visited the British front in June 1916.[26]

The authorities laid on a grand tour of the British, Italian, and French fronts so he would write an encouraging essay on their efforts, and by and large he did. But the man who created Sherlock Holmes noticed other interesting facts as well, proof of why the high commands of the two armies only grudgingly allowed outsiders to see the war, even at a distance.

> There was one little gun which fascinated me, and I stood for some time watching it. Its three gunners, enormous helmeted men, evidently loved it, and touched it with a swift but tender touch in every movement. When it was fired it ran up an inclined plane to take off the recoil, rushing up and then turning and rattling down again upon the gunners who were used to its ways. The first time it did it, I was standing behind it, and I don't know which moved quickest—the gun or I (89–90).

So here it was, June 1916, and the French were still using mechanical-recoil field guns.

Not that one can blame the gun crew Doyle observed. They had to fire something at the enemy, and that was all they had. As General Gascouin observes, modern heavy guns in any quantity did not begin to reach the troops until late 1917 or even early 1918.

Yes, by the end of the war, the Allies had weapons that were just as good as the ones the Germans had, and by and large they had learned how to use them. But the qualifier of "by the end of the war" is hardly an insignificant detail.

MANPOWER AND DENIAL

Now, as we have seen, Joffre's plan was based on the assumption that the Allies were getting steadily stronger, and their opponents were getting steadily weaker. Not only did the Allies have more and more weapons at their disposal, but there were more and more British soldiers in France, a growing force that more than compensated for French losses.

Besides—and perhaps more important—German losses were such that they were simply incapable of doing anything more than hanging on, if that. We have already seen the Allied (mostly if not entirely French) estimates, running into the millions, the most recent being the one reported by Colonel Repington in January 1916: 3.5 million.

So what the GQG argued was the casualty exchange ratio was the basic warrant for Joffre's repeated offensives, including his great *coup de bélier* scheduled for summer 1916. In fact, upon reflection, it is clear that the Allied advantage in the casualty exchange was the key assumption on which everything else was predicated.

Consider the following hypothetical. Suppose that the cabinets in both London and Paris had believed that the central powers had access to unlimited resources in manpower and munitions, that their armies were powerful enough to fight on three or four separate fronts all over Europe. These men were hardly idiots. It is difficult to imagine that they would have continued to launch their ambitious schemes of flank attacks in the Balkans and Italy had that been their perception. The whole idea of the amphibious invasion of Turkey, of bribing Italy (and laying plans to bribe Romania), the incursion into Greece, the initial dependence on the

Russians, all of these notions were predicated on the idea that the Germans had very limited resources that a war on multiple fronts would stretch to the breaking point.

So too with the reluctant support given to the British and French high commands in their determination to launch repeated offensives on the Western Front. From December 1914 to November 1915, basically a year, there were no less than four separate offensive operations in Champagne and Artois. It really beggars the imagination to suppose that London and Paris would have let those multiple attacks continue had they not really believed that their armies were inflicting far more damage on the German defenders than they were incurring.

Rather obviously, the Allied advantage in the casualty exchange to a great extent smothered embarrassing questions about the lack of modern weapons, the shortage of shells, and, above all, the failure to make significant territorial gains during these offensive operations.

Of course, this last was neatly trumped by a certain sleight of hand. As we have seen, the GQG seemed to think that objectives were taken in the same way that goals are scored in football games. It was sufficient to get the ball across the goal line. So the fact that the remnants of a few infantry units managed to get a toehold on one end of the Vauquois, or Les Éparges, or occupy the first line of German trenches somewhere was always accounted a victory. That in tactical terms absolutely nothing had been accomplished was treated as being a matter totally beyond the pale.

It was only as the summer of 1915 came to an end that the criticisms began to coalesce, which was why in October the government fell and was replaced. But it is clear from reading the diary of the new minister of war that not even a wily old soldier like Marshal Gallieni really understood how badly the GQG was misrepresenting the situation.

But Gallieni, like everyone else, was dependent on what the army was telling them were the losses.

It will be remembered that in February 1915, the French minister of war had told the secret committee that army casualties up to that point were 151,900 dead, 217,500 missing, and 368,500 wounded.[27] There were two problems with those figures. The first difficulty is that they grossly understated French losses. The actual numbers: 528,000 dead or missing, and at least 580,000 wound cases.[28] So the report Millerand gave was thus erroneous by roughly 30 percent.

The surprisingly high number of those soldiers in the category of missing should have set off alarm bells. "Missing" is an interesting category, since it includes both the living and the dead. Some soldiers are missing because they've fallen into enemy hands, and are very much alive. Others are missing in the sense that their bodies have not been recovered, while still others—a small number—are missing in the sense that they deserted.

In one sense the breakdown is irrelevant. In any brief time period, soldiers who are dead, who are missing, or whose wounds have caused them to be evacuated are no longer available for combat. But by February 1915, the army should have been able to reduce the number of the missing considerably, that is, to assign them to one of the three groups, at least provisionally.

Doing so is not simply an exercise. The number of prisoners lost is generally regarded as an important indicator of your enemy's success. Either your soldiers have given up, or they've been caught by surprise, surrendered to keep from being slaughtered. One of the first questions General Grant always asked after an engagement was how many prisoners had been taken.

When there are more men missing than dead, there are two highly probable conclusions to be drawn, neither of them very encouraging. Either your army can't keep track of its casualties, or a good many of your men are surrendering.

Now, in the case of the French army, we have a good deal of evidence to establish the former, from the astoundingly high number of men still in the category of the missing well after the war (nearly a quarter of a million), to the candid admission that the number of wound cases in the opening months is simply unknown, to the incomplete identifications on the grave markers in the cemeteries.[29]

The French army did a rather poor job of keeping track of its soldiers, just as it did a terrible job of caring for them. The observation is really indisputable, and has never been questioned.

But then, although the army couldn't count its own losses accurately, the cabinet was being asked to believe that their estimates of enemy losses were highly accurate. There was, in other words, a failure in the short term to connect the dots.

So what exactly were the relative loss figures? We now know that by the end of 1914, French casualties came to 528,000 dead and missing.[30] As the French at this point did not separate out the dead and the missing, we'll combine the two categories simply for the sake of the comparison. Doing that, we get a figure for the British of 115,333, and for the Belgians, 62,000. So the total Allied dead and missing for 1914 came to 708,000 men.

For the same period, the German medical services reported 223,766 dead and missing, a figure for the Western Front only.[31] So if we express the casualty exchange ratio, restricting it only to the dead and the missing, the advantage is slightly over three to one for the Germans.

Now, before proceeding further, it should be observed that in these figures the wounded have been omitted. The reasons are simple, but the failure to realize them is a difficulty that has dogged historians and analysts for most of the century.

The medical services did not count individuals, but evacuations (the actual word the French used), and the German medical services were quite explicit that their data was compiled the same way: cases, not people.

Logic suggests the reason why: a soldier can be wounded more than once. In fact, he can be treated for his wounds and then eventually either get killed or go missing. We know, from the wound analyses conducted by the United States medical services, that this idea is not simply theoretical; the army actually tabulated the number of men who were wounded more than once, and discovered that the figure was significant. The same is true for other armies as well.

Michel Huber sums the situation up perfectly for his own army.

> The evaluation of the number of wounded and sick is much more uncertain than that of the dead or the missing, because the statistics for admissions to medical facilities contain numerous examples of double counting, most often owing to multiple transfers from one facility to another (*France*, 429).

In fact, if we simply add up the number of wound cases for each year, the resulting number (9,382,000) is much greater than the total number of men inducted into the army during the entire war. When the French went over their admissions figures, they reduced the nine million figure down to 3,481,000 wounded, which gives a good idea of how misleading the figures can be.

Lumping the dead, the missing, and the wounded together is reasonable when discussing the losses in any one engagement, particularly for the commanders of the units involved, since it gives them an idea of how many soldiers they have left at that point. But when longer time periods are considered it becomes a considerable distortion, since a certain percentage of the wounded are patched up and sent back to their units.

That may seem a rather obvious point, but what it sometimes disguises is that a wounded soldier's chances of recovery were significantly higher if he was treated by the German medical services than by the French. The author of the official Australian medical services report discussed this differential in detail, so again, we have the data to support the idea.

However, given the importance of the issue, here are the relevant figures for 1914: French wounds cases came to 635,000, British to 52,969, Belgian to 15,000, for a total of 702,969 wounds cases. German wounds cases were 471,923.

Given the Allied deficiencies in heavy artillery, we should expect the Germans to have a higher ratio of wounded cases to deaths, because more of them would be exposed to bullets than to shells, which would also mean a lower rate of mortality. A comparison of the wounds sustained, conducted by the medical services involved, supports this notion: there were significantly more Allied casualties caused by shell fire than there were German.

Sven Hedin, the famous Swedish explorer, provides us with anecdotal evidence that confirms this idea. He visited the Argonne in 1914, courtesy of the German government, and recorded that the wounded German soldiers he observed had much less serious wounds than their French counterparts.[32]

This asymmetry is important, but before going into it further, here are the figures for the next period of the war. At the end of 1915, French casualties were as follows: 439,000 dead and missing, and 696,000 wounded cases. British losses were 90,971 dead and missing, and 224,963 wounded, for a total of 529,971 dead or missing and 920,963 wounded. We have no figures at all for the Belgians, although during at least half of the year, their forces were actually larger than the British. So the Allied totals are clearly on the low side.

The corresponding German figures for the Western Front were 186,306 dead and missing, and 660,618 wounded cases, which gives a ratio of almost three to one, again favoring the Germans.

Of course, the total German casualties were higher than these figures, since there were German troops fighting in Russia and the Balkans. As we have already seen, the Germans were quite energetic in shifting their units around, and the Allies were generally wrong in their estimates of who was where and how many (to put it crudely).

So obviously they also had grave difficulties in assigning casualties to the various fronts, which is probably one reason their estimates were so wildly wrong: they ended up counting German losses on all fronts, and comparing those with Allied losses just on the Western Front.

However, without going any further into these calculations, it is pretty clear that the Allied notion that they were slaughtering the

Germans, who would soon run out of men, was not only wrong, but it was actually the other way around. So one of the most important assumptions on which the direction of the war was based, the warrant on which virtually everything else depended, was completely backward.

For the French the consequences of this fundamental failure were catastrophic. France was smaller than Germany. Before the war, it had maintained a standing army of an equivalent size by applying the principle of universal military service much more rigorously than was the case in Germany and Austria-Hungary. But once the fighting started, there was a ghastly arithmetic at work. The French had a smaller pool of men to draw from, so they could not afford to lose them at the same rate as their opponents. Already, as 1915 came to a close, their depots were emptying out.

At the start of hostilities, France had been able to mobilize about three million men to add to the existing peacetime army.[33] The next draft into the depots, concluding in January 1915, was therefore much smaller, slightly over a million. Then came the ominous part: the draft that concluded in January 1916 was only 850,000. It was not terribly difficult to predict the numbers available for successive drafts, and the actual figures are scary: 505,000 for the next period, and only 219,000 were available for 1919.

To a certain extent the implications of this were masked by various factors, so the actual size of the army was not decreasing so dramatically, or even within the same time frame. Demographic analysis of this sort is always confusing, so the failure of the government to grasp it is understandable. But the bottom line makes the situation clear enough: once the war started, millions of men were called up and put in uniform, but the actual size of the army only increased by about 10 percent—and then it slowly began to decline.

By contrast, not only were the Germans not running out of men, but the size of their army was increasing. Not just in divisions, but in terms of men. So the Allies had that estimate backward as well. The basic reason the Germans were creating more divisions was that they had more men. That the divisions were, in terms of infantry, smaller was really irrelevant.

Here are the numbers. In October 1914, 1.7 million men were in arms, and the ration strength in the west was 1.633 million. By May 1915, the ration strength was nearly 2.2 million, and by the end of the year, it was 2.6 million.[34]

So the Allies had the situation absolutely backward. Abel Ferry's gloomy prediction was absolutely correct. But the GQG persisted in its illusions, the British command in France drank from the same bottle, and across the channel in London, the cabinet perforce believed them.

Now, the reader who has carefully studied the various English-language accounts of this war will find these numbers perplexing, because they contradict almost everything that has been written. In fact, after the war, the assumption that the Allies were winning the casualty exchange was incorporated into all the standard accounts of the war.

Initially, there was a good reason for this. On the one hand, by the end of 1918, Germany had basically dissolved, owing to the collapse of the Kaiserreich and the ensuing civil war. There was no agency around to issue any figures, so historians were still largely dependent on Allied estimates.

Very reliable French data was available early on—by 1919, in fact—and the British War Office published a very thorough statistical summary in 1922. By contrast, it took the Germans a very long time to sort through the data, and their voluminous and typically Germanic report appeared only in 1933, by which time the Great War was a distant memory indeed, given the state of Europe.

This report therefore vanished into almost complete obscurity. One never finds it mentioned in any of the standard accounts of the war, either in French or English, with one exception.

Now, the disinterested reader will surely find this exception exceptionable: Winston Churchill.

When Churchill set out to write his account of the war, which he called *The World Crisis*, he realized that the casualty exchange ratio was a vital component in any assessment of what had actually happened. So he did the most obvious thing that any competent researcher would surely do: he asked the Germans what their figures were, as he had found out that they were compiling away.

He had a particular interest in this issue, since the man writing the British Army's official history of the war had made a rather astonishing claim, to the effect that the Germans didn't count their lightly wounded, and so their claimed totals were deliberately misleading.

Of course, this notion more or less flies in the face of our general idea of German behavior, so Churchill, not surprisingly, asked Edmonds what the basis was for his claim. Where was the evidence?

The answer he got really transcends the casualty issue, as it reveals the mind-set of several generations of historians. The thing was so obvious he hadn't bothered to inquire, was the answer. Everybody knew the Germans were lying.

And indeed, given the success of Allied propaganda, the notion was certainly feasible. Indeed, in the concluding chapter of this book, we will take a cursory glance at the various myths and distortions that have passed into the historical record, simply to point out that the general idea of Verdun is only one among the many. The depressing thing about these distortions and misrepresentations is that they were not confined to the uneducated. On the contrary, the totally false claims made by distinguished historians are on a par with the crudest sorts of wartime propaganda. And they are the most destructive, given the reputation of the person making them.

So Edmonds had plenty of company, and when Churchill published his account, he was roundly smeared by his fellow countrymen. We tend to forget that in the 1920s and 1930s, the reputation of the man who became his country's greatest wartime leader was truly abysmal.

Although the Second World War either salvaged Churchill's stature or established it, his reputation as a competent historian was never truly accepted by British historians, and to this day, the notion that the German army was much more efficient in combat than the British or the French is guaranteed to be met with withering scorn.

A grimly amusing book could be written about the torturous logic, ad hominem arguments, and sneering innuendo that are used when the myth of how the British Army won the First World War is in any way challenged. The casualty exchange situation is only one facet of this fairy tale, and facts have nothing to do with the case.

Understanding the outright denial and the torturous explanations of the clear German superiority on the battlefield by successive generations of historians is not simply an excursion into historiography.

It allows us to comprehend the mind-set of the Allied high commands, who simply dismissed the criticisms and misgivings of men like Driant and Ferry with withering condescension. The false emphasis and the rhetoric also allow us to grasp the atmosphere inside London and Paris, to understand the extent to which they were helplessly adrift.

When we grasp that blindness, that denial, we can then begin to comprehend the effect of the German offensive of February 1916 at Verdun on the military leadership of France. Suddenly, the light at the end of the tunnel was revealed to be the headlight of the oncoming locomotive.

DISQUIET ON THE WESTERN FRONT

We have already observed how, as reports filtered up from the front, the news became progressively changed, until finally, at headquarters, it began to look like the complete opposite of reality. Even President Poincaré had noticed this, and had complained to

Abel Ferry about it. This progression is worth repeating, because it allows us to understand how it was that the GQG failed to comprehend the nature of the struggle.

> At the GQG, they tell me "Everything is going well in the Argonne: success!" At the army group headquarters, they tell me, "We're advancing, but with trouble." At the army corps headquarters, General Gérard tells me, "We're losing 100 meters a month, the Germans are gnawing us, and the letters from the soldiers are discouraging" (Ferry, *Carnets*, 35).

Seen from Chantilly, the war seemed to be going well. Seen from the viewpoint of the combatants, it was going very badly indeed. The idea of being gnawed on, with its unpleasant connotation of rats, is not a pleasant idea—for those who feel they're being gnawed.

But at the headquarters of the two commands—and hence in London and Paris—almost everyone clung to the opposite notion with the determination of a shipwrecked sailor holding on to a piece of driftwood. True, they couldn't penetrate the German defensive system in the west. True, Serbia, Italy, and Russia had all failed to give them the relief that they had anticipated. True, the expeditions in the Balkans and the east were bringing them the eagerly expected results. However, they naturally clung to the idea that they were winning a war on the most basic level: through attrition, what the French called the *guerre d'usure*.

Colonel Repington, the correspondent for the *Times*, a man with access to every level of both governments, recorded in his diary a highly reliable estimate that the Germans to date had lost 3.5 million men.[35]

If President Poincaré was suspicious, General Fayolle, who had to live with Joffre's staff, and saw the results of their complacency on a daily basis, was bitter. Here he is commenting on the situation at the start of 1915.

An extraordinary thing, that must be held to the account of the GQG and its inexactitudes, is that the official bulletins of information recount nothing but jokes. They say, and all newspapers repeat, that we took 500 meters of German trenches. However, we didn't take anything at all. The generals want at any price to have successes, so they invent what they want to believe. Do they even understand the situation? I doubt it.[36]

Indeed, Fayolle's concluding sentence hits the proverbial nail on the head: it was not as though the GQG was openly and consciously lying. They believed what they were saying, and failed to realize the extent to which their eagerness—and the inexperience of Joffre's subordinates at Chantilly—not only precluded their understanding, but warped the information they were receiving.

Fayolle, already a corps commander, was skeptical. Abel Ferry, a lowly infantry lieutenant who happened to be a member of the Chamber of Deputies, was outraged. Like everyone else in the government, the only figures he had were the ones the GQG had provided, but he knew what he had seen—and it flatly contradicted the rosy picture. Here is the key part of his June 1915 discourse to the secret committee.

One speaks of a "war of attrition," but we have not lost fewer men at Les Éparges than the Germans. In Champagne we have lost more than they did. In front of Marcheville, since 18 March, 3,000 men fell: 500 Germans were casualties. Even more than an avowal of our strategic impotence, and a preview of a devastated France, the war of attrition, a journalistic rather than a military formula, *the war of attrition goes against us*. Fifty voices have told me. I have reviewed my regiment. On 18 March, an heroic folly animated them. Out of my company of 250, 20 men returned. In the 8th company, it was the same. They found, in the German trench they seized, then abandoned, *not a single dead German. . . .* As this wastage continues, the day is near when the offensive value of our army, already fatally weakened, will be destroyed.[37]

No translation can capture the compressed and eloquent fury of this passage, and the phrases Ferry uses are much more sinister and disturbing than their English counterparts. *Guerre d'usure*, with its connotations of usury, is much more brutal than the idea of attrition, and the word *gaspillage*, with its subtext of profligate squandering, is rhetorically much more effective than *wastage*. But, lacking access to the numbers, Ferry had no choice but to use rhetoric to make his point.

The cabinet received his note in dismissive silence. But by July their attitude had changed. And then in August came the bombshell: a letter written to Paul Deschanel, who was president of the Chamber of Deputies. Unlike the other governmental positions, this one tended toward stability: Deschanel had been president before (1898–1902), was now serving his second term, which had begun in 1912. He would remain in that position all through the war. He was thus an important political figure in France.

But then, so was the man who wrote the letter of 23 August 1915—Émile Driant—and his letter was truly a bombshell.

Like Abel Ferry, Émile Driant was a member of the chamber, and a man with intimate ties to important people. Ferry was the nephew of Jules Ferry; Driant was married to the daughter of the late General Boulanger. But Ferry was a politician who happened to be a soldier. Driant had graduated from the military school at Saint-Cyr (fourth in his class), and had served with distinction in three African campaigns. He had been a battalion commander by 1896, but Louis André (the current minister of war) had no more interest in seeing Boulanger's son-in-law advanced to the higher grades than he did in allowing defiantly Christian Roman Catholics to become senior officers.

But when the war broke out, Driant was a colonel commanding

the 1st Battalion of *chasseurs*, one of the crack regiments of the French army. He had been at Verdun since the start of the war, had fought on both sides of the Meuse. So, briefly, he and Ferry were neighbors, as the newly minted lieutenant's regiment, the 165th, was part of the Verdun garrison, was on the right bank as well, where it got slaughtered as the Bavarians pushed farther into the Woëvre in the first months of the war.

By July 1915, Driant had lost 26 officers and 1,300 men in six separate engagements. In addition to being a member of the chamber and a career officer, he was also a well-known writer. So his was not a voice to be easily dismissed, and here is what he charged.

> The German wave is going to return. The Russians will be out of action for six months. Here we think that the next blow of the hammer will be delivered on the line Verdun-Nancy. What a moral effect would be produced by the fall of one or both of these! It would be worth the price, and they have already proven that they know how to sacrifice 50,000 men to carry a place, if they are able to succeed.[38]

That belief was bad enough, but Driant had much more to say, all of it bad. However, before going on to that, two points are worth remarking.

One of them is simple enough: the idea that the Russians would be out of the picture for six months, and the connection of these sentences is clear: since the Russians are out of the picture, the Germans can now attack us.

The phrase Driant uses is significant: *coup de bélier*, the hammer blow, the same idea that Joffre was pushing for the summer. Both in that, and in the remark that the Germans had already demonstrated they were willing to sacrifice 50,000 men for an important objective, Driant was adhering to both the concept of the battle of annihilation and as well to the belief of heavy German losses. His tactical thinking, in other words, was very much of a piece with the mind-set of the GQG.

Where he departed from them was in his conception of strategy, because he emphasized the effect on morale—to use the inexact English synonym. His concern was not that the French would lose a battle; his concern was the effect the loss of the position would have on the country at large.

However, Driant then delivered a troubling assessment of purely military matters. His commanding general, he averred, is a good man, is trying to foresee all possibilities. But there is little he can do, because of the lack of means. The phrase Driant uses, *le manque de bras*, seems deliberately ambiguous, particularly since he emphasizes it in the letter. However, the point is clear enough. He lacks the means to do what is required—and that is the point of the sentences that follow. Thus the reason for Driant's letter: He is asking that Deschanel call this to the attention of the minister of war, because

> If our first line is overrun by a massive attack, our second line is insufficient. We have gotten to this point because of a lack of workers and, I add, a lack of barbed wire. . . . If this is not done, we will not be ready when the wave returns. . . . Of artillery and above all machine guns, we only have a minute quantity, but I don't speak of those, because more have been promised (180).

In return Driant received a rather blandly inconsequential note, but Deschanel promised to bring the letter to the attention of the minister of war, "either tomorrow or the day after" (181).

But there is no record of anything much being done. In fact, for the next two months (22 August to 26 October), the cabinet was preoccupied with the grand strategic plan to send an expeditionary force to Greece that would, together with the Greek and Serbian armies, mount a powerful offensive that would do what the previous three attempts (Russia, Italy, and the Dardanelles expedition) had failed to manage.

Like the earlier schemes, this one ended in a series of disasters:

von Falkenhayn, having temporarily ejected the Russians from the field (as Driant noted), now turned his attentions to the Serbians. A joint Austro-German and Bulgarian offensive in early October destroyed the Serbian army and forced its evacuation to offshore Greek islands, and thence to Greece. The forced alliance with Greece was collapsing, the British troops stayed put, and General Sarrail's French expeditionary force accomplished nothing at all, although the good general managed to alienate all and sundry.

But by then—mid-October—the government was fighting for survival, so the Greek fiasco was simply another nail in its coffin, and on 29 October the Viviani government fell.

As with most of these governmental crises—and quite unlike the situation in Great Britain or the United States—there was much less to the changes of government than met the eye. The conscientious reader will recall that Joffre had been elevated to chief of staff by Adolphe Messimy when he was minister of war in June 1911. Five changes of government later—it was only June 1914— and he was minister of war again. But in the panic of late August, the government fell again, and Messimy was replaced by Alexandre Millerand, who had already succeeded Messimy once before, in 1911.

So in October, when Poincaré asked Aristide Briand to form a new government, it was his third turn as prime minister, which suggests how little things had changed. However, in an uncharacteristic burst of rationality, Briand named as his new minister of war Joseph-Simon Gallieni, the real architect of the victory that Joffre had let be called the Battle of the Marne, and France's most distinguished soldier, prewar.

Now, Marshal Gallieni was personally extremely unhappy about the way in which Joffre's staff had tried to deny him any credit at all for the Marne; nor was he impressed by what he had seen thus far at Chantilly. "The GQG is a machine with an engine that doesn't run," is a quote from his diary that pretty much sums up his attitude.[39] Nor was he much of a fan of the civilian leadership. Before the war he had lobbied for heavy artillery, and he personally blamed the

Chamber of Deputies for blocking the appropriations to develop proper weapons. As minister, he had to attend cabinet meetings and sessions of the chamber, and his descriptions of them are scathing, as a few snippets from his diary make clear.

> At the Council of Ministers, discussion confused, as always (10 November)
>
> Council. Always words, never decisions. Poincaré, Briand . . . talk continually, and about everything. Nothing is ever resolved (11 November).
>
> At the Chamber [of Deputies]. Interminable babbling (12 November).[40]

However, Gallieni was not simply some crotchety oldster. A certain contempt for a government that has had seven ministers of war—in 42 months—hardly seems hypercritical. Particularly when most of the time the new prime ministers and most of their cabinet were simply being recycled from the same parties that had been in power for decades.

Moreover, Gallieni had an argument to make about the reason the GQG was a machine that lacked a working motor. His argument was in two simple parts, both of which revealed a shrewd insight into the problem.

During the first month or so of the war, Joffre had sacked almost all the senior generals. By 6 September 1914, by his own admission, he had removed about a third of the senior commanders from their posts: two army group commanders, 9 of the 21 corps commanders, 33 of the 72 division commanders, and 5 of the 10 cavalry commanders.[41]

Their successors were men who were new to their rank, colonels who were now having to be division and in some cases corps commanders, brigadiers who were having to coordinate units much larger and more complex than infantry divisions. The learning curve was steep.

At the same time, Joffre had surrounded himself with relatively junior officers who had no experience either in the field or in combat. Maurice Gamelin, for example, was a major in 1914 who had never commanded more than a battalion, and that only briefly. Most of his military service had been doing staff work. Although Ferdinand Foch was not only older, but was actually a corps commander in 1914, he had held the job only briefly, as he had spent most of his recent career at the École Militaire. Like Gamelin, he was somewhat of a theorist, had written a book that was rather pretentiously entitled *On the Principles of War*. Among its many gems was the notion that victory could only be achieved by engaging in hand-to-hand combat, that, in an atrociously ambiguous phrase, "victory floats above the enemy's bayonets."[42]

But these new men felt themselves vastly superior to everyone else, even though they had no substantive experience. "The GQG, perpetually incorrigible, lives in an atmosphere of unreality," Gallieni observed (*Carnets*, 239). Given that major battles such as the Woëvre were planned in a way that revealed complete ignorance of the terrain, that costly and futile attacks were launched on strongpoints that clearly were beyond the means of the units involved, that information was carefully massaged to reflect the preconceptions of the headquarters, Gallieni's remark seems fair enough.

Then there was the aging marshal's idea that Joffre was in fact being managed by his staff, rather than the other way around. His experiences in September 1914, watching as these same men glorified the commander in chief, building him up as the great military strategist who had defeated the Germans at the Battle of the Marne, rankled, and not least because of the way in which his role as military governor of Paris had been dismissed.

The whole thing was smoke and mirrors, Gallieni thought. "Was there a Battle of the Marne?" he wondered, meditating on the four separate battles, spread out from north of Paris to south of Verdun, that had all been rolled up into one battle and given the name of a French river.[43]

Perhaps the most disturbing thing about the Marne was how the name was assigned. At Chantilly, there was considerable discussion about this. General Berthelot suggested "Bataille des Champs Catalauniques," an obscure and rather bookish reference, although one with some vague historical resonance.[44] General Belin suggested a more prosaic but accurate tag: "La Bataille Paris-Verdun." To which another officer retorted that the name sounded more like a bicycle race than a battle. Then Gamelin, still a major, and very much a junior member of the staff, came up with the idea of calling it the Battle of the Marne. Joffre, who had contributed nothing to the discussion, agreed.

Now, the French, left in possession of the battlefields, were entitled to claim a victory, and certainly to call it whatever they wanted. But this process is a perfect encapsulation of the problems at the top: a great concern with appearance, a rather passive supreme commander, discussions dominated by junior officers. But neither civilians at the top nor the uneasy officers lower down had access to the data that would enable them to substantiate their unease, their distress. They were forced to argue either on the basis of anecdotal information or abstract principles such as the faulty theories or the ignorance of modern warfare.

But now, at about the same time that Gallieni was appointed minister of war, there was a new development that helped to bring matters to a head.

Since the staff at Chantilly was sitting on all the information, only doling it out as they saw fit, there was no way anyone on the outside could win the argument as it was being framed. But there was leakage. Driant apparently wasn't the only source for the cabinet. Here is Gallieni's entry recording the discussion of 16 December.

> Morning, Council of Ministers, discussion about Joffre and the trenches. Disquiet about the next German attack. Wrote Joffre. In some places, the defensive works are not in good condition. The thing is grave. Do what is necessary from Verdun to Toul, between Berry-au-Bac and Soupir. The first line easily broken through, there aren't enough

troops there. At 1500 or 2000 [meters] very little in the way of a second line of troops.

So that same day, Gallieni wrote Joffre a letter, laying out his—and the government's—fears about Verdun and adjacent areas:

Some differing sources have come to us giving accounts of the organization of the front and signaling some points of faultiness in the system of defense. In particular and notably in the regions of the Meurthe, Toul, and Verdun, the network of trenches is not completed as it is in the major parts of the front. This situation, if true, risks posing the most severe inconveniences.[45]

Translating from the habitually understated and generic language of the military bureaucracy: *We hear there aren't any defenses in this area and that's a big problem, because we're talking about a big piece of our front line, everything from Verdun down to Toul.*

Now, Joffre could easily brush off the potshots taken at him by members of the chamber who just happened to be officers and so were immune to military discipline. They didn't understand these matters, had no grasp of military theory or of modern warfare. But whatever he thought about Gallieni, he was minister of war. So, within 24 hours, Joffre promptly answered him.

I can give the government assurance that, across the entire front, there are at least two main defensive lines, furnished with the necessary passive obstacles required to assure all the required resistance. In this region there exist three or four successive defensive positions, finished or on the road to completion. The organization is, on the whole, much better and more complete than that of our adversaries. . . . I consider that nothing justifies the fears you have expressed in the name of the government in your dispatch of 16 December.[46]

Joffre could hardly have been clearer. *These people don't know what they're talking about. Everything is in order. Shut up and let me win the war.*

Of course, the difficulty here is that after four months of pounding away on the right bank, it was hard to see just what the French defensive positions actually had been, but the consensus among the men who were there is that Driant was largely right: that Joffre's claim was largely and fatally untrue.

Now comes the puzzle. To give Joffre credit, he did actually visit the front on occasion, when he could fit it into his schedule of eating and napping, and during 1915, he inspected Verdun almost every month. That raises an interesting and unanswerable question. He went there, he presumably looked around. He surely must have noticed that the defensive positions in no way corresponded to the letter.

What's curious is that, as we all know, bureaucrats usually give themselves escape clauses when their pronouncements are parsed carefully. But there is none here. Joffre could not have been more emphatic.

Of course, France's military ruler had always been prone to making sweeping declarations. In January 1915, he had told President Poincaré that "in six months, the Germans would no longer be in France," that he would be in hot pursuit of them.[47] But his wildly optimistic views were to a considerable extent shared by the civilians, who believed—as did Joffre—that Italy's entrance into the war (in May 1915) would have a great effect on its outcome.

Colonel Herbillon, whose diary is a fascinating record of these blissful moments, was less sure. In July 1915, as everyone was still rhapsodizing about the impact of Italy and the prospects of a great breakthrough in Champagne-Artois, he said frankly to the prime minister and the president, "I do not believe that the war will be over by this winter [1915–1916] and that by that point we will have run the enemy off our territory" (*Souvenirs*, 1:162).

There followed a spirited exchange, in which Poincaré observed that he hoped Herbillon was a bad prophet, because if the army didn't at the very least win some sort of tactical victory [in Champagne in September], "I can't answer for the Chamber, or for the country," and the president went on to characterize Joffre and his "entourage" as being out of touch with the mood of the government.

Joffre was not in the least bit abashed by the failure of his January prediction. On 18 July 1915, he told Herbillon how pleased he was with the results of a meeting with Prime Minister René Viviani, Millerand (minister of war), and Alexandre Ribot, the minister of finance. "He had declared that, in three months, there would be no Germans in France. I hoped so, but I regretted his words," Herbillon confided to his diary, drawing the obvious conclusion that if his confident forecast proved false, everyone would turn against him (*Souvenirs*, 1:169).

But although Herbillon was generally very restrained and cautious in his assertions to the president and the prime minister, he too was dependent on the information the staff was giving him, and he naturally assumed they were telling him the truth. Conscientiously, he queried General de Castelnau about what he had seen when he visited Verdun in January, and the general assured him that the defenses were well along and in good order.

By now—early February—everyone assumed that there would most likely be a German offensive at Verdun, to the extent that on 15 February, both Poincaré and Viviani revealed their unease about the situation. Their concern was not about whether there would be an attack or not; it was much more pessimistic: If there was an attack, would it be successful?

Back in September 1914, as Poincaré was hearing about the Bavarian offensive at Saint-Mihiel, he had instantly jumped on the notion that the Germans aimed to take Verdun by force, and had told Herbillon what a disaster that would be, owing to its effect on the morale of the country. So now he was naturally even more concerned.

But Herbillon, having talked to de Castelnau, could only say what he had in turn been told, and that assumption—that he had been told the truth—led the good colonel to climb out on a fatal limb.

Yes, Herbillon agreed, "the attack is certain." He went on to explain that they had information from deserters about a great offensive, intelligence from a spy, accounts from workers, all this just recently received, all pointing to a great offensive, and Herbillon was doubtless being quite truthful when he said that the French would be in for "a rude shock."[48]

The interchange between the colonel and the prime minister is interesting, as it suggests just how unreal the atmosphere at the GQG really was. Herbillon admitted that the French would be in for a "shock," and that he didn't doubt that the Germans would get into the first line of trenches, "like we did in Champagne." But there's no need to panic when that happens. "General Joffre has been preparing for this for a long time. He has brought in more troops, increased the heavy artillery, although there's no doubt it will be difficult."

Briand had only one question: would Verdun hold? Because if it didn't, "that would be a disaster" (*Souvenirs*, 1:243).

So the French waited, Joffre with his usual sangfroid, the civilians nervous, and Gallieni simply biding his time.

7

The German Gamble

A bold stroke of this nature depends absolutely for success on a dog or a goose.

—Napoleon[1]

Judging from the book he wrote about his tour of the front in 1916, H. G. Wells was a terrible observer with a very poor understanding of the war. But he was not a bad judge of human beings, and one of his more intriguing remarks about the war was this:

> One of the larger singularities of the great war is its failure to produce great and imposing personalities, mighty leaders, Napoleons, Caesars. I would indeed make that the essential thing in my reckoning of the war. It is a drama without a hero; without countless incidental heroes no doubt, but no star part.[2]

One supposes that when he wrote those lines he was thinking both of Joffre and his own Sir Douglas Haig, commander of the expeditionary force in France. The historian Phillip Guedalla put it much better when he wrote that "the combination of high office with incapacity is peculiar to these islands. It is only foreigners, decadent Latins or unwieldy Teutons, who seek out able men to be their governors."[3]

Certainly by comparison with Haig, Joffre was a mental giant, albeit a slothful one. The point being that as they were not able to say much that was flattering about their own supreme commanders, the Allies took refuge in a time-honored political expedient of heaping abuse on the leaders of their enemies.

The characterizations of the German commanders are both extreme and extremely foolish. They call to mind nothing so much as Somerset Maugham's remark about the biographer of his fictional modernist painter: "You may be sure that if Charles Strickland left a laundry bill unpaid it will be given you *in extenso*, and if he forebore to return a borrowed half-crown no detail of the transaction will be omitted."[4]

A particular virulence is reserved for Erich von Falkenhayn, the German chief of staff from September 1914 to August 1916, probably because he was clearly the most successful and by far the most intelligent of the three commanding generals. That may sound like faint praise, given Haig and Joffre, but von Falkenhayn's record is formidable: the successful attack on Saint-Mihiel, the seizure of Antwerp and the channel ports, the breakthrough offensive of May 1915 against the Russians, the near absolute destruction of the Serbian army that same year, the steady progress in the Argonne that so disturbed President Poincaré.

Then there was the creation of the virtually impregnable positions in the west, with the resultant serial suicides of the Allied attacks, from the First Battle of the Somme, to the failed offensives we have already seen (the Vauquois, Les Éparges, the Woëvre). And this list is seriously incomplete, as it does not include the failed offensives in Champagne and Artois, the slaughters of the Hartmannswillerkopf and the Lingekopf in the Vosges. That the GQG and its English counterpart hid the bad news, wildly inflated the German losses, and managed to spin the result of every engagement does not alter the basic fact that London and Paris both perceived there was a bloody stalemate on the Western Front.

Smearing your opponent as a substitute for admitting his success and your weakness is a standard ploy in politics. Since all the leaders involved, whether they were in uniform or not, were basically politicians, the idea was reflexive, went hand in hand with the hate. The venom distracted them from studying their opponent, understanding his weaknesses. It was, at bottom, the distorting lens of a nationalism that became racism—the same myopia that led to a dismissal of the Japanese military before Pearl Harbor and Singapore.

None of which should be taken to imply that the Germans did not have their own problems. By the autumn of 1915, their commander in chief was a man sorely beset.

VON FALKENHAYN'S DIFFICULTIES

Despite this string of actually rather impressive successes, the German chief of staff found himself in an extremely precarious situation. Paradoxically, the more successful his armies were, the more precarious his situation became. In that sense the German commander was the antitype of Joffre. The reasons are not difficult to comprehend.

As we have seen, there were two reasons why Joffre, despite the growing antipathy of the government, remained firmly in control as a sort of half dictator. On the one hand, there was no one around to replace him, and on the other, the instability of the governments of the Third Republic, with its revolving-door ministries, allowed him the luxury of cultivating his image undisturbed. This was true even as the animosity of the cabinet grew during the summer of 1915, since by October they had all been replaced. Ironically, as their hostilities increased, so did their general unpopularity with the voters, while Joffre became steadily more popular.

He and his staff also took care to make sure that there were no possible successors on the horizon. After the wholesale purges of fall 1914, there were really only two senior generals remaining in the army who could be seen in that light. Auguste Dubail and Maurice Sarrail just happened to be the two generals responsible for French forces on the flanks of Verdun, and both came to grief as their offensives there foundered. Dubail had been formally tagged as Joffre's eventual successor, but he was made a scapegoat for the fiasco of the Woëvre offensive in spring 1915, just as Sarrail was for the failures in the Argonne that summer.

Whether or not either general was more than minimally competent, given the absolute lack of heavy guns and even sufficient stocks of the shells for the few guns their soldiers possessed, it is hard to imagine how anyone could have done much better. But in the unreal world of Chantilly, a world in which offensives were planned as though the Germans had no artillery at all, hurling masses of infantry into battle on their own was a perfectly sensible tactic, and the general whose troops failed to prevail was clearly incapable.[5]

Sarrail was even more of a radical than his old patron, Louis André, the minister of war who had instituted the political inquisition that had essentially wrecked the officer corps, so he was, as one of Joffre's biographers sarcastically remarks, the "darling of the left."[6] Given the paranoia of the government about Joffre's control of the war, he was the ideal replacement, at least as far as politics went. So Joffre, rather smoothly, managed to have him shunted off to the black hole of the Balkans. He figured, astutely enough, that this assignment would put an end to any thought of Sarrail replacing him. He was right: out of sight, out of mind, apparently. If Joffre had been as good at fighting the Germans as he was at dispatching potential rivals and successors, the war would have been over in six weeks.

This brief appreciation of his opposite number allows for a better understanding of the German chief of staff's basic problems.

By contrast with republican France, the constitutional monarchy that was Germany exuded stability. Wilhelm II was a popular monarch with his people, and although his powers were extremely limited he had a significant role to play in the government. This role was complex and is even today poorly understood. The complexity and reality of it is explained below, but for the moment, it is only important to understand that he liked von Falkenhayn, despised Ludendorff, and was intimidated by von Hindenburg and von Mackensen—along with the other senior generals who had served under his grandfather and von Moltke the Elder.

That was important, because the easterners were champing at the bit to get rid of von Falkenhayn, were doing everything they could to trip him up. Part of that was professional jealousy of the usual sort, but at bottom it also reflected a genuine difference of opinion on how to win the war, a split in the officer corps that had been simmering for decades. When von Moltke the Younger failed to secure a quick victory in the west in August 1914, and when von Falkenhayn, who replaced him, opted for a more defensively oriented strategy there, the conflict came out into the open.

The debate was a reasonable one, but so long as his chief of staff could offer up reasonable prospects of success in this ghastly war, Wilhelm would stand by him. But as opposed to that, there was the matter of the stalemate in the west, particularly when offset by what the easterners were claiming was an unbroken string of triumphs against the Russians. Their position was simple: "Look what we can do, even when stuck with the hapless Austrians as allies, and then imagine what we could accomplish if we were running the war."

Von Hindenburg, the nominal commander of the German forces in the east, was as astute as Joffre in self-promotion, the proof being that he ran for president in the new German republic, was elected, and remained in office the rest of his life. And, unlike Joffre, he actually had a string of military successes under his belt. So his position was secure to the point of invulnerability.

In effect, the easterners had von Falkenhayn in a double bind. They excused any shortcomings by claiming they weren't getting what they needed, and blamed the Austrians, this last always being a successful ploy in Berlin.

Whatever his feelings for the easterners were, von Falkenhayn actually was obsessed with winning the war, and what his command decisions mostly reveal is a man trying to balance the two factions. He was also, sensibly enough, concerned about the situation of Germany's chief ally, Austria-Hungary.

Its early disasters had mostly been a function of the extremely small size of its armed forces: the army had fewer men in the field in 1914 against the Russians than they had deployed in 1866 against the Prussians. But the empire had a population of 50 million, so it was not as though they were running out of men; it simply took time to draft and train them. But their early losses had been heavy, and by April 1915, with Italy about to enter the war, with the Russians making headway in Galicia and the Bukovina, with the Serbians still in the field, there was a certain amount of panic in both Berlin and Vienna.

So in spring 1915, von Falkenhayn turned his attention to the east, worked with his opposite number in Vienna, Conrad von Hötzendorf, to come up with a grand offensive operation against the Russian forces in Galicia. That offensive began on 2 May, with a bombardment the like of which the Austrians had never seen before, one that simply pulverized the Russian lines.[7]

The key German general in this operation was August von Mackensen, a spry and energetic veteran of 1870 who was in command of the Eleventh Army, a force of eight German and four Habsburg divisions. This attack was very much a joint affair, as von Mackensen was flanked on each side by an Austro-Hungarian army, but, like von Hindenburg, the Eleventh Army's commander wasn't at all shy about taking credit for the resulting success.

The May offensive was certainly successful enough. The dazed Russians immediately began to retreat, and when the offensive finally wound down in July, not only had the Russians been run out of Galicia, but the new front stretched from just outside of Riga in the north, all way past Pinsk and Tarnopol, and on to Czernowitz in the Bukovina.

So von Falkenhayn's (or Conrad von Hötzendorf's) plan resulted in a major victory, far greater than anything achieved thus far by von Hindenburg and Ludendorff in the north. This victory was why, when Driant wrote his letter to Paul Deschanel, he began by observing that the Russians were out of action for six months. In fact, Driant's time frame was eerily prescient. If anything, it was understated. After the collapse of May 1915, the Russians had only enough left for two more offensives, one in February 1916 and the other in June.

So Austria-Hungary was now off the hook, and in fact, the army of Franz Josef, despite the universal contempt in which it was held by friend and foe alike, proved remarkably resilient. Although von Falkenhayn had been nearly as distressed as Paris was enthusiastic about Italy's entrance into the war in May 1915, as the summer wore on events turned out somewhat differently both from his fears and from Allied hopes.

The Italian ambassador to Paris had proclaimed enthusiastically to the French cabinet that his country had the "formula for a rupture," which they hopefully took as meaning that the Italians would smash through the Austro-Hungarian positions almost immediately.[8] But Tomaso Tittoni was as ludicrously out of touch as Joffre. Within twelve months the Allied government was dispatching friendly witnesses like Wells and Conan Doyle to the Italian front to help them justify what any objective observer could see was simply another stalemate, the only accomplishment of which was the slaughter of the hapless Italian infantry. Far from collapsing the Habsburg empire, what the subjects of Franz Josef perceived as Italy's stab in the back was repaid with interest—even by the allegedly unreliable Slavs.

But triumph in the east, and the failure of Allied hopes on the Italian front, hardly solved von Falkenhayn's problems. In fact, it only made them worse. His successful actions in the east—actions for which von Mackensen, von Hindenburg, and the Austrians all promptly claimed the credit—only made the stalemate in the west all the more discouraging, and thus made his position all the more precarious.

Marshal von Haesler, the octogenarian former commander of von Mudra's Sixteenth Army Corps—who was still on hand in the Argonne to make sure this brash young sexagenarian was up to the mark—expressed the view perfectly when he exploded about the whole idea of trench warfare. It was a disaster that destroyed the army's chances for victory: "And it should never have come to this, if we had not been led with such deplorable incompetence."[9]

But this was unfair. As the war had worn on, von Falkenhayn was beginning to grasp something that the vast majority of the generals, regardless of their nationality, failed to grasp: The armies of this war, backed by the great industries of the combatants, were simply too large for the traditional idea of warfare to work. Joffre claimed that the Marne was a great French victory, just as von Hindenburg did the same for Tannenberg. But both battles were fought in September 1914, and here it was, going on a year of warfare, and the Germans were still in France and the Russians were still in the fight.

Driant's estimate really hit the nail on the head. Despite their defeat, despite being on course to lose the incredible figure of a million men taken prisoner, and with equally staggering casualties, the Russians were not disposed to quit the war.

For that matter, the same could be said of the Austrians. Annihilation worked reasonably well if your opponent was Serbia or Belgium. Those countries were not very large in terms of population or area. Their small size meant that they could be physically occupied, and both had small armies. Serbia's was larger and more experienced, but in the context of this war it was possible to overwhelm a few hundred thousand men.

As we noted earlier, by October 1915, that was basically what had happened in the Balkans. The Serbian army had largely been destroyed, the country overrun. But when a country had a population of 30, 50, 60, 100 million—and the industry to match it—the thing was either impossible, or not achievable in any reasonable amount of time.

The easterners, in other words, were pursuing a chimera: the idea that one more great victory would force the Russians to quit the war. In that sense, the only difference between von Mackensen and von Hindenburg on the one side, and Joffre and Haig on the other, was competence. Fundamentally, they all believed in the same thing: the great battle of annihilation that, with its consequent massive breakthrough, would bring a speedy end to the war and the defeat of their opponents.

But as the months went by, von Falkenhayn decided that was not going to work.[10] The only way to win was to destroy your opponent's will to fight, what the French called his *moral*, a word that means something slightly different from its English equivalent, morale, as it implies a sort of backbone as well as a state of mind.

Possibly, von Falkenhayn had gotten this from pondering the American Civil War, as, like all professional German officers, he had studied that conflict. Or it may have been the result of his experiences in China, or his knowledge of how the British, despite their bumbling, had finally beaten the Boers. The common thread was that in each case, your opponent simply decided to quit, came to the realization that nothing was worth the continued sacrifice.

The generals on both sides were mesmerized by Waterloo, forgot all that had happened in the previous decade: that despite all his great victories over them, Napoleon's adversaries had never really quit, had simply regrouped and then come back to rejoin the battle, until finally, at the end of one fine June day, the Corsican had simply given up.

Increasingly, technology had transformed the battlefield. Everyone paid lip service to that fact, although when the war started the Germans were the only ones who had actually embraced it wholeheartedly. But no one had grasped that there was also a conceptual shift required. The route to success was not to bash your enemy in some great battle; it was to make him realize he couldn't win, that the cost was too high.

Of course, the difficulty was in hitting on the means to accomplish that. As with all theories, the difficulty lay in the practical application. The failures of 1914 were proof of that. Von Moltke's ambitious scheme of a complex double envelopment of the French armies, his own more modest plan of doing the same thing at Verdun, so those grandiose and complex schemes, Conrad von Hötzendorf's equally grandiose plans, all had been frustrated because of their very complexity.

By contrast, the old-fashioned and rather primitive ideas of the easterners had been surprisingly successful. The plan for the May offensive had hardly been sophisticated. In that sense Joffre had the right idea; his difficulty was he lacked the means to carry it out. He had the men but not the firepower.

Moreover, the French weren't like the Russians, willing to take astronomical losses to no avail. At some point the army was going to crack, reach a tipping point as they threw themselves against the defensive positions without ever actually conquering them, their only achievement horrific losses.

The trick was to find that point.

Now, as he pondered the Western Front and how best to win the war, at some point it occurred to von Falkenhayn that there was a way to effect a solution. He was struck by a curiously destructive pattern of French behavior. In September 1914, local commanders on both sides of Verdun had simply vacated important bits of territory, the Vauquois and Les Éparges being the most significant. Nor did the GQG seem to grasp what was happening on both banks of the Meuse until it was far too late. The front to the northeast of Saint-Mihiel had been held by elements of a few reserve divisions, so his plan for the envelopment had been a victory achieved on the cheap.

But after the fact, the French high command, having grasped the importance of what they had lost—and in some cases simply thrown away—became obsessed with recapturing the territory. The crown prince, nominal commander of the German Fifth Army, had been appalled by the extent of French losses in the repeated assaults. And that was for obscure pieces of real estate the possession of which was only of theoretical importance, if that. Yes, the Vauquois was a key position, but Les Éparges? Yet the French had lost what, the equivalent of two or three divisions of good infantry in suicidal attempts to wrest it from some aging reservists?

That was definitely food for thought.

What would they risk to recapture something of real importance, something whose significance even the dimmest *poilu* or politician could grasp?

His troops had Verdun in a stranglehold still. The French had been totally unable to relieve the grip, had shifted their attentions to another section of the front. Why not clinch the deal?

How would the French react if his troops were to seize a big piece, engineer another Saint-Mihiel? Based on their behavior in the past, they'd throw every last man into an effort to retake the lost ground. And since he had both sides of Verdun in his grasp, the result would be another slaughter, Les Éparges on a grand scale.

It would be like waving a red flag at a bull. The French had spent decades building up the position, making it the center point of their defenses. Nobody in Paris had ever heard of those two buttes out in the wilds of Lorraine, but Verdun was a different matter entirely. Losing it would have an incalculable effect on their morale; it would be like the collapse of the Liège forts and Antwerp for the Belgians.

That was the point: to destroy morale, make the French realize there was no way they could win. They couldn't retake the Vauquois. They couldn't retake Les Éparges. They couldn't get back Saint-Mihiel. They couldn't wrest the two key German positions in the Vosges away from the Germans. Their offensives in Artois and Champagne had been costly failures. They couldn't keep von Mudra from chewing his way steadily through the Argonne.

At some point, the French would realize there was no way they could win, that all they could accomplish was killing off their infantry. That was the tipping point: the realization that a blank wall was staring them in the face.

Of course, it was possible that there was a learning curve, that having taken the losses they had been taking these past months, someone in the government would come to his senses and simply walk away. That was the rational decision, and it might happen.

But if they did, that would come to the same end: the realization that there was no way France could win this war. Besides, if they walked away from Verdun, refused the bait, he doubted the country would stand for it. The government would fall—once again—and finally, eventually, a new government would become sensible, agree to a peace. But then again, if they tried their best, there was no way they could win, and the loss would be an even greater catastrophe. They'd realize the only way out was to quit the war. 1915 wasn't like 1870; they could come to reasonable terms.

But time was of the essence. As the French campaigns unfolded elsewhere, it was easy to see Joffre's idea. Assemble a gigantic army and try to break through the German line. And at some point in 1916 he'd have enough British troops to manage it, probably by early summer. The disaster of the spring offensive in the Woëvre had probably made him realize that early spring was not good, and the GQG had squandered its best shot during the summer, when von Mudra had beaten Sarrail to the punch in the Argonne.

No, the thing was clear enough. Joffre would lick his wounds and wait until he had enough British troops to mount a huge offensive of the same sort that he'd been trying steadily since December 1914. It was predictable, unimaginative, a useless wastage of valuable infantry.

So there was a window of opportunity. Wait until the ground was good and hard; then just move in for the key forts of the right bank, attack them directly. Winter was good, because it would make it next to impossible for the French to dig in. Not that they'd try. They'd panic, abandon half their positions, and then mount a desperate attempt to get them back. That was the pattern that had been established.

The best-case scenario: a whole section of the front would simply cave in, and the Germans would split the French armies in two, and drive deep into the heart of France. The worst case: Joffre's troops would simply move their defensive line forward, sit there and let the French destroy themselves. Either way, at some point they'd come to their senses and realize they couldn't win.

THE SECRET

Now, to the outsider—to someone in London or Paris—there was an obvious flaw in von Falkenhayn's notion. It was like the mice talking about belling the cat.

Verdun was the largest and most powerful assemblage of fortifications in the world. The reinforced concrete carapaces of its key forts were proof against the heaviest German shells. In front of the outer ring was a dense network of lesser defensive positions: three lines of trenches, anchored by concrete blockhouses. In fact, Verdun was the only part of the French side of the Western Front where the defensive network was comparable to the German one. It was anchored by Douaumont, the largest concrete structure in the world, a position that was the textbook definition of *impregnable*.

So how on earth did von Falkenhayn think his plan would succeed?

The answer is as simple as it is incredible. Gabriel Bichet sums the matter up succinctly and bitterly.

Douaumont illustrates in effect the errors of the French high command in the matter of fortifications. Not only were the forts not activated during the mobilization in 1914, but a year later, 5 August 1915, a decree practically prescribed their dismantling. In virtue of that decree, the independent fortified complexes were suppressed, integrated into the general disposition of the armies. As a consequence, their armaments, their provisions, were withdrawn. Theoretically, this was done chiefly to furnish the field armies with their artillery—one uses the word as an alibi—because that was lacking. Practically, that recovery only produced a number of guns very insufficient to meet the needs, difficult to adapt to service in the field. But as opposed to that, the fortifications lost the totality of their efficacy.

In the forts, no more garrisons: the only thing left in place were the guns in the turrets, weapons with a short range, not usable elsewhere. Finally, orders were given to prepare mines in all the forts, so they could be destroyed in the case of an enemy advance.[11]

So von Falkenhayn knew beforehand that his troops could simply walk in and take the forts—provided they could break through the French defenses in front of them.

Based on the French experiences, that was still a tall order. The first line of trenches was nearly ten kilometers north of Douaumont, and that was only the first line. Getting past all three, and then penetrating the ring of the outer forts, would be a success all on its own, and the GQG reckoned it was impossible.

But there again, von Falkenhayn had reason to be confident. Over on the left bank, in the Argonne, von Mudra's reliance on massive firepower had been steadily forcing the French back, as their divisional commanders admitted. But thus far, von Mudra's high-explosive offensives had been choked off, owing to the needs of the gunners in other parts of the front.

But there was nothing wrong with the concept: Simply scale it up, use even more heavy guns, and the infantry would be able to work its way through the devastation before the French could rush in reinforcements. Uniquely on the Western Front, the German lines were closer to the outer ring of forts than those forts were to where the bulk of the French troops were.

And von Falkenhayn's staff, working with Fifth Army, was proposing an artillery barrage in depth. The massive arsenal of heavy guns the plan called for required prepared sites, ammunition bunkers, tethering points for the observation balloons, quarters for the gun crews. And a great deal of concrete.

In the late summer, Captain Hans Marguerre, an engineering officer, began laying out an enormous development deep in the forest to the northeast of Verdun. Ultimately Camp Marguerre would cover some 50,000 square meters, a sprawling complex of concrete buildings: living quarters, ammunition bunkers, repair facilities.

Marguerre started, sensibly enough, with a concrete plant, so the building materials could be fabricated on-site. Although rarely if ever mentioned by historians, the remains of Camp Marguerre still exist, and we know from contemporary photographs that buildings were going up by August of 1915.[12]

By September, the Germans had set up a 38-centimeter gun in the Bois de Warphemont. Guns of this size were hardly mobile. The site was approximately 25 kilometers to the northeast of Verdun, slightly to the south of the village of Mangiennes, a few kilometers outside of the tiny hamlet of Duzy.[13]

"Big Max," as it was known, fired a 750-kilogram shell containing 183 kilograms of explosive over a range of 35 kilometers, so it could easily range over the entire right bank. The dense forest shielded the construction from aerial surveillance, and indeed it remained unscathed throughout the war, and was finally abandoned in October 1918.

Now, this installation was a serious affair. The gun itself was mounted on a circular concrete platform about 20 meters in diameter and five meters deep, enabling it to have a wide angle of fire horizontally. The cavity is now partly filled with water, so it is difficult to give its exact dimensions, but the installation is impressive. In addition to the enormous concrete base and pit for the gun, there are three separate bunkers to store the ammunition, and a narrow-gauge trolley line to convey the assembled shells to the gun.

Once the installation was complete, in October, the gun began firing shells. As was often the case when it came to heavy artillery, although the French observers realized what was being lobbed at them, they apparently didn't understand the procedure, chalked up the shelling as yet another instance of German barbarism, since many of the shells landed in the town itself.

Unfortunately, no one bothered to keep a chart of the hits, so the information is scanty. But we do know that one of them hit Fort Vaux, knocking a good-size chunk out of it—and confirming what the engineers already knew: that even the heaviest artillery was not going to make much of a dent on the newer forts.

The others hit in areas likely to be used by troops moving up into the heights of the right bank. This detail is usually overlooked. But troops coming up from either the south or the west, headed for the heights on the right bank, would have to go directly through the town itself. The relatively steep slopes of the heights looking down on the city meant that shells fired from any reasonable distance would pass harmlessly over troops as they ascended the heights. This natural feature of the terrain, which gunners referred to as a dead angle, meant that the only effective way to interdict reinforcements moving up to the defensive positions on the heights was to shell the city streets. That accounts for where the 38-centimeter shells landed: the gunners were checking the range. After firing 16 rounds, the shelling stopped—until 21 February 1916, when the gun began firing again.

A brief consideration of the distances explains the reason why the gunners were so interested in the environs of the town. The French decree of 5 August meant that the forts were not only stripped of their artillery, but were abandoned. It was a good ten kilometers as a crow flies from Douaumont to the northernmost command post of the infantry in the forward positions. So the infantry holding the trenches in front of the forts would be left up in the air, deprived of any artillery support, since the forward trenches would be out of range of French guns. Nor would there be any counter battery fire from the French side: minus the observers in the fort and the heavy guns behind them, the distances were simply too great.

The abandonment of the forts meant that instead of sheltering infantry in reserve behind the initial position, reinforcements would be located another ten or more kilometers behind the outer forts. The infantry would have to make its way up into the heights either from the town or from positions along the river to the north of it—two equally unpleasant prospects, if there was an in-depth artillery barrage.

And the Germans were definitely planning for such an event. In addition to two more 38-centimeter weapons, whose positioning required the longest lead time, they assembled 11 of the Austrian 305-centimeter weapons, and 13 of the big 42-centimeter German ones.[14] Nor was that all. In addition, Fifth Army deployed 400 howitzers of 15 and 21 centimeters, and another 100 howitzers in smaller sizes, together with about 100 guns of 10, 12, and 13 centimeters. It was a vast arsenal, but the plan was to saturate the entire area in depth, simply annihilate the defenders in one massive blow, and make sure that the attacking infantry could get through the defensive positions well before a counterattack could develop.

The entrance to Fort du Camp des Romains, buried in the woods south of Saint Mihiel. The capture of this fort, taken by direct assault on 25 September 1914, cut off one of the two rail links into Verdun.

The ruins of Fort de Troyon, north of Saint Mihiel. The energetic defense of an obscure French captain named Heym thwarted the initial German plan to surround Verdun.

Fort Vaux, still mostly intact. Damage is impressive but superficial. The garrison surrendered because through negligence they ran out of water.

In this view of the top of Fort Douaumont, the observer's cupola (*foreground*) and the retractable gun turret can be clearly seen, unscathed by all the shelling, and proof that properly designed fortifications were basically invulnerable. Douaumont fell because it had been abandoned.

The French 155-millimeter gun was the heaviest weapon the army had in quantity. A state-of-the-art weapon of 1878, but by 1914 it was sadly obsolete. Note the absence of any recoil mechanism.

The German 21-centimeter howitzer was the most potent artillery piece on the battlefield. Unlike its Allied counterparts, it could be towed, and its hydraulic recoil mechanism allowed for extreme accuracy.

The war had been raging for years before the French infantry received modern mortars. This 51-millimeter example typifies the problem: too little and too late.

A French 240-millimeter howitzer. Like the 155-millimeter gun, these weapons dated from the late 1870s. The absence of a recoil mechanism made them essentially worthless on the battlefield, but the war was nearly over before the gunners had a modern version in any quantity.

The 10.5-centimeter howitzer gave German gunners a modern weapon whose high angle of fire made it perfect for the terrain, at a time when their opponents relied exclusively on smaller weapons incapable of such fire.

The Allies had nothing comparable to the German 15-centimeter howitzer in terms of transportability and range. These weapons, available to German gunners in large numbers, were the forerunners of the standard weapons used today.

The French 75-millimeter gun was the first modern field gun. Its recoil mechanism gave it accuracy and a high rate of fire. But it was incapable of firing its shells at the steep angles required in modern warfare. Incredibly, the army blocked the development of the modern heavy weapons their soldiers desperately needed.

The German 17-centimeter mortar. Fitted with wheels, it could be pulled into position or even manhandled. The war was nearly over before French soldiers had anything remotely comparable.

All that remains of the village of the Vauquois. Artillery fire directed by German observers atop the butte severed the main rail line into Verdun. For reasons still not clear, the tracks were never relaid out of range. Instead, there were futile attempts to seize the position, at first by assault, and then by mines. These craters are the result.

The intact remains of this German trench make clear why French assaults always failed. Only direct hits from heavy guns could damage the position, and the French lacked that capability. When the barrage ceased, the infantry crawled out of their shelters and massacred the attackers.

Part of a veritable city of German bunkers in the Argonne forest, outside Varennes. Elaborate constructions like these astounded French soldiers, who generically referred to them as the "shelters of the Crown Prince."

The American monument on the butte of Montfaucon, rising out the ruins of the village. Together with a similar memorial on the butte of Montsec in the Woëvre and numerous obelisks, it celebrates the liberation of Verdun by the American army in 1918.

THE PLAN BEGINS TO EMERGE

The staff of the Fifth Army had been agitating for another attack since the success of the Saint-Mihiel offensive in September 1914. They kept pointing to the way von Mudra was steadily chewing his way through the Argonne. By late August, he had basically forced the French out of the forest proper. They were hanging on to positions on the southern edge, and instead of reinforcing the troops there, Joffre had shifted his attentions up to the northwest, and was obviously planning another senseless attack in Champagne and Artois.

That attack was duly made in September, with pretty much the same lack of results as all the others. Strategically, the offensive was senseless. There was no important objective behind that section of the front. All the Allies could accomplish was to run up the body count the same way they had been managing it so far. The point, insofar as there was one, was the Allied delusion that they were killing lots of Germans, when in reality it was the other way around.

But the lack of any meaningful objective meant that when the attacks failed, they could quit, claiming they had done something important. And in that sense, time was on their side. The French and the British, with their vast colonial possessions, had unlimited manpower, and thus far it appeared that they were nearly as callous as the Russians about squandering it.

But these bloody French efforts on the flanks of Verdun were instructive. At some point—after they had carelessly thrown them away—the French high command realized they were important, mounted attack after attack in a desperate and determined effort to recapture them.

And now, in August, the Germans were seeing a repetition of that on a grand scale, with the virtual abandonment of the Verdun forts. This was the war for the buttes on a grand scale indeed. There was no way the French could bear the loss of Verdun. The army might be willing to write it off, but the population at large, the government, wouldn't stand for it, just as Poincaré had told Colonel Herbillon in July 1915.

So the opportunity was too good to pass up, and the staff of the Fifth Army was convinced that they had the formula for success, and would simply repeat what von Mudra had been doing in the Argonne—what to a lesser degree von Mackensen's Ninth Army had done in Galicia in May: a stupefying artillery attack that would completely erase the enemy's positions, so that the infantry would simply be moving through the ruins of the enemy positions.

The heights of the Meuse above the city would be the basis for a formidable defensive position, so when the French responded by trying to retake their lost territory, they'd be slaughtered. Given the interdicted rail lines, and the denuding of the forts, the French would hardly be able to succeed, as their situation would be considerably worse than it had been when they tried to retake the buttes.

The loss of Verdun would strike deep into the heart of France, and when they realized they couldn't get it back, that their sacrifices were futile, they'd come to their senses, agree to a reasonable peace.

Unlike the earlier operations, which all involved flank attacks, this one would be a direct frontal assault on the forts of the right bank. But the main weight of the attack would consist not of soldiers, but of high explosives, just as had been the case in the Argonne. The staff planned for a massive artillery barrage that would simply erase the French positions. At the same time, the artillery assault would not simply be aimed at the initial lines, at the forts and the entrenchments in front of them, but would have great depth, so that the defenders would be unable to counterattack.

The 38-centimeter gun was only the first of a whole phalanx of heavy weapons. Two more of the 38-centimeter guns were installed, along with 13 of the 42-centimeter guns and 11 of the Austrian 30.5-centimeter weapons, and 210 smaller guns.[15] That was in addition to the 140 21-centimeter howitzers and the usual complement of divisional howitzers in 10.5 and 15 centimeters (354 of them).

As the munitions were being shipped in and the gun emplacements prepared, the troop movements began as well. General Buat's scrupulous recording of the movements of German divisions in and out of the fronts shows a pattern nicely synchronized with the emplacement and firing of the 38-centimeter gun.

In September 1915, four divisions were shifted from Germany to the Western Front, probably in response to the Anglo-French offensive in Artois and Champagne, or at least that was General Buat's inference.[16]

But then, in October, no less than 11 divisions were moved into line, and on 3 November more were added, raising the number of divisions on the Western Front from 107 (in September) to 117. The numbers don't add up because there were also divisions being transferred from the Western Front, as the German high command kept shifting its resources back and forth, as well as in and out of the line.

However, the most revealing point here is that the bulk of the troop movements to the west came in October 1915. For the previous year—that is, from September 1914 to September 1915—the average number of German divisions in the west had fluctuated between 99 and 107. Most months it had been 104.

But now, suddenly, in October it shot up to the highest it had been, and in November it climbed another notch. By contrast, in December and January only one division was added, and three more were added in February.

The pattern makes sense when we realize that General Herr, the French officer in immediate command of the troops at Verdun, believed he would be attacked on 16 January 1916, nearly five weeks before the actual attack.[17] Unusually strong winter storms interfered with the original timetable, and gave the GQG and the French local commanders at Verdun ample time to prepare.

But aside from General Herr, no one seemed particularly concerned about the notion of a German offensive. In Paris, the theaters had finally reopened, although judging from the diaries maintained by Gallieni and Abel Ferry, the best theater in town was to be found at the cabinet meetings. Out in Chantilly, Joffre professed himself quite satisfied with the state of the defenses. Even though 1915 had brought the Allies an almost completely unrelieved strain of checks and disasters, their feelings in midwinter bordered on a dangerous complacency.

THE LETTER

Now that the offensive was set, the arrangements largely complete, von Falkenhayn took the last step. He notified the emperor of the plan. Now, clearly, given all the activity to date, the decision to attack had already been made, and the preparations were complete. So the notion implicit in all accounts of this letter is highly misleading. The letter, which openly hostile writers seized on, is not a proposal; it is a piece of internal public relations. Von Falkenhayn knew the importance of keeping the emperor on his side, as his continuing in the role of chief of staff depended on Wilhelm's willpower.

He also knew his master's peculiarities, as did everyone who worked closely with the monarch, so he wrote with a specific audience in mind. That audience explains both the parts of the letter that subsequently became infamous, or anyway notorious, and it also explains the surprising omission.

However, with these reservations, the key paragraph of the letter is really quite revolutionary.

> Moreover, the lessons to be deduced from the failures of our enemy's mass attacks are decisive against any imitation of their battle methods. Attempts at a mass break-through, even with an extreme accumulation of men and material, cannot be regarded as holding out prospects of success against a well armed enemy whose morale is sound and who is not seriously inferior in numbers.[18]

This point is exactly the one that neither Joffre nor the easterners had yet grasped. Writing to a man whose knowledge of tactics and strategy was minimal, von Falkenhayn did not go into the detailed reasons why a "mass break-through" was impossible. For that we must turn to the musings of General Fayolle, who had spelled it out very precisely the previous summer.

In this war it is not sufficient to open a breach, one must open a gap of twenty kilometers or so, so that there is no response on the left or right. One must do this with an entire army, and then have another ready to pass through the breach. And that is not simple.[19]

Having now dismissed the ideas of the easterners that more vigorous action would carry their armies to a final victory in the west, von Falkenhayn now explained his idea in very simple terms.

The only way to win in the west was to make the French realize that there was no way they could ever hope to prevail, or, as von Falkenhayn put it in the letter, when "it is clear to the eyes of the French people that, militarily, they have nothing to hope for. Then will their limit be surpassed."[20]

The precise antecedent of "their" is one of the two most important parts of this often quoted document. Judging from how the reference is invariably parsed, one would conclude that historians are rather weak at grammar. But for those who are not grammatically impaired, the word clearly and unambiguously refers back not to the French army, but to the French people, and hence to France itself. Or, more precisely, the government and the people, the two entities that President Poincaré had invoked in July 1915.

By December 1915, the Germans had begun to realize that the French army was apparently willing to fight far past the point of rational calculation. France's generals had already established that, as they ordered assault after assault on German strongpoints all along the line. Given the almost total lack of modern heavy artillery, the shortage of shells, any objective observer would conclude these attacks were doomed in advance. They all failed. But in each case, the GQG insisted on more attempts, the local commanders obeyed, and the slaughter continued.

The assaults on the butte of the Vauquois that began in 1914 continued into March 1915. That set the pattern. It was continued all along the line. The attempts on the flanks of Verdun were tactically some of the most senseless and futile. Indeed, judging from the accounts of the survivors, the efforts to wrest the butte of Les Éparges resulted in some of the most horrific combats of the entire war. But the desperate and unsuccessful attempts elsewhere were more of the same.

The struggle for the two buttes was simply the beginning. In the Argonne, in the Woëvre, in the Vosges mountains, and in Champagne-Artois, the GQG launched infantry attacks in successive attempts, with only the most perfunctory artillery support at best. The losses, carefully concealed, were horrifying. The gains, tiny and insignificant at best, were carefully spun. Well might von Falkenhayn conclude that his opponents could be baited into destroying themselves.

But thus far, there was no sign that the willingness of France's soldiers to die in vain assaults was diminishing. To the contrary, as Wilhelm was reading the famous letter, the steep slope that led to the crest of the Hartmannswillerkopf, not far distant from his summer castle in the Vosges mountains, was littered with the dead of the elite French alpine troops, as they tried to seize the German position. France's best soldiers were taking losses at the rate of 50 percent of the men engaged; senior officers and generals were killed as they tried to exhort their battered men.[21]

Although the German defenders had not reached the point of their Austrian allies in the Alps, who would call out to the Italian infantry not to attack, as they would be cut down to the last man by machine-gun fire, the situations were precisely similar: just one prolonged and futile bloodbath.

But the attitude of the French nation, or, more specifically, of the rulers of that nation, was a different matter entirely. Both the country at large and its elected officials were being fed a steady diet of soothing reassurance, as epitomized by the slogan on a widely disseminated French postcard, featuring a suitably heroic-looking soldier proclaiming, "We are progressing day by day."

The rigorously suppressed casualty figures, the wildly inflated estimates of German losses, the clever way that each engagement was turned into a victory of one sort or the other, combined with the obscurity of the positions named, gave the nation an utterly false sense of optimism.

As we have seen, there were men inside the government itself who were hardly optimistic, who were beginning to see behind the comfortable facade. There was not, in fall 1915, any thought of coming to terms.

Although both then and later, it was claimed over and over again that this was because democracy had to be saved from German militarism, totalitarianism, and repression, the real reason was rather less heroic. The two governments were now so deeply immersed in their own lies that if they tried to act rationally, began to negotiate, they would be howled out of office as traitors. Colonel Repington's observation about the state of popular opinion in Great Britain is worth repeating.

> The ignorance of the people concerning the war, owing to the Censorship, is unbelievable. Lunching at the Hautboy [where] . . . the proprietor—a good-class intelligent looking man—told me that the Serbians were going to beat the Germans; that there was nothing in front of our Army in France; and that we were going to be in Constantinople in ten days' time. These are the kind of beliefs into which the country has been chloroformed by the Censorship.[22]

But what if the patient woke up, discovered that instead of removing his tonsils, the doctors had actually removed his kidney and his lung?

This was the proverbial elephant in the living room, which was such a horrifying prospect for the politicians of both countries that it didn't bear thinking about. So they didn't.

But to put matters quite simply—as, given Wilhelm, they had to be—von Falkenhayn proposed to wake them up. Verdun, he observed, was a position of such importance to France that the nation could not stand to lose it. It was, just as Pétain would later observe, the *"boulevard morale"* of the country. After half a century of fortifying it, after pouring millions of francs into it, the country simply could not stand for the loss.

Nor could that loss be concealed. Very few Parisians knew exactly where Les Éparges or the Hartmannswillerkopf was, and if their knowledge of the obscurities of their national geography was such that they did, they also knew that these places were rather insignificant.

But everyone knew where Verdun was, and most people had a pretty good idea of the area encompassed by the great arc of the forts. This was one elephant in the room that could not easily be converted into a piece of furniture and covered over with a rug.

So as a result, when von Falkenhayn observed that "the French leadership would fight to the last man to get it back," he analyzed the situation precisely, and rather astutely.[23]

But note the abstract nature of the sentence. There is nothing here about the French army; he is speaking about the leadership of the country. Rightly so: he already knew that his opposite number had already written Verdun off, had stripped it bare, and were ready to evacuate it entirely if need be.

And indeed, as we shall see—leaping ahead to those critical days of February 1916—that proved to be precisely the reaction of the French leadership. The GQG was cheerfully willing to write the whole area off, but the government realized that if they did, that would be the end of the war. The country would collapse. What was worse, their careers would be at an end.

Basically, then, given the situation after over a year of fighting, von Falkenhayn's appreciation was correct. Indeed, it was perhaps more fundamentally correct than he realized, so far as the idea of a breakthrough went. Even when the attack was tactically a success, resulting in a deep penetration into enemy territory, that success did not bring the enemy to the bargaining table. Since the Allies never had anything approaching a breakthrough on the Western Front, they naturally glossed over this rather basic point. But if one steps back, looks at all the fronts, the two patterns are quite clear.

On the one hand there were the theaters where there was a stalemate, just as Lord Hankey had perceived a year earlier: Italy, the Western Front after October 1914. On the other, on the Eastern Front, enormous territorial gains were achieved with commensurate casualties, but failed to bring the war to an end. It has always been fashionable to denigrate the armies of Russia, of Italy, and of Austria-Hungary, all three of whom suffered enormous losses during the war. But Russia did not finally quit the war either because of some great military defeat or because their enemy had conquered their country. On the contrary, the last great action of the Russian army—the offensive of June 1916—was by any standard a massive breakthrough of precisely the sort that both the Allies and the easterners in the German army assumed would end the war.

The difficulty was that it didn't, any more than the equally impressive breakthrough offensives of the Germans in France in spring 1918. So von Falkenhayn was quite correct insofar as the situation at the time, and largely correct in his judgment for the entire course of the war. The only practicable goal was to create a situation where your opponent realized the impossibility of victory, and was thus willing to quit.

Having established that it was a given that the French leadership would fight to the last man for Verdun, von Falkenhayn now made a nice rhetorical flourish. He wrote two consecutive sentences, each beginning with the same phrase, the only shift being that the second sentence uses a negative, so the result is a rhetorical expression that can be simply expressed: "if he does/if he does not."

The rhetorical device is even more important to an understanding of the plan than correctly parsing the antecedent for "their." In fact, it is the most significant part of the letter. Nor is there any particular difficulty in grasping the point. Anyone with a rudimentary grasp of rhetoric recognizes this construction. There are only two alternatives, and either one leads to the same end.

The French cannot afford to lose Verdun. If they fight for it, their losses will be so heavy that they will have to quit the war. If they do not fight for it, the effect on the country at large will be such that they will be forced to quit the war.

Military success has nothing much to do with the end result. In fact, von Falkenhayn is quite clear that it makes no difference whether or not the French would be able to hang on to Verdun or to recapture it. The consequences of losing Verdun would certainly have an enormous effect on French morale: Von Falkenhayn describes this effect as *ungeheuer*, a German word with all sorts of nasty connotations: frightful, ghastly, and horrific, as well as enormous, huge, and monstrous. Again, leaping forward to the panic in Paris in late February, it should be observed that he was quite correct.

Now comes the one phrase in the letter that several generations of Allied apologists have seized upon, have indeed made the exclusive basis for their appreciation of the plan. Out of this abstract and sophisticated piece of grand strategy, they extracted one phrase, and then used it to claim that von Falkenhayn's aim was to win the war through attrition.

Now at this point, the thoughtful reader who is familiar with the traditional interpretations of this letter will begin to see that those interpretations rest on a series of basic grammatical or rhetorical errors. There is the failure to identify the antecedent of *their*. There is the fatal conflation of the general concept of the leadership of the country, with the more specific notion of the army. Then there is the failure to grasp the rhetorical device of the key sentences.

And then the whole train of error culminates in the most critical, in which a key phrase is incorrectly translated. If the French decide to fight, regardless of the outcome, von Falkenhayn avers, the result will be heavy losses. Then comes the key phrase: in that case, then will *Frankreichs Kräfte verbluten*. This phrase is the basis for the whole notion that von Falkenhayn's aim was to win the war through attrition.

Unhappily for the contentions of several generations of historians, it may be easily dismissed. The idea of winning through attrition rests on a basic grammatical fallacy. *Frankreich* is obviously the German word for France, so it modifies the word *Kräfte*. Now this word denotes, quite simply, strength, or force, which may either be physical or spiritual/psychological. In point of fact, it is the same term that is used in physics for the English word *force*, and is the basis for a whole series of compound words that make German such a joy for foreigners, words such as motorcycle (*Kraftrad*) and motor fuel (*Kraftstoff*), for instance.

The point is that the word represents power, or strength, or force as an abstraction. To the educated person who has struggled through courses in philosophy, trying to understand Heidegger or even Kant or Hegel, that should hardly be a surprise. To put it quite simply, and in basic English: *Force* is an abstract noun, while *blood*, clearly the root of the word *verbluten*, is a concrete one.

By linking them, von Falkenhayn is either resorting to a rather obscure and incomprehensible synecdoche, or he has in mind another definition of the word. Because, although the primary definition of *verblutet* is, as the cognate of *blut/blood* suggests, bleeding or draining, only a corporeal organism can be drained of blood. So to use that meaning of the word, to couple it with *Kräfte*, is a species of false personification.

As we know, words have multiple meanings, one of the reasons dictionaries are so big, as lexicographers try to list them all. So it is here. The secondary meaning of the word is precisely correct. It means draining or hemorrhaging.

To the native English speaker, the word is certainly colorful, but German is, after all, a language where veal is called *Kalbsfleisch*, a compound that to the English speaker immediately suggests a

rather unpleasant phrase, *calf flesh*, as opposed to our rather re-
fined word *veal*. Another equally standard word, *Schweinefleisch*,
is hardly more appetizing. A restaurant in the United States that
advertised "roasted swine flesh" on its menu would probably have
potential customers in a stampede for the exit in short order. For
that matter, as anyone struggling with the intricacies of French
cuisine discovers, the French word used to describe rare beef is
likewise rather unappetizing: the primary meaning of *saignant* is
bloody, derived from the same root as the word *sanguinary*. But
that word is in little use, so the derivation does not strike the ear
quite as unpleasantly.

So the whole idea that von Falkenhayn saw Verdun as a way to
win the war by killing enormous numbers of Frenchmen rests on
one phrase in his letter, which is then rendered as a rhetorical
absurdity.

In addition, it has the inordinate difficulty of ignoring arithmetic. If that was his aim, all he really had to do was remain on the
defensive. Given French losses to date, he hardly had to go to the
trouble of staging a major offensive.

By the end of 1915, France, with a population half the size of
Germany's, but with losses two or three times higher, was already
facing the prospect of running out of men, which was the main
reason Joffre now had to wait patiently until enough British soldiers arrived to allow him to stage a major offensive—six months
into the future.

Of course, given the way the casualty figures were suppressed,
misrepresented, and then denied, it is easy to see why this conclusion is superficially appealing. If one believes the Allied fantasies
about crippling German losses, then everything becomes reversed.
The Germans become desperate, and so forth.

Now, this intrusion of logic and rhetoric into historical narrative may well make the reader nervous, even if he is willing to grant
the basic fact of the lopsided nature of the casualty exchange. So at
this point, let us shift slightly. Here is what people actually said.

Three months into the 1916 battle, von Falkenhayn's aim had already been incorporated into a neat little trope that was being disseminated all around. His aim was, quite simply, to win the war through attrition—that is, to win by killing off enemy soldiers—and this was expressed through the catchy phrase *to bleed France white*, a memorable metonymy in which the nation is turned into a person.

This idea was advanced not by historians writing long after the fact, but by propagandists busily doing their job. How do we know this?

Proof isn't hard to find. Here is the creator of Sherlock Holmes, who visited the French, British, and Italian fronts in June 1916, speaking of his visit to the French sector. Notice the date: June 1916.

> Germany set out to bleed France white. Well, she has done so. France is full of widows and orphans from end to end. Perhaps in proportion to her population she has suffered the most of all. But in carrying out her hellish mission Germany has bled herself white also.[24]

There, in four simple English sentences, is the whole Allied spin on the 1916 battle for Verdun—written while the fighting was still going on.

Now then, compare what Conan Doyle wrote in June 1916 with what the eminent historian A. J. P. Taylor wrote nearly a half a century later. In discussing von Falkenhayn's plans for Verdun, he concludes with this statement:

> He therefore proposed to bleed the French white. . . . This was not a strategy. It was a policy of attrition, just like that of Joffre and Sir William Robertson, but more scientifically calculated. Falkenhayn did not seek a spot where victory would bring him a strategical advantage. He wanted only a symbol which would be a challenge to French pride.[25]

A more perfect example of how propaganda becomes sober historical fact would be difficult to find.

Since the French controlled the figures of their losses, they were easily able to spin the 1916 battles to their advantage. As Winston Churchill would point out later, the French always won what he termed the "war of communiqués."[26] In terms of a rhetorical strategy, the idea was excellent: assign an aim or a position to your opponent that he doesn't actually have, and then insist that he be judged for failing to meet the goal you have falsely assigned him. Everyone who has studied rhetoric in the past two thousand years knows this is a fallacy, but the reason it was identified early on, and given a name, is because it turns out to be an extremely effective debating technique.

Apparently it works pretty well for historical narratives as well. But then, as the British historian Phillip Guedalla observed, "It was Quintilian or Mr. Max Beerbohm who said, 'History repeats itself: historians repeat each other.'"[27]

A FAILURE OF COMPREHENSION

Defending von Falkenhayn, or the Germans, is a forlorn enterprise in which the facts have no particular weight, given the refusal of so many historians to acknowledge even the most obvious and fundamental facts, like the casualty imbalance.

The difficulties, or risks, with the plan had little or nothing to do with either the morality or the practicality of "bleeding France white." And the idea that it was possible to get a nation to quit a war without winning some spectacular battle was sound enough.

Like the cherished British notion of a blockade, however, there was an enormous gap between the theory and actual practice. The blockade believers, like the subsequent bomber barons and airpower apostles who rose to prominence in the 1930s, were never able to get the results they claimed could easily be achieved, and this no matter how skillfully they manipulated the facts.

The blockade worked very well—from November 1918 through June 1919, after the war had supposedly ended. Interestingly enough, the proponents of massive bombing of the cities who came along afterward used the estimates of deaths caused by the block-ade to argue that strategic bombing actually killed fewer people. So the two ideas are in a curious way related.

Moreover, both are means of reaching the civilian population of your combatant, affecting his morale, so the civilians will agitate for an end to the war. That is to say, the British navy aimed to do the same thing through the blockade that von Falkenhayn aimed to do through the Verdun offensive, and that the Royal Air Force later tried to do in the next war through bombing cities.

That relationship, which seems clear enough, suggests a motive. Given the highly problematic morality of blockades and the bombing of cities, revealing that von Falkenhayn's aim was pretty much the same (or in fact exactly the same) would lead people to the reflection that the Allies were morally no better than their opponents.

Since the entire basis of the Allied position was based on the idea that they were as morally unimpeachable as the Germans were wicked and treacherous, that would hardly do. The writing of history can be a way of uncovering the past, but it can also be a way of burying it.

The aim here is not to defend von Falkenhayn, but to get as close to actuality as we can. So having said how his aims were considerably shrewder than his opponents have allowed, and hence that by comparison with the Allied generals he was a mental giant and a competent strategist (although given his opponents, that is not much of an accomplishment either), it should be said that in several key respects his idea was extremely risky.

Although von Falkenhayn was correct in his assessment about the theoretical possibilities, he erred in seeing the results as being almost axiomatic. He came of a generation of military and civilian thinkers who had quite forgotten Napoleon's fatalism, Bismarck's wariness, and Grant's pragmatism.

Nations enter and exit wars for reasons that are exceedingly complex, to the point of being irrational. Once half a century of propaganda is stripped away, France's position in June 1940 was certainly no worse than it was in September 1914, and indeed in some ways substantially better. But the perception, the belief, on the part of the government and of much of the country was that their cause was lost. They acted accordingly, and lost their country.

There was no way that von Falkenhayn could predict that France would reach its breaking point in the immediate future as a result of Verdun. Yes, the idea was sound, and in May 1917, that breaking point actually arrived—a year too late for the German commander's hopes, and in the army, not the country.

Therein lies the difficulty. He could predict with confidence the country's response. Although he phrased it in such a way that the logic suggested the possibility that the French might not fight, he clearly assumed they would, and he was correct.

However, whatever his strategic acumen was, he failed to grasp two basic points about the governments of his opponents. Failing to understand civilians and their institutions is not an unusual failure in generals, of course, but since his strategy was directed at the governments, he should have reasoned more closely or observed them more intimately.

The first failure was the failure to grasp that both London and Paris were caught in a trap of their own devising. The two traps were different, but in each case, the government could not withstand the revelations that would ensue about their deception and ineptitude in the years before the war, and their incompetent impotence once it began. Politicians have great difficulty in placing the interests of their country (or of their constituents) over their careers—not so much out of selfishness, but because they generally confuse the two.

But however we categorize that error, calling it hubris or wickedness, it is a powerful force. To expect the leaders of the political parties that had dominated French political life for half a century to admit that their decisions had ruined the army, that their alliance with Russia had blown up in their face, and that they then sat around having endless meetings while their citizens were massacred, was unrealistic to the point of delusional.

If France quit the war, it would hardly be ruined as a nation. France had lost North America in the eighteenth century, Napoleon had eventually been defeated, and the Second Empire had collapsed in 1870. In the last two cases the country had been not only defeated, but occupied by foreign troops. But very few Frenchmen would have argued that they were worse off in 1900 under the Third Republic than in its earlier iterations or under Napoleon.

Nor is there the slightest shred of evidence to suggest that the Germans had any intention of territorial expansion into Western Europe. This was a war that, in terms of the well-being of its citizenry, France could survive rather easily. It had done so in 1871, and it would do so in 1940.

But the same could not be said for its leaders. Their careers would suffer; possibly even their lives would be forfeit. They would either vanish into the obscurities of national history, or survive as examples of national failure and perfidy along the lines of Napoleon III or, by 1944, Philippe Pétain.

So it's hardly surprising that the French repeatedly refused even to come to the bargaining table, and were unwilling even to discuss the idea. It is well to strip through that particular piece of misrepresentation, to realize that the Germans were willing to talk peace, that it was London and Paris who refused, justifying their refusal on demonstrable falsehoods.

Indeed, as the truth gradually leaked out, the confidence in the government evaporated. By spring 1918, it was already largely gone. Here is the offhand remark by a young American woman resident in Paris for the entire war: writing in early 1918, she speaks dismissively of "the falsehoods concerning German military strength that had been spread consistently for three years," by which she meant the steady diet of wildly exaggerated claims of their losses and of Allied successes.[28]

In other words, von Falkenhayn was extremely naive to believe that anything within his powers would bring Paris to the table. A curious defect, since von Moltke the Elder had gotten stuck in the quagmire of France in 1870. He had defeated their armies, captured their leader, had their capital surrounded, and they refused to quit. That it took nearly five months before they did should have suggested the perils of dealing with the French political class as though they were rational.

That was one failure. It was intimately connected to another: the failure to realize the extent to which both governments were enmeshed in their own lies. Educated Germans who took the trouble could find out what their losses were, as they were regularly reported in the Reichstag, and the newspapers listed names, albeit tardily and somewhat erratically. One can hardly say the Kaiserreich was transparent, but by contrast with its opponents it was a pane of glass compared to a fog in a swamp.

A swamp into which the civilian leaders of the two governments were steadily sinking. If they agreed to any sort of terms, they would have to admit that everything the public had been told was a lie. So instead they resorted to the standard techniques of shady politicians. They covered up their failures and demonized their opponents.

During the war, the convergence of anti-German propaganda and emerging Marxist theory combined to turn the German empire into a feudalistic, repressive, militarist state. All of that was nonsense, as any halfway competent survey of what was written about Germany in the decades before 1914 quickly reveals.

Nowadays it is difficult for us to grasp the corrosive distortions generated by Allied propagandists about the German government and the German emperor once the war began. The following passage is an excellent illustration, since it comes as an almost offhand remark.

Even in Germany, the most rigid of Absolute Despotisms, a phantasm of political liberty was allowed to flit about the Halls of Parliament. But through the cunning of Bismarck the Socialist masses were bound all the more tightly to the Hohenzollern Despot.[29]

That this completely untrue and gratuitous swipe occurs in the middle of a biography of Theodore Roosevelt only drives the point home more effectively. Nor is this an isolated comment. In a later chapter, the author tells his readers:

> The German attack on civilization, which was openly delivered in 1914, revealed to the world that for twenty years before the German Emperor had been secretly preparing his mad project of Universal Conquest (Thayer, 216).

The man who wrote these lines was not a minor journalist or some eccentric conspiracy theorist. He was the president of the American Historical Association, a member of the governing board of Harvard University, and an established historian. The remarks come dangerously close to professional malfeasance, and really escape only because they are patently ludicrous.

But given the author's profession, and his professional reputation, it is no wonder that this sort of nonsense has proven remarkably durable, particularly among military historians, to the point that one of the emperor's more distinguished English biographers has been compelled to make the following, rather blunt remarks:

> Nor do I consider that the Kaiser really did run the country. . . . Ideas about what happened in 1914 must not be influenced by knowledge of what happened afterwards. The German military and civilian leaders were not thinking in terms of 1918 and 1940 so much as of 1866 and 1870. . . . Other countries as well as Germany could have averted the outbreak of war in 1914 by adopting different courses of action.[30]

If the reality was totally fraudulent, the intensity was equally real. During the war the Allies demonized the German emperor, to the extent of branding him a war criminal and making a surprisingly feeble effort to arrest him and bring him to trial. He fled to the Netherlands, and the Dutch, quite sensibly and morally, re-fused to see him extradited; the whole sorry affair demonstrated the extent to which the whole vicious campaign had been simply another aspect of the four-year hate.

Unfortunately for von Falkenhayn's career, Wilhelm II was simply another constitutional monarch, rather more like his cousin George in London than like his more distant relatives in Bulgaria and Romania. Long before the start of the war, he had been relegated to the sidelines. As another of his biographers remarks, his "ignorance of the true na-ture of the struggle in which Germany was engaged was profound and his utility to the military leaders quite limited," and a much more hostile writer admits that his behavior had already "convinced the vast majority of the generals that the Kaiser was not capable of playing a decisive part in any future war."[31]

But what Germany actually was, was a state governed with remarkable naïveté. Bismarck's successors were an equally remark-able collection of idealists and academics, whose common trait was a lack of any practical political sense.

Von Falkenhayn realized that the easterners were extremely naive in their ideas about how to win a war. He was equally naive in his notions of how France worked. The politicians were too ineptly narcissist, the people too blindly ignorant of the truth, for his strategy to have any chance of working. Indeed, as we shall see, the army had little difficulty in spinning Verdun into yet another French triumph: the facts of the case had little to do with it.

People had not yet grasped that governments frequently lie to their citizens, generally when the lies are necessary to keep the members of the government in power, but also to keep them from fomenting revolt, or giving in to counsels of despair.

THE CONSEQUENCES OF LOSS OF SURPRISE

Like any document, von Falkenhayn's letter has a subtext of the sort that contemporary literary theorists are always stretching to extract. But in this case the subtext seems straightforward enough: there was a narrow window of opportunity for the Germans, and their only real chance at winning was to exploit it.

Everyone knew that the British forces in France were steadily expanding, that the shipments of munitions from the United States were increasing. The thousands and thousands of hectares of fertile Ukrainian land that the easterners were conquering would suffice to keep them in food indefinitely. But manpower and armaments were a different matter.

If von Falkenhayn had been as calculating as his critics and subsequent historians (the former and the latter being the same) claim, arguing that he could win the war by killing more Frenchmen, he was a remarkably stupid fellow: the manpower resources of the two Allied empires was even greater than that of Russia. Germany's only real hope lay in the next few months.

That militated for an attack at the earliest possible moment, but the weather refused to cooperate. January came and went, and by February the French were alarmed. Although the initial German success was such that there is often an undercurrent in accounts of the battle suggesting that the French were surprised, even by then they had no idea the Germans would attack the right bank at all. That idea is yet another part of the propagandistic narrative of the war, in which the only German successes (which, according to the Allies, were very limited) came as the result of surprise or some sort of wickedness, such as poison gas or the violation of Belgian neutrality.

On the contrary, both the local commanders and their superiors had a wealth of information indicating that the attack was imminent. As the analyst who made a careful examination of the French intelligence data makes clear,

> Not only were the troops holding the Verdun front perfectly aware of the imminent nature of the German attack, but in addition (and this is much more interesting), the officers had a perfect account of certain details of the actions

along the front in their sector, multiple indices received by ground observers who give us proof that is undeniable.[32]

Of course, one problem inherent in depending on ground-based observation was that the observers were unable to look down into the area behind the lines, so they couldn't see for themselves what was being built where.

From the very start of the war, the Germans had made heavy use of aircraft to direct artillery fire. One French gunner described this technique with a certain professional admiration: "The enemy has perfected his aerial arm to the degree of virtuosity, and unfortunately our seventy-fives are almost useless against them."[33] Very early on, both the French and the Germans made heavy use of aerial photography.

The problem on the French side was not, therefore, an absence of photographs that would reveal in detail the enormous expansion of German positions and hence allow for accurate counter battery fire. It was a serious lack of men to interpret them. Nor were the divisional staffs trained to make use of them. In fact, it was not until February 1916 that the GQG got around to creating topographic sections even at the corps level.[34]

Failures of this sort make pretty clear the extent to which neither Joffre nor his subordinates really grasped the nature of modern warfare, just as they never really understood the employment of heavy artillery. At a postwar conference arranged for Swiss army officers, Henry Corda explained that "the most important tactical lessons of Verdun concern artillery and aviation"; having failed to grasp the importance of either one, Verdun was a rude shock that promptly became a disaster.[35]

However, within the framework of a somewhat stunted imagination, Chantilly did what it could. Joffre was concerned sufficiently with Verdun to visit it once a month during 1915. In January 1916 he was reassuring his nervous subordinates that all was well, and he was worried enough about the offensive to order the Thirtieth Army Corps, consisting of the 39th and 153rd divisions, to move up in mid-February. When the offensive was launched the forces were still deploying at Bar-le-Duc, and thus were 53 kilometers south of the city of Verdun, with the only way to get there a narrow country road. In the event, most of them went into combat on foot.

Given the forces at Verdun, this was a substantial reinforcement. The left bank was held by the Seventh Army Corps, but its two infantry divisions, the 29th and the 67th, had only arrived there in early February. Curiously, given the section of the front they were holding, corps headquarters was all the way down the Meuse at Souilly, 22 kilometers from Avocourt. By contrast, the headquarters of the entire German Fifth Army, downstream from Verdun at Stenay, was only a kilometer or so farther from their side of the front. French corps commanders, removed from their troops both physically and psychologically, were simply too far back to be able to direct their units in the event of an attack.

On the right bank, the main section of the front was held by the Thirtieth Army Corps. This unit was a considerably more powerful corps than its colleague on the left bank, as it consisted of the 14th, 51st, and 72nd divisions, plus the 212th Brigade of territorial troops. Its headquarters was thus considerably closer to the front, as it was located at Fort Souville. At less than ten kilometers behind his troops, General Chrétien was thus in theory able to take command in the event of an attack, but his proximity to the front meant that he was also well within the range of the German guns. But again, these troops had arrived at the front only in the last days of January, were still discovering the nature of the defensive network.

Below the Thirtieth Corps, the front was held by the 2nd, which was very much a mixed bag. The 3rd and 4th divisions were, as their numbers indicate, first-line units; but the 312th was composed of men who really had no business being in uniform, and, like their partners up north, this corps also had a brigade of territorial troops (in this case the 211th).

When one ponders the dates for the arrival of all these units, one deduction seems difficult to avoid: If the German attack had been delivered on 21 January instead of 21 February, the outcome would have been completely different. In those first weeks of 1916, the GQG did actually make attempts to reinforce the front, one reason why Colonel Herbillon was so sanguine in his assurances to the government, why he soothed their nerves by saying that at most the Germans would penetrate the front lines, just as the French had done in Champagne in the fall.

ON BALANCE

The weather had shrunk the German window considerably, thus reducing the amount of time they had to effect the great sea change von Falkenhayn desired. At best he had five months, but now he only had four—a significant reduction. A less cautious general would not have delayed, would have said weather be damned.

On the other hand, the fact that the French were moving reinforcements into Verdun was by no means bad for the plan. On the contrary, it meant their resources were already stretched, even before the fighting started.

Once again, it must be pointed out that the French problem in manpower is not very well understood. As far as men and guns went, Joffre absolutely did not have the resources necessary to mount an in-depth defense. Indeed, this is the point of departure Pétain takes in his own account of the 1916 fighting.

This rather dry and laconic accounting strikes to the root of France's problem. In a few sparse pages the marshal lays bare the roots of the stunted final victory.

At the end of 1915, Pétain observes, six Belgian and 39 British divisions were holding a 180-kilometer stretch of the front.[36] Against those 45 divisions, the Germans opposed only 32. Moreover, there were four French divisions in the Belgian sector, and 14 in the British, leaving only 87 for the other 500 kilometers of the front.

So, sensibly enough, the French tried to keep a substantial force in reserve, the result being that the front line was actually only held by 58 divisions, since 29 were being held back. Although the Germans had roughly the same number of divisions opposite the French (80 to 87), their superiority in armaments and in concrete, their methodical construction of successive lines of defenses, meant that they could afford to hold far fewer units in reserve. The end result was that when units holding the fronts were considered, the Germans actually outnumbered their opponents decisively: Pétain's estimate is 70 to 58.

Now, applied to Verdun, what the French weakness in manpower meant was this: at any one point on the line, the Germans would always have a local superiority. The only way the French could match that was to commit their reserve units. But the more they committed in one area, the less they had available in the others.

The situation was exacerbated by the asymmetry in firepower. In consequence, the Germans didn't need some crushing superiority in men; that was more than compensated for by the artillery available to them.

At Verdun, the German Fifth Army had carefully assembled the greatest concentration of modern heavy weapons that had yet been seen: 246 15-centimeter howitzers, 140 of the extremely effective 21-centimeter howitzers, and thirty of the superheavy guns in sizes greater than 28 centimeters, for a total of 800 pieces, none of them the relatively ineffectual 7.7-centimeter field gun.

In sheer numbers, the French situation seems reasonable: over 600 guns of all types on both banks, evenly divided between left and right, while on the right bank there were approximately 100 pieces of heavy artillery.[37]

However, the raw numbers conceal a horrifying imbalance. What the positions on the right bank actually consisted of was 245 of the 75-millimeter field guns, 35 of the elephantine long-recoil 155-millimeter howitzers, and 34 genuinely heavy weapons of various types and vintages, whose chief characteristic was their enormous weight and consequent immobility. The rest consisted of antiques from the 1870s. Basically, without stretching the point, when it came to heavy weapons, the French were outgunned by the ratio of about 20 to 1, which was definitely not good.

But in January 1916, that was basically all the French had available, in terms of both firepower and men. On the key 10- to 12-kilometer section of the right bank where the commanders supposed, correctly, that the main thrust of the attack would fall, there were 12 battalions distributed in centers of resistance (reinforced concrete shelters and command posts). As the GQG reckoned such things, this was an ample force. The weakness was of the usual sort: of the 131 field guns deployed there, 42 were antiques from the last century, while of the 140 guns that could technically be called heavy artillery, only 14 were in any sense modern, which suggests the true nature of the disadvantage.[38]

Compounding the problem was the fact, carefully concealed until long afterward, that the defensive positions on the right bank were very sketchy. When Colonel Herbillon had assured the government that at most the Germans would get into the first line of trenches, he forgot to add—probably because he didn't know himself—that there really wasn't much else on the right bank behind the first line.

As Pétain recalls in his typically understated and laconic way: "Between the forts and beyond, everything was in a state of dilapidation. Trenches had collapsed, the network of barbed-wire . . . was in pieces, roads had turned into swamps, and matériel lay scattered about."[39]

There were bits and pieces of a second line, but the third line was nonexistent, just marks on a map. If the Germans broke through the first line of trenches, could work past the outermost forts, the defenders would be in a very awkward position indeed. Lacking mobile artillery with the correct angles of fire for the heights of the Meuse, and heavy guns in general, they would be forced to resort to the same tactics they had been using since the start of the war—again, not a very promising position to be in.

So although the plan was a gamble, a calculated risk that the

Germans could make the French quit the war before the lumbering Joffre and his dim-witted British colleague managed to organize their great summer offensive, it was by no means an act of desperation. That the plan failed to bring about the desired results in the predicted time does not mean it was doomed, or that it was seriously flawed.

Or, to put it another way, it was no worse than Isoroku Yamamoto's plan of attack at Pearl Harbor was a gamble. The Japanese naval genius was dubious about the outcome of a war with America, which was why he gambled so recklessly.

Moreover, von Falkenhayn's plan came considerably closer to success than Yamamoto's. Verdun really did shake the French government to the foundations, set off a chain of events that reduced the country to dire straits indeed. And as France went down, it took Great Britain with it.

Prince Barnhard of the Netherlands, speaking of Operation Market Garden in September 1944, remarked sarcastically that his country could never withstand the "luxury" of another such "success."[40] Another Verdun would have destroyed France, and it was no real fault of the German chief of staff that finally, the fates conspired against him.

But then again, as Napoleon observed, victory can depend on a dog or a goose.

8

The Most Famous Battle:
February–March 1916

Frenchmen love an heroic legend.

—Paul Lintier[1]

The German assault began on 21 February 1916, with a massive artillery barrage of the sort that nowadays we associate almost exclusively with the Great War. The geysers of the earth and the moonscape of craters that resulted are visually striking. To a great extent they epitomize the war.

In actuality, however, 21 February was the first of the great artillery attacks. But then, this bleak February day saw a number of other firsts as well. For the first time, tactical bombing was coordinated with ground fire. In the infantry assault that followed, German troops appeared for the first time wearing their now famous steel helmets, and, more horrifyingly, began the first systematic and widespread use of the flamethrower.

The new hardware was accompanied by new tactics. As with much else about this war, hardly any of this penetrated, although in defense of the French, it must be said that the chaos of the opening battle and the virtual annihilation of the defenders were a considerable obstacle to understanding what had happened.

THE BARRAGE

Although the barren and cratered landscape is probably the most memorable image of the war, the process that led to that end is imperfectly understood, even today. A few Allied officers had grasped the point of the tactic early on, even though the scale was in no way commensurate with what happened at Verdun in 1916. On 8 September 1914, General Fayolle had confided to his diary, "The method of the Germans is simple: to eliminate our ability to respond through their heavy artillery fire."[2] It was only necessary to paralyze your enemy, not to destroy him outright.

Moreover, such total destruction was not a very likely outcome. Although direct hits from explosive shells landing on earthen works at steep angles could destroy them, just as shells bursting in air directly above the trench could kill or maim the soldiers huddled there, direct hits of that sort demanded a level of precision that was extremely difficult to achieve at ranges of 5,000 and 6,000 meters or more. Statistically, if you fired enough shells, some of them would land on the trench; some would fall short of the target; others would land behind it. Indirect fire at any distance was not in any way the same as aiming a rifle or a pistol. Small variations in the actual amount of explosive in the shell, the condition of the barrel, even currents of air, all had an effect. This was so even if the gunners were using modern guns with hydraulic recoil mechanisms. With the older weapons, putting *accuracy* and *indirect fire* in the same sentence is an oxymoron.

One of the calculations artillery officers made was to try to figure out how many shells had to be fired at any given target in order to destroy it, and what sort of target they could actually destroy. Trenches were one thing; reinforced concrete bunkers, often dug into the ground, were quite another, and the modern forts were basically an impossibility, as the Germans had discovered in their sporadic shelling during 1915.

The difficulty, then, lay in the damage done by all the shells that missed, as the majority of them did. The craters that would now lie in front of the first line of the defensive trenches would create serious obstacles for the advancing infantry. They had to proceed from their lines to the enemy lines on foot. Fire enough shells to obliterate your opponent's initial positions, and your infantry's already hazardous and physically exhausting trek would degenerate into the worst sort of obstacle course.

Although we often speak in a way that implies that each side had one line of trenches, as we have seen, there were supposed to be three successive lines, each anchored by strongpoints that were impervious to artillery fire. So the shells that landed between the successive lines only made the assault even more difficult.

Given the large number of shells that missed their targets entirely, an artillery barrage could almost be said to have been a case where the cure was worse than the disease—as far as the infantry were concerned. They had to work their way through this obstacle course in order to occupy the enemy trenches. The defenders only had to emerge from their strongpoints and shoot them down as they clambered across.

It should also be remembered that although vast craters are visually impressive, most of them represent misses. When a shell explodes, the forces generated spread out in a sphere. To be optimally effective, the shell should explode in the air slightly above the target. The shell that creates a big hole in front or behind does nothing but impede the infantry advance.

Gunners were aware of this problem. The preferred shell therefore had a timing mechanism so it would, in theory, explode to do maximum damage. But these shells were delicate and expensive, and the Allies had very few of them. The vast majority of French shells operated on a much simpler principle: when the nose of the shell impacted a hard surface, it ignited the explosives in the warhead. A hard surface: concrete was ideal, a rock or boulder would do, and soft earth was not so satisfactory.

No one knows how many of the shells fired during the war failed to explode, and simply buried themselves in the earth. But the unwary or the foolhardy have been getting blown up with depressing regularity as they gambol about on the battlefields of northeastern France ever since.

The main point here is that a cratered landscape means a great many misses. A waffled and corrugated landscape, devoid of vegetation, is an infallible indicator that the infantry assault across it was fruitless—that instead of a breakthrough, there was a massacre.

Given their lack of heavy weapons, French gunners had not yet had to grapple with this issue, although as Fayolle's comment reveals, the men who were actually directing the attacking infantry had become aware of it rather quickly.

Now on the right bank, the Germans faced a peculiar problem. Although as we have seen, the successive defensive positions formed by the trench lines were rudimentary to nonexistent: neither the forts nor the reinforced concrete strongpoints that anchored the initial line of defense were vulnerable to artillery fire. A few direct hits would not destroy them, and in the case of modernized or recent forts like Douaumont, which was the most forward of the forts on the right bank, destruction was physically impossible.

However, the proper sort of bombardment, which extended far behind the first defensive position, could paralyze the enemy, isolate him in his strongpoints, deny him reinforcements, and prevent him from sending or receiving orders.

However, in order to grasp the effects of the bombardment at Verdun on 21 February 1916, we must realize that, in the words of one French officer, it was "a preparation of artillery, the violence of which surpassed anything that had been experienced up to that time," a terse phrase that is perfectly true.[3] Verdun was the first time such a massed artillery attack had occurred in the history of warfare. No one had experienced anything like it before. The barrage extended from Avocourt on the left bank all the way across to the easternmost forts on the right bank, and then down into the Woëvre, so the section of the front it encompassed was unprecedented.

Given the mixture of heavy weapons, the Germans were able to reach far behind the first line of defenses. Shells fell as far back into the salient as the town itself, and the bridges across the Meuse were targeted, rendered impassable.

By midday, visibility had increased, so the artillery fire became heavier, since observers were able to see the fall of the shells more distinctly. In this they were aided immensely by aerial observation.

TACTICAL AIRPOWER

As we have seen, German gunners were relying on aerial observers from the start of the war. Given the state of early aviation, they relied on a mix of airplanes and balloons. As the front stabilized at the end of 1914, observers in balloons became more and more important. They were cheap, relatively stationary, allowed the observers in the air to communicate directly with the ground by telephone.

The disadvantage of the balloons was that the observer was actually behind the lines, while planes could fly directly over the enemy positions. Whenever possible, the Germans therefore used both. For Verdun they had gathered together seven balloon units, each operating two balloons, and six units of fixed-wing aircraft.[4] The generic German designation for such units, Abteilungen, is not a reliable indicator as to the size, so the exact number of aircraft involved is unknown, but probably between thirty and forty.

The tripartite division of the fledgling air forces of the war is routinely noted: observers, bombers, and fighters. However, most of what has been written in the histories of early military aviation focuses on fighter planes, while the airpower theorists who emerged in the 1920s in Italy and Great Britain wrote as though the idea of strategic bombing were something new and untried. Not so—both sides tried to bomb the opposing cities early on.

The reason this aspect of the air was minimized was twofold. First, it was an area in which the Germans had a considerable advantage: their planes were bombing London and Paris with reasonable frequency, while the Allies rarely were able to get even across the Rhine. Second, the results were minimal. Although the Germans inflicted 6,608 mostly civilian casualties in their raids on the two capitals, their losses were surprisingly heavy, particularly given the rudimentary ground-to-air defenses that were hastily organized.[5] To the extent that when the war was over, the Germans concentrated on tactical as opposed to strategic bombing: the new German air force that emerged during the Hitler years was almost entirely a tactical arm—that is to say, air-to-ground attacks were directed at military targets behind the enemy lines, and were simply an extension of the artillery barrage. So Verdun was yet another first in the history of warfare. On 21 February German aviators swarmed the skies over Verdun. As French officers were forced to admit, their enemy had complete mastery of the air.

On the one hand, that enabled the observers to work undisturbed. The reason that the barrage intensified in the afternoon was that improved visibility meant the effects of the morning shelling could be observed, and fire could be corrected—directed on objectives that had been missed, or on new ones that had emerged.

To protect the observers, over 60 fighter planes were used, divided into ten fighter units. Although from the viewpoint of the fighter pilots, their duels in the air were what early aviation was all about, the truth is more prosaic. Fighter planes were used either to protect observers or to destroy them. Battles with other fighter planes were incidental to that aim.

Although as the battle developed, French fighter squadrons fought back vigorously, in this, the all-important opening of the offensive, they were caught off guard, so the Germans were able to proceed without any opposition at all.

Their mastery of the airspace over Verdun allowed the Germans to deploy two of their five squadrons of strategic bombers. These units had the blandly misleading designation of Kampfgeschwader der Deutsche General Stabs Staff, which, abbreviated as Kagohl, perhaps confused Allied observers. However, the five squadrons of Kagohls were Germany's strategic bombing force.

As any student of the next war knows, strategic bombers can carry enormous loads of bombs over great distances. Alternatively, they can carry even heavier loads over short distances. But in the Second World War, neither the British nor the American bomber commands were much interested in infantry support. They felt their mission was strategic bombing, and that tactical air support, to be done by someone else, was a distinctly lesser priority.

During the First World War this idea was still being developed, and the Germans never really took to it. So at Verdun they made use of the roughly 80 heavy bombers they had assembled. As the weather cleared, in addition to the artillery barrage, the French were subjected to some surprisingly heavy bombing.

Verdun was the first time bombers had been used in conjunction with artillery fire.

Now, by comparison with the bombers of the next war, the payload of these early planes was minuscule. Over the first week, the Kagohls only managed to drop roughly 500 bombs on the entire area, or slightly under 5,000 kilograms. No surprise there: in late February visibility is poor, so the planes were able to operate only sporadically.

But this figure should be put in the context of the war. From the first raid of 30 August 1914 to the last, on 15 September 1918, the German air force dropped only 30,000 kilograms of bombs on Paris.[6] By that measure, managing a sixth of that in one week is impressive.

A bomb dropped from an airplane has two significant advantages over an artillery shell. By comparison, the bomb is almost entirely composed of high explosive, and it comes straight down. Given the slow speeds and low altitudes of these early planes, together with the absence of coordinated ground-to-air defenses embedded in the infantry divisions, level bombing was not only practicable, but surprisingly accurate.

Moreover, just as the infantry had never been subjected to a barrage of this intensity and scope, they had never been attacked from the air in this fashion. So although the fact of the attack was not in itself a surprise, the scope and intensity of the attack definitely were. Marc Bloch, the brilliant French medieval historian, a veteran of this war, noted that surprise often led to panic, that hardened veterans who had never flinched under enemy fire would suddenly panic and run when startled by the unexpected.[7]

The physical destruction was very real, and significant. There was the destruction of infantry positions in the open, the wrecking of prepared fields of fire, the destruction of bridges and ammunition dumps, and the consequent loss of wired links back to the various headquarters. But the effect of this unprecedented type of offensive, new in its violence, in its accuracy, and the means employed, had a shattering effect on the defenders. When, late in the afternoon of 21 February, the German infantry began to probe, the French, despite heroic efforts, were disorganized, demoralized, and in no position to mount a coherent defense.

THE ASSAULT ON THE RIGHT BANK

In the popular view, once a bombardment lifted, thousands of heavily encumbered infantry struggled out of their trenches and advanced in waves across no-man's-land, hoping they would survive the machine-gun fire, or, as they fell into the first trenches, engaging in hand-to-hand combat.

This idea was to a great extent true for the Allies, considerably less so for their opponents. The notion of dense waves of Germans swarming the battlefield was basically a myth. It was partly based on mirroring: that was how the Allies conducted their assaults, so therefore it was assumed the Germans did the same thing. The myth was created early on in the war, and was the basis of the wildly inflated German losses the French claimed to be inflicting.

And, of course, since Verdun was the first large-scale German assault since September 1914, the idea seemed logical enough. One solid assumption that permeated the ranks of cabinet ministers, armchair strategists, and historians was that there was no development of infantry tactics or even weaponry during the war.

In reality, German infantry tactics, which were never understood very well by the Allies, had evolved enormously. Not everywhere on the front, but in the enormous section that was technically controlled by the Fifth Army, there had been dramatic changes. One we have already seen being employed in the Argonne. A small piece of the front trench line would be targeted. Heavy artillery would simply obliterate it to the degree that was possible; then the infantry would close in on the debris, eliminate the dazed survivors, and consolidate their gains. Then the process would begin all over again.

When the beleaguered French infantry in the Argonne spoke of being gnawed, that was what they meant. They were losing territory meter by meter, in a process that was as inevitable as a bucket draining water through a leak. And the French had no idea how to stop it.

At the other end of the sector, in the Vosges mountains, a variant of this was being developed. Instead of a platoon of riflemen, backed by machine gunners and artillery, the Germans put together mixed groups: specially selected infantry, combat engineers, and machine gunners. Instead of a direct frontal assault, these small and heavily armed groups would work around the objectives, attack from the sides. When they encountered strongpoints that could be easily be reduced by grenades, the engineers would deploy their formidable 17-centimeter mortars, while the machine gunners would counter French attacks.

As these tactics became known to the Allies, they were associated with the famous "storm troopers," a name derived from the German designation of Sturmabteilungen. The tactics, composition, and purpose of these units are fundamentally misunderstood.[8]

Once the tactics were perfected, the units were deployed across the front, the idea being that they would teach the other soldiers what they had learned. The ideal was to inculcate the entire army with this new idea.

A more helpful way of describing the result would be to characterize the units that were thus formed as combined-arms units, since they brought together soldiers who historically had operated in complete independence of one another. In August 1914, infantry platoons were organizations armed entirely with rifles. They were entirely separate and distinct from the companies of machine gunners, and the companies of combat engineers, even though these last controlled some of the deadliest weapons available to the infantry: mortars and flamethrowers.

The British and French continued to go down this line, maintaining rigid separations. Heavy artillery was exclusively controlled by the corps or the army group command. Divisional commanders only had control over the field guns. The result, which Marshal Fayolle termed a "gross error," was that decisions on how to employ the heavy guns were made by men far from the front, completely unfamiliar with local needs. It was, he concluded, "completely crazy."[9] He was right.

The Germans had long since abandoned this idea, parceling out their heavy weapons to the commanders who needed them. So, for example, the 7th Reserve Corps, which would mount the main infantry assault on the section of the right bank roughly between Consenvoye and Flabas, was not only supported by a vast artillery park of heavy guns, mostly 15- and 21-centimeter howitzers, but actually had control of them.

That is, the infantry commanders could ask directly for supporting artillery fire on targets they wanted destroyed, whereas in the French system, that same commander would have to transmit his request all the way up the chain of command, where it would approved or rejected, even if he was a divisional commander.

Integrating combat engineers, machine gunners, and riflemen was simply the next logical step.

So in the late afternoon, instead of hordes of infantry charging (stumbling and staggering, actually) across a blasted and cratered no-man's-land, we should instead envision small groups working their way cautiously through the fallen trees, maneuvering around the shell holes that were the inevitable result of misses. The caution was because there were no trenches extending from the main German positions toward the French. The distances were considerable, so the troops moved slowly, feeling out the centers of resistance that still remained, which they then destroyed with grenades and this new and horrifying weapon, the flamethrower.

This was not an assault; rather it was a mopping-up. The French divisions holding the first line of trenches were simply overwhelmed, and the reinforcements that were trying to reach them now became hopelessly intermingled. At the woods of Herbebois, for instance, one of the key German objectives, the advancing Germans of the 64th Infantry Regiment were opposed by 15 companies of infantry from four different French regiments. Given that degree of confusion, there was no possibility of a coordinated action.

At dawn the next day, with the snow falling everywhere on the right bank, the assault continued. The objective to the immediate western flank of Herbebois was Caures. The name, like that of Herbebois, indicated a patch of forest, not a town or a fort. But Caures was one of the key positions, the center point of the right-bank trenches. As such it was held not by regular infantry, but by two battalions of *chasseurs*, the 56th and 59th.

By one in the afternoon, troops from the German 87th and 89th infantry regiments had forced the *chasseurs* back to the southwestern end of the woods. By four, the two battalions had essentially been annihilated: of the 1,800 men, only 70 were still in action. Their commander was Colonel Émile Driant, the man who had first protested the lack of proper defenses at Verdun.

In one of those grim ironies, he was one of the first senior officers to fall in combat at Verdun. The advancing Germans, soldiers of the 21st Infantry Division, stopped long enough to bury the colonel, their enemy, in the woods, marking his grave with a rude cross. One of the officers collected his personal effects and sent them, via Switzerland, to his widow. Driant was a well-known writer, a member of the chamber, and something of a celebrity. Still, his death and burial is a strange counterpoint to the horrific struggle that was going on all around him.

The advances of these first two days were not deep: about two kilometers on a 12-kilometer front. But the situation was extremely alarming. This was the peak, or crown, of the positions on the right bank. If the Germans succeeded in pushing through it, they were well past the first line of trenches in this sector. That was bad enough, but this part of the front was essentially due north of the city itself, as the zone of attack stretched from the Meuse eastward. Envision a fist smashing down on the center of a ball of rising dough. Keep on going and the sides will collapse.

Now, in the not inconsiderable French experience with assaults, getting into the first line of trenches was a not unusual occurrence. The losses were high, and the gains usually ended up being minimal, because the Germans would attack and reconquer much of what they had lost. Colonel Herbillon had explicitly evoked that comparison in making the army's reassurances to the government.

What he didn't say, probably because he didn't know himself, was that there were no successive defensive positions. Practically speaking, when Driant was forced to retreat from the woods of Caures, the survivors had to go all the way back to Vacherauville. That this fort was actually on the left bank basically sums up the emerging French dilemma. Unlike in Champagne, where the German defenders had simply fallen back to their next line, the French retreat was entirely up in the air. The only thing to do was to try to get the positions back.

So on the twenty-third, the 37th Infantry Division made the attempt. There were a few local successes at first, but by the end of the day, the Germans had pushed forward. The advance was insignificant, a few hundred meters. But it meant the absolute loss of the first defensive line, and the fatal compromise of the rudimentary second. In other words, the counterattack had not only failed to push the Germans out, but it had actually resulted in the evacuation of what had been contested ground the day before.

As the evening approached, the French were forced to evacuate all of the woods of Herbebois to avoid being encircled, and later that night they abandoned most of Samogneux as well.

The start of the day had begun with the evacuation of Brabant. It ended with desperate attempts to construct a defensive line based on the heights of Talou, of Hill 344, and the woods of Fosses and Louvemont.

But there was a dangerous momentum building. At no point had the French been able to stop the advance. And the next day the attack pressed on. By now the left flank of the advance was right down to the Meuse, so for the first time, the gunners on the left bank, relatively unscathed, were able to provide supporting artillery fire for the infantry on the other side of the river.

But as Colonel Chaligne observes, "In reality, they maneuvered by infiltration, under the protection of heavy fire from their artillery," and when their advance was blocked by strongpoints or advancing enemy troops, "they did not try to continue, they waited until shellfire had resolved the problem posed by the terrain, or until the advance of one of their neighbors had opened a way forward."[10]

The terse description of this senior French officer makes a nice contrast with the subsequent fantasies of historians. Here is how one of the more distinguished of their number characterizes the opening phase of the assault. It reveals, he says,

a deep, endemic fault in the German system of war. At bottom this stemmed from the contradiction between Falkenhayn's large object—the destruction of the French army—and the small means by which he hoped to procure it. . . . The German bombardment of February 21st was more destructive than anything yet seen . . . and yet, when the time came to follow it up, the Germans appeared to lose faith. Very slowly, preceded by large patrols and probing parties, the infantry came forward.[11]

Indeed. But, to paraphrase Jean Norton Cru, war is not a game in which points are scored by getting across the goal line regardless of the cost; the true goal of any competent general is to secure objectives with the least possible loss of life, bloodthirsty civilians and amateur poseurs to the contrary. The general who wishes to hurl his men into battle in such a way that enormous casualties are the sadly predictable result is not a great warrior, but an incompetent.

So, despite their refusal to march toward the French positions in serried ranks and get slaughtered in the requisite numbers desired by historians, the Germans were advancing—slowly but inexorably, as they had done in the Argonne. Although the French succeeded in limiting the German advance, the actual territory gained by the end of the day was the largest slice yet: two ominous bulges down into the French positions, reaching down on either side of Louvemont, while on the eastern end, the advance was right up against Bezonvaux.

The events of the night of the twenty-fourth were a mixture of confusion and error. It will be recalled that the 20th Army Corps had been arriving at Bar-le-Duc just before the attack. Now, in the evening, two full brigades, having made an astonishing 36-hour march up the road, arrived at Souville. They were promptly dispatched to hold the section of the front to the north of Fort Douaumont. But in one of those typical confusions that happen on the battlefield, they took up positions in the village of the same name, a good distance behind the massive fort. Nor were they able to discover the whereabouts of the nearest French unit, which was holding Hill 378. What was worse, they apparently did not realize that the Germans were already in the forest of the Vauche.

BAD DECISIONS

Such mishaps occur on the battlefield; nor are they necessarily irremediable. But that evening, Fernand de Langle de Cary, commander of the Armies of the Center, made what may well be the single worst command decision of the Great War, although admittedly the competition for this dubious honor is steep.

He decided that to abandon the Woëvre entirely, and to form a front based on the Côte du Talou in the northeast, through Louvemont, then to the forts of Douaumont and Vaux. However, this drastic move was simply the preparation. At eight that night, he telephoned the GQG to inform them that he planned to evacuate the entire right bank, lock, stock, and the few remaining barrels. To that end, he stopped the remainder of the 20th Army Corps at Fort Regret. The order for the successive abandonments, General Order Number 18, was actually sent out.

Georges Lefebvre terms this decision a "criminal fault" (*Verdun*, 108–9). But although the result pushed the army right to the edge of the abyss, de Langle de Cary was actually only carrying out what had been prescribed months earlier when Verdun had been downgraded and folded into the front.

Of course, the self-identified experts at the GQG thought the idea that the Germans would attack to be highly unlikely, because, as they condescended to explain to a mere colonel who was only on the staff of a lowly corps commander, "One does not attack into a salient."[12] But should this highly unlikely event occur, the most sensible option was to abandon the right bank entirely, just as de Langle de Cary was ordering.

Of course, at that hour—eight in the evening—Joffre was engaged in one of his most important duties as commander in chief of the French army, but an hour later, rising from the dinner table, he sent word to de Langle de Cary that he was to hold the right bank at all costs.

It is worth pointing out that Joffre's decision to fight on the right bank completely undercuts his later assertion, made in his

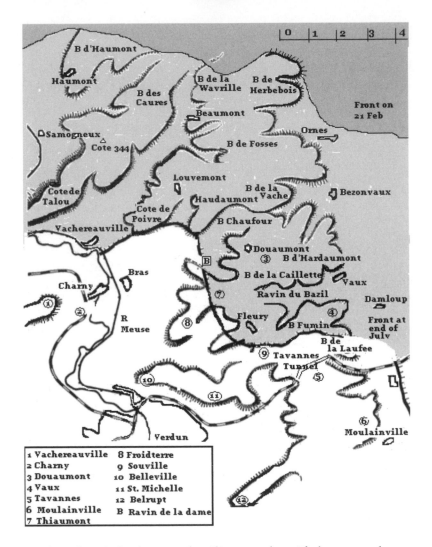

1 Vachereauville	8 Froidterre
2 Charny	9 Souville
3 Douaumont	10 Belleville
4 Vaux	11 St. Michelle
5 Tavannes	12 Belrupt
6 Moulainville	B Ravin de la dame
7 Thiaumont	

memoirs, that it had no real military value. If that was the case, why did he overrule de Langle de Cary? The simple answer was that he had some vague idea that abandoning Verdun was probably not going to go over very well with the president, the prime minister, and the minister of war.

But then, probably because he felt it necessary to placate the man he had overruled so decisively, he authorized the withdrawal from the Woëvre. Of course, in Joffre's rather limited playbook, the cardinal fault of any general was a lack of proper enthusiasm for the sort of aggressive actions that showed the proper Napoleonic spirit. His army commander was clearly a defeatist, and had panicked.

So Joffre dispatched General de Castelnau to Verdun to take whatever measures he found necessary. Traveling by car, he could reach Verdun by the next day if he didn't dawdle, and would see what needed to be done. There was no particular hurry. Having done his bit to inject even more chaos into the situation, Joffre retired for the night, conscious of having discharged his duty as supreme commander.

But before doing so, he made one of the very few sensible decisions of his military career. He told the staff to find General Philippe Pétain and have him report to headquarters early the next morning. Having dispatched de Castelnau to the front, he now decided to send Pétain along behind, to take command of the French forces struggling there. And then, satisfied, he went to bed, his duties fulfilled: he had sent someone out to do something.[13]

He had also effectively removed de Langle de Cary from the chain of command. That is, even though as commander of the armies of the center he was in theory superior to the corps commanders at Verdun, de Castelnau was now going to exercise command independently, since he would be reporting directly to Joffre. And since it would be hours and hours before de Castelnau got there, another whole day before Pétain could possibly arrive, the key decisions would all be in suspension, as no one was exactly sure who was in command or what orders they were supposed to carry out.

Sometimes lost in the genuine distress about order 18, however, is the subtext—one that everyone involved tries to finesse by a verbal sleight of hand. Instead of saying that de Langle de Cary ordered the army units to abandon Verdun, the phrase *evacuate the right bank* is used. This is a distinction without a difference. True, a goodly part of the city of Verdun is technically on the left bank of the river. But as anyone who glances at a map can see rather clearly, the river runs right through the city, and the heights of the Meuse are less than a kilometer distant. The engineers of the last century, looking at the terrain, had concluded that the city was no longer in any way a defensible strongpoint, which was why the forts were all built out on the heights, ten or more kilometers to the northeast. True enough, most of the important buildings, and the citadel, are on the left bank, but to pretend that after a withdrawal from the right bank the city would be nicely divided on the order of Minneapolis and Saint Paul, or Buda and Pest, is absurd.

So in reality, evacuating the right bank was the same thing as abandoning Verdun, both the city and the defensive position. All that would be left would be the forts on the left bank. Given the angles of the ridge there, those positions could then be shelled from the rear, where they were the most vulnerable. Moreover, the order to evacuate the right bank clearly did not mean the entire stretch of the right bank between Toul and Verdun, but what, precisely, did it mean? Without the northern section, the part of the heights of the Meuse below the city was hardly defensible. The key fort there, Troyon, had only survived by luck, and the courage of a junior French officer.

The most cursory inspection makes all this painfully obvious, thus presenting us with a vexing question: what on earth were any of these people thinking? The sad answer is that they were firmly held in the grip of extremely theoretical ideas about warfare, ideas in which an analysis of the terrain, like any consideration of morale or politics, played no part.

Although Joffre's decision was really the only possible decision, decoupling the right bank from the Woëvre was a really bad move. It shortened the German lines on the right bank, as the main bulge to the east was in the Woëvre. It rendered useless all the struggles of 1915 around Les Éparges. It eliminated what the German crown prince had, with surprising insight, called the postern gate, the prime sally port out of which the French could strike due northeast and actually, if fortune favored them, strike into Germany itself. And it moved the heavy German guns a good ten kilometers closer in.

Now comes the really bizarre part of this chain. When Joffre said no, the order was countermanded. But the next day, for reasons that have never been explained, General Balfourier, the local commander of the positions in the Woëvre, who had before him an order prescribing that the right bank was to be held position by position, refused to transmit this new order.[14]

As a result, the whole southeastern sector was simply abandoned, together with about 5 percent of Verdun's heavy weapons.

Nor is there any valid reason why it shouldn't have been held. The opposing German forces south of the Verdun–Étain road consisted of one cavalry brigade and five Landwehr regiments. The area had been bombarded, but some of the shelling was misdirected—although some of the abandoned guns had already been destroyed, the French could certainly have held their ground here. The evacuation of the Woëvre was a costly mistake, clear proof that the French army was still infected with the same disease that had cost it so dearly in 1914, when fortified positions (Lille) and strategic sections of ground (the Vauquois, the butte of Mont Sec) had been abandoned almost without a shot being fired.

Leaving aside the tactical value of the area, trying to order a selective evacuation in the middle of a battle only adds to the confusion, lowers morale, and precipitates panic. Sure enough, the decision helped to trigger just those responses, particularly when coupled with the indecision, the change of command, and, above all, the discovery that there really was nobody in command on the French side.

When the GQG decided to get rid of the whole notion of the fortified *place*, integrate into the front, and haul off all the ammunition and guns, they created exactly this sort of potential chaos. So now, on the evening of the twenty-fourth, the stage was set for a play in which all these factors would come together to form a perfect storm. The French couldn't stop the advance; they had hopelessly intermingled their units. No one knew who was in charge, or what actual orders were to be carried out. Some units were told to advance, others to evacuate; others were abruptly halted.

Not surprisingly, on Thursday, 25 February, the perfect storm appeared. Four days into the offensive, the Germans had really honed the liaison between the infantry at the head of the advance, and the gunners far behind. Still, the day began inauspiciously enough. On the western edge, the Germans were having difficulties, and in the center Louvemont was captured and lost several times.

In November 1915, the French had decided that they needed a third defensive line, and this was defined as a line running from the Côte du Talou, right beside the Meuse, along the Côte du Poivre and then through Hill 378 and on to Bezonvaux. By the evening of the twenty-fourth, the Germans were still more than a kilometer from 378 and twice that distance from Bezonvaux. So the French situation was passable, although not exactly "brilliant," to resort to a bit of Gallic military irony.

But the French line, precariously held and badly led, was like a levee. One crevasse and it would collapse. Thus far, despite the shelling, there had been a steady flow of reinforcements up into the heights. But de Langle de Cary's order to the 30th Army Corps to hold at Regret essentially stopped that flow. True, it was only a temporary stoppage, but given the obvious confusion, it is understandable how the troops bearing the brunt of the repeated advances began to feel that they had been abandoned, and that they had no positions left to fall back into.

THE COLLAPSE

The cracks first began to show in the east, where the 2nd *chasseurs* (one of the elite units of the army) was completely infiltrated by German infantry advancing carefully through the woods of the Vauche. The *chasseurs* retreated toward Douaumont fort, abandoning their colleagues in the 208th Infantry Regiment, who were promptly surrounded. Some made their own way back down the heights; most simply surrendered.

It was now three in the afternoon, and as the Germans cautiously advanced, they were approaching the great fort of Douau-mont, the centerpiece of the Verdun defenses. That was the idea still presented to a credulous world. But as we have seen, in August, the largest concrete structure in the world suffered the same indignities as its lesser brethren. The garrison left and it was largely disarmed, except for two turrets where the guns were permanently mounted.

So when the attack commenced, the two turrets of the great fort were subordinated to a lowly lieutenant located off in the woods of Caillette. The fortlet he commanded was well on its way to being demolished by the morning of the twenty-fifth, but the lieutenant managed to send orders to Douaumont, directing them to fire in the general direction of the Vauche forest.

There were forty or so aging territorials in the fort, elderly men who had most likely done their conscription two or even three decades earlier. Inside the enormous structure, they were performing little more than maintenance, although there were a few artillery observers on hand. But the noncommissioned officer in charge of the 155-millimeter turret obediently began firing toward the trees. As they began firing, detachments from two Brandenburg regiments were working their way toward the fort. As they went through the forest of the Vauche, they began rounding up members of the French 208th Regiment.

But Brandeis, a junior lieutenant in the 8th Company of the 24th Brandenburgs, began working his way toward the southeastern corner of the great fort. His assault team inched its way around, trying to get down into the dry moat and find an opening. But they were wary, and assumed the fort was fully manned. After all, the 155-millimeter turret was still firing.

After several false tries, the Brandenburgs finally managed to find an opening close by the other turret, and, although an officer was hit by stray machine-gun fire from Douaumont village, the Germans were now inside.

Following close behind Brandeis was a captain in the same regiment, and Hauptmann Haupt now began an exploration of the fort. The handfuls of territorials inside were astonished to discover the Germans had gotten in, but, confronted with a handful of heavily armed and nervous enemy soldiers, they surrendered meekly enough. There were no combat soldiers in the garrison, if we can dignify the motley group by that name. It was basically cooks and electricians, mechanics, a few artillery observers, and a core of retirees.

Thus were all the hopes and dreams of a series of great French engineers and strategists confounded by the boneheaded idiocy of a group of inexperienced junior officers at the GQG, who had decided that they knew everything and no one else knew anything.

The fall of Douaumont was not the cause of the abrupt collapse; rather the two events happened almost simultaneously, were independent of one another. But by the evening, the remaining key positions on the right bank were all in German hands.

In five days the Germans had advanced over ten kilometers on an ever-expanding front that was perhaps 15 to 20 kilometers across. And that was not counting the nearly 200 square kilometers of the Woëvre that had been handed to them on a platter.

In these first few days the three French divisions that bore the brunt of the fighting lost about 17,000 dead or missing, with another 3,000-odd wound cases; the attrition was roughly 30 percent, or perhaps higher, and the alarming thing about the figures was that more than 95 percent of the first category were simply listed as missing. No one knew what had actually happened to them.

9

Panic, Politicians, and Pétain: April–July 1916

> It is a terrible advantage to have done nothing, but it
> must not be carried too far.
>
> —Jean Dutourd[1]

The Germans lost no time in announcing the fall of Fort Douaumont, even as their soldiers were steadily advancing beyond. The news was released on Friday, 26 February.

> The armored fort of Douaumont, the northeastern pillar of the chief line of permanent fortifications of the Verdun strongpoint, was taken by assault yesterday afternoon by the 24th Brandenburg Regiment. It is completely in the power of German troops.

This precise and accurate account, which, as one French historian observes, is an "exact description" of the importance of the fort, drew a quick response from the French high command.

> A bloody struggle took place around the fort of Douaumont, which is an advanced element of the ancient organization of Verdun. The position was taken in the morning by

the enemy after numerous fruitless assaults, that cost very high losses and was passed by our troops, who repulsed all the attempts of the enemy to throw them back.[2]

With that the battle lines were drawn. While grudgingly acknowledging what was impossible to deny, the GQG at the same time began to elaborate on a marvelous fantasy world that completely inverted the situation on the battlefield.

Yes, the Germans had made gains, but at a horrific cost. For the first part of the battle, the GQG solemnly averred that the Germans had lost 400,000 men, and this incredible fantasy was believed even by cynical generals like Fayolle, while far up to the north, on the same date that the irascible French general was recording the figure in his diary, a brilliant young English officer wrote complacently:

> Things are going quite well for the French at Verdun and they are not the least bit anxious about it. . . . They have not yet used any of their reserves and they have the show well in hand. It is part of our policy to let the Germans beat themselves to death against the stone wall. . . . The Germans have lost enormously and they can't afford to.[3]

Regardless of how they were doing on the battlefield, in the imaginary war the French high command was creating to justify its decisions, Verdun would be turned into yet another disastrous German setback. One imagines that had the Germans gotten to the outskirts of Paris, the GQG would blandly dismiss the event as a few stragglers who had been rounded up by the police.

Meanwhile, in the real world, the German advance continued.

PÉTAIN TAKES COMMAND

Tall, trim, sarcastic, and condescending, Pétain had hardly endeared himself to the government or to the army high command before the war. When it began, he was only a colonel, was in the same boat as Driant, although the causes were different. In fact, it is far from clear why Pétain was never promoted further: the one biographer who has researched the matter thoroughly confesses he has no real idea.[4]

In his extensive teaching experiences, Pétain's emphasis on the importance of firepower certainly put him in the minority of theorists and lecturers. We know he tangled with the various politically correct minions of André during the attempts to purge the officer corps of everyone who was not properly Republican. There is a famous but doubtless apocryphal story that when he was asked to reveal the names of those of his officers who attended mass, he supposedly retorted that as he sat in the front row and never looked back, he had no idea.

The anecdote, whether true or not, accurately reflects both the chaos generated by the André regime, and, perhaps more to the point, Pétain's sarcastic wit. We know for a certainty that he told President Poincaré that of anyone, he must surely know that France was neither led nor governed.[5]

Or perhaps it was the bachelor's truly personal life, which was, almost uniquely among field-grade French officers, filled with escapades involving other men's wives. Whatever Pétain's professional problems were, women found him attractive. When, on the night of the twenty-fourth, he was routed out of bed, he was not by himself, although the identity of his female companion has never been revealed.

But by 1916, there were very few French officers who had proven themselves as competent at high command as Pétain. Moreover, he was a soldier's general. They liked him, if no one else did, the main reason being that he was distinctly unenthusiastic about ordering them to charge the enemy en masse and get butchered. He was dubious about the prospects of the various assaults demanded by the GQG, and enthusiastically embraced by Foch, and a British officer was impressed both by his emphasis on firepower and his sense of humor, although he added that it was "deeply concealed under his frozen exterior."[6]

Promptly at eight the next morning (the twenty-fifth), Pétain appeared at Joffre's headquarters. By his own account, Joffre had little in the way of advice. The situation was serious, but not alarming, he said; when Pétain got there, de Castelnau would fill him in. Given the situation, the few words speak volumes, and there is a slight hint of sarcastic humor in Pétain's characterization of Joffre's "long sentences," that despite being "a little agitated," he was able to preserve his customary calm.[7]

Given the roads, Pétain did not arrive at Souilly, where de Langle de Cary and de Castelnau were, until that evening. He promptly drove to Dugny, the headquarters of General Herr, there to learn of the loss of Douaumont. Unlike the GQG, he understood what a disaster this was.

Late that night (at eleven) Pétain formally took command, and notified both Balfourier (right bank) and Bazelaire (left bank) that he was now in command. One imagines that they were both relieved to find that someone finally was, given that the attack was now going into its fifth day.

The new commander promptly laid out a defensive line on both banks. His intention was to hold fast to those lines, and to do so, he could rely on three new army corps that were en route: the 21st, the 23rd, and the 33rd. With those, and with those units that were still intact and holding the battlefield, his forces would be more than equal to the Germans in terms of manpower.

The pressing need was organization, a word that the army had basically forgotten, if it had ever known it. Nothing was foreseen, and everything was improvised, hurriedly thrown together at the last minute, a technique that the soldiers referred to sarcastically as "plan D"—those who were still alive, anyway. Fortunately, there was time.

Now, simply by looking at the map, it was easy to see a developing German problem, insofar as further advances went. One of the stupidities of abandoning the forts was that it let the Germans move up their relatively short-range howitzers so they could cover the initial defense positions in considerable depth. But the German advance had now put the infantry out of range of all but the heaviest of their artillery. Paradoxically, the advance meant that the French guns on the left bank, located behind the ridge with the main forts, could now be brought to bear on the area around Douaumont.

So the German gunners now faced the difficult task of moving their barely portable weapons up into the heights themselves. This was not in the plan, which assumed that the French would either quit outright (the de Langle de Cary option) or they would come charging up the heights to retake what had been lost (the Ferdinand Foch approach). But Pétain refused to be drawn. Having seen firsthand the logistical problems of breakthrough offenses, he knew that there were unavoidable pauses. Troops had to be rotated; ammunition had to be replenished; guns had to be repositioned. Even though the Germans had bashed away for five, now going on six straight days, there was a limit that had been reached, was in the process of being reached.

Having studied the German defenses all through 1915, Pétain had grasped the idea of a defense in depth that was based on interlocking strongpoints, and that was what he proceeded to construct.

The main defensive line on both banks was created, a line that was to be held at all costs. It ran roughly from Avocourt to Hill 304, then to the ridged forest of Mort-Homme, jumped the river to Thiaumont, cut down to Fort Vaux, and hence to the downward slope of the heights of Meuse due east of the city of Verdun. The line was essentially based on the original fortifications, and these were rearmed and put in the first class. From the left bank going across the river, the positions were des Bruyères, Bourrus, Marre, Belle Epine, Vacherauville, Charny, Froidterre, Souville, Vaux, Tavannes, Moulainville, Lauffé, and Déramée.

Then there was a second position, anchored by Choisel, Belleville, Saint-Michel, Rozelier, and Belrupt. Those were known, colloquially, as the *forts du Panic*, as there would be a real panic if they attacked, given their position.

Behind that was a final position: Chana, Sartelles, La Chaume, Regret, Landrecourt, Dugny, Falouse, Haudainville, Saint-Symphorien, and Génicourt.

Each of the forts in the first and second groups was given a garrison and a commandant, integrated into the lines of defense.

Pétain then turned to the thorny matter of supplies. Belatedly, work began to effect a bypass for the main west–east line, still interdicted by the German position on the Vauquois. But that would take weeks and weeks to complete, so the army was totally dependent on the country road running up from Bar-le-Duc, and the narrow-gauge railway that ran alongside.

From his headquarters at Souilly, Pétain could see the work on the road being done so it would support the round-the-clock convoys into and out of Verdun, and the road gradually began to take more and more traffic, which peaked at 3,900 trucks every 24 hours.[8] Almost 200,000 French soldiers marched up that road, and Pétain stood on the sidewalk and watched them as they trudged past, so close that they could have reached out and touched him.

However, the single most important command decision was this. Pétain refused to be drawn. He took a page from the German defensive manual, established a good defensive position, and waited for his opponent to try to take it.

This was not at all what von Falkenhayn had envisioned. Pétain's resolve to hold fast was a calamity, as far as the Germans were concerned. Given how obligingly they had been trying to fight their way up hills and clambering across no-man's-land, it apparently had never occurred to anyone in Berlin or Stenay that this would change. So they were, temporarily, stymied.

Moreover, the crown prince, the commander of the Fifth Army, whatever his failings, whatever the realities of the complicated system of command in the German army, had imbibed one important lesson of generalship: the need to conserve the lives of your troops. Of course, for men like Foch and Haig, and certainly for their admirers, this was not at all in accord with the manly sport of war. But the sort of man who receives a letter from a woman that says,

"[O]f all the feminine hearts you have conquered, there is none (am I too bold?) which understood you more, which devoted more faithful admiration, fervent tenderness," clearly has no need to assert his masculinity in other ways, and certainly not with the false manhood of sending men to their deaths while hiding out in the rear.[9]

So the Germans were frustrated, and inevitably, they turned their attentions to the left bank, just as Pétain anticipated.

PANIC IN THE GOVERNMENT

Gallieni, the minister of war, was slowly dying, and he was quite aware of it. Unfortunately for France, the attack at Verdun seems to have coincided with that sense of detached remove, of viewing the world from a distance, that often occurs to those in the final stages of illness. His colleagues in the government misinterpreted it, complained about it, and his admirers were disturbed, because they assumed that the attack would result in Joffre being replaced, preferably by the aging marshal himself.

On the twenty-sixth, the cabinet spent a heated 90 minutes discussing Verdun. They grilled Pénelon, who was the liaison between the GQG and the government, who of course gave all the usual answers. At some point his repeated references to the "battle" irritated Gallieni, and he nailed the issue head-on. "Why speak of a battle; are there even any defenses? Why aren't there more troops there, given that you're opposed by seven army corps? Why change commanders at the last minute?"[10]

Judging from his notes, the implication seems to be, How can there be a battle when you don't have any defenses, very few men, and no commander? However, the dominant impression one gets from reading Gallieni's increasingly terse and gloomy notes is of a panic, but a panic without any direction or purpose, indicative of a government that has no idea what to do.

Despite Poincaré's animadversions in private about Joffre and the GQG, and the fury of the prime minister, the government really had no choice but to close ranks and support Joffre. Gallieni's jibe about changing commanders at the last minute had struck home. Besides, Gallieni was clearly not able to continue serving as minister of war, so the position would have to be filled. There was a widespread suspicion inside the government, particularly if we include the members of the chamber of deputies, that Briand was deeply supportive of Joffre, and sure enough, when Gallieni was forced to resign for reasons of ill health, he was replaced by Pierre Auguste Roques, a colonial solider, an engineer, and in consequence a friend of Joffre's.

While the cabinet was wrangling and the chamber was simmering, the German offensive, after a few days' respite, abruptly came to life, so events quickly left the government behind, as had been the case throughout the war.

Now, it is true that France had the misfortune to be in the hands of politicians of the lesser sort. Even the reputation of the best of them was based on what Robert Louis Stevenson once derisively referred to as resting on the more cultivated among the ignorant. But it is almost impossible to overestimate that ignorance. Poincaré offers a wonderful snapshot of how, in the face of impending disaster, the military responded.

A month after the fighting began, he assured the president that the Germans had already lost nearly a quarter of a million men, the French only 65,000; the figures the Germans were publishing for prisoners were completely false.[11] This charade continued, with the army giving ever more precise figures. Possibly the French had slightly over 100,000 casualties of all sorts, but the Germans had suffered nearly 300,000, the president was told in early April (*Service*, 8:187–88). Poincaré kept insisting. He wanted more precise figures. De Castelnau pulled a piece of paper out of his pocket. As of 25 April, 125,000 prisoners, 16,594 dead, 57,142 wounded, and 51,000 or 52,000 missing, figures that Poincaré greeted with incredulity, since they "did not agree with those given previously" (*Service*, 8:209). When pressed, de Castelnau admitted that it was not impossible that the Germans actually had taken the number of prisoners they were claiming.

A month later, the president was given an entirely new set of figures, broken down into categories that seemed expressly designed to confuse, since in order to derive the actual numbers, Poincaré would have to do sums on the fly, as it were. But it came down to 23,343 dead, 54,000 missing, and 74,844 wounded. But now Poincaré had been doing some fieldwork, as it were, and challenged the data. There had been a good 135,000 wounded and sick evacuated from Verdun, which was far higher than what the army was admitting (*Service*, 8:242–43).

But the contradiction was shrugged off. The government and the army had thus reached a standoff. No one really believed anything that the army's generals said, but they had no way to disprove it through data; the only man among them who had any real military expertise was missing, gravely ill (Gallieni); the only person who knew enough to do any analysis of the numbers was no longer in the government (Ferry); the only insider secure enough in his position to speak out had been killed early on in the fighting (Driant).

Moreover, to make matters worse, at moments of crisis, the generals tended to close ranks. Interestingly, in Poincaré's quest for the truth, he was foiled by three senior generals (Joffre, de Castelnau, and Pétain), none of whom much cared for one another. But their contempt and dislike for the successors of the men who had persecuted the officer corps during the André regime was a powerful institutional memory. For decades, the Republicans had hated and feared the army, only to be outraged that they were viewed with contempt.[12]

So the government drifted along, suspicious and impotent, too divided to exercise an authority it had long since lost any moral claim to possess and at bottom more concerned about its own welfare than the fate of the nation. As the unhappy Louis-Philippe, the last real king of France, observed toward the end of his reign: "All things are possible for France, but one thing is impossible, that any of those things should last."[13]

THE SITUATION ON THE LEFT BANK

Pétain's refusal to mount offensive operations against the newly held German positions on the right bank forced a change in plans. There were four reasons why the initial thrust had been aimed at the positions on the right bank. The existence of Douaumont, the way the heights sloped down to the river, the difficulties of reinforcing the forward position all made it the obvious choice. Perhaps most important, the angles formed by the French position lent themselves to exactly the sort of attacks that allowed the new infantry tactics to work. They could approach the sides of a section of trench, and work their way around.

By contrast, the positions on the left bank formed a reasonably straight line—straight enough that it would be difficult for these tactics to be employed. At some point, the infantry would have to make a direct frontal attack. However, the angle of the line was promising. The northernmost part was right on the Meuse, just opposite the village of Brabant. The French positions then continued at a slight southwesterly turn, with a bulge between the villages of Béthincourt and Malancourt.

The bulge was roughly five kilometers across and about three kilometers deep. Some four kilometers back from the initial positions was a more or less continuous ridge with two distinctive humps, although the dip between the bulges is wide enough to be thought of as almost a valley, or a pass. In 1916, that was where the village of Béthincourt was located—the operative word being the past tense of the verb. But, of course, by now there were a good many *villages détruits*, or destroyed villages, on this section of the front. The village of the Vauquois only had the honor of being the first.

The two bulges are not very high. The eastern one, closest to the river, is only 260 meters, while the western one is 294 meters.

To add further to the confusion of French place names, this 294-meter hill was designated as Côte 304, the result of a surveying error. That the infamous Hill 304 was not in reality 304 meters high is an excellent illustration of the general conflation of error, myth, and downright confusion that characterizes the battles for Verdun.

Speaking in purely military terms, the ten-meter error is not inconsequential, particularly when one realizes that the irregularly shaped ground that the hill rises out of is itself a good 280 meters above sea level. The Germans were not, therefore, attacking up a butte, as was the case for the French infantry at the Vauquois and Les Éparges; rather they were advancing up an irregular slope with an inclination about one meter or so for every 100.

The eastern hump was lozenge-shaped forest. The forest bore an ominous name: Mort Homme, "the forest of the dead man." Although by the start of the war the appellation was lost in the distant past, it would prove strangely prophetic. In 1916 it would live up to its name and then some.

From the Mort Homme, artillery spotters could see across the river and onto the reverse slope of the Côte du Talou. So as the German infantry carefully closed in on Pétain's defensive line, they became more aware of the danger posed by these positions.

The danger was very real. Two kilometers behind the ridge of the Mort Homme was another tree-covered ridge, known as the Bois Bourrus. It was on that ridge that the engineers had constructed the main forts of the left bank. The intention was that the observers in the forts could direct artillery fire down onto any troops advancing up the next ridge to the north. Although there were some guns housed in the forts, the real firepower lay behind the ridge, in the valley. Essentially the forts provided cover for the gunners behind them.

The orientation of the left-bank forts on the ridge of Bois Bourrus and their supporting guns was entirely to the north, but, directed by spotters on the Mort Homme, the gunners behind the ridge were able to pour fire onto the right bank.

The forts themselves, however, were actually the third defensive position. The second was anchored by Hill 304 and the Mort Homme, while the first, and most advanced, was based on the structures of the villages that lay in front of the ridge: Forges, Malancourt, the Raffécourt mill, and Béthincourt.

When Pétain had taken command, not much had been done to organize this defense in depth, and there was a limit to what could be accomplished in a week; nor did he have enough men. To defend the entire 15-kilometer stretch there were only two divisions, each reinforced by a brigade, with a third in reserve.

This structure, by the way, appears to be a drastic departure from how the GQG operated. By this point in the war, the German army was well along the road to a drastic simplification of the unit system. Initially, each division had artillery, cavalry, machine gunners, engineers, and infantry. We might therefore think of each infantry division as an army in miniature. Or, to look at it another way, that it was only at the divisional level that a combined-arms force existed.

As we have seen, the French not only had stuck with this organization, but maintained it even more so. French engineers were not organized into combat units, and French heavy artillery units were held back at the army group level (two levels up).

In 1915 the Germans began eliminating the brigade entirely. The division had three regiments, a reduction in the number of riflemen. But that was accompanied by a dramatic increase in firepower, as howitzers began to replace field guns, more machine guns were added, and the combat engineers were given more mortars and, now, flamethrowers.

What all this meant in practice was that increasingly the German regiment became more like a miniature division. The next step, already under way in 1916, was to turn the regiment into a purely administrative construct. Think for a moment of the battlefield as a board game, with the units represented by pieces. Initially, each piece represented a division. The direction the Germans were headed in would mean that each piece represented a battalion, with more and more of the battalions being divided not into the traditional company of riflemen, but into a combined-arms Abteilungen.

To say that the Allies simply failed to see this transformation is a gross understatement. Not only did they misinterpret what they saw, see it as a proof that the Germans were running out of manpower, but they failed to grasp its significance, never really understood that the key to success on the modern battlefield was autonomous units with fewer men and much more firepower, units whose commanders had been trained to act on their own, not wait for orders that might not ever arrive in the pre–wireless communication era.

Given the French losses in manpower, they had been forced to rely more and more on brigades, simply out of necessity. Their heavy losses were dragging the theoreticians, kicking and screaming, into the modern era. But it appears that just as Pétain, in his prewar lectures and his actual combat commands, had emphasized firepower, he grasped the need to move in the same direction. For the French army, however, with his emphasis on logistics and organization, the new commander at Verdun was not only atypical, he was positively heretical.

Still, his problem remained the same. He had too few men, hardly any modern guns, and neither men nor guns were being given sufficient supplies and ammunition. To a certain extent, the insane obsession with offensive actions of the sort that had characterized the army since 1914 had allowed them to shortchange all the vital logistical elements that are now taken for granted. French soldiers lacked proper medical care. They were not being given enough food, hardly ever saw a hot meal, and were not allowed proper rest. In a good many respects, the army treated its soldiers the same way Napoleon had, and largely left them to fend for themselves—the difference being that his soldiers had been able to live off the territories of their enemies.

There was a sad but simple reason why the system hadn't broken down by spring 1916: losses. The army had many fewer active-duty soldiers to supply.

These problems must be borne in mind to appreciate what happened on the left bank, just as the increasingly asymmetrical nature of the two sides makes us appreciate Pétain's accomplishments.

THE ASSAULT

Reluctantly, the crown prince agreed to the expanded German offensive, and so on 5 March, the artillery began firing, aiming chiefly at the batteries lying behind the forts. The defensive zone on the left bank was a much smaller area than on the right bank, so German gunners could concentrate their fire. They ignored the frontline positions, concentrated on the ridge and on the artillery behind it, grimly aware that unless those positions were neutralized, their infantry would be massacred.

The result was a barrage of much greater intensity than the one of 21 February. French observers described the two positions as being flattened. Hardly anything remained except craters. At ten in the morning on 6 March, the infantry launched the first assault. Their plan was painfully obvious: to start at the easternmost section of the first line and simply enfold it. So they attacked the area between Béthincourt and Forges, roughly five kilometers, using the same tactic of infiltration that they had used on the right bank.

In general, the end results over the next few days were the same as in February. That is, each day the German infantry surged forward, driving their opponents back, and simply erasing positions with accurate artillery fire. The bombardment on 7 March was even worse than the first one.

But there was a difference. This time in response to each attack, the French countered it with their own. They were, in other words, imitating the German system as best they could. In each case the position was eventually lost: Raffécourt and Béthincourt on the sixth; then the Corbeaux woods; then Cumières, which changed hands several times; then the Côte d'Oie. Finally, on 10 March, the French unit bearing the brunt of these attacks, having lost almost its entire complement of officers, retreated. The greater part of the first line had been lost.

By 14 March, the Germans launched the first of their assaults on the Morte Homme, as they now had the whole eastern end of the first line. But the attack was beaten off. Pétain was moving artillery up to replace what had been destroyed, was conducting an aggressive defense of exactly the same sort the Germans did. His troops were not as well armed, his artillery woefully inadequate, but he had grasped the principle, and it was working.

Two days later, another assault was repulsed, but the Germans kept on, each time adding more and more firepower, broadening the frontage, until finally, on 21 March, they succeeded, more or less. There certainly was no more possibility of artillery spotting from the ridge.

But the Germans had now been at Verdun for a month. This was not how matters were supposed to go. Pétain's refusal to be drawn into fruitless assaults, his emphasis on the same details that had distinguished his opponents, was paying dividends. Strategically, the Germans were in serious trouble. As we have seen, their plan had been predicated on one of two things happening. True, the French were losing the casualty exchange, but this was nothing new. The panic of February had vanished, and as von Falkenhayn knew, with the coming of April, spring was on the way, summer not far behind—a summer during which he could look forward to enemy offensives on every front and then some.

Tactically, however, the situation on the left bank was encouraging. The German attacks of 20 to 22 March simply eliminated the top of the bulge and collapsed the western side running from Avocourt to Malancourt. A new wave of attacks, beginning on 28 March, resulted in the loss of all the initial positions, including Malancourt, and the Germans were now on the western slopes of Hill 304. Gradually, they were collapsing the French line, forcing it back in on itself. An aging monument outside the ruins of

Malancourt gives an idea of the scale of the fighting: It commemo-rates the losses of the French 69th Infantry Division. Between 30 March and 5 April 1916, six companies of the division "completely disappeared" in the struggle to defend the sector from Lamcourt to Haucourt.

This was repeating the same step-by-step advance that had been so destructive to the French in the Argonne; no matter how hard they fought, they were unable to stop the advance. Once the Germans finally wrested a strongpoint, they held on to it—not nec-essarily the first time, but within a day or so, it became theirs.

In February 1915, General Sarrail had admitted to Colonel Herbillon that

> in the Argonne, the Germans have a superiority of morale. They conquer parcels of terrain where the gains or losses are of minimal importance, but those operations allow them to maintain an ascendancy of their morale.[14]

In the end, in the face of the French fall offensive in Cham-pagne and Artois, von Mudra had been forced to call off opera-tions. But here, on the left bank, the Germans simply seemed to keep on coming, regardless.

From Pétain's point of view, the fact that the attacks kept on coming was even more alarming than their modest success. He was convinced that the left bank was the real key to Verdun, and later argued in his account of the battle that if the Germans had at-tacked on both banks in February, the whole position would have been lost.

This argument, although it reflects a very narrow view, has a great deal of merit. The left-bank front was roughly 15 kilometers across. The Germans already were right on the southern edge of the Argonne forest to the west. Moreover, the left-bank position was vulnerable at the western end. The engineers had wanted to build a fort there, but had lacked the funds. As a result, the posi-tion could be turned, outflanked, and the German superiority in heavy artillery meant that they could isolate the forts and reduce them one by one.

Once across the ridge of Bois Borrus, there was no real way they could be stopped. They could roll down the left bank, turn Verdun into a pocket, and drive a wedge deep into France. While none of this had been in von Falkenhayn's plan, opportunistically it was too good to pass up. So on 4 April, two entire German divisions attacked the Mort Homme and got control of the top. It will be recalled that to defend the whole left bank, Pétain only had two divisions and three brigades, and his losses were, not surprisingly, heavy. He needed more men.

Although the German offensive on the left bank was the crucial event now, there had been violent attacks on the right bank as well, beginning just before the first German assault of 6 March. On 4 March there was an offensive directed against the remnants of the Twentieth Army Corps, whose soldiers had borne the brunt of the February attack.

Sensibly enough, given the way French artillery could reach the attacking Germans on the right bank, this new German assault was aimed squarely at the part of the front lying between Douaumont and Vaux, and by 8 March the fighting had intensified. The village of Vaux was attacked at least a dozen times, and the two French regiments defending the sector were almost completely destroyed: Between them they lost over 2,500 men in a few days of combat.

So Pétain simply did not have the men he needed to contain these simultaneous offensives. He had already told Poincaré that he would not hesitate to abandon the positions on the left bank if that was what it took to save his troops, to which the president replied that it would be a "parliamentary catastrophe," which he judged to be far worse than a national one, judging from the way he phrased it.[15] First and foremost a politician, he was more concerned about the collapse of the government than of the country.

It would be hard to find a better example illustrating von Falkenhayn's naïveté than this one. When push came to shove, the cabinet and the president were just as willing as Joffre and the

GQG to fight to the last Frenchmen. Neither group appreciated Pétain's position, in either sense of the word.

It was at about this time that he sent Joffre a telegram saying that without more men, he would be obliged to retreat from the left-bank positions. He had no intention of retreating, but he was certainly blackmailing the GQG into sending him more troops.

As March passed, the fighting continued. On 4 April, nearly a month after the first attacks on the left bank, the Germans launched yet another round. The 12th and 22nd reserve divisions cleared the whole of the forest of the Mort Homme. At the same time, the Germans began a series of attacks that, by 9 April, had gained them the crest of Hill 304.

But the French were still hanging on, and that led to the subsequently famous order of the day, with its slogan, *On les aura!*—the implication being that the attacks had failed and the defense had triumphed. Pétain had hesitated to sign this order, remarking to Serrigny that the phrase was not correct French, but then relented.

Unfortunately, like many catchphrases, this one covered up the reality. The Germans now had long since passed over the first line, and were now firmly in command of the second. They had eliminated the menace of the spotters, which was one of the main reasons for the assault.

The hope, which was in accordance with standard army doctrine, was that now that they had seized the position, the French would try to take it back, which was, it will be remembered, the whole point of the offensive in the first place. So there was no need to go any further, especially since they commanded the ground between the ridge of Hill 304 and the Mort Homme as well as the ridge of Bois Bourrus, where the forts were.

So declaring that the defense had prevailed was simply more of the same sleight of hand that had been employed all through the war. But in modern warfare, if you had the proper heavy artillery, once you seized the crest of a ridge, there was no need to fight your way across a valley.

Whether they knew it or not, both the Fifth Army staff and the

German high command had guessed correctly. In one of those marvelous coincidences that no novelist would dare to put into his story, on the very day that the left-bank fighting reached its desperate crescendo, 9 April, Pétain received a peremptory telegram from Joffre, urging him to reestablish the situation with "a vigorous and powerful offensive to be executed with only the briefest delay."[16] Given the situation during the first week of April, the timing of the telegram was grimly amusing. Far from being able to go over to the offensive, French troops were hardly able to contain the steady advances of their opponents.

But this lunacy was consistent with how the GQG felt war should be waged: full speed ahead and damn the machine guns; forget about losses; charge up that hill and wrest it from the enemy at the point of a bayonet. War à la Ferdinand Foch, in other words.

Now, to be fair to Joffre, just before that telegram, he had gone a round with the prime minister. Briand was a career politician; he understood the mood of the chamber. It was beginning to dawn on them that what was really happening was not at all what the army claimed was happening. In February 1915 the GQG had boasted that the Germans were running out of men, and would soon have to quit the war. Here it was, a year later, and not only were the Germans still fighting, but they had so many men that they could afford to lose 400,000 of them in one battle.

There was clearly something wrong somewhere. But now, when pressed, Joffre simply blandly dismissed the whole thing. Verdun was a minor military objective. If need be, they could simply abandon it. Briand went ballistic. If Verdun fell, the government would fall; everyone except the GQG would realize it was a defeat. Implicit in the explosion was a threat: If Briand went, he would take Joffre with him. Stung, Joffre comforted himself with a good meal and a telegram ordering Pétain to put together an attack.

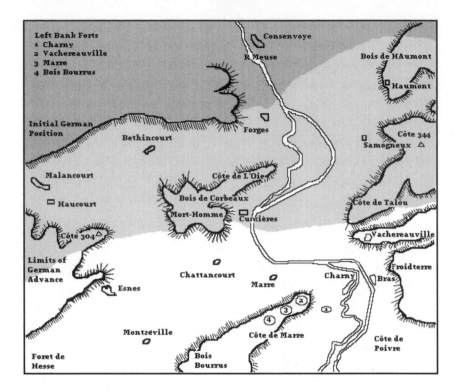

Left Bank Forts
1 Charny
2 Vachereauville
3 Marre
4 Bois Bourrus

THE DESPERATION BEGINS

By mid-April, the French were exhausted. But the Germans were beginning to have second thoughts. Although their casualties throughout the offensive were significantly lower than the French, their generals were more inclined to worry about heavy losses than anyone in Paris. The crown prince was particularly disturbed. His army had sustained more than 50,000 casualties (including wound cases) in a fight that the plan had never envisioned.

The disadvantage of a decentralized system of command was that local commanders understandably tended to make judgments on the basis of the situation directly in front of them. From their point of view, the steady string of advances, and the relatively low casualties incurred, suggested they were on the verge of a break-through. Generally speaking, in the French army, the pushback of unit commanders was essentially passive-aggressive: That is, they dragged their feet in an effort to keep all of their men from being killed. As Norton Cru remarks, "If orders had been obeyed to the letter, the entire army would have been massacred by August 1915."[17]

On the German side, the pushback was more positive: local commanders, scenting victory, and having been trained to be aggressive, naturally wanted to continue. There is sometimes the suggestion in attempts to construct a narrative of the fighting for Verdun that the battle simply spun out of control. Not so; in the earlier battles the French kept on attacking because of the obsessions of the GQG, which saw failure as a want of the proper aggressive spirit. Their opposite numbers kept on attacking because they were encouraged by their successes.

On both banks, the obscurity and confusion of geography tends to obscure the fact that the Germans were steadily advancing. Nor were these advances secured at some horrifying cost. The entire German army on the Western Front only had 17,355 soldiers killed or missing in March, a monthly total that was nowhere near being the worst month for the army.[18]

Moreover, there were signs that the French were beginning to crack. As we noted above, the French position on the left bank was highly defensible (by comparison with others, anyway). But in the initial thrust around Avocourt (20 March), a curious event took place. When the Bavarians attacked, the units of the French 29th Division holding this section of the line simply surrendered.

After the war, an army court established that they had surrendered without a shot being fired. In the rigid world of such affairs, no allowance is made for motivation: surrender is surrender. So no one knows the actual cause. But the act speaks for itself. There has long been a story (or legend) that the French soldiers trudging up the country road toward battle would bleat like sheep. Whether true or not, the collapse and abrupt surrender of the men of the 29th Division suggests that the army was reaching its breaking point.[19]

But if the local commanders were encouraged, the crown prince was still dismayed, and although von Falkenhayn never revealed his thoughts about the actual battles for Verdun, he certainly could not think that his plan was achieving its goal of getting France to quit the war. We can divine both the drift of his thoughts and the difficulties he was having by a simple accounting. At the end of February, when the offensive seemed unstoppable, three additional divisions were moved to the west. All three were from the Balkans. In March, one unit was pried away from von Hindenburg, and a fourth unit came from the Balkans. A second division was transferred from the Russian front in April, and a fifth from the Balkans in May.

But the total number of divisions remained the same: 172. The only way more troops could be brought to Verdun was to take them from somewhere else. By the end of May, having transferred all the troops that were available from the Balkans, von Falkenhayn was stalled. The easterners, who viewed the whole idea of Verdun with suspicion, hemmed and hawed, claimed they had no men to spare. When the offensives on the left bank temporarily came to a halt in April, therefore, von Falkenhayn was reduced to the hope that finally the French would start behaving the way his plan called for them to behave: that is, either quit entirely or go over to the offensive.

As we have seen, they came very close to the former. Indeed, the Nachrichtendienst, the army's intelligence service, may have gotten wind of how the idea was being debated. If so, the Germans were now in for a pleasant surprise, as von Falkenhayn's wishes now more or less came true.

Joffre was just as political as Poincaré, only more so. That was how he had managed to land the job. It certainly was not because of seniority or a distinguished career. But his position was precarious. Deep in his heart, he really believed that a vigorous offensive action was the answer, no matter what the question was.

He was already under fire for the constant replacement of officers. If it hadn't been for this madcap scheme in the Balkans, he would still be stuck with Sarrail—and the chamber would be pushing him forward as a replacement. But Pétain was an obstacle. You could hardly sack the man who everyone felt had saved the day at Verdun. Besides, the present government would never agree to him as commander in chief, especially not Poincaré, after the general's sarcastic barbs. So in that sense, Pétain was a good man to have around. Competent enough, but inclined to defeatism. What was required at Verdun was someone who'd get out there and attack!

Politicians craft political decisions, and Joffre now crafted an elegant one: He promoted Pétain. He would now be commander of the Central Group of Armies, namely, the Second Third, Fourth, and Fifth. This was a major step up, and de Castelnau, who had been tasked with belling the cat, observed that given the scope of the command, the GQG would run Second Army, responsible for Verdun directly.

That allowed Joffre to replace Pétain with someone directly in charge of the battlefield, a younger officer who had more dash, more offensive spirit. There was also a military reason. Despite the huge drain on his resources, Joffre was determined to launch the great joint offensive, now scheduled for July, that would end the war. So what was required at Verdun was some vigorous offensive action to rattle the Germans, send them reeling, push them back, and make them go on the defensive.

Pétain was hardly fooled. He knew exactly what would happen, and he was right. His replacement at Second Army, Robert Nivelle, was as convinced of his brilliance as he was committed to the doctrine of the all-out attack. The difference between Nivelle and Foch, other than several dozen points on the intelligence scale, was that Nivelle really did understand the importance of firepower, realized that howitzers were preferable to bayonets.

The difficulty was that the theory was all very well and good, but the French army still lacked the firepower required. Like many theoreticians, Nivelle failed to bridge the gap between theory and practice. Undaunted by mere technicalities, Nivelle proceeded to oblige the Germans by launching an assault on Douaumont.

Late in April, Charles Mangin, the general commanding the 5th Division, had suggested a plan to recapture the fort. It will be remembered that it had been taken by a few junior officers and part of an infantry company. Mangin estimated it would take four divisions, with proper artillery support.

The idea was so preposterous that its details are universally passed over in near silence. The structure of the fort was still completely intact; the Germans held the areas around it, had established their positions there, and owned all the ground behind. Presumably, judging from his later actions, Nivelle believed that if he brought enough firepower to bear on the area, the infantry could secure it. So the infantry force was cut in half.

As best can be figured out from what actually happened, Nivelle and Mangin believed that their guns would simply punch holes in the fort, allowing the infantry to break in and overpower the dazed defenders. After all, this was the French impression of what had happened to the Belgians in 1914, what the army press releases said had happened to Douaumont in February. After an artillery bombardment there had been a direct assault that had carried the fort.

If either general had studied the aerial photographs closely, or had talked to an engineer, he would have realized that the idea was physically impossible. Moreover, the terrain surrounding, although relatively unscathed in February, was now, owing to the fighting there in March, the worst sort of cratered ground over which to mount an assault. Moreover, the only way to get to it was to attack it head-on, so the infantry would be exposed to fire from three sides.

Nevertheless, on 22 May, troops from the 5th and 36th divisions stormed the fort, after what observing officers felt was the most well-coordinated artillery barrage they had yet managed. The French had temporarily blinded the German gunners by shooting down six of their observation balloons. As a result, the advancing infantry were on top of the fort in eleven minutes.

But what then? The carapace was now almost completely bare, nothing but blasted concrete with steel cupolas and turrets, hardly a good place to be in the middle of a battle. Brandeis and Haupt had found a way in by carefully going around the dry moat, which in February was still intact. There was no comparable entrance from the top; nor did the French possess a gun that would effect one (neither did the Germans, for that matter).

This approach was like that of a man trying to dig his way through a steel plate with a plastic fork. It was doomed to failure from the outset. The soldiers who reached the top were stranded, killed off one by one. By the evening of the next day, the attacking force had either been killed or had surrendered.

Incredibly, after nearly two years, there were still French generals who believed that the solution to a failed attack in which everyone got killed was another attack. Charles Mangin's colleagues had a very low opinion of him, as did many junior officers. One of them famously quipped that he was only fit to lead an army of monkeys.[20] However, in this case another attack was too much even for Mangin. He flat-out refused to launch another attack. But then, he had nothing left with which to attack. His division was now essentially destroyed: in a few days' fighting with what Joffre and the GQG believed to be the proper offensive spirit, it had lost 130 officers and 5,507 men, or about half its strength.[21]

Mangin's losses had shaken Nivelle sufficiently that he reversed course. Besides, it was now the end of May, and Joffre was beginning to assemble his forces for the Somme. So the French went back to the defense, frustrating von Falkenhayn's plan. The window was closing rapidly.

CALAMITIES ALL AROUND

On June 4, the Russian general Alexei Brusilov began his grand offensive in Galicia. Initially, this offensive seemed destined to bring the war in the east to an end. The Russians penetrated deep into the Habsburg empire, and there was panic in Vienna, alarm in Berlin.

Conveniently for the easterners, that now gave them the perfect excuse. The imaginary conveyor belt that moved troops from one front to the other now had to be thrown into reverse. Four divisions were sent to the Russian front, and the loss was partly made good by sending two units in the interior of Germany to the west.

June thus saw a curious paradox. On the one hand, the fate of the Brusilov offensive suggested, perhaps even proved, that von Falkenhayn was correct. Despite enormous territorial gains, despite the panic it generated, it did not bring the war in the east to a conclusion. On the contrary, the easterners rallied, the advance stalled out, and the war went on. In retrospect, the Brusilov offensive was the death rattle of the Russian army. It was also confirmation of von Falkenhayn's observation that the principle was flawed, something the Allies were shortly going to find out the hard way, on the Somme.

On the other hand, however, events meant that the Germans had to change plans. Hence the paradox: they now went over to the offensive at Verdun once more, trying to bring the battle to an end before the July offensive began.

Of course, strictly speaking, the German attacks on the right bank had never actually stopped. But these operations were more in the nature of consolidations, were of an entirely different sort from the initial assault on the right bank and the subsequent one on the left.

At the beginning of March the Germans had been about 3,000 meters from Fort Vaux, and 4,000 from Fort Souville. Their eventual aim was to envelop the northeastern quadrant of the forts by exploiting a sort of fissure that existed, marked by the railroad line that ran from Verdun toward Étain and thence on to Metz. The rail line marks a drop-off in the heights. If the Germans could exploit an opening there, they would be in a good position to isolate the forts that controlled the area, notably Vauz and Tavannes. Then they could drive straight to the river.

The climax of this effort, however, only took place in June. By the end of May the Germans were close enough to mount an attack of Fort Vaux, and on 2 June, after a heavy bombardment, they attacked the fort directly. Unlike in the French assault on Douaumont, the Germans were well equipped, but in six days of what were basically combat mining operations, they were unable to break into the fort.

Commandant Raynal, the irascible commander of the fort's garrison (500 men plus about 100 stragglers) was ultimately defeated, mainly because he was out of water. On 8 June 1916, with no reinforcements—and no water—he surrendered.

Thus encouraged, the Germans began working to create a large wedge-shaped opening that encompassed the area stretching from Vaux all the way up to the rubble that marked where the hamlet of Fleury had once stood.

In the first week of June, as the situation around and inside Fort Vaux worsened, General Nivelle ordered an attack to rescue the fort. Four companies of infantry, who for some reason were specially equipped with scaling ladders, were to conduct the attack, which went in on 6 June. But the same conditions prevailed around Vaux as at Douaumont. When the attacking troops were slaughtered, Nivelle proposed a second attack, in which a brigade would be pulled from the left bank, trucked across the river, and then thrown immediately into action.

Although the loss of Vaux and the surrounding territory hardly changed the overall situation, it considerably heartened the local German commanders, who took their success there as an indication that one or two more vigorous assaults would win the day. That phrase is trite, but it expresses the idea perfectly.

So on 21 June, the Germans attacked once more, opening up the wedge still further. The artillery barrage there now took a horrifying turn. German gunners began firing gas shells, and in the face of this new and disturbing weapon, the French were thrown back. After ten days, regardless of how hard they fought, the French had lost another sizable piece of Verdun: the *ouvrage* of Thiaumont, what remained of the ruins of the village of Fleury, and all of the Vaux-Chapitre woods.

So on the right bank, the French were now hanging on to the

edge of the heights of the Meuse, were reduced to what was basically the last defensive line, comprised by the oldest and most vulnerable forts. Thanks to the Nivelle-Mangin assaults, the French were also woefully short of men.

Helpless, removed from immediate command, Pétain was grimly pessimistic. He had good reason to be. Since the start of the battle, every German offensive operation had ultimately succeeded. Each one chewed off a slice of the defensive positions, using the same approach that von Mudra had pioneered in the Argonne—not surprisingly, since he had been brought over to direct operations on the right bank.

Insofar as von Falkenhayn's plan went, these conquests were beside the point. However, that was not the case of the battlefield itself. The German commanders were optimistic, their opposite numbers depressed. So was Pétain. It would do Joffre little good to break through on the Somme if at the same time the Germans surged out of the right bank. It would be like the revolving door of August 1914 in reverse.

So the final assault, on 11 July, was a moment of desperation on both sides. Mangin—by now promoted to command of an army corps—simply ordered counterattacks with no apparent concern for losses or results. On 15 July, he ordered the 37th Division to retake Fleury, which was now held by the Alpenkorps, who had consolidated German control of the area the week before.

Mangin's attack was such a disaster that on the eighteenth, Pétain, as commander of the center group of armies, and thus technically still in charge of Verdun, stepped in and stopped all further attacks except in cases where he was assured the preparations had been adequate.

The July fighting degenerated into a confused melee of mutual attacks, and when it was over, thirteen days later, both sides exhausted, nothing much had been accomplished.

The most famous battle for Verdun was at an end—not so much with a bang, but with a gasp. The word *ironically* is greatly overused. But in this case it is hard to avoid. Of all the battles fought at Verdun, this one, despite being the most famous, ironically achieved the least.

Curiously, then, the great plans of both commanders in chief collapsed at almost the same time. By the third week in July even the perennially optimistic Joffre had to admit that the great offensive on the Somme had failed. There was no breakthrough. Nor was there likely to be. Fayolle, the army's point man for the French attacks there, promptly wound the offensive down. Haig soldiered on, his main achievement being to get still more of his men killed, and to ruin the advent of the tank as a surprise weapon.

The Allies secured some territory, a good deal more than they had managed in their earlier offensives in Champagne. But their losses were horrific. By contrast, total German losses in dead and missing for July—a month that encompassed both the last gasp of the Verdun offensive and the brunt of the Somme—came to 58,960 (*Sanitätsbericht*, 3:150). By comparison with their opponents, the Germans won this casualty exchange as well, but they were dismayed: July was the second-worst month of the war in terms of losses.

It is vaguely possible that had the final German assaults on the right broken through completely, that event, taken in conjunction with the collapse of the two Allied offensives in the east and west, might have achieved something close to what von Falkenhayn had envisioned. But the operative phrase here is the qualifier after the verb. It is vaguely possible, which is to say not very likely.

10

Revanche and Revision:
October 1916–August 1917

What all this comes down to is that the enemy's
losses on all fronts are not appreciably greater than
our losses on our one front.

—André Maginot[1]

So the most famous of the Verdun battles—in the minds of most
people the only battle—ended in a curiously anticlimactic way.
The attention of everyone, from peasants to historians, was diverted to the horrific spectacle of the Somme, which began on 1
July 1916, and whose losses, both the real losses of the Franco-
British forces and the imagined losses of the Germans, rapidly
eclipsed the bloody spring of 1916.

Nor was the Somme the only great event. June began with the
death rattle of the Russian armies in their great offensive in Galicia, and this success was in turn dwarfed by the Somme, which in
turn was partially eclipsed by Romania's entry into the war.

In each case the governments trumpeted the event as a great
triumph that heralded the impending doom of the Central Powers.
At Verdun the Germans had been worsted. Their nefarious scheme

to bleed France white had backfired. The Austrians were on the verge of collapse in the east. Finally the Russian alliance was bearing fruit. The Somme offensive would smash the Germans into the ground. Romania's entry into the war would collapse the Balkans, fatally weaken the Germans, who were already on the ropes, owing to their catastrophic losses at Verdun and the Somme.

This was the narrative: like the French army's complacent assessment of the casualty exchange at Verdun, and its insignificance as a military objective, no amount of contrary fact could dislodge it. Denial is not simply a river in Egypt. Moreover, by September 1916, the war had clearly entered exactly that phase predicted by von Falkenhayn: three powerful offensives in a row, the entry into the war of an entirely new ally, and except for the loss of a few bits of ground here and there, nothing much had changed.

Von Falkenhayn's plan represented a new way to look at the concept of battle. Perhaps not totally new, but then nothing is. However, in the context of the emphasis on decisive battles of annihilation, of great breakthroughs that would destroy your enemy, of a sort of pseudoscientific idea of warfare, it was a major departure, an early attempt to square the circle, taking into account the enormous potential of the major powers. The former German commander in chief had attempted the same end that would motivate the strategic airpower theorists postwar. They were enormously more successful, although their theories hardly worked much better than his.

At the end of the summer, von Falkenhayn resigned, was forced out, the Germans having the curious and novel notion that when something failed, the man responsible should be held responsible. Joffre followed him in the late fall, finally forced out as the government belatedly began to realize the extent to which the army high command had deceived them.

When von Falkenhayn went, his ideas went with him. Most German generals shared the view of their opponents that set-piece battles that destroyed your opponent represented the end-all and be-all of warfare.

In that sense, von Hindenburg, who now replaced von Falken-hayn, was no different from Joffre, right down to a curious similar-ity in their appearance. Both men had clearly spent a good deal of time enjoying their meals. The only real difference between them was that von Hindenburg was better at it. Joffre's great offensives never worked, no matter what yardstick was used. By contrast, under von Hindenburg, the Germans and their Austrian ally won precisely the sort of battlefield victories everyone was aiming to achieve.

Of course, this last is routinely denied by Allied apologists to this day, but anyone who looks at the front lines before and after the German attacks can see the thing clearly enough. As Tolstoy has one of his fictional characters observe after the Austro-Russian defeat at Austerlitz, "We civilians, as you know, have a very bad way of deciding whether a battle was won or lost. Those who re-treat after a battle have lost it is what we say."[2] Although not in-variably true, it is true enough. And since von Hindenburg went on after the war to win election for the presidency of the new republic, he was much better at politics as well.

That does not however alter the fact that the basic idea was wrong, and that von Falkenhayn was right. Not surprisingly, ev-eryone was delighted to distort his ideas and consign him to the memory hole. Even Kaiser Wilhelm, who in nearly 300 pages of memoirs manages to avoid once mentioning his name.[3]

But now, with the German chief in disgrace, sent to languish on the Romanian front (where he promptly destroyed the Romanian army and occupied 90 percent of the country), everyone could go back to their old ways, carefully readjusting reality to fit the narra-tive, and in a way to escape all censure. In London, the shock of catastrophic losses was only beginning to sink in. But in France the peasants—that is to say, the chamber of deputies—were collecting tar and feathers and ordering up the pitchforks. Something had to be done.

REVISIONS: (1) FUDGING THE FIGURES

As we have seen, all through the war, the army had issued wildly inflated estimates of German losses, and had been remarkably reticent about its own. When Poincaré started prying out the figures, he was actually accomplishing a good deal. At Verdun, the immediate reaction of the GQG was to do more of the same. On the one hand they denied the importance of what was lost, and on the other, they wildly inflated German losses.

And as the final weeks of fighting at Verdun were submerged in the horrors of the Somme, the situation became so confused that constructing an alternative view was tolerably easy. Since when the Germans finally called off their offensive, in mid-July, they had not broken through the last French defensive line, had not taken the city itself (which, of course, was irrelevant to both sides), it was easy to spin the battle into a great defensive victory for the French.

Since the Germans were the ones attacking, and since the conventional wisdom was that the attackers always took more casualties, the next step was likewise simple. That, taken together with all the understandable confusion about what Verdun actually was, allowed the Allies considerable leeway. Conceptually, they converted the 150-plus-kilometer stretch of the front, almost a fifth of it, into a small town on the Meuse. It was an excellent public relations and marketing concept.

The difficulty in all this was that it required people to now believe the opposite of what they been told, a sort of early counterpart of the manipulations Orwell portrayed in *1984*. During most of the war up until Verdun, the French had claimed that they were mounting successful offensives, not only gaining ground, but killing lots and lots of Germans. So the first Allied meme had linked offensive actions with small gains to heavy losses on the part of the defenders. But now, during Verdun, this was all reversed. The army went back to the meme of August 1914: The Germans were sustaining horrible losses precisely because they were attacking, but without getting anything in return.

As we noted earlier, in mid-March, General Fayolle was under the impression the Germans had lost 400,000 men. He wasn't the only one who was being deceived in this fashion. The analysis from the *New York Times* is remarkable.

> The Germans once more used the massed formation, hurling forward whole divisions of men at a time and having them slaughtered in thousands. In the valleys between the hills and other points of vantage, for the possession of which hundreds of thousands of lives were sacrificed, the dead could be seen lying in heaps literally as thick as flies.[4]

So the 400,000 figure was easy enough to believe. The army realized, of course, that given its previous predictions that the Germans were running out of men, someone might wonder how they could manage to sacrifice hundreds of thousands more. Like any good writer, the government propagandists had a reasonable answer.

> Two questions at once arise as to this effort. The first is why it was made at such a time, and second, once it had been decided to make it, why was Verdun, the strongest point in the whole French line, chosen as the point of attack? . . . Germany's manpower is dwindling. There can be no question of that. The available number is much less than that of the allies, and unless Germany can inflict losses on her enemies out of all proportion to those which she herself sustains in the process, sooner or later she will be worn out. This is merely a matter of arithmetic (*Times*, 45).

Why indeed, and what to believe?

Now, to any educated man or woman, the answer was quite simple—to André Maginot and Abel Ferry in 1916, Winston Churchill ten years later: look at the casualty figures, and compare the totals.

An idea simple to articulate, but almost impossible to calculate.

It is relatively easy to compare the grand totals for the entire war. Indeed, when in June 1916, Maginot went through the computations before the astonished and incredulous chamber, that is exactly what he did. Let us assume, he argued, that our army is telling us the truth about our losses, and the German army is doing the same to our opposite numbers. Voilà! Here are the figures. It had been announced in Germany that as of 29 February 1916, German losses in killed amounted to only 667,833, with another 357,835 missing and 1,658,457 wound cases. But, Maginot pointed out, on 31 March 1916, the deputies had been told that as of that date the French had suffered 625,323 known dead, and the army had admitted that the figure was actually probably 760,000. So even if we assume that all the German missing are dead, and that the army's figure includes all our missing presumed dead, then it is obvious that our losses are nearly the same as theirs.[5]

But, Maginot went on to say, the situation is actually much worse than you think, because the German figures are for all the fronts their army is fighting on. Our losses are only for the Western Front.

Pandemonium ensued, since for years the army had claimed that German losses exceeded French losses by some ordinal factor, i.e., three or four to one. At Verdun the army had repeatedly said that the Germans were losing men at the rate of three to one. As noted earlier, that was pretty much the exchange ratio throughout the war, the only problem being that it was the other way around.

But it was some time before Maginot's figures were proofed, even on the French side. Later on in the year, Ferry went through a more elaborate series of calculations, trying to explain to the government (he was now back in) why the army's calculations that the Germans were weakening and so one more attack would do the trick.

However, that did not necessarily deflate the army's claims about the losses at Verdun. That was far beyond the capacities of anyone while the war was going on, particularly given the fact that in 1916, 180 different French divisions had fought there (the French rotated whole units in and out of the line; the Germans simply replaced the losses).

Nevertheless, several analysts made the attempt. Louis Gillet weighed in early, with an estimate of German losses that he had derived from their official lists. His accounting was precise, in that it gave a time period (the end of 1916): 68,500 dead, 8,500 prisoners, 226,500 wounded, 23,000 missing, and 2,000 who died of illness; the total comes to 328,500.[6]

Now, the interesting thing about this figure is that it is not far off from what is now recorded at the German military cemeteries as posted by the *Volksbund Deutsche Kriesgräbenfürsorge*. Here are the figures recorded at the military cemetery at Mangiennes, north of Verdun: 41,600 died in combat, 13,165 died of wounds, and 26,739 missing, for a total of 81,504. These totals are very close to the data compiled by the German medical services after the war. For the period February through June, they list deaths for the entire Western Front as 72,237.[7]

That eliminates the wounds cases, which, as we have seen, is mandatory. Nor does it specify whether the missing are the missing or presumed dead, or does that total includes prisoners (presumably it does). However, making allowances for that, the current figure of 26,739 missing is surprisingly close to Gillet's derivation of 23,000. Given the difficulties of such computations, the figure of 54,775 is reasonably close to 68,500, and it's possible that in some way Gillet managed to double-count, added the missing to the total of those killed in action. This is a common computational error, the numerate parallel to the innumerate one of lumping everything together and then claiming the grand total represents deaths.

The French were understandably curious about the matter themselves, and in 1919, a commission of the chamber established that 263,000 French soldiers had died or gone missing.[8] This figure is unsatisfactory in various ways, as it appears to lump the various categories of the missing together. Probably the real figure—that is, for the dead alone in the various categories (including those missing presumed dead)—is the one extracted from the report by Huber, who puts it at 179,000 for the period of 1 February to 1 July.[9]

Figures thrown into the discussion by historians long after the fact, particularly when they are not accompanied by the necessary stipulations, have no particular value, regardless of their source. And as we shall see in our concluding chapter, serious attempts were made after the war to inflate the death tolls at Verdun into the stratosphere.

So, accepting for the moment that these earlier analysts have it about right, then the casualty exchange rate works out to somewhere between three and four to one. Depending on which way one looks at that ratio, it either suggests that insofar as von Falkenhayn aimed to "bleed France white," he did an excellent job, or, alternatively, that Verdun was just more of the same: all through the war the Germans won the casualty exchange. Not that it mattered in the long run.

REVISIONS: (2) HIDING THE OBVIOUS

Unlike the English, the French admitted early on that the Germans were formidable adversaries, although to a certain extent they did so in order to rationalize their own defeats and checks. But then, the idea that the German army was, by comparison with everyone else, an efficient and effective killing machine is obvious to most people.

However, at Verdun, most of the real German successes were the result of French bungling, and had little to do with efficiency, leadership (except in the sense that there wasn't any at first), or even superior firepower.

Chronologically, the first of these stupidities was General Order 18, which signaled an evacuation of the Woëvre. As noticed earlier, the order was actually transmitted before being countermanded, and the key individual in charge then stuck to the original order. As a result, the Woëvre plain was simply abandoned. So the largest single piece of ground the Germans gained in the fighting, they gained as a result of what we might call an unforced error on the part of the French. All the opposing Germans had to do was walk in and take over.

The fall of Douaumont was the result partly of a muddle—the troops sent to the position mistook the village for the fort—but it was primarily caused by the absurd decision to abandon the forts the GQG made in August 1915. It is all very well to justify this decision by pointing to what happened to other forts in Belgium and on the frontier. But given how many of these structures there were, finding one that supports the idea at hand is just another form of cherry-picking.

Both these decisions can ultimately be traced back to the incompetence of Joffre's staff, and the way he passively let such decisions be made. Pétain and Fayolle had it about right, Pétain when he observed that nothing is more dangerous in war than theoreticians, and Fayolle when he wrote, "cretins!" in his diary.

Despite initial attempts to downplay its loss, everyone knew that Douaumont was important. A desperate Joffre tried to get it back in May, and the reconquest of the fort—and Nivelle's recapturing it in late October of 1916—probably propelled him directly into his brief tenure as French commander in chief, about which more below.

Then comes the real bungling. Reynal had to surrender Fort Vaux because someone had forgotten to keep his water supply topped up. Otherwise, he would have held out indefinitely. Nor were the Germans inclined to go in and get him. So a minor failure handed the Germans a second triumph, and at an extremely inopportune moment.

The worst of these disasters occurred during the fall interim period. On 4 September, there was a terrible accident in the Tavannes rail tunnel. Since the rail line going toward Étain was unusable, had no purpose at all, thanks to the evacuation of the Woëvre, the tunnel was used as a combination aid station and shelter, with electricity being supplied by gasoline engines.

So the tunnel was a mixture of men, explosives, and gasoline.

The wires carrying the electricity weren't insulated. The Tavannes tunnel was a disaster waiting to happen, and when it did, somewhere between 500 and 600 men died.

Now, accidents certainly happen. On May 8, there was a horrific explosion inside Fort Douaumont: The remains of the 679 German soldiers who died in the explosion are still buried there. But the Tavannes tunnel was not simply an unfortunate accident of the sort that sometimes happen; it was negligence and carelessness, pure and simple.

While this incident is hardly in the same category as the others, it suggests a lack of order in the French army. The Germans were routinely castigated for their ferocious discipline, obsession with detail, and overzealous punctiliousness about minutiae. More sober observers spoke of the Germans as being "well organized."[10] In a well-organized and properly run army, events like the Tavannes tunnel fire don't happen. That they were happening in September 1916 is not a good sign. Or, to put it another way, the May explosion is duly noted. The tunnel is not.

REVANCHE: THE NIVELLE OFFENSIVE

With their final failures of July, as far as Stenay was concerned, the battle was over. Nivelle made sporadic attempts to persuade them to fight, but his Second Army was almost completely out of artillery. It had only 185 75-millimeter guns for its theoretical complement of 170 batteries, and one of its best divisions, the 3rd Colonial Infantry, had only 15 working guns.[11] The manpower situation was equally dire, so although Nivelle did his best to spar with the equally exhausted Germans, making sure that there were no further assaults, the battle was basically over.

However, once the GQG realized that the Somme offensive was simply a repeat of their earlier offensives in Artois, that too trailed off, and high command began to regroup. By now it was obvious to everyone that Joffre was on the way out, but one last offensive was ordered up. So an attack on the right-bank positions was planned for the end of October 1916.

Nivelle, prodded by Pétain, now was able to assemble the bulk of the army's heavy weapons. There was the usual sleight of hand with the number available, but a third of Nivelle's 300 heavy guns were modern, so the French were, relative to their earlier situation, in good shape.

The Germans, by contrast, were considerably weaker. All of their relatively sparse reserves had been sent to the Somme in July, and when Romania entered the war at the end of August, six divisions had to be sent to that section of the front right off.[12]

Besides, von Hindenburg, who was now in command, had resolved on an entirely new approach to winning the war. He was now supreme commander in the sense that von Falkenhayn had never been; that is, he controlled all the fronts. His plan was simple and old-fashioned. First, the bulked-up German forces in the east would drive the Russians completely out of Galicia, working in tandem with a joint force in southeastern Hungary that would defeat the Romanians, drive across the Carpathian mountains, and occupy their country.

Von Hindenburg aimed to win the war in the east outright first. Afterward he would smash the Italians, and then, able to bring an overwhelming force to bear, he would end the war once and for all by a great offensive in the west. He had absolute confidence in his soldiers, and an equal amount of confidence that he had enough time to accomplish this. At the very worst, he was convinced he could fight the war to a draw.

The first part of his plan certainly went well enough. The British had high hopes for the Romanians. Like the French, from whom they were getting most of their hard intelligence, they had bought into the notion of catastrophic German losses, of dwindling manpower reserves. Apparently the secret deliberations of the Chamber of Deputies, where a very good approximation of the truth was revealed, remained one of the few secrets of the war.

By the end of 1916, von Falkenhayn, who was directing operations in Romania, had driven their army back into the northeastern corner of the country.

Now, the point of this brief summary is this: for von Hindenburg, the Western Front would have to wait its turn. He assumed, correctly, that the Somme offensive had failed, that the German defensive line in the west was basically invulnerable. In July, the British and French had given it their best shot, and had not broken through. They had conquered some territory, but his experiences in the east had made him quite aware of how illusory such gains were. Victory in war was not a function of acquiring a few hundred square kilometers at random.

So in other words, the German army commanders in the west were basically on their own. Although the actual number of divisions available increased slightly, so that by October there were 128 of them, what was basically happening was that Berlin was moving its better units out of France, replacing them with units that were either newly formed or composed of less fit soldiers, and hence substantially less combat capable.

The French barrage began on 20 October, and for the first time was reasonably effective. Most of the German defensive positions constructed outside the existing forts and blockhouses were destroyed, and nearly a third of their guns knocked out. On the twenty-fourth, the infantry assault went in, the soldiers stumbling through a dense fog, and in and out of craters filled with rainwater.

The spearhead of the thrust was the *infanterie coloniale du Maroc*, which was, despite the misleading name, not a division of African troops. The colonial infantry were basically the French equivalent of the American and British marines. There were, however, African troops in the assault, mostly from Senegal.[13] The spearhead drove on through the initial lines for two kilometers, and by about three in the afternoon of the twenty-fourth, the colonial infantry retook the fort. On 4 November, the Germans evacuated Vaux, which fell into French hands.

The defending Germans were already in a poor state of morale, as evinced by the number of prisoners taken (more than 6,000), and in general German resistance was feeble. But then, the best troops had been sent to the east; the ones left were not capable of the effective counterattacks that had thus far stymied the French. And that was leaving aside that for the first time at Verdun, Second Army had sufficient artillery. Moreover, it was difficult for the Germans to get worked up about hanging on to the position anchored by the forts. After the May explosion, the interior was wrecked; the forts had no firepower, and were simply infantry shelters dependent on the guns behind them and, to a great extent, the infantry in the surrounding areas.

Suitably cheered by their success, the French spent the next six weeks carefully building up the infrastructure to support two more attacks, one on the left bank and another on the right, as Nivelle aimed to recapture the left-bank positions.

The bombardment began on 9 December. Despite having assembled even more heavy weapons, the results were significantly less, as the battlefield was shrouded in snow clouds, snow was falling intermittently, and there was heavy fog. As a result, aerial observation was extremely difficult. But the defenders were seriously demoralized, as evinced by the number of prisoners: over 11,000.

Nivelle, who was no slouch when it came to self-promotion, was now the man of the hour. He had the "formula," as he announced triumphantly to Pétain over lunch in October.[14] He was the man who reconquered Verdun, had driven the Germans back to where they had started in February.

Except that he hadn't.

First of all, the dependence on heavy artillery was not Nivelle's idea at all. It was Pétain's. As commander of the central group of armies, he insisted on a careful and methodical preparation. How else to explain the abrupt shift in tactics? In May and July, Nivelle had been cheerfully willing to pursue the same suicidal infantry assaults that had been employed all along.

But by late autumn, Joffre was in eclipse, and Pétain was able to exert his authority. He was, after all, Nivelle's superior, at least for the moment. In fact, by October there was basically no one in charge at all at the higher levels of command, so the army group generals were doing as they pleased. Interestingly, it was only in October that the first detailed description of a true supreme commander's duties and responsibilities began to circulate, the genesis being a letter from Charles Dupuis to Poincaré. After two years of war, it would be another seven months before the idea was implemented.

The one part of the GQG motor that functioned perfectly was the machine that ground out misleading or totally false news about the army's progress. Having retaken the two forts, which now were acknowledged as the key oppositions on the right bank, the army encouraged everyone to believe that the reconquest was complete. And since the army said so, and the people saying so probably believed what they wrote, everyone subsequently took it to be true. Indeed, the idea that by the end of December the Germans were right back where they had started is both the guiding principle of the standard English account of the battle and its explicit conclusion.

The reality on the ground was rather different. On the right bank, the Germans were still firmly in possession of the Woëvre, as well as all the territory that lay between Douaumont and their original lines in January 1916. Given that advances on the Western Front tended to be measured in kilometers, and sometimes in meters, the nearly 8,000 of them that lay between the battered hulk of the great fort and the remains of Driant's command post were hardly trivial. Just getting back to where Driant's *chasseurs* had been deployed would be a considerable feat.

Because although Douaumont afforded a great view of the sloping terrain ahead of it, the fighting behind the fort had made the terrain virtually impassable. Infantry could work their way through, had indeed done so in the October assault. But bringing heavy artillery close enough to the fort to be able to shell the German lines was basically impossible. The fact that Nivelle had switched the second offensive to the left bank is basically an admission of that.

Now, given what Abel Ferry had sarcastically referred to as war waged for the communiqué, it is difficult to escape the idea that these two French offensives were mostly designed to support the army's claim that they had won the battle, the idea being that once they recaptured the two forts, everyone would think they had ejected the Germans completely from Verdun.

If Nivelle had stopped there, had remained as commander of the Second Army, one would be inclined to be more charitable about his accomplishments, see him as a competent general who had taken Pétain's tactics to heart and applied them, although the nagging doubt would still remain about a general so indifferent or insensitive to the condition of the terrain and the effect of bad weather on planning.

Unfortunately for France, the government was desperate to get rid of Joffre, had been frustrated since June and furious since July; was blocked only because they couldn't find anyone they would agree to appoint to the job. The obvious choice was Pétain. But just as before 1914, the politicians in the war ministry had basically said "over my dead body" to his promotion, and the same intensely partisan strain gripped the government, egged on by scurrilous gossip from Joffre's staff about his defeatism, his pessimism. Plus— and this was true—Pétain, like most older French generals, not only did not speak English, but he had very little use for the British. The derisive German expression that characterized the British army, "Lions led by jackasses," was one he would have wholeheartedly endorsed; indeed, it pretty much expressed his views of the high command of his own army, and of the politicians of the Third Republic.

So the cabinet pinned its hopes on Nivelle. He was younger, he was full of self-confidence, he had the "formula," and he spoke English. What could go wrong? What could go wrong indeed— Nivelle promptly led the army to a disaster in Champagne that dwarfed all the previous disasters of French offensive operations there. The results of the attack on the ridge of the Chemin des Dames in April 1917 was so awful that his generals went over his head, demanded his replacement, and thus the infamous mutiny began. The army had endured years of senseless and costly attacks. Enough was enough.[15]

So von Falkenhayn's idea thus came true, although in a twisted and curious way. Despite all the claims made about the significance of Verdun, despite its real military value, its most lasting contribution to France was that it catapulted Nivelle to power, and then, in the resultant disaster, established Pétain as the man who saved France. For the second time, his command at Verdun being the first. The staff gossips could say what they wanted, the average soldier wasn't fooled: This was the man who saved France, and in May 1917, he saved the country again.

Unfortunately, June 1940, when he was called to the helm for the third time, would not prove so felicitous, either for the aging marshal, or for France. Jean Dutourd famously remarked that "the choice is always between Verdun or Dachau," but it would be more correct to say that the former led directly to the latter.[16]

REVANCHE: THE LEFT-BANK OFFENSIVE OF 1917

Although it is often said, or anyway hinted, that after May 1917 the French army was incapable of carrying on the war—a convenient excuse for Haig's gradual destruction of his command—the idea, no matter how expressed, is absolutely untrue.

Over the summer, Pétain carefully reorganized the army, arranging for better logistical support for the infantry at every level, and preparing for a great assault on the left bank, where Nivelle's attack had been frustrated. French reconnaissance revealed that the Germans had not been entirely idle. After the last attacks in December, they had begun a series of three tunnels into the reverse slopes of their forward positions behind the Mort Homme. The idea was that their infantry would take shelter there during any bombardment, then emerge to massacre the attackers as they struggled to reach them.

Now for reasons obvious to the more cynical reader, Pétain's offensive of August 1917, like numerous other French engagements, has been generally passed over in silence, since it doesn't fit the narrative that at the end of 1916 the Germans had been thrown back to where they started.[17]

However, not only was there an offensive, but the scale of it was enormous. Pétain deployed no less than four complete army corps: two on the left bank and two on the right. But this by no means inconsiderable force of infantry was dwarfed by the guns. There were 2,200 artillery pieces taking part in the offensive, which set a record of sorts. In some areas, gunners outnumbered the assault troops by over two to one.

If the French preparations were far different, so were the Germans, who reacted energetically. By now (late summer 1917), von Hindenburg was slowly beginning to shift focus away from the east, given the state of the Russian army and the chaos inside the short-lived provisional republic (the czar having abdicated in February). So three divisions were added to the left bank, while on the right, in addition to the four divisions now holding the front, there were two more in reserve. Along with the infantry came more artillery, so the German commanders had reason to be confident.

The artillery barrage began on August 13, and went on intermittently for a week. It should be understood that this did not mean the guns were firing continuously. It took time for aerial reconnaissance to survey the damage and select new targets. But for the first time the system worked for the French, and quite well. When the infantry assault started on the twentieth, the left-bank assault, spearheaded by the Legion and the colonial infantry, quickly overran the entrances to the tunnels before the German infantry could emerge, and in a few hours, the main defensive position had been taken, with only Hill 304 remaining in German hands. In the advance positions, the infantry found mostly nothing but corpses. An attack on the twenty-fourth delivered the hill back into French hands.

On the right bank, the French had a more difficult time of it, probably owing to the condition of the terrain, but early on they occupied the woods of Beaumont and des Fosses. On the twenty-sixth the French cleared out the woods of the Chaume (not that there were any trees left; the terms had become simply memories of what once had been). A final attack, on 6 September, delivered Bois des Caurières.

The August offensive was a considerable success. By any reasonable measure, it was the first unequivocal and unambiguous French victory of the war. There were 10,000 prisoners, the infantry took all of its objectives, and losses were very light.

The two humps on the left bank were the equivalent of the two forts on the right, but had considerably more tactical value: Reconquering them was a serious achievement. On the right bank, getting back the Côte du Talou was probably more significant than possession of the forts.

The success of the offensive, immediately followed by another in Champagne, the site of Nivelle's disaster, did wonders to restore the morale of the army, and it's a pity that the GQG, having lied in December 1916 about Verdun, was thus unable to publicize a real as opposed to a fictional victory. People had begun to catch on: They couldn't very well say they had gotten Verdun back, when they had already claimed that eight months earlier.

But does the August victory mean that finally the French had reconquered what they had lost in spring 1916? Colonel Chaligne puts it this way: "We had almost returned to our positions of 21 February 1916," and he concludes his account by invoking a French verb, *degager*, whose primary meaning is "to liberate," as in delivering the wounded from captivity.[18]

A polite way of saying no, not quite: Pétain had removed the threat posed to the French positions; he had not attempted to restore the original positions. The technical distinction is subtle but important. The best way to explain it is in this fashion: If, in July

1917, von Hindenburg had decided to mount a massive offensive on both banks, his forward positions—the positions identified above—would have given him a significant, perhaps even an overwhelming advantage. So Verdun was now freed from that menace.

On the other hand, if, for whatever reason, the Germans had decided to attack there in force a second time, say February 1918, they would have been in a considerably better situation than in February 1916. The lines were closer together, and the positions, particularly on the right bank, would enable excellent staging areas for infantry assaults.

In an oft-quoted passage in his memoirs, the German crown prince terms Verdun a postern gate. Pétain disagreed completely. But then, he despised military theorists, and the Fifth Army's commander was speaking theoretically. In that sense he was quite right. The shortest route into Germany proper was a diagonal going from the right bank to the northeast. Given the German lines from 1914 on, a breakthrough in that direction would be a catastrophe.

Not only were the distances immensely shorter than from the British lines or from Artois, but an army that started out on the right bank would not be faced with the obstacle of the Meuse. The British belief that the war could be won by beating the Germans back through Belgium was a conceit concocted by men whose experiences did not include studying the terrain, who relied entirely on flat maps, who thought contour lines were there just for decoration. This was hardly a uniquely British failing: the same sort of error had dogged the French staffers all through the war, Nivelle's blithe unconcern with the December weather being only the latest in a whole series of similar miscalculations.

However, regardless of who made it, it was a major error. Belgium was not the Argonne, an area small enough that gnawing your way through it was feasible, especially if the cost was minimal. But a thrust up out of the right bank could cut the German position in two, force a general retreat, since the attacking force would be behind the greater part of the German army.

So the crown prince was actually correct. The reason Pétain disagreed was simple: He knew the impossibility of the French putting together the force required. His succinct analysis of the distribution of their forces on the front is a revelation. By the end of 1915, losses had been so high that such a massive offensive was simply not possible. Even Joffre had figured that one out, which was why he had pinned his hopes on the Somme. It was the only place where a joint offensive against the same sector of the front could occur, and it was only with the assistance of the British forces that the attacking armies would be big enough.

That the offensive on the Somme failed does not mean that Joffre's idea was wrong, any more than the failure at Verdun means that von Falkenhayn's idea was. Similarly, the notion of a sally port or postern gate that the crown prince advanced was theoretically correct, exactly the sort of problem that should be worried about. Or, to put it another way, he paid the French the compliment of believing them competent strategists. Pétain knew better.

11

The Last Battles: September–October 1918

Major Griesel, chief of the war press bureau in
Berlin, keeps three American shells on his desk by
way of welcoming American correspondents, and
then to make them feel at home he adds he was
wounded by one of them.

—Herbert Bayard Swope[1]

As the epigraph to this chapter suggests, America had been involved in the war long before the actual declaration. However, it
was not until the spring of 1918 that American troops saw serious
combat, were present in large enough numbers to make a difference on the battlefield.

But the combat capabilities and the objectives of those troops are
often misunderstood. That is hardly surprising, given how much of
what happened during the war was either hidden, misrepresented,
ignored, or denied. But then, alliances are chancy affairs. The Germans and the Austrians cordially disliked one another, even though
to a great extent they had a shared language and culture.

So it's not surprising that the French and British had mixed
feelings about the enormous American force that was assembling
in France. Their presence contradicted the growing British legend

of how they won the war all by themselves, and although the French were realistic about their needs, they were at bottom no more inclined to give the Americans credit for stopping von Hindenburg's final 1918 offensive than the British were.[2] They were simply more polite about it.

THE BASIC MISUNDERSTANDING

It can hardly be said that the two great American offensives of fall 1918 are unknown, or that we are unfamiliar with their intense combats with the Germans.

However, their place in the Verdun battles is overlooked almost entirely. The British commanders were obsessed with Flanders, and the French were desperate to get back all the territory they had lost in spring 1918, when the Germans had gotten so close to Paris. So by the summer, the only Allied strategy seemed to be to attack the Germans in every way possible. There was no real thought given to where. In truth, the British commanders had no real strategy at all; they were simply following along behind the German general retreat.

In consequence, American operations were seen as merely a small simply part of the general bashing and chasing, particularly since the British never really understood what was going on in the 80 percent of the front the French controlled.

However, in reality, the two great American offensives had a clear purpose: to continue what the French thought of as the battle of the wings, the two flanks of Verdun.

The names given them are in themselves quite revealing. The first offensive is known as Saint-Mihiel, the second as Meuse-Argonne. Rather obviously, the first term refers to the German bulge on the right bank established in September 1914, while the second is simply another way of identifying the left-bank positions of Verdun, what the French called the battles of the wings—that is, the German attempts to bypass the Verdun forts, cut them off, and move deep into France, attempts that as we have seen led to a series of additional battles as the French tried to take the ground back.

But since the Battle of the Woëvre and the fight for Les Éparges were attempts by the French to eject the Germans from their gains on the right bank, then by definition so was the American offensive of 1918, as it covered exactly the same section of the front. The only difference between the American attack in 1918 and the French one in 1915 was that the latter was a disaster, the former a victory.

Similarly, in the second offensive, the Americans battled up through the Argonne, just as General Sarrail had attempted in 1915, crossing the Meuse directly above Verdun in their successful drive to the north. In fact, the American maps for these two offensives can be overlaid directly on the corresponding French maps for the earlier engagements.

Different names, but battles for the same end: Verdun.

SAINT-MIHIEL: ROLLING UP THE RIGHT BANK

While Foch and Haig deluded themselves into believing they could eventually beat the Germans on their own, Pétain was doubtful. In his view, the only real chance the Allies had for beating the Germans was to wait until the Americans arrived, and as their divisions appeared, he tried, as best he could, to slot them into what in his experience was the key section of the front: behind Verdun and the Saint-Mihiel salient.

Some American units had the misfortune of being seconded to the British sector, but the bulk of the American army in France was south of Verdun (and in the Vosges, where the troops could get actual experience).

The reader who has been patiently following this account of the fighting for Verdun will thus not be surprised that the Saint-Mihiel salient was chosen for the first great Franco-American offensive. Moving up the right bank was by far the best route both to bypass Verdun and to prepare for an assault into Germany.

It was at this point that the implications of the muddle that had lost them the Woëvre began to dawn on the French high command. The Germans did what they had done in 1917: withdrew from a bulge in the front, thus shortening their section of it and improving their supply lines in consequence.

Just as the GQG had planned to evacuate the right bank if attacked, the Germans now planned to evacuate the part of the right bank they held around Saint-Mihiel. Once again, the issue boiled down to a simple one: timing. As the Germans planned their withdrawal, Pershing and Pétain planned their offensive.[3]

Although this offensive is simply known as Saint-Mihiel, the area of operations extended from Haudimont south to below the town of Saint-Mihiel, and then straight across the Woëvre to Pont-à-Mousson. Given the French disasters here in 1914 and all through 1915, a successful offensive would do for the two allies what Pétain's earlier 1917 offensives had done. Yes, the territory had a certain military importance, but it was more important for the boost it would give the two armies. It would show the Americans they could operate successfully where the French had failed, erase the black marks on the French record, and shake the defending Germans.

The performance of the American troops in stopping the great German advance of summer 1918, although it certainly was good for France, brought Foch and Haig (and their staffs) to a horrifying realization: What if the Americans, whose forces were growing at a dizzying rate, actually beat the Germans in the field? Given the size of the American units, that they were lavishly equipped with French equipment and assisted by some of France's best troops, the possibility was quite real. And horrifying: if the Americans succeeded at Saint-Mihiel, while the British and the northern French armies were battering away fruitlessly up in Artois and Flanders, who knew what the result might be?

Foch had no interest in letting the Americans do anything on their own. So he wandered into Pershing's headquarters and suggested that the operation be canceled. The whole idea of operating as a self-contained army was foolish; Saint-Mihiel was a terrible idea.

Instead the American units should be dispersed among the French and British, who would then mount a great offensive in Artois. If this offensive succeeded, the Allies would then be . . . in Artois.[4]

By this point in 1918, Pershing had been fending off absurd and insane demands by the British and French for over a year, the most incredible being the serious British proposal to feed the Americans into existing British units, where they could get massacred in proper British fashion. So Pershing was accustomed to batting off ideas that were militarily ludicrous and politically disastrous; by mid-1918, even the Anglophiles like President Wilson were becoming wary of the British.

Besides, Foch had no real authority, either over Pershing or over Pétain, as the two senior generals actually commanded the troops. So he said no, the offensive would go ahead as scheduled. Desperate, Foch then began a campaign right on the spot to browbeat Pershing into mounting another offensive immediately, as soon as possible, on the left bank, in support of a French offensive in eastern Champagne (the theater immediately adjacent to the Argonne). This offensive was already set for September, Foch insisted, blandly proposing that the Americans mount two major offensive operations in different areas in two successive months.

The difficulty in evaluating Foch is that it is almost impossible to tell whether he was extremely crafty and sly, or simply incapable of grasping modern warfare. In either case, he clearly felt he had thrown Pershing into an impossible situation; nor was anyone pleased when Pershing promptly called his bluff.

So the Saint-Mihiel offensive was duly launched on 12 September. The Germans had begun to withdraw, but their timing was off, so they were caught at the worst possible moment: some units had withdrawn; others were still there. Had Pershing followed the lumbering pace of his allies, this would not have been a problem. But after a short, massive bombardment that covered the entire salient, there was a coordinated assault all along the line. Given the size of the salient, the scale of the assault surpassed anything that had been done to date by either side.

The weakness of the German position was obvious: An assault on two sides could break through the base, cut off the defenders. That was the French aim in 1915, but they lacked both the resources and the tactical competence to achieve it. In this, Joffre's theory was correct: only an overwhelming assault on a broad front would succeed. Otherwise the defenders would move reinforcements along laterally from the areas not threatened to those that were.

But there was more to it than overpowering force. As the Germans had shown over and over again, speed of deployment was all-important, whether one was playing defense or offense. Speed was one thing, the close coordination of artillery with the infantry advance another. With the exception of Pétain's two offensives in 1917, the French and the British had never been able to do this on any scale in sustained fashion.

Despite the best attempts of staff gossips and their fellow traveling historians, the result was a major success. Von Hindenburg thought Saint-Mihiel was a smashing major defeat, and Ludendorff, his greatly touted by British historians chief of staff, basically had a nervous breakdown.[5]

In one great dash, the Americans had cleared the lower portion of the heights, gone up the right bank, were now very close to the original battle line of early September 1914.[6] So the right bank of Verdun had finally been completely freed.

Now, the next logical move would have been the one the crown prince had worried about: a mighty thrust up the right bank and into Germany. But for Haig and Foch, it was more important to be seen winning on their own than to beat the Germans. Besides, they really believed that they could engage them in a classic battle and defeat them outright.

So the insistence on the Americans now tackling the left bank was partly to support what Haig felt was the main thrust. But given the terrain, the way the Germans had beaten the French like a rug there all through the war, the Argonne seemed like a good place to teach the newly arrived Americans the realities of combat.

RECONQUERING THE LEFT BANK

Given the experiences the French had there, it is not much of a surprise that the Americans found it tough going as well. If they broke through, they could cut the main lateral rail line the German army needed to keep the front supplied. They could then keep on going all the way up the Meuse, flowing around Verdun. A major breakthrough here could be catastrophic for Germany.

The American speed at switching from one offense to the other had stunned the British and heartened the French. But once the offensive began, and the AEF had tough going, a host of military experts declared them completely inept. The slow progress through the Argonne, as the Germans gave way elsewhere, allowed the British in particular to suggest that they won the war and the Americans were merely helpful.

Those claims are the window dressing to disguise a ferocious internal attack spearheaded by British officers. Having failed to prevent the formation of an American army as a unitary force, they engaged in serious attempts to destroy it. Back in London, General Wilson (the fellow who had told Lloyd George he was too stupid to understand military matters) tried to get Pershing's Saint-Mihiel offensive canceled. The campaign went all the way over to Washington, and in Paris, Georges Clemenceau did his part, demanding that Pershing be removed from command, even going so far as to appeal to Lloyd George.[7] Postwar, the internal intrigues were largely covered up, only to surface as the evaluations of British historians intent on preserving the fiction that their army won the war almost entirely on its own, and that the Americans were totally inept.

All through October the Americans slowly fought their way through the Argonne, systematically reversing the gains von Mudra had made in 1914 and 1915. If Belleau Wood was one of the bloodier engagements in the history of the American army, then Meuse-Argonne was certainly one of the bloodiest campaigns. In September, the AEF had about 5,000 soldiers killed outright, and in October the number climbed to 22,000. The American cemetery at Romagne-sous-Montfaucon has 14,240 graves; it is bigger than the cemetery at Normandy.

But on the other hand, the BEF, which was essentially just chasing the German withdrawal like a dog chasing a car, had 29,000 men killed and missing in September, and 44,000 in October. The French, who were encountering serious resistance in eastern Champagne, and in some cases were fighting side by side with American units, had 23,000 men killed and missing in September and nearly 40,000 in October—and it should be realized that at this point the nominal combat strengths of the three Allied armies were nearly equal.[8]

But the outcome of the struggle was victory. The Americans crossed the Meuse above Verdun, as attested by divisional markers at Brieulles and Velosne. That marks the definitive end of the battles of Verdun. Just as the Germans had attempted in 1914, the Americans had managed it in reverse, flowing around Verdun and on both sides.

There is a certain bizarre symmetry. The battles for Verdun began in 1914, but were folded into obscurity when Joffre's staff created the somewhat fictional Battle of the Marne. They finally ended with the great American offensives, whose familiar names of Saint-Mihiel and Meuse-Argonne likewise obscure the relationship to Verdun. But then, as the patient reader has by now probably realized, everything about Verdun is in one way or the other obscured.

VON HINDENBURG'S APPRECIATION

The performance of the American troops in this war has been roundly savaged by British historians and their followers on this side of the pond, while even the defenders are handicapped by their lack of knowledge about the two main theaters of operations. Hopefully the story thus far has made the connection clear enough. From the very first, the battles for Verdun were conducted on the flanks. It was only in 1916 that there was a direct assault.

As to the significance of the American involvement, von Hindenburg sums it up perfectly in his rather lumbering and ponderous way, as he attempted to answer a question posed by an enterprising American journalist who had commandeered a car and driven straight to his headquarters in November 1918. The question was simple: "Who won the war?"[9]

> "I will reply with the same frankness," said Hindenburg, faintly amused by our diplomacy. "The American infantry in the Argonne won the war. . . . Without American troops against us, and despite a food blockade which was undermining the civilian population of Germany and curtailing the rations in the field, we could still have had a peace without victory. The war could have ended in a sort of stalemate. And even if we had not the better of the fighting in the end, as we had until July 18, we could have had an acceptable peace. . . . Even the attack of July 18, which Allied generals may consider the turning point, did not use up a very important part of the German army or smash all our positions. . . . But the balance was broken by the American troops. The Argonne battle was slow and difficult. It was bitter and used up division after division. We had to hold the Metz-Longuyon roads and railroad. . . . From a military point of view the Argonne battle as conceived and carried out by the American Command was the climax of the war and its deciding factor. . . . I repeat, without the American blow in the Argonne, we could have made a satisfactory peace at the end of a stalemate or at least held our last positions on our own frontier indefinitely—undefeated—the American attack won the war."[10]

As indeed they did, although one would never know it from reading the British accounts. But then, one would never know what Verdun was about or what happened there. There are limits to writing histories based on government press releases.

12

A Conclusion of Sorts: The Temptations of Myth

> The truth must be always repeated, because errors
> are preached over and over again, and not just by a
> few individuals, but by the majority. In newspapers
> and encyclopedias, in schools and universities, error
> predominates, and takes comfort in the knowledge
> that the majority is on its side.
>
> —Goethe[1]

Verdun is a disappointing battle. Its beginnings were submerged in the start of the war, the middle parts deliberately obscured by the French army, and the 1916 battle trailed off in a bloody melee that was quickly eclipsed by the Somme, sputtered to a life in the late fall, only to be appropriated by French propagandists. The ending is equally obscure, so it is fitting that after four years of intense battle, the only real victors, the Americans, would find their part reduced to a mere supplementary note, their contributions to winning the war dismissed as mere logistics, their combat record the subject of derision.

So almost every part of Verdun is buried somewhere or jumbled in with something else. In that sense the heaps of bones scattered underneath the great ossuary on the battlefield are a wonderful metaphor for the struggles there, made all the more poignant by the remains still hidden deep in the forests that now cover the heights of the Meuse, and the battlefields of the left bank.

People who study battles wish to find winners and losers. In that sense, Waterloo is the great battle of the modern age. True, there are still debates. Napoleon's many admirers come up with ingenious solutions to explain his defeat, and British students of history often seem to forget that it was the arrival of Blücher and his Prussians that brought about the victory. However, Napoleon himself conceded defeat, and no one has ever suggested he won.

Nitpicking the victor is a distressing habit of the modern age. Wellington never lost a battle, was clearly the greatest British general since Marlborough, but their hard-earned reputations are often obscured. By any standard, Grant was the architect of victory at Shiloh. The Confederates retreated, their leader mortally wounded on the field. But Grant was savaged nonetheless, while academics later devoted ingenious efforts to rehabilitate Henry Halleck. So it is understandable that when a battle, or series of battles, really is inconclusive, everyone tries to convert it into something definite. Usually they do so at the expense of the facts, preferring instead to weave myths.

THE CASUALTY MYTH

The first and in some ways the most enduring myth that rose out of Verdun was the myth of some incredibly bloody struggle with astronomical casualties. Since the war had gone on for years after the 1916 battle that the French insisted had resulted in a stalemate, the only lesson to be drawn from Verdun was that it was a meaningless bloodbath, an idea that the pacifists who came to prominence in 1918 lost no time in elaborating on.

Immediately after the war, the *Basler Nachrichten* published an advertisement for round trips to the Verdun battlefield. The copy makes for interesting reading.

> Not only to the French mind is it the battlefield *par excellence* on which the enormous struggle between France and Germany was finally decided. . . . If the entire war cost France 1,400,000 dead, almost one third of those fell in the sector of Verdun, which comprises a few square kilometers. The Germans suffered more than twice the number of casualties there. In this small area, where more than a million men—perhaps a million and a half—bled to death, there is not one square centimeter of ground that has not been torn up by shells.[2]

It is always tempting to dismiss advertisements as gross exaggerations, figments of a fevered copywriter's brain. But in this case, the key numbers can easily be traced to a much more authoritative source.

After the war, Monsignor Ginisty, the Roman Catholic bishop of Verdun, began raising money for a great memorial to be erected on the battlefield. The costs would be paid by subscribers. The fund was authorized by the government on 3 December 1919. A committee was formed under the joint presidency of Marshal Foch, former president Poincaré, and Cardinal Dubois, former bishop of Verdun and at that time archbishop of Paris. That was the honorary committee. Then there was the executive committee, whose honorary president was Marshal Pétain.

The committee sent out letters inviting people to subscribe to the fund, to the tune of 500 francs. The opening paragraph is definitely worth reading.

> The battlefield of Verdun is certainly the greatest and most bloody on the whole European front. Millions of men struggled here in a gigantic duel: *four hundred thousand French soldiers* fell on a front of 12 miles, about 300,000 of whom, according to official records, have never been identified.[3]

So now we know, more or less, where the figure came from. Four hundred thousand became half a million. During the 1916 fighting, the French had claimed that German losses were three times theirs, so suddenly we're at 1,500,000 dead.

It is worth pointing out here that all of these figures are wild exaggerations of one sort or another, with one curious exception. The official French data for losses in the war is—or rather was—1,070,000 deaths, and 314,000 missing presumed dead. Michel Huber, after analyzing these government figures, concludes that 1,400,000 dead should be considered the minimum, but in the context of his analysis, it is clear that he's simply being painstakingly precise: the true (and probably unknowable) figure is only a few tens of thousands higher than that, if indeed it is that high.[4]

So where did the good bishop's figures come from? The most probable explanation is that two mistakes were made. The first was that the total figure for the missing presumed dead for the entire army over the whole course of the war was used for the total of the missing for Verdun. That is to say, 314,000 total missing became 300,000 missing at Verdun.

The second mistake was to conflate the figures for all casualties incurred in the various categories: the dead, the wounded, and the missing. Many historians routinely do that, even though, as we explained earlier, it is only appropriate as a measure of loss when speaking of one engagement. But terms like *losses* or *casualties* are then misinterpreted to mean the totals for the dead. Yves Buffetaut observes that at the joint ceremony held at Verdun in 1990 between Germany and France, the journalists present did precisely that: they added all the figures up and then said they represented the dead, which he quite rightly terms a "gross error."[5] There is a historical precedent for that, so the committee was hardly alone.

And, of course, the bishop wanted to raise money, and the best way to raise money was to attract people's attention. But clearly these totals are wild exaggerations.

Now, it is certainly possible that if one were to try to total up all the losses over the entire war for all of the battles that were for the Verdun sector as described in this book, it might well be true that nearly a third of their total losses were incurred there.

But as our narrative and the accompanying maps have hopefully made clear, these battles took place in a large section of the Western Front. The French section of the front was, on average, 583 kilometers, so it is not hard to believe that if we take the section from the Argonne through the Woëvre we get very close to a third of that distance. Moreover, an appreciable portion of that 583 kilometers ran through the Vosges mountains. The fighting in the rough terrain there was bloody enough, but the number of troops engaged was, by comparison with the other areas, very small. So if the entire sector is considered for the entire war, maybe.

But to say that those casualties were all incurred on a 20-kilometer stretch of the front is absurd. So is the notion one often hears in France: that the cemetery in front of the bishop's ossuary is the largest French military cemetery of the war. Not so—that sad distinction belongs to the Notre-Dame de Lorette, in Artois.

It is claimed that the ossuary beneath the memorial that the fund built contains the remains of over 120,000 men. But this is both unlikely and unknowable. Humans have duplicates of some parts. Then there is the grisly joke of the French veteran who used to show visitors the ossuary and remark jovially that he had come to see his leg; he was sure it was in there somewhere.

Historians may sneer at these exaggerations, just as they unconsciously look down on mere journalists, but gradually these popular ideas seep into the narrative, begin to form their assumptions as well, perhaps unconsciously. The result is discoverable only by looking at the subtext of the narrative, assumptions often disguised by waffling and qualification.

The early French historians gave very precise figures for their own losses in the 1916 battles, and these numbers are all more or less in agreement. Interestingly, however, with each decade, there seems to have been a sort casualty creep, as though each successive historian feels the subject is diminished if the body count is not significant. And since none of these gentlemen define the time period and the area with any particular accuracy (unlike the first group), almost any number could be justified in one way or the other.

The myth of incredible losses and a bloody struggle during 1916 help to propel a narrative that emphasizes the futility of the whole enterprise, the cold-blooded calculations of the Germans, and how their plan to bleed France white was foiled, which in turn leads to the idea that in December everyone was back where he was in January.

Perhaps without even realizing it, the narrative is created so as to conform to those preconceptions. Clearly, given the complexities of the fighting there, the host of obscure and vanished place names, the mysteries of the terrain, and the obfuscations of the government, one can come up with any set of facts one chooses.

THE PROBLEM OF FALSE IDEAS

When the issue of learning from historical experience comes up, the famous adage that the only thing history teaches us is that no one learns anything from it comes irresistibly to mind. That may be true, but military history presents us with a more particular, or peculiar, difficulty. When looked at closely, the events are so confusing, the causes so complex, the effects so difficult to discern, that anyone can find support for almost any idea he chooses to advance.

What makes the situation trickier is that in this particular area, the fox is generally put in charge of the poultry. The 1920s saw the rise of the strategic airpower theorists, who believed that bombing the enemy's cities and his factories (objectives that more or less meant lots of civilians would be killed) was the most effective way to wage a war. The men who advanced these theories, primarily in Italy and Great Britain, constructed an argument at the expense of certain facts. They created a world in which, in August 1914, hardly anyone had any airplanes, or even any trucks; they avoided any meaningful discussion of the extensive strategic bombing campaigns of the war; they did not discuss the extent to which ground-to-air defenses were extremely effective against bombers.

Either out of genuine ignorance or cunning, they simply pretended that none of this happened. But it did. That the evidence was ignored hardly means it did not exist. It was ignored because it contradicted the basic idea the theorists were trying to advance. The Germans looked at their strategic bombing campaign, decided it wasn't worth the losses incurred, and saw airpower as an adjunct to traditional ground operations.

At the end of the next European war, surveys were conducted that "proved" the effectiveness of the strategic bombing campaign against Germany, even though those surveys hardly pass muster as such, are mostly exercises in circular reasoning. The fox is not only guarding the chickens, but he's in charge of the investigation to find out why they keep disappearing.

Now, this example can by no means be taken to mean that the idea was wrong, that it was foolish or even immoral. The point is that dramatically opposing ideas can emerge from a study of the same situation, and particularly when it comes to war. In an ideal world, the British bomber barons would have looked at the data, studied the Germans, and realized that if your loss rate really was close to one out of every three bombers you sent up in the air, you definitely had a problem. The Germans should have studied the hysteria in London (during the First World War) their bombing raids caused, and concluded that possibly the effects were worth the risk.

Instead, both sides sailed (or rather flew) on, serenely confident that they were right, and merrily ignoring any contrary evidence. Iceberg? What iceberg?

The historians who then wrote the accounts that the bomber barons had thoughtfully provided them with the data for, simply developed the meme further, putting on it the imprimatur that it was history, and therefore true. But both the primary data and the subsequent accounts were all generated to support an argument, no more represented an objective look at the situation than did the claims of government propagandists.

Even when there was some skepticism, similarly unsubstantiated ideas kept hovering in the background. In the case of the Great War, for instance, from the very first days of fighting, the French began to describe the Germans as attacking in enormous hordes of massed infantry, wiped out by French (and British) musketry and bayonets. As we noticed in an earlier chapter, the description was still being used for the battle of Verdun. It was being fed to observers like H. G. Wells, and decades later historians who should have known better were describing the German infantry at Verdun exactly the way they had been described during the war by French government propagandists.

Why should the historians have known better? Because early on, French analysts went through all the records available to them trying to find a confirmation of this tactic, and failed. Joseph Bédier found only one example of German infantry advancing en masse: soldiers of the 21st Division attacking the Bois de Marfée above Sedan.[6] Given the casualties (established conclusively by French and German researchers), given the absence of examples based on properly verified witnesses, and given the extensive evidence available as to the evolution of German infantry tactics during the war, the whole idea is a myth. But it persists.

THE ABSENCE OF LESSONS TO LEARN

There were general lessons to be derived from the Great War that all the combatants absorbed and then applied, but very few of them were derived from Verdun. Arguably the fighting there over the course of the war convinced even the most retrograde gunners that their basic weapon should be the howitzer firing explosive shells, not the field gun firing shrapnel, but this lesson would probably have taken whether or not there had been any fighting on the Meuse at all.

Interestingly, both the French and the Germans emerged convinced of the value of concrete fortifications. They both realized that, properly supplied and garrisoned, even weaker forts, the smaller and less protected ones that were known collectively as *ouvrages*, were basically invulnerable. The French engineering effort that resulted, popularly (and incorrectly) known as the Maginot Line, was the result.

Given the abrupt fall of France in June 1940, there was a mad rush to demonstrate how the idea was not only flawed, but revealed a defective mentality. It was only long after the war that a series of meticulously researched accounts revealed the extent to which all those claims were false.

At the same time, perhaps spurred on by French research into their own fortifications, other researchers pointed out that the Germans had constructed their own equivalent.[7] The collapse of the Soviet empire provided us for the first time with glimpses of the fortifications built by the Czechs and the Russians themselves. It may well be that precision-guided munitions have made such forts obsolete, but so far the evidence is inconclusive.

Given the obscurity, misrepresentation, and outright confusion that surrounded the fighting for Verdun, there is a certain irony in seeing how the combat histories of the direct descendants of the Verdun forts met the same fate—yet more proof of how hardly anything about Verdun was properly understood.

THE SEARCH FOR COHERENCE

We are all conditioned to look for Waterloo or Gettysburg or Hastings. Faced with a bewilderingly complex battle that began in geographical obscurity, ended in confusion, and did not in any way resolve the struggle between France and Germany, it is only natural to try to find something there to give it meaning, and thus the origins of a horrific struggle with millions of dead, all to no purpose whatsoever.

For all those people who firmly believe that war never solves anything, Verdun is therefore a wonderful symbol—one that the city has certainly exploited, since it bills itself as the "world center of peace." But that is to overlook almost entirely the fact that Verdun was the key to France, as Pétain observed. If one wants to find a symbol of the senselessness and futility of war, visit Les Éparges.

Although it is possible, in rather tortuous fashion, to ascribe certain other lessons to the battles there, other than convincing both sides that fortifications, properly managed and equipped, were invulnerable, there are none.

The coherence—the story, if you will—does not lie on the heights of the Meuse. It is the intimate connection between what happened there and the effects it had on the government of France.

Those effects were profound, and no less so for being misunderstood. The Third Republic can be accused of all sorts of vices and defects, but the one thing it cannot be accused of after 1918 was neglecting national defense. In 1939 the army that went to war was well equipped with modern weapons of all types—a striking contrast with its condition in 1914.

That it quit the war in six weeks is true enough, but the reasons given are wrong. That it quit was because of the other lesson that the politicians of the Third Republic absorbed, mainly from Verdun.

Verdun brought to a climax a crisis. Who was in charge of the country: the army or the government? The parties of the left had, unwittingly, created the situation that they had feared so greatly, so the government drifted along in 1916, finally mustering up the courage to dismiss Joffre—only to replace him with someone who was even worse.

But the lesson was learned. When the next war began, the civilians who had been elected (after a fashion) to govern France were definitely in charge. The generals took their orders from them. Unfortunately for France, the government of 1940 was even more inclined to panic than the government of 1914. The only real difference was that in 1940 the panic was final. Paris lacked a Gallieni; France lacked a Joffre. What it did have was a plethora of clever politicians who, having surrendered the country in a panic, managed to cast the blame for the loss on the army.

They succeeded perfectly, mainly because all the agencies involved were in agreement. The British wanted to blame the French to excuse their own miserable performance on the continent. The Germans wanted the world to believe they were invincible. The leaders of post-1940 France wanted everyone to believe that the outcome was preordained, inevitable. The leaders of France after 1945 agreed, as the idea turned them into heroic figures of resistance. That in the process they turned their country into a global laughingstock as a great power never occurred to them.

The collapse of 1940 reminds us of the other direct link with Verdun. The defense of Verdun in 1916 catapulted one minor general among the hundreds to national fame: Verdun made Pétain. Unfortunately, it also made Robert Nivelle, and Nivelle was the man who brought the French army to its knees in 1917. That in turn led to the elevation of Pétain, and we all know the rest of that tragic story. But without Verdun, the meteoric rise and fall of Robert Nivelle would never have occurred. Nor would the emergence of Pétain as by far the most influential and important man in France during the final decades of the Third Republic.

Nor is it particularly far-fetched to make the same observation about Paul von Hindenburg, whose ascent was a function of von Falkenhayn's failure at Verdun. The situation is a good deal more complicated, but the link is there. In different ways Verdun made each general a greater-than-life figure who then presided over the moral disintegration of his nation.

Of course, all of this was entirely unintentional and unforeseen, beginning with Bismarck's attempt to create a lasting peace, a decision that led to the importance of Verdun, and everything that followed. History may not be written for the convenience of historians, but it often seems to prove Thomas Merton's observation about the law of unintended consequences.

ENDNOTES

1. Battles Known and Unknown

1   Herbert George Wells, *The War of the Future* (London: Cassel, 1917), 8. Wells, along with Arthur Conan Doyle and Rudyard Kipling, was one of the leading public figures given an extensive tour of the British, French, and Italian fronts as the Allied governments desperately tried to gin up support for the war, largely as a result of the negative impact of the February 1916 German offensive at Verdun.

2   Jean Bernier, *La Percée* (Paris: Albin Michel, 1920), 46. Unless otherwise noted, all translations, however wretched, are mine. The French phrase Bernier uses is *je grignote*. In fairness to Joffre, it's never been established that Joffre actually said that. See Louis Guiral, *"Je les grignote . . ." Champagne 1914–1915* (Paris: Hachette, 1965), ix.

3   That is certainly the impression the casual reader gets from the otherwise excellent account of Jules Poirier, *La bataille de Verdun, 21 février—18 décembre 1916* (Paris: Chiron, 1922),15–18. Poirier never says directly why the battle was fought. See as well the numerous illustrations and photographs reproduced in the opening pages of Jacques-Henri Lefbvre, *Verdun: la plus grande bataille d l'histoire racontée par les survivants*, 10th edition (Verdun: Éditions du Mémorial, 1960). These are all of the city, thus leading the reader to conclude that Verdun was like Ypres.

See as well the reference to the "fortress town" in the Army Historical Section, *American Military History*, rev ed. (Washington: Center for Military History, 1989), 368. This latter is one of the best succinct summaries of the conventional wisdom about the battle.

4   Population figures taken from *Guide Michelin* (Paris: Albouy, 1900): Belfort, 82; Lile, 163; Nancy, 194; Reims, 225; Verdun, 271. The nearest town with more than a few thousand people was Saint-Mihiel, with 5,250—little more than a village (244). The other neighboring villages—Étain, Stenay, Clermont—were so small they were omitted from the guide altogether.

5   Jules Poirier, *La bataille de Verdun, 21 février—18 décembre 1916* (Paris: Chiron, 1922), 58. Poirier is counting the flanks of Verdun, which extended down the heights of the Meuse on one side, and into the Argonne on the other. His point is that when the 1916 attack came, the French troops were widely dispersed, not in a position to respond to the attack en masse.

6   See the table in Michel Huber, *La population de la France pendant la guerre* (New Haven: Yale, 1931), 112. It should be stressed that Huber's compilations are critical abstracts of official government documents.

7   Gabriele Bichet, *Le role des forts dans la bataille de Verdun* (Nancy: Imprimerie Georges Thomas, 1969), 17–19. Bichet was at the time the director of the historic Verdun Citadel, and his monograph was issued by the Centre National d'étude et de Conservation de la Fortification Permanente. He was not simply a maverick historian, in other words. For the discussion of what to call the Battle of the Marne, see Raymond Recouly, *Joffre* (Paris: Éditions des portiques, 1931), 165.

8   Jean de Pierrefeu, *G.Q.G. Secteur 1, édition définitive* (Paris: les éditions G. Crés et cie., 1922), 13. See as well the discussion in Jean Galtier-Boissière, *Histoire de la grande guerre* (Paris: Le Crapouiilot, 1932–33) [Paris: Coquiler, 1919], 295.

9   David Lloyd George, *War Memoirs* (London: Odhams, 1938), 2.1313.

10   Lloyd George (1: 546). In *The Price of Glory* (London: Macmillan, 1962), Alistair Horne simply recapitulates this

conclusion (13), without bothering to inform the reader that he is simply repeating what Lloyd George was told by Asquith.

11 "On September 14, the Germans reached the Aisne," is how A. J. P. Taylor describes their retreat in 1914 in *Illustrated History of the First World War* (New York: Penguin, 1966), 34. Given the course of the river, apparently the Germans were retreating sideways. In *The First World War* (New York: Knopf, 1999), John Keegan repeats this assertion, making the geography even more erroneous, as he says that the Germans "retreated to the Aisne" (13). These are not simply slips of the pen; they indicate a basic lack of knowledge about key features of France, as though a Civil War historian were to speak of the Ohio River flowing into Lake Superior.

12 The notion of the enslaved peoples of Alsace-Lorraine—and the French desire to return them to the fold—was a staple of wartime propaganda. Like much else in this war, the facts are complex and obscure. However, the notion that the natives were enslaved, or being repressed, like the notion that the French were desperate to free them, hardly stands up to the facts. See, among the many, the analysis of Jean-Jacques Becker, "*L'opinion publique française et l'Alsace-Lorraine en 1914*," in *Boches ou tricolores? Les Alsaciens-Lorraines dans la grande guerre*, edited by Jean-Noël Grandhomme (Strasbourg: la Nuée bleue, 2008), 39–44.

13 Jules Verne, *Celebrated Travels and Travelers* (London: Gilbert and Rivington, 1880), 2:113.

14 Indeed, when I used the phrase "Champagne-Ardennes" in a conversation with a highly educated Frenchwoman, I was sharply corrected, lectured on all the reasons why Champagne was not in any way to be connected with a bunch of trees (the Ardennes is indeed mostly forest). She was not pleased to see a photograph of an official highway marker welcoming visitors to "Champagne-Ardennes." For ten years—up until her retirement—I worked with the president of the French Film and Television Critics Association, who became a good friend. I loved this middle-aged woman dearly, and my affection for her was exceeded only by my respect. But her prideful ignorance (she was a true Parisian) about her own country was a source of constant amusement. I

should add that the natives who live out there in the boondocks, in *France profonde*, heartily reciprocate.

15 All the distances computed under 15,000 meters are computed using the very large-scale (1 centimeter equals 250 meters) maps of the Institute Géographique National. These maps clearly show important landmarks, elevations, contour lines, and, where relevant, the exact locations of fortifications and trenches.

16 The length of the Western Front, and the amount of it held by each Allied power, shifted over the course of the war. The variation in the actual length is insignificant: At the end of 1914, it was 785 kilometers, and at the end of 1917, 750. In 1914, the French controlled slightly more than 90 percent of the front, but their share went steadily down: In 1916 it was 80 percent, and by 1917, 70 percent. See the table in Huber (112), whose figures are derived from official army documents.

17 *The New York Times Current History, The European War* (New York, 1917) 2:175. The interesting part of this comment is when the writer cheerfully speaks of "the uses" of journalism, that is to say, the extent to which journalism could be harnessed to the service of the state.

18 Elizabeth Latimer, *France in the Nineteenth Century* (Chicago: McClurg, 1892), 244–49.

19 Ernest Alfred Vizetelly, *My Days of Adventure: The Fall of France, 1870–71* (London: Chatto and Windus, 1914), 252.

20 Charles Inman Bernard, *Paris War Days* (Boston: Little, Brown and Company, 1914), 79–80. The preface is dated October 1914.

21 George Seldes felt this was one of the greatest scoops of his long career. His account of the German expedition appeared in *You Can't Print That! The Truth Behind the News, 1918–1928* (Garden City, New York, 1929), 24–40. To my knowledge no historian has made use of this interview. Seldes's career spanned the century, and when his accounts were repackaged and issued as *Witness to a Century* (New York: Ballantine, 1987), the book became a bestseller, and was praised by the *Columbia Journalism Review*. Needless to say, the von Hindenburg interview was reprinted in *Witness* (96–101).

22 M. L. Sanders and Philip M. Taylor, *British Propaganda During the First World War, 1914–18* (London: Macmillan, 1982), 143.

Endnotes

23   Charles á Court Repington, *The First World War, 1914–1918, Personal Experiences of Colonel Repington* (London: Constable, 1920), 1.56–57.

24   Jean Norton Cru, *Témoins* (Paris: les Etincelles, 1929 [reprinted Nancy: Presses universitaires, 1993]), 17–18.

25   As reported to Abel Ferry and recorded in his *Les Carnets Secrets d'Abel Ferry, 1914–1918* (Paris: Grasset, 1957), 35. Note the late date of actual publication; like the secret notebooks of Marshal Fayolle, Ferry's notes came to light long after the war.

26   Paul Allard, *Les dessous de la guerre révélés par les comités secrets* (Paris: les Éditions de France, 1932), 15. I'm paraphrasing. As reported, Maginot actually said that the Germans had lost fewer men than the French.

27   Martin Samuels, *Doctrine and Dogma: German and British Infantry Tactics in the First World War* (New York: Greenwood, 1992), 52. See as well the analysis of how this conception shaped German strategy in Jehuda L. Wallach, *The Dogma of the Battle of Annihilation* (Westport, Connecticut: Greenwood, 1986), 97.

28   Basil Liddell Hart, *The Real War, 1914–1918* (Boston: Little Brown, 1930), 216. Of course, this point is generally passed over in silence, as it contradicts one of the great propagandistic memes of 1914: that the Germans were trying to envelop Paris. As I pointed out in *The Myth of the Great War* (New York: Harper Collins, 1999), if the German commander von Kluck was actually trying to do that, he really needed a better map, as his actual position before the general retreat could hardly be squared with the idea (13). But the historians of this war are rarely bothered by actual facts if they get in the way of the myth.

29   Fernand Gambiez and Martin Suire, *Histoire de la première guerre mondiale* (Paris: Fayard, 1968), 1.79–80. On 297 there is an exhaustive list of what the authors term "secondary" operations. In this table isolated bits and pieces of the Verdun battles are mentioned.

30   Not all of the 56,056 soldiers were dead: 12,543 were wounded, and another 13,028 simply missing; but in the short term those losses meant seriously understrength units. Here is how one of the few detailed analyses puts it: "Of the 84 British battalions on 1 November, 18 had fewer than 100 men, 31 fewer than 200, 26

had 200-300, 9 only exceeded 300 but none had more than 450, that is, half strength." Peter Young and J. P. Lawford, *History of the British Army* (New York: Putnam's Sons, 1970), 215. Detailed figures taken from War Office [United Kingdom], *Statistics of the Military Effort of the British Empire During the Great War, 1914–1920* (London: His Majesty's Stationery Office, 1922), Table 3:253.

31   Winston Churchill, *The World Crisis, 1916–1918* (New York: Charles Scribner's Sons, 1927), 1:26–29. Although viciously attacked by British historians, and oftentimes quite wrong as to his deductions, Churchill's account of the war is not to be despised. The main reason for the attacks is that he made arguments that totally contradicted the delusional complacency of the conventional accounts of the war—as we shall see, notably in chapter seven.

32   *The Price of Glory* (London: Macmillan, 1962), 13. Subsequent accounts of the matter have simply elaborated on this summary; hence the epigraph to this book.

2. How Political Geography Dictated Strategy

1   Phillipe Pétain, *La bataille de Verdun* (Paris: Payot, 1929), 15.

2   Data taken from Charles Heberman, editor, *The Catholic Encyclopedia* (New York: Appleton, 1907) 1:342; Dominus Mondroe and Marius Culp, editors, *Encyclopaedia Catolica* (Vatican City: Vatican Press, 1948), 1:915. An enormous number of studies have appeared dealing with the complexities of the area and its relationship to Germany and France. See, among the many: Francis Roth, *Alsace Lorraine: Histoire d'un "pays perdu" de 1870 a nos jours.* (Nancy: Éditions Place Stanislas, 2010); Jean-Noel Grandhomme, *Boches ou tricolores? Les Alsaciens-Lorrains dans la Grande Guerre.* (Strasbourg: La Nuée Bleue, 2008); Eugene Riedweg. *Les «malgre nous». Histoire de l'incorporation de force des Alsaciens-Mosellans dans lármee allemande.* (Strasbourg: Éditions du Rhin, 1995). Note that all of these titles—and others too numerous to list—are published locally, and not widely available anywhere else. Even the most skeptical reader will find the

analysis of the popular folk songs of the region convincing. See Carl Engel, *Musical Myths and Facts* (London: Novello, Ewer, and Company, 1926) 1.8–22.

3   Herbert George Wells, *The War of the Future* (London: Cassel, 1917), 12. A reader of one of my earlier books wrote me and, rather humorously, observed that I was guilty of "Germanophilia, which is much worse than pedophilia."

4   See his extensive and candid revelations in Adolphe Thiers, *Memoirs of M. Thiers*, translated by F. M. Atkinson (New York: James Pott, 1916), 269–328. For the Gladstone quote, see Lord Newton, *Lord Lyons: A Record of British Diplomacy* (London: Edward Arnold, 1913), 2:334. The British government found the 1870 war, from beginning to end, profoundly embarrassing, as they were unable to admit openly that they were agreeable to the one thing that would resolve the matter—loss of territory.

5   A. J. P. Taylor, *Bismarck: The Man and the Statesman* (London: Hamish Hamilton, 1955), 62.

6   As quoted by Gerhard Ritter, in his edition of von Schlieffen's writings, *Der Schlieffenplan: Kritik eines Mythos* (München: Oldenbourg, 1956), 54.

7   Both quotes from Taylor, *Bismarck*: "dying man" quote (167); Pomeranian musketeer quote (105). For some reason the former sentiment is always repeated incorrectly: Bismarck actually said "Pomeranian musketeer," not "grenadier." The former term was still being used in the German Army in 1914 to 1918, as anyone who studies the markers in their military cemeteries can see rather easily.

8   There is an extensive bibliography on the history of the Maginot Line and its performance in combat in France. See Emmanuel Bourcier, *L'Attaque de la ligne Maginot* (Paris: ODEF, 1940); Roger Bruge, *Histoire de la Ligne Maginot I: Faites sauter la ligne Maginot* (Paris: Libraire Fayard, 1977), and *Histoire de la Ligne Maginot II: On a livré la Ligne Maginot* (Paris: Fayard, 1975); Paul Gamelin, *La Ligne Maginot: images d'hier et d'aujourd'hui* (Paris: l'Argout, 1979); Jean-Yves Mary, *La Ligne Maginot: ce qu'elle etait, ce qu'il en reste* (Paris: SERCAP, 1980); André Gaston Prételat, *La destin tragique de la Ligne Maginot* (Paris: Berger-Levrault, 1950); J. J. Rapin, *Une organization exemplaire: l'artil-*

lerie des ouvrages de la Ligne Maginot (Lavey, Switzerland, 1977); Michel Truttmann and Alain Hohnadel, *La Ligne Maginot* (Paris: Tallandier, 1989); Jean-Bernard Wahl, *La ligne Maginot en Alsace* (Steinbrunn-le-Haut: Éditions du Rhin, 1987). The effects of the German aerial bombardment of Schoenenbourg may easily be seen to this very day: a few eroded craters. The structures were completely undamaged. For an account of fortification building before 1939 and of Patton's fiasco at Metz, see John Mosier, *The Blitzkrieg Myth* (New York: HarperCollins, 2003), 28–42 (fortifications); 257–61 (Metz).

9   The best single account of Séré de Rivières and the forts is Guy Le Hallé, *Le système Séré de Rivières* (Louviers: Ysec Éditions, 2001). But see also Henri Ortholan, L*e général* Séré de Rivières (Paris: Bernard Giovanangeli, 203); Phillipe Truttmann, *La barrière de fer* (Thionville: Gerard Kopp, 2000).

10 Data taken from Le Hallé (*Le système*, 62–64). Two hundred and seventy-eight batteries were constructed between 1870 and 1885, but afterward there were so many that Le Hallé is unable to give a precise figure (63). For the importance of the 1885 date, and why that is used as a dividing line, see chapter three below.

11 General James Marshall-Cornwall, *Grant as Military Commander* (London: B. T. Batsford, 1970), 87. A point echoed, or copied, by John Keegan in speaking of Shiloh: "It was a tract of territory, indeed, on which no European army would ever have offered or given battle. . . . It was an entirely American landscape, one of those wildernesses which settlement as yet had scarcely touched," in *The Mask of Command* (New York: Viking, 1987), 167.

12 Général J[ean-Joseph] Rouquerol, *Les hauts de Meuse et Saint-Mihiel* (Paris: Payot, 1939), 31.

3. The War of the Engineers

1   Gabriel Bichet, *Le role des forts dans la bataille de Verdun* (Nancy: Imprimerie Georges Thomas, 1969), 1.

2   Report of the Surgeon General for 1920 (w1.1:920/1), 49. In this sense the Civil War was a modern war. French medical services recorded casualties from edged weapons at roughly one-third of 1

percent. See Michel Huber, *La population de la France pendant la guerre* (New Haven: Yale, 1931), 431. The German medical services went one step further and didn't even bother to record these cases.

3   See the rather technical discussion in Jules Paloque, *Artillerie de campagne* (Paris: O. Doin et fils, 1909), 142–54.

4   For the technical discussions of artillery, and the estimates of relative numbers, see General Firmin Émile Gascouin, *L'evolution de l'artillerie pendant la guerre* (Paris: Flammarion, 1920), 18–21; 38ff. There is a brief but extremely relevant discussion in the appendix to the English-language edition of Joffre, *The Personal Memoirs of Joffre, Field Marshal of the French Army*, translated T. Bentley Mott (New York: Harper, 1932), 2:597–600. See also the essay by Colonel Kauffer in Service Historiques des Armeés, *Inventaire Sommaire des Archives de la Guerre (N 24 and N25)* (Troyes: La Renaissance, 1967), 143–59.

5   Daniel Reichel implies that these guns were the divisional artillery. See his "History of Artillery in the Last Century, 1871–1971," Joseph Jobé, editor, *Guns, An Illustrated History of Artillery* (New York: Crescent, 1971), 171–72. This view is echoed by Ian Hogg, whose caption of the German 77 says it was the "mainstay of divisional artillery during the latter half of the war." See *A History of Artillery* (London: Hamlyn, 174), 138. Even the standard reference by Dastrup has only a very perfunctory account of the importance of medium artillery and mobility in his introductory essay: Boyd L. Dastrup, *The Field Artillery: History and Sourcebook* (Westport, Connecticut: Greenwood Press, 1994), 45–50.

6   Bruce I. Gudmundsson, *On Artillery* (New York: Prager, 1993), 29–30.

7   As even his most devoted biographer concedes, Sarrail's behavior in Greece alienated everyone, but Joffre, who believed (correctly) that the whole idea was militarily disastrous, probably thought that was simply a bonus. See the treatment by Jan Karl Tannebaum, *General Maurice Sarrail* (Chapel Hill, North Carolina: University of North Carolina Press, 1974), which treats the political situation entirely from the point of view of the left, but is forced to admit that Sarrail's career was marked by gaffes and blunders.

Sarrail was closely linked to André, one reason why Joffre couldn't simply sack him outright, even though his command in the Argonne was a disaster.

8   Marshal [Joseph Jacques Césaire] Joffre, *Mémoires du maréchal Joffre* (Paris: Plon, 1932), 4. There are substantial differences between the original French text and the standard English translation. Whole chapters in the French are not in the English: those on artillery, munitions, training, and budgets, which appear at the start of the text, as well as the detailed listing of Plan XVII.

9   Data taken from the archives, published as *Service Historiques des Armeés, Inventaire Sommaire des Archives de la Guerre (N24 and N25)* (Troyes: La Renaissance, 1967), 154. It is an illuminating comment on how little the British knew about their allies that in the official handbook the French army issued to their officers, the 105-millimeter howitzer was listed as in service at the divisional level. As the army had only 586 of these in service by the end of the war, the claim is hardly true.

10   See André Duvignac, *Histoire de l'armée motorisée* (Paris: Imprimerie nationale, 1947), 248.

11   General Staff [of the United Kingdom, War Office], *Handbook of the French Army, 1914* (London: War Office, 1914), 256–57. An excellent illustration of how poorly informed the British were about their ally.

12   Data take from Felix Martin and F[ernand] Pont, *L'armée allemande: étude d'organisation* (Paris: Chapelot, 1903), 495–97.

13   Fayolle, *Carnets secrets de la grande guerre*, edited Henry Contamine (Paris: Plon, 1964), entry of June 13, 1915, 111–12.

14   Although it is assumed that the French were mad for the concept of the offensive at all costs, the situation is much more complicated than that. As Douglas Porch explains in detail, the real problem was not that the army was committed to the wrong idea, but that it hardly had any agreed ideas at all. See *The March to the Marne: The French Army, 1871–1914* (Cambridge University Press, 1981), especially 249–54.

15   The first quote is from Ferry's entry of May 6, 1916 (*Carnets*, 160), the second from his entry of April 13, 1918 (*Carnets*, 271).

16   Georges Blond, *La Marne, Verdun* (Paris: Presses de la Cité, 1966), 13.

Endnotes

4. The September Wars for Verdun

1   Jean Dutourd, *Les Taxis de la Marne* (Paris: Gallimard, 1956), 33.

2   Data from Michel Huber, *La population de la France pendant la guerre* (New Haven: Yale, 1931). Mobilization figures: 96–105; casualties: 412–13.

3   See the table that classifies all the major engagements of the war in *Service Historiques des Armeés, Inventaire Sommaire N Groupes de divisions* (Troyes: La Renaissance, 1967), Annexe: 627–30. Despite the theoretical emphasis on archival research in contemporary history training, it often seems that a great deal is missed.

4   Maurice Genevoix, *Ceux de 14* (Paris: Flammarion, 1950), 61. This quote is from his journal, originally published in 1916 as *Sous Verdun*, literally *Under Verdun*, a significant title. Heavily censored, it was still considered for the Prix Goncourt; had it not been so mutilated by the censor, it would have probably have won. See the discussion by Norton Cru in *Témoins* (Paris: les Etincelles, 1929), who says, "Among all the writers of the war, Genevoix incontestably occupies the first rank" (142–54; quote from 142). His five-volume account of his eight months in combat, in reality one long narrative, was eventually combined into one text with the title *Ceux de 14*. For some strange reason, in the postwar editions of this classic narrative, the title page suggests it is a novel.

5   Gabriele Bichet, *Le role des forts dans la bataille de Verdun* (Nancy: Imprimerie Georges Thomas, 1969), 23.

6   A. J. P. Taylor, *Illustrated History of the First World War* (New York: Penguin, 1966), 38.

7   By January 1915, the front had stabilized to a measured length of 773 kilometers, of which roughly 170 looped around Verdun from the Moselle over to the western edge of the Argonne, and another 180 kilometers across Lorraine and then down the Vosges to Belfort. The BEF held 5 percent of that line, or 40 kilometers. The straight-line-as-the-crow-flies distance from the edge of the RFV to the western edge of the Argonne is more than 60 kilometers. Figures from Senate [of France] Report 633:186, as summarized by Huber (112). See also Ferry (167–70).

8   There are numerous photographs that show the existence of large forested areas even as late as July of 1915, e.g., in the 1974 edition of Pezard's *Nous autres à Vauquois*. Photograph 24, of the ancient Roman road through the forest, reveals a landscape on July 14, 1915, that looks remarkably like it does today. So does photograph 23, simply labeled "Argonne." See André Pézard, *Nous autres à Vauquois* [1915–1916] (Paris: Ranaissance du Livre, 1917; revised and amended: ([Aurillac: Imprimerie Moderne, 1974]).

9   The only account of the Argonne battles of 1914–1915 in English is J. M. Scammel's redaction of some rather propagandistic French sources, "The Argonne 1914 and 1918," *Infantry Journal* (October 1929), 354–61. Scammel is apparently unaware of what happened after September 12, 1914, as his account stops there. The best short account is in Buffetaut (*de Verdun, de l'Argonne a la Woëvre*, 31–36). The most comprehensive treatments are from General Rouquerol, *La guerre en Argonne* (Paris: Fayolle, 1931) and a very early monograph by Bernhard Kellermann, *Der Krieg im Argonnerwald* (Berlin: Julius Bard, 1916).

10   See the extensive analysis of French and German artillery in General [Firmin Émile] Gascouin, *L'evolution de l'Artillerie pendant la Guerre* (Paris: Flammarion, 1920). Classifications taken from page 28.

11   Marshall [Joseph Jacques Césaire] Joffre, *Mémoires du maréchal Joffre* (Paris: Plon, 1932), 71. As Gascouin points out, there was a further problem with the French guns. The German 10.5-centimeter howitzer had the same range as the Rimailho 155, and the heavier German guns all outranged the French weapons (*Evolution*, 18–20).

12   The flamethrower in the accepted sense of the term wasn't used until February 1915 at Malancourt, north of Verdun. Eyewitnesses seem to be talking about some sort of incendiary device used by the Pioniere, a larger and more cumbersome unit that is referred to briefly in Paul Heinrici, *Das Ehrenbuch der Deutschen Pioniere* (Berlin: Wilhelm Rolf, [1931]), 516.

13   The medium *Minenwerfer*, a 17-centimeter weapon that tossed 12 kilograms of high explosive out to distances of 900 meters, was a fairly heavy weapon for men to lug around, although it could certainly be carried by its gunners. The new 7.6-centimeter light

mortar delivered only about a kilo of explosive, but it was much easier to transport, and represented the first true infantry weapon for the Germans.

14   A marker a few meters south of the monument at the *haute che-vauchée* marks the spot. Gouraud is interred in the Navarin ossuary in Champagne, along with 10,000 other French soldiers.

15   Général J[ean-Joseph] Rouquerol, *Les hauts de Meuse et Saint-Mihiel* (Paris: Payot, 1939), 31. Details of the September fighting taken from Roquerol, 36–53; Yves Buffetaut in *La bataille de Verdun, de l'Argonne a la Woëvre* (Tours: Éditions Heimdale, 1990), 10–12; Henri Ortholan, *Le général Séré de Rivières: le Vauban de la revanche* (Paris: Bernard Giovangeli, 2003), 529–30.

16   Raymond Poincaré, *Au service de la France* (Paris: Plon, 1931), 5:327.

5. The French Riposte: October 1914–July 1915

1   Abel Ferry, *La Guerre vue d'en bas et d'en haut* (Paris: Grasset, 1920), 35.

2   Marshal [Joseph Jacques Césaire] Joffre, *Mémoires du maréchal Joffre* (Paris: Plon, 1932) 433.

3   The computations, listed in Ferry (*La Guerre*, 53) are taken from his report to the Secret Committee [of the war cabinet] of June 17, 1916. Ferry's elaborate calculations of French casualties were based on official army reports, and indeed are basically the same as those used later by French historians, e.g., Michel Huber, *La population de la France pendant la guerre* (New Haven: Yale, 1931), 410–12.

4   Joffre, (*Memoires*, 4). The standard English translation puts it slightly differently, but the meaning is the same. See Joffre, *The Personal Memoirs of Joffre, Field Marshal of the French Army*, translated by T. Bentley Mott (New York: Harper, 1932), 1:4. In his secret diary, Gallieni observed that he had been trying to get modern heavy weapons into the army as well: Joseph-Simon Gallieni, *Les carnets de Gallieni* (Paris: Albin Michel, 1932), 79.

5   A fact noted by John Buchan, *A History of the Great War* (Boston: Houghton Mifflin, 1922), 1:137. This is an excellent early history

of the war, and a fine example of British propaganda, as Buchan, a respected minor novelist, was employed by the government to advance the official story. The publication date of the American edition is extremely misleading. The first volume actually appeared in early 1915. The British were writing the history of the conflict while it was still going on.

6   Joffre, *Memoires* (76–77). Of course, the chief motive behind Joffre's account is to justify himself and lay the blame on the government. But the general attitude of the parties of the left, who governed the Third Republic, was a profound distrust, amounting to a fear of the army, an attitude with serious consequences, of which much more later.

7   There is a summary of the tests in Bruce I. Gudmundsson, *On Artillery* (New York: Prager, 1993), 30.

8   The explosives required for shells were all derived from coal and coke, just as coal was required for the blast furnaces. Before the war, France was heavily dependent on imported coal and ore, the bulk of which came from Germany and Belgium. See Arthur Conte, *Joffre* (Paris: Oliver Orban, 1991), 261.

9   Général [Alexandre] Percin, *L'artillerie aux manouevres de Picardie en 1910* (Paris: Berger-Levrault, 1911), v.

10   Georges Boucheron, *L'Assaut: L'Argonne et Vauquois avec la 10e division* (Paris: Parin, 1917). His description of the October attacks is found on pp. 59–80.

11   Joffre, *The Personal Memoirs of Joffre, Field Marshal of the French Army*, translated by T. Bentley Mott (New York: Harper, 1932), 2:343.

12   Boucheron mentions only the 270, but implies that there were also 155-millimeter guns involved, as well as the ancient 95s. There is a certain amount of confusion here, since Buffetaut speaks only of the mortars; in addition he speaks of a "batterie of obusiers de 200," which is curious, since there was no gun of that size in the French inventory. Presumably he's referring to the 220-millimeter weapons, which, given their caliber, could be termed howitzers (*obusiers*). To muddy the waters still further, Boucheron speaks of a gun of 150 millimeters, when presumably he means 120, since again, no such weapon existed. The confusion is probably typographical. See Yves Buffetaut in *La bataille*

de Verdun, de l'Argonne à la Woëvre (Tours: Éditions Heimdale, 1990), 35. This is the best short account of the fighting yet written. For the definitive list of the French artillery park, see General [Firmin Émile] Gascouin, L'evolution de l'Artillerie pendant la Guerre (Paris: Flammarion, 1920), 18–19, 29.

13 André Pézard, Nous autres à Vauquois (Paris: La Renaissance du Livre 1917), 63.

14 Service historique, Armées Françaises dans la grande guerre (Paris: Imprimerie Nationale, 1922), 2:520. Note that the volume numbers of this work are misleading; the work is actually divided into tomes, and each one is multivolume (in the normal sense of both words).

15 Gérard Canini, La Lorraine dans la guerre 14–18 (Nancy: Presses universitaires, 1984), 82.

16 General J[ean-Joseph] Rouquerol, Les hauts de Meuse et Saint-Mihiel (Paris: Payot, 1939), 131. Rouquerol also observes that the position had no real value (113). Both to General Rouquerol, writing in 1939, and to Yves Buffetaut in 1993, the position had no military value whatever, which unfortunately seems a fair judgment (Buffetaut, 51).

17 Maurice Genevoix, Les Éparges in Ceux de 14 (Paris: Flammarion, 1950), 565–69.

18 Service historique, Armées Françaises dans la grande guerre (Paris: Imprimerie Nationale, 1922), 2:501. Contrary to what is sometimes implied about official histories, the French one treats losses in surprisingly candid fashion.

19 Quote taken from the official marker at the entrance to the butte: a reminder of how much of the real history of this war is as much archeological as documentary.

20 See, e.g., Michelin Guides, The Battle of Verdun, 1914–1918 (Clermont-Ferrand: Michelin, 1919), 5. The claim has been repeated steadily since then. See the maps in Pétain (from whence most maps come), La bataille de Verdun (Verdun: Fremont, [1931]), 40–41. AEF maps are in American Battle Monuments Commission, American Armies and Battlefields in Europe: A History, Guide, and Reference Book (Washington: U.S. Government Printing Office, 1938).

21 Information on Henri Collignon taken from the marker erected at the Vauquois. He was 58 years old.

22 The front from the Verdun–Étain road to where it crossed the Moselle above Pont-à-Mousson is almost exactly 96 kilometers, but the upper end of this line, about eight kilometers, was apparently not part of the offensive. The Somme was less than 50 kilometers of front.

23 Including four batteries of 120-millimeter Longs, four batteries of 120-millimeter Shorts, and 155-millimeter Rimailho guns. Data on artillery strength comes from General M. Daille, *Histoire de la guerre mondiale: Joffre et la guerre d'usure, 1915–1916* (Paris: Payot, 1936), 2:41, 110, 179. See also Joffre, *The Personal Memoirs of Joffre, Field Marshal of the French Army*, translated by T. Bentley Mott (New York: Harper, 1932), 2:343–44; General J[ean-Joseph] Rouquerol, *Les hauts de Meuse et Saint-Mihiel* (Paris: Payot, 1939), 119.

24 The best discussion of this new structure is in Pierre Joseph Camena d'Almeida, *L'armée allemande avant et pendant la guerre de 1914–18* (Paris: Berger-Levrault, 1919), 208–19. Allied intelligence, optimistic as always, saw this as proof the Germans were desperate for men. For details on how the Germans formed more divisions, see Eugene Carrias, *L'armée allemande: son histoire, son organisation, sa tactique* (Paris: Berger-Levrault, 1938), 101–6.

25 Yves Buffetaut, *La bataille de Verdun, de l'Argonne a la Woëvre* (Tours: Éditions Heimdale, 1990), 46. See as well General J[ean-Joseph] Rouquerol, *Les hauts de Meuse et Saint-Mihiel* (Paris: Payot, 1939), 116.

26 Paul Cazin; this excerpt is taken from his diary, which he called *La humaniste a la guerre* (Paris: Librarie Plon, 1920), 117–26. Along with other members of the regiment, he took part in the attacks around the ruins of Régnéville and the bois Le Prêtre, and then returned to Apremont. On 23 July 1915, after four and a half months at the front, Cazin had a nervous breakdown and was taken to the hospital. Released in September, he served as an army interpreter, working with Polish prisoners of war. Although the *récit* Cazin titled "The Evil Night" reads like a work of fiction, it is actually a piece of reportage, since it was written a few days after the actual experience. The French historian Jean Norton Cru (the source for this biographical information on Cazin) authenti-

cated it as written shortly after the experiences in April of 1915, probably on April 22, since the passage is inserted between two brief entries marked April 23 and 24.

27 Georges Boucheron, *L'assaut: L'Argonne et Vauquois avec le 10ᵉ division* (Paris: Perrin, 1917), 95–96.

28 *Histoire d'une Division de couverture* (Paris: la Renaissance du Livre, 1919), 186.

29 [Colonel] Bernard Serrigny, *Trente ans avec Pétain* (Paris: Plon, 1959), 41.

30 Technically, the eight cemeteries contain 35,902 remains, but the ossuary of La Gruerie supposedly contains 10,000 of these, and one learns to be suspicious of ossuaries with 10,000 remains (or in the case of Verdun, with 100,000 remains). By contrast, about 17,000 soldiers are buried in the 15 Meuse cemeteries, about 112,000 in the 18 Champagne graveyards, and another 56,000 in the 21 cemeteries of Verdun.

31 As German cemeteries were consolidated from wide areas, comparisons are difficult. However, the sum total of all German war dead buried on the left bank of the Meuse through the Argonne—including the consolidated cemetery of Servon-Melzicourt, which includes about 6,000 remains removed from Champagne, and Brieulles, which is mostly devoted to Verdun dead—comes to only 34,000 remains, a figure that is all-inclusive through 1918.

32 British data from the official history, corrected for certain omissions and displayed in more elaborate form in Arthur Grahame Butler et al., *The Australian Medical Services in the War of 1914–18* (Melbourne: Australian War Memorial, 1930–43), 2:261. French data from Service Historiques des Armeés, *Inventaire Sommaire des Archives de la Guerre (N24 and N25)*, (Troyes: La Renaissance, 1967), Annexe 6, corrected for live prisoners of war according to reports made to the Chamber of Deputies as redacted and analyzed in Michel Huber, *La population de la France pendant la guerre* (New Haven: Yale, 1931), 135. German figures are found in Heeressanitätsinspekion des Reichsministeriums, *Sanitätsbericht über das deutsche Heer in Weltkrieg 1914/18*, (Berlin: Reichsministerium, 1935) 3. Tables 155–58.

6. France's Winter of Dreams and Discontent

1   *The Rise of the Roman Empire*, translated by Ian Scott-Kilvert (London: Penguin, 1979), Book 36, part 17, 538 (the last sentence but one of the work).

2   Lord Hankey, *The Supreme Command* (London: Allen and Unwin, 1961): his awareness of the defects in the artillery (139); the surprise about Antwerp (200); importance of the Channel ports (207). Possession of the channel ports enabled the Germans to begin submarine warfare using their rather short-range undersea craft, as these vessels would have been extremely ineffective if forced to rely on German home ports.

3   The key word is *modern*. All subsequent tanks in every nation followed the basic design of the Renault tank, with its rotating turret. In the last years of the war it was in mass production, with more than 3,000 produced, and was "a staple of French arms exports after the war. It also saw more combat use in the inter-war years than any other tank." Quote and data from Steven Zaloga, *The Renault Light Tank* (London: Osprey Publishing, 1988), 33. Although in the Anglosphere the notion of the tank is usually credited entirely to a British initiative, the French, working independently, were developing a tank at basically the same time.

4   The Gallipoli disaster has been written about extensively, largely because most of the resources committed there were from the Commonwealth, the Greek and Italian fiascos considerably less so. For Italy see Mark Thompson, *The White War: Life and Death on the Italian Front, 1915–1919* (New York: Basic Books, 2009). The view from the other side of the Alps is Gunther E. Rothenburg's uniformly excellent *The Army of Francis-Joseph* (West Lafayette, Indiana: Purdue University Press, 1976). For Greece, see George Abbott, *Greece and the Allies, 1914–1922* (London: Methuen, 1922). Both Abbott and Thompson write scathing critiques of the events they describe. Interestingly, however, when these campaigns are analyzed, their net impact on the main theater of the war is in various ways minimized.

5   *The New York Times Current History, The European War* (New York, 1917), 1:246.

6   4:1042–43 (comments by the British correspondent Beach

Thomas); 5:255 (an analysis by the American general Greene); 5:321 (an analysis by Edgar Crammond); 6:924 (summarizing an article in *The Economist*); 6:45 (an analysis by J. W. B. Gardiner); 7:705 (summary of an article by E. J. Dillon in *The Fortnightly Review*); 9:450 (summary of a study by the War Study Society of Copenhagen).

7   Charles á Court Repington [colonel], *The First World War, 1914– 1918, Personal Experiences of Colonel Reppington* (London: Constable, 1920), 1:112.

8   Fayolle, *Carnets secrets de la grande guerre*, edited Henry Contamine (Paris: Plon, 1964), entry of 26 June 1915, 117.

9   David Lloyd George, *War Memoirs* (London: Odhams, 1938), 1:545.

10   Data here and in the paragraphs immediately following taken from the exhaustive tables compiled by General Edmond Buat, *L'armée allemande pendant la guerre de 1914–18* (Paris: Chapelot, 1920). For 1914, see 30–34; for 1915, 113.

11   Joffre, *Memoirs*, 352.

12   J. F. C. Fuller, *Tanks in the Great War* (London: John Murray, 1920), 309; with numerous examples on the following pages.

13   Even though the importance of the one Allied innovation, the tank, was endlessly proclaimed, both by theorists like Fuller and numerous historians coming along afterward. In *The Myth of the Great War* (New York: HarperCollins, 2001), I examined the development of the tank and its effect on the battlefields, explaining how little was actually accomplished (229–32; 297–99). The point here is that although on the one hand the Allies were boasting about one technological innovation, they simply ignored all the other ones—probably because they were German. As a fine example, see the treatment of German aviation in William Lockwood March, *A History of Aeronautics* (London: Collins, 1921), where, in his discussion of aviation during the war, significant German innovations—e.g., the synchronization of the machine gun with the propeller—are systematically ignored (chapters 19 and 20). Some of this cherry-picking comes from genuine technical ignorance, as is probably the case with the recoil revolution, but to a great extent it is part and parcel of a determination to see the war through a distorting nationalism and Germanophobia.

14   *The New York Times Current History, The European War* (New York, 1917), 4:1043.

15   The impact of these fantastic notions on our understanding of the war is discussed in the conclusion to this book.

16   Abel Ferry, *Carnets secrets, 1914–1918* (Paris: Bernard Grasset, 1957), 52 (the note is in annex 6, page 248). Interestingly enough, this data is omitted in the recent edition edited by Nicolas Offenstadt (Paris: Bernard Grasset, 2005), 248.

17   Joffre, *The Personal Memoirs of Joffre, Field Marshal of the French Army*, translated by T. Bentley Mott (New York: Harper, 1932), 2.599.

18   As quoted by A. J. P. Taylor, *Illustrated History of the First World War* (New York: Penguin, 1966), 104.

19   Taylor (*First World War*, 120–21). A wonderfully sarcastic and succinct passage. One is reminded of Phillip Guedalla's remark about the famous British historian Thomas Babington Macaulay: "The comment recalls the writing of Macaulay alike by its eloquence and by its inaccuracy." Phillip Guedalla, *Supers and Supermen* (Garden City, New York: Garden City Publishing, 1924), 88.

20   Arthur Conan Doyle, *A Visit to Three Fronts, June 1916* (New York: George Doran, 1916), 66. An enormous part of Abel Ferry's work with the secret committee directing the war (actually, trying to get direction of the war) consists of a rather lucid exposition on how densely the British were packed into their section of the front, and how much of it they could actually take over.

21   The reader who finds this remark to be an unwarranted generalization should consider the numerous examples given in Ernest R. May (editor), *Knowing One's Enemies: Intelligence Assessment Before the Two World Wars* (Princeton: University Press, 1984).

22   The army was not anxious to advertise the extent to which it had no modern gun in service in quantity except for the 75. General Daille sums it up neatly enough. Of the "3,538 heavy weapons in service, modern matériel was represented by one 105-millimeter howitzer, of which the armies possessed no more than 78 examples" in June 1915. Quote taken from General Maurice Daille, *Histoire de la guerre mondiale: Joffre et la guerre d'usure, 1915–1916* (Paris: Payot, 1936), 2:179. See also the accounting on 2:41.

These figures agree with the ones Joffre himself proffers in the French edition of his memoirs. See Marshal [Joseph Jacques Césaire] Joffre, *Mémoires du maréchal Joffre* (Paris: Plon, 1932), 71.

23 See the technical discussion in General [Firmin Émile] Gascouin, *L'evolution de l'Artillerie pendant la Guerre* (Paris: Flammarion, 1920), 38. However, Gascouin goes to great lengths to demonstrate the gross inferiority of French weaponry.

24 Gascouin is a difficult writer, explaining a very technical subject. The sentences quoted are an attempt to render the gist of two pages of explanation. See Gascouin (*Artillerie*, 115–16).

25 Entry of January 22, 1919, as recorded by General Émile Fayolle, *Carnets secrets de la grande guerre*, edited by Henry Contamine (Paris: Plon, 1964), 323.

26 Arthur Conan Doyle, *A Visit to Three Fronts: June 1916* (New York: George Doran, 1916), 36. Doyle's account is the classic instance of what a thoughful and educated observer can see. He was careful not to draw any negative conclusions from his observations, which is why they passed through the censorship. But the details are significant—in the best Sherlock Holmes sense.

27 Those numbers were given to the cabinet by Millerand on February 4, 1915, as recorded by Abel Ferry, *Carnets secrets* (Paris: Grasset, 1956), 52. Note: The date was omitted from more recent editions published by Grasset.

28 The data taken from a report Ferry made to the government on November 1, 1916, as part of an attempt to compare the losses of the combatants. See the table in Abel Ferry, *La Guerre vue d'en bas et d'en haut* (Paris: Grasset, 1920), 120. These figures are very close to the ones compiled and published after the war.

29 The cemeteries containing the dead from the 1914 battles around Verdun are revealing in this regard. See, among the many: Lironville (one kilometer south of Limey-Remenauville, which is 15 kilometers west of Pont-à-Mousson); Les Islettes (on N3 between Clermont en Argonne and Sainte Menéhould); Buzy-Darmont (one kilometer north of the village on D167—the town is on N3, between Étain and Conflans). Markers with only a surname, or a few letters of the name, are not atypical of French cemeteries, particularly if they were contemporaneous with the

action. Similarly with the enormous numbers of unknown dead whose remains are in the communal graves. For example, in the cemetery at Esnes en Argonnes, there are 3,587 graves and two common graves, each with 1,500 remains. There are several graves with two or three sets of remains. Although French grave markers in theory have the name and unit of the deceased, and the date of death, in this cemetery there are numerous markers with no date, or even the unit.. The relatively few dated identifications run from 1914 through 1918. There are unknown soldiers with individual markers, plus unknowns buried with identified remains (two or three to a marker). These cemeteries suggest—correctly—a dysfunctional army.

30   Allied casualty data for 1914 and after comes from the following sources. For the United Kingdom, War Office [United Kingdom], *Statistics of the Military Effort of the British Empire During the Great War, 1914–1920* (London: His Majesty's Stationery Office, 1922), as subsequently corrected by Arthur Graham Butler, *The Australian Army Medical Services in the War of 1914–1918* (Canberra: Australian War Memorial, 1940). Both are official government sources. For France we have both Ferry's 1916 data in *La Guerre vue d'en bas et d'en haut* (Paris: Grasset, 1920) and the final figures in Michel Huber, *La population de la France pendant la guerre* (New Haven: Yale, 1931). Both are derived from the army's records and are universally accepted by French historians. For Belgium the situation is more complicated, but the information in Henri Bernard, *L'an 14 et la campagne des illusions* (Bruxelles: la Renaissance du livre, 1983), seems as close to an official accounting as it is possible to get. Bernard was a professor in the Belgian military academy, and his father was a battalion commander in August 1914 who later became a general.

31   The official German data is to be found in Heeressanitätsinspektion des Reichsministeriums, *Sanitätsbericht über das deutsche Heer in Weltkrieg 1914/18* (Berlin: Reichsministerium, 1935), 3: tables 8 and 55. When Churchill wrote his account for the war he sent research assistants to Berlin to confer with the men who were working up the data, which he then used to make his point about the relative superiority of the Germans in combat. See the

discussion in Robin Prior, *Churchill's World Crisis as History* (London: Croom Helm, 1983), 212–13.

32   Sven Anders Hedin, *With the German Armies in the West*, translated by H. G. de Walterstorff (London: J. Lane, 1915), 41. See his description of German wounded: "As a rule it is the left forearm and especially the hand that has been pierced by a bullet, the arm being carried in a sling. Here and there a man had an unimportant flesh wound in the shoulders, or his head had been grazed by a bullet . . ." (87–88).

33   The exceedingly complicated tables for mobilization are all displayed by Huber, but without any real explanation (*Population*, 96–105). But the conclusion is obvious, and made by several French historians: The French were running out of manpower.

34   Troop strengths from *Sanitätsberich* (3: table 55). The totals agree broadly with those given by von Falkenhayn in his memoirs: *Die Oberste Heeresleitung, 1914–1916* (Berlin: Mittler, 1920), 247–48.

35   His source was the former Dutch minister of war, the date of the entry 25 January 1916. See Charles á Court Repington, *The First World War, 1914–1918, Personal Experiences of Colonel Repington* (London: Constable, 1920), 1.112.

36   Fayolle, *Carnets secrets de la grande guerre*, edited by Henry Contamine (Paris: Plon, 1964), entry of January 1, 1915: 72.

37   The complete discourse as he gave it to the committee is in Abel Ferry, *La Guerre vue d'en bas et d'en haut* (Paris: Grasset, 1920), 35. In his secret diary, he records the response: Basically it fell flat. At that point no one believed him. It was only in July that their attitude changed. See Abel Ferry, *Carnets secrets, 1914–1918*, edited by Nicolas Offenstadt (Paris: Bernard Grasset, 2005), 99–103.

38   The complete text of the letter is reprinted in Gaston Jolivet, *Le colonel Driant* (Paris: Librairie Delagrave, 1918), 179. Jolivet reproduces almost all of Driant's letters during the war, and bits and pieces are usually quoted by French historians. As for the impact of the August letter, see the discussion in Jacques-Henri Lefebvre, *Verdun*, 10th edition (Verdun: Éditions du Mémorial, [1993]), who, rather troublingly, quotes Liddell Hart at length (22–26). The standard discussion in English is in Alistair Horne, *The Price*

of Glory: Verdun, 1916 (New York: St. Martin, 1963), 61–62, who, like Liddell Hart (whom he quotes), uses a somewhat scrambled translation of Driant's letter.

39 [General] Joseph-Simon Gallieni, *Les carnets de Gallieni, publiés par son Fils Gaëtan Gallieni,* notes by P. B. Gheusi (Paris: Albin Michel, 1932), 220.

40 The successive quotes are in Gallieni (*Carnets,* 217, 220).

41 Marshal [Joseph Jacques Césaire] Joffre, *Mémoires du maréchal Joffre* (Paris: Plon, 1932), 421.

42 Fernand Foch, *De principes de la guerre* (Paris: Berger-Levrault, 1921), 321.

43 As recorded by Jean Galtier-Boissière, *Histoire de la grande guerre* (Paris, Crapouillot, 1932), 240. As Galtier-Boissière points out, Joffre admitted that the name was decided upon because the battles fought all in some general way were fought in the Marne valley. Galtier-Boissière thoroughly debunks the myths of the battle in a chapter titled "The Truth about the Marne" (240–46).

44 This account is in Raymond Recouly, *Joffre* (Paris: Éditions des portiques, 1931), 165. Notably, Recouly is one of Joffre's more sympathetic biographers, and he had access to numerous eyewitnesses.

45 The relevant portions both of this letter and Joffre's answer (directly below) are to be found in Lefebvre (*Verdun,* 23) and in Blond (*La Marne, Verdun,* 273–74).

46 Blond adds an important detail to the exchange of letters: that Joffre "threatened the bearer of the news" (*La Marne, Verdun,* 274).

47 President Poincaré related this to his liaison, Colonel Herbillon, on 15 February 1915: Colonel [Émile Emmanuel] Herbillon, *Souvenirs d'un officier de liaison pendant le Guerre Mondial* (Paris: Tallandier, 1930), 1:116.

48 As we have seen from these brief snippets, Herbillon appears to be a reasonably cautious and prudent fellow, and although this is his diary, much of which is not verifiable, it hardly seems that he would have recorded how wildly off he was about the offensive when he was reassuring the president how events would play out unless it was the truth. Witnesses don't generally testify to infor-

mation that makes them look bad unless it happens to be the truth, and this interchange (*Souvenirs*, 1.243) certainly does that.

7. The German Gamble

1   As recorded by Louis Antoine Fauvelet de Bourrienne, *Memoirs of Napoleon Bonaparte*, edited by R. W. Phipps (1891), 2.13

2   H. G. Wells, *War and the Future: Italy, France, and Britain at War* (London: Cassell, 1917), 16.

3   Philip Guedalla, *Supers and Supermen* (Garden City, New York: Garden City Publishing, 1924), 132.

4   W. Somerset Maugham, *The Moon and Sixpence* (New York: Grosset and Dunlap, 1919), 14.

5   "It appears as though the effects of modern artillery were passed over in silence. . . . They reason as though German artillery did not exist" is how General Gascouin put it in *L'evolution de artillerie pendant la guerre* (Paris: Flammarion, 1920), 18–21. See as well the analysis in Pierre Waline, *Les crapouillots, 1914–1918: naissance, vie et mort d'une arme.* (Paris, Charles-Lavauzelle, 1965), 23, which also cites other references to the notion.

6   Raymond Recouly, *Joffre* (Paris: Éditions des portiques, 1931), 235.

7   See in particular the account of Gunther E. Rothenburg, *The Army of Francis-Joseph* (West Lafayette, Indiana: Purdue University Press, 1976), 185–86; and Norman Stone, *The Eastern Front, 1914–1917* (New York: Charles Scribner's Sons, 1975), 122–33. The authors of the two standard works on the subject both are in agreement that the plan for the May offensive was von Falkenhayn's and Conrad von Hötzendorf's, and most emphatically not von Hindenburg's.

8   Ferry transcribed the Italian ambassador's remark in his diary for a meeting of April 27, 1915 (*Carnet secret*, 105). For an analysis of just how bad the situation was for the Italians, see Mark Thompson, *The White War: Life and Death on the Italian Front, 1915–1919* (New York: Basic Books, 2010), the best and basically the only account in English of this part of the war. Like the studies by

Norman Stone and Gunter Rothenburg referenced above, Thompson provides a valuable corrective to the received wisdom about the war in the east, in Italy, and in the Balkans.

9   As quoted by Herbert Rosinski, *The German Army* (New York: Harcourt, Brace, 1940), 146, in support of his own argument that "the 15th [of September 1914], the morning on which Falkenhayn decided against a return to the mobile strategy of the first weeks, *that must be considered to be the real turning point of the war*" (148: italics in the original).

10   In the discussion of von Falkenhayn that follows I am relying on Pierre Conard, *Trois figures de chefs; Falkenhayn—Hindenburg—Ludendorff* (Paris, E. Flammarion, 1923); Lothar Wilfried Hilbert, *Falkenhayn: l'homme et sa conception de l'offensive de Verdun* (Verdun: Actes du Colloque international sur la bataille de Verdun, 1976); D von Wienskowski, *Falkenhayn* (Berlin: Siegismund, 1937). The conclusions, however, are my own. I cite these works simply as a counter to the very superficial and uninformed comments in the standard English-language accounts.

11   Gabriele Bichet, *Le role des forts dans la bataille de Verdun* (Nancy: Imprimerie Georges Thomas, 1969), 26.

12   Enthusiasts have been mapping and photographing the site for some time. See, for example, www.ww1battlefields.co.uk/verdun/marguerre.html. Although the road to the site off the highway is marked, it is quite a drive through the forest, and, except during the late fall and winter, the trees and brush obscure the numerous structures almost completely. Standing in the parking area, one finds it difficult to believe there is anything man-made around, as the buildings are completely invisible.

13   The site is still there, and can be accessed by a narrow road that leads through the tiny hamlet of Duzy, off of Departmental Road 105. The dates of this installation are clearly displayed on signs at the site. This gun is not the one described by T. Ehret in Trancheée, 11 (November 2012), 50–57. That weapon, also of 38 centimeters, was emplaced in the forest outside of Muzeray, slightly south of Duzy.

14   French and German artillery figures all taken from Alain Denizot, *Verdun, 1914–1916* (Paris: Éditions Latines, 1996), Annexe 2 (French) and 3 (German).

15   Totals taken from Alain Denizot, *Verdun, 1914–1918* (Paris:

Nouvelle Éditions Latines, 1996), Annex 2, 271. Unfortunately, Denizot (or the copy editors) converted all the German gun sizes to millimeters, so the result is extremely difficult to comprehend: For example, the actual dimension of the German 15-centimeter howitzer was not 150 millimeters, but 149.7, so the table has to be decoded.

16 All this information is taken from the elaborate tables in Edmond Buat, *L'armée allemande pendant la guerre de 1914–18* (Paris: Chapelot, 1920), 34–35.

17 [Lieutenant Colonel] Raoul de Thomasson, *Les preliminaires de Verdun (aôut 1915–fevrier 1916)*, (Nancy: Berger-Levrault, 1921), 137. Notice the date in the title: August 1915.

18 Erich von Falkenhayn, *The German General Staff and Its Decisions, 1914–1916*, no translator given (New York: Dodd, Mead, 1920), 243. The passages that follow are my translation, taken from Erich von Falkenhayn, *Die Oberste Heeresleitung, 1914–1916* (Berlin: Mittler, 1920).

19 In order to make this passage more readable, I have omitted a complicated qualifier that Fayolle used. He speaks of this war as a "*guerre de siège de campagne*," by which he means war in which heavy artillery has the same importance that it would in traditional siege warfare, even though it is not technically the siege of fortifications, since in gunnery *siège* and *campagne* were thought of as opposites. Fayolle, *Carnets secrets de la grande guerre*, edited by Henry Contamine (Paris: Plon, 1964), entry of 1 June 1915, 109.

20 Von Falkenhayn, *Heeresleitung* (181).

21 Not an exaggeration: On 21 December 1915, the 5th, 7th, 27th, and 78th battalions of *chasseurs alpines* had launched a final fruitless attack against the German positions on the Hartmannswillerkopf, a minor tactical strongpoint up in the Vosges mountains. During that attack, the general commanding, Serret, was mortally wounded and died a few weeks later. See the account in Jean Mabire, *Chasseurs alpins: des Vosges aux Djebels, 1914–1964* (Paris: Presses de la Cité, 1984), 150. Speaking of an earlier and even less successful attack in July, Mabire used the term *massacre* (145).

22 Charles á Court Repington, *The First World War, 1914–1918, Personal Experiences of Colonel Repington* (London: Constable, 1920), 1:56–57.

23   The whole sentence: "Behind the French lines there are many strong points, for possession of which the French leadership would fight to the last man to hang on to." The French leadership: *französische Führung*, the word derived from the same root as *Führer*, a German word that everyone knows (Falkenhayn, *Heeresleitung*, 181–82).

24   Arthur Conan Doyle, *A Visit to Three Fronts, June 1916* (New York: George Doran, 1916), 61.

25   A. J. P. Taylor, *Illustrated History of the First World War* (New York: Penguin, 1966), 121.

26   Winston Churchill, *The World Crisis, 1916–1918* (New York: Charles Scribner's Sons, 1927), 2:89.

27   Philip Guedalla, *Supers and Supermen* (Garden City, New York: Garden City Publishing, 1924), 13. Rather hilariously, he has the quote wrong. Beerbohm actually said something quite different: "History does not repeat itself, historians repeat each other." See Sir Max Beerbohm, "1880," in his *Works and More* (London: John Lane, 1930), 113. Add this factoid as an appendix to the consecutive quotes from Conan Doyle and A. J. P. Taylor, and you have everything that is wrong with historical writing in this century.

28   Helen Davenport Gibbons, *Paris Vistas* (New York: Century, 1919), 293.

29   William Roscoe Thayer, *Theodore Roosevelt: An Intimate Biography* (Boston: Houghton Mifflin, 1919), 165.

30   Michael Balfour, *The Kaiser and His Times* (New York: Norton, 1972), 527–29. These remarks are taken from the afterword appended to the 1972 edition, and not found in the 1964 original. This is an extremely important miniature essay on the numerous errors of modern German historians, and the snippets quoted do some violence to the sophistication of the argument, although not at all to the basic point here being made.

31   First quoted phrase taken from Lamar Cecil, *Wilhelm II* (Chapel Hill: University of North Carolina Press, 1996), 2:212. The second is from Martin Kitchen, *The German Officer Corps, 1890–1914* (Oxford: Clarendon, 1968), 19–20.

32   Charles Paquet, *Dans l'attende de la ruée: Verdun (janvier-février 1916)* (Paris: Berger-Lavrault, 1928), xi.

33   Lintier (*Ma pièce*, 107). Significantly—and ominously for the

Allies—this observation is taken from his diary entry for August 30—of 1914. The technique was simple: The aviators dropped flares marking the positions, which, given the low speed and altitude of aircraft in those days, made hitting the target rather easy; the gunners then observed the fall of the shells by their proximity to the flares.

34   Information from Paquet (*Verdun*, xii). Actually, the situation for Verdun was considerably worse. As Pacquet admits, the Central Army Group apparently had no specialists in the interpretation of aerial photographs at all (8).

35   Henry Corda, *La bataille de Verdun, 1916: ses enseignements et ses consequences: conferences faites en 1921 aux sociéte d'officiers suisses* (Paris: Gauthier-Villars, 1921), 35.

36   Phillipe Pétain, *La bataille de Verdun* (Paris: Payot, 1919), 14–16. There is a decent English translation of this account (London: Matthews & Marrot, 1930), but with different maps. Interestingly, the maps in the British translation show this distribution of forces quite clearly. The alert reader will notice that this figure disagrees with the figure cited earlier. In January 1916, the Belgians held 27 kilometers and the British 96, for a total of 133. So Pétain is being generous; the difference, however, is accounted by the 18 French divisions that were in the Anglo-Belgian sector. Official kilometrage from Michel Huber, *La population de la France pendant la guerre* (New Haven: Yale, 1931), 115.

37   Figures taken from Jules Poirier, *La bataille de Verdun, 21 février–18 décembre 1916* (Paris: Chiron, 1922), 62–65. The accounting given by the various experts is confusing, mainly because it's never exactly clear what area is being defined: the actual front (itself confusing) or the entire area going all the way down to Bar-le-Duc. And, of course, the time period is significant. Once the battle began, the French began moving in more guns, which explains why the extensive data given by some historians doesn't agree with Poirier's figures. To reconcile the two it is necessary to realize that Poirier is giving the count on February 20, 1916; the higher figures often used are for the end of the month. Compare his data with that given in Denizot, 226–27, although the arithmetical errors in Denizot's tables hardly inspire confidence.

38   See the very precise but somewhat bewildering summary of the

French positions in Fernand Marie Chaligne, *Histoire militaire de Verdun* (Paris: Charles Lavauzelle, 1939), 162–63. As a field-grade officer, his summary is preferable to those of civilians.

39   Pétain, *Verdun*, 21–22.

40   The actual quote: The Netherlands could "never again afford the luxury of another Montgomery success," as said to Cornelius Ryan, *A Bridge too Far* (New York: Simon & Schuster, 1974), 597. There is a curious parallel here between Montgomery and Joffre. The French commander never admitted his mistakes at Verdun, insisting that the objective had no military value. Long after the fact, Montgomery insisted that the operation, if "properly backed from its inception," would have succeeded: "I remain Market-Garden's unrepentant advocate." Quote taken from his autobiographical *Montgomery of Alamein* (London: Corgi, 1974), 267. It should be pointed out that although Ryan's book is a wonderful account, the catchy title is extremely misleading. The Arnhem Bridge was not the last bridge needed to cross the Rhine. There was a second bridge farther on. Although universally ignored, it was a very real bridge. Also, the last bridges were the whole point of the operation, which was to get across the Rhine: Failing that objective, there was no real point. The First World War was not the only war where one standard was applied to the Allied side, quite another to the German (and especially to the Italian).

8. The Most Famous Battle: February–March 1916

1   Paul Lintier, *Ma pièce* (Plon, 1916), 25.

2   The verb Fayolle uses, *abrutir*, does not mean "destroy" or "obliterate"; it means to render incapable of doing anything. In the next sentence (not quoted above), he links the French failure to the insufficiency of their artillery. Quote taken from Émile Fayolle, *Carnets secrets de la grande guerre*, edited by Henry Contamine (Paris: Plon, 1964), 28–29.

3   Fernand Marie Chaligne, *Histoire militaire de Verdun* (Paris: Charles Lavauzelle, 1939), 153. This is an excellent and succinct account, written from the point of view of a field-grade officer. In

the narration that follows I have depended heavily on it, but also on the following: Louis Gillet, *La bataille de Verdun* (Paris: G. Van Ouest et Cie., 1921); Jules Poirier, *La bataille de Verdun, 21 février–18 décembre 1916* (Paris: Chiron, 1922); Gabriele Bichet, *Le role des forts dans la bataille de Verdun* (Nancy: Imprimerie Georges Thomas, 1969); and Jacques-Henri Lefebvre, *Verdun, le plus grande bataille de l'Histoire, 10ᵉ Édition* (Verdun: Éditions du Mémorial, 1993), which is a reprint of a much earlier edition. The third edition, the earliest I have been able to find, was published in 1960, by the Paris firm of Durassié.

4   Even though, as noted above, Henry Corda observed that "the most important tactical lessons of Verdun concern artillery and aviation," hardly anything has been written about the topic. See the exceedingly brief essay in Alex Imrie's *Pictorial History of the German Army Air Service* (London: Allan, 1971), 30–33. For the Corda quote, see *La bataille de Verdun, 1916: ses enseignements et ses consequences; conferences faites en 1921 aux sociéte d'officiers suisses* (Paris: Gauthier-Villars, 1921), 35.

5   Casualties computed by Jules Poirier, *Les bombardements de Paris (1914–1918)* (Paris: Payot, 1930), 15–16. John McConnell at the United States Naval Academy has computed that German losses during daytime raids approached 30 percent.

6   Poirier (*Les bombardements*, 15–16). Total tonnage dropped on Verdun from Imre (German Air Force, 33).

7   Marc Bloch, *Strange Defeat: A Statement of Evidence Written in 1940*, translated by Gerard Hopkins (New York: Norton, 1968), 43.

8   See the extensive discussion in Martin Samuels, *Doctrine and Dogma: German and British Infantry Tactics in the First World War* (New York: Greenwood, 1992), which is one of the three or four best books written about the war. History of the evolution of the *Sturmabteilung*, 18–25; used as training units, 27; inability of British to grasp tactics, 53–55; failures of historians to grasp structure of army, 17–19.

9   The complete passage is his diary entry from June 13, 1915. See Émile Fayolle, *Carnets secrets* (Paris: Plon, 1964), 111–12.

10   Chaligne (*Verdun*, 167). It should be noted that this characterization completely contradicts the dramatic picture painted by British

accounts of this day's fighting, which describes French gunners firing point-blank into dense masses of Germans on the slopes of the right bank. How the gunners managed to get their elephantine and elderly weapons to the tops of the ridges on the left bank remains a mystery, although it is one anyone who hikes up the ridges will easily resolve: It is logistically impossible, geographically erroneous, and flies in the face of the accounts written by the French themselves.

11   John Terraine, *The Great War, 1914–1918* (New York: Macmillan, 1965), 208. And yet these very precise and detailed step-by-step accounts of the battle by French officers and historians had been in print for decades. Gillet's study appeared in 1921; Poirier had published his detailed study in 1922; the compilations of Lefebvre and the more restrained military perspectives of Chaligne appeared before the start of the Second World War.

12   The lowly colonel was Serrigny, the general Pétain. See the account in Bernard Serrigny, *Trente ans avec Pétain* (Paris: Plon, 1959), 56.

13   That is one version. There are others, even less creditable to Joffre, in which everything is de Castelnau's doing. See the summary by Herbert Lotttman in *Pétain: Hero or Traitor* (New York: William R, Morrow, 1985), 53. Lottmann references Abel Ferry's *Carnet secrets*, in this case not a convincing source, since Ferry was out of the government after the fall of the ministry in October 1915. Nor does the reference particularly support the contention.

14   The only extensive discussion is in Jacques-Henri Lefebvre, *Verdun, le plus grande bataille de l'Histoire,* 10ᵉ Édition (Verdun: éditions du Mémorial, 1993), 108–11, although there is a brief summary of the situation in Jules Poirier, *La bataille de Verdun, 21 février–18 décembre 1916* (Paris: Chiron, 1922), 108–9.

9. Panic, Politicians, and Pétain: April–July 1916

1   Jean Dutourd, *Les Taxis de la Marne* (Paris: Gallimard, 1956), 95.

2   All three quotations are taken from the excellent short account of Yves Buffetaut in *La bataille de Verdun, de l'Argonne a la Woëvre* (Tours: Éditions Heimdale, 1990), 63. He concludes by remarking

that "not a single word [of the French communiqué] corresponds to reality."

3   The lieutenant was Bernard Law Montgomery, who became famous in the next war as the general who beat Rommel in the desert. To be fair to Monty (not that many British historians are), he later annotated this letter: "My views on the fighting at Verdun were not in any way in accordance with the true facts." Both the letter and the annotation quoted by Nigel Hamilton in his excellent multivolume biography, *Monty: The Making of a General, 1887–1942* (New York: McGraw-Hill, 1981), 103.

4   Herbert Lotttman, in *Pétain: Hero or Traitor* (New York: William R. Morrow, 1985), concludes his summary account of the marshal's prewar career with a question: Was the reason for the blocked promotion "personal or political, or both?" (43).

5   See the observations by Serrigny (*Pétain*, 82). None of Pétain's wit comes through in his rather dry and bland account of Verdun, a book that makes Grant's memoirs of his role in the Civil War look like a flashy popular novel.

6   The officer was Colonel Edward Spears; the quote is taken from Lottman (*Pétain*, 49). In November 1914, Pétain was actually able to convince Foch to hold off on one of his massacres, and in May 1915, in Champagne, he was equally unenthusiastic—and quite correct. But in the eyes of the GQG, being right was a capital offense.

7   Philippe Pétain, *La bataille de Verdun* (Paris: Payot, 1929), 45. The word he uses to describe Joffre's demeanor is curious: It suggests a man who is struggling to maintain an outward appearance at odds with an inner panic. Regardless of what Joffre pretended, or what he thought about the military situation, there is no way he did not realize the political implications of the attack, given the correspondence with Gallieni in December.

8   See, in addition to André Duvignac, *Histoire de l'armée motorisée* (Paris: Imprimerie nationale, 1947), 100–5; Chaligne (*Verdun*, 178). The road up, the *voie sacrée*, is justly famous, like the legendary taxis of the Marne. But in reality, the French relied on motor vehicles to a much greater extent than is generally realized. Nearly 10,000 vehicles were immediately pressed into service upon mobilization in 1914, and the army was moving large units

entirely by truck before the end of October. On the other hand, none of the heroic measures of 1916 would have been necessary if the GQG had bothered to reroute the main railroad at the Aubréville curve. Given that it had been cut since October 1914, they had plenty of time to fix the difficulty. A point to remember when pondering Pétain's withering contempt and thinly disguised scorn.

9   Letter quoted by Lottmann (*Pétain*, 41) who cites private correspondence as his source and does not identify the lady. Although some generals (Grant, Fayolle) were devoted and uxorious husbands, it is interesting to note that some of the greatest generals had quite an eye for ladies, regardless of marital status (on either side), and that it was warmly reciprocated. Both Napoleon and Wellington come to mind, this last despite a certain primness foisted off by his biographers. The same is true of Pershing, after the horrific death of his wife. But many of the generals of this war seem ambiguous characters. In a Freudian world, it is difficult not to entertain certain suspicions. One can either laugh or sigh at Joffre's gourmandizing, but there's nothing creepy about it.

10   Joseph-Simon Gallieni, *Les carnets de Gallieni* (Paris: Albin Michel, 1932), 273.

11   Raymond Poincaré, *Au service de la France* (Paris: Plon, 1931), 7:143.

12   For a good many historians of those years, the framing of Alfred Dreyfus as a German spy justifies everything. Not only is this a gross oversimplification of a complex situation, but it commits the cardinal sin of evaluating 1900 in the light of 2000. France was arguably the most anti-Semitic country in Europe, and it remained so for a long time. "If someone had come to me in 1914 and said that one country would attempt to exterminate the Jews, I would have said then 'no one can be surprised at the depths to which the French can sink,'" George Mosse is quoted by Yehuda Bauer, as discussed by Ron Rosenbaum, *Explaining Hitler* (New York: Random House, 1998), 345.

13   As quoted by Elizabeth Latimer, *France in the Nineteenth Century* (Chicago: McClurg, 1892), 13.

14   Colonel Herbillon, *Souvenirs d'un officier de liason pendant le Guerre Mondial* (Paris: Tallandier, 1930), 1:106.

15 An exact translation of the French; the anecdote is found in Bernard Serrigny, *Trente ans avec Pétain* (Paris: Plon, 1959).

16 As quoted by Yves Buffetaut in *La bataille de Verdun, de l'Argonne à la Woëvre* (Tours: Éditions Heimdale, 1990), 72. No one else refers quite so explicitly to this telegram.

17 Jean Norton Cru, *Témoins* (Paris: Les Etincelles, 1929), 20.

18 According to the monthly totals maintained by the German medical services and reported in "Verluste und Ausfall bei dem Deutschen Feldheere im 1 Kriegsjahre 1916/17 auf dem Westlichen und Östlichen Kriegschauplatz," in Heeressanitätsinspektion des Reichsministeriums, *Sanitätsbericht über das deutsche Heer in Weltkrieg 1914/18* (Berlin: Reichsministerium, 1935), 3: Table 150. Interestingly, the only Anglo-American history of the war that makes any reference to this book is Winston Churchill's *The World Crisis* (New York: Charles Scribner's Sons, 1927). Churchill derived most of his numbers on German losses from the officials in Berlin who were working on this text, as publication was some years away.

19 Stephan Ryan, in his excellent and well-researched *Pétain the Soldier* (Cranbury, New Jersey: Barnes, 1969), argues that it was a result of negotiations between the two sides, which is to say treason, probably brought about by defeatism (93–94). Buffetaut argues that it was panic (71).

20 Henry Morel-Journel, *Journal d'un officier de la 74e division* (Montbrison: Brassert, 1922), 327.

21 Figures Georges Blond, *Verdun*, translated by Francis Frenaye (New York: Macmillan, 1964), 165. It always seems that historians assume that Allied units in these situations were at their theoretical strength. This was hardly likely.

10. Revanche and Revision: October 1916–August 1917

1 Speaking to the Chamber of Deputies, as reported by Paul Allard, *Les dessous de la guerre révélés par les comités secrets* (Paris: Les Éditions de France, 1932), 15. Actually, they were considerably less, particularly when the British and Belgian losses were added to the French.

2 The quote is found in Book 5, chapter 7, of Leo Tolstoy, *War and*

Peace, translated by Aylmer Maude (New York: Norton, 1966), 406–7.

3   Kaiser Wilhelm II, *Ereignisse und Gestalten aus dem Jahren, 1878–1918* (Berlin: Koehler, 1922). See the detailed index (294–309). By contrast, von Hindenburg gets an entire paragraph.

4   *The New York Times Current History, The European War* (New York, 1917), 7:iii.

5   The arguments made in the chamber are to be found in Allard, *Les dessous.*

6   Louis Gillet, *La bataille de Verdun* (Paris: G. Van Ouest et cie., 1921), 201.

7   Heeressanitätsinspektion des Reichsministeriums, *Sanitätsbericht über das deutsche Heer in Weltkrieg 1914/18* (Berlin: Reichsministerium, 1935), 3:140–41. The difference probably derives from the fact that the medical services apparently adhered to an absolute month-by-month computation. A soldier wounded in March who died in July would appear on the total for July. Medically, that obviously makes sense. However, if we're trying—vainly—to assign deaths back to actual engagements, obviously it presents a problem.

8   As reported in detail by Jules Poirier, *La bataille de Verdun, 21 février–18 décembre 1916* (Paris: Chiron, 1922), 294.

9   Michel Huber, *La population de la France pendant la guerre* (New Haven: Yale, 1931), 420.

10   A direct translation of the expression *"bien organisée"*; interestingly, in June of 1994, a French grounds supervisor at the cemetery of St. Thomas en Argonne used the same phrase in a conversation in which he was describing the administration of German military cemeteries versus his own.

11   Bernard Serrigny, *Trente ans avec Pétain* (Paris: Plon, 1959), 101.

12   See the charts in Edmond Buat, *L'armée allemande pendant la guerre de 1914–18* (Paris: Chapelot, 1920), which record the movements of German divisions from front to front, identifying each one. June–November 1916 (113).

13   See the marker on the wall of the fort. This division also had a number, 38, which accounts for the apparent contradiction on the plaques. The top plaque speaks of the colonial infantry and the 46th Battalion of the Senegalese and Somalis; the bottom refer-

ences the 38th Division. From what we know happened to the African troops in the April 1917 offensive on the *chemin des dames*, they were probably used as cannon fodder in the assault.

14   The source is Colonel Serrigny, the exact words: "We have the formula! We will beat them with it!" Bernard Serrigny, *Trente ans avec Pétain* (Paris: Plon, 1959), 113.

15   The mutiny was greatly exaggerated. First, as noted, it began at the top, with generals refusing to order more attacks and demanding Nivelle be replaced. The French term *collective indiscipline* is a more accurate designation. The units remained at their posts; they simply refused to charge off and get killed. Proof positive: There were approximately 700 soldiers executed during the war; about 50 were as a result of the "mutiny." But since the army refused to let anyone look at the records until the 1960s, the confusion is understandable. Nor is it clear that the records are very helpful. The standard French account is by Guy Pedroncini, *Les Mutineries de 1917*, 3rd edition (Paris: Presses universitaires de France, 1996). See the careful summary in David Englander, "Mutinies and Military Morale," *World War I*, edited by Hew Strachan (New York: Oxford University Press, 1998), 191–94.

16   Jean Dutourd, *Les Taxis de la Marne* (Paris: Gallimard, 1956), 13.

17   There are only two accounts of this offensive: Louis Gillet, *La Bataille de Verdun* (Paris: G. Van Ouest et cie., 1921), 253–74; and [Colonel] Fernand Marie Chaligne, *Histoire militaire de Verdun* (Paris: Charles Lavauzelle, 1939), 214–19. Gillet, like many French writers in the immediate postwar period, had access to much data since destroyed, and the battlefield was still largely intact, so his recapitulations are invaluable. Chaligne's brief summary is more restrained, but gets to the heart of the matter, particularly in his conclusions.

18   The pedant inclined to quibble is advised to consult any one of the standard French dictionaries used by high school students. The illustration of how the verb is used in the text is taken straight from the pages of the *Larousse poche 2008* (Patis: Larousse, 2007), 218.

11. The Last Battles: September–October 1918

1   Herbert Bayard Swope, *Inside the German Empire* (New York: Century, 1917), 113. Hopefully it is clear that Swope is referring to an incident that happened before America entered the war in 1917.

2   The best account of the Americans in France is John S. D. Eisenhower, *Yanks* (New York: Simon & Schuster, 2002).

3   In the midst of the spring 1918 German offensives, the Allies had finally decided they needed a joint commander in chief. They chose Foch. However, although he was the supreme commander, he did not have the authority to order the commanders of the three main armies to do anything—neither Haig, Pétain, nor Pershing. Foch's supremacy was thus largely fictional, but then, so was Foch.

4   Amazingly, a whole series of British and American historians have bought into this bizarre notion, attributing to Foch and Haig a level of military competence hardly supported by their records as generals, but certainly consistent with their press releases. See, among the many, the sympathetic account of what Foch was proposing in Donald Smythe, *Pershing: General of the Armies* (Bloomington: Indiana University, 1986), 174–75, a classic instance of how the failure to understand geography leads to errors in evaluating strategy. See the extensive analysis in James H. Hallas, *Squandered Victory, The American First Army at St. Mihiel* (London: Praeger, 1995), especially 261–65.

5   See the entertaining summary in Smythe (*Pershing*, 187), who quotes the impression of a German officer who said that Ludendorff was "so overcome by the events of the day as to be unable to carry on a clear and comprehensive discussion." The reader who has been led to believe that Ludendorff was the key figure is advised to study his record after 1918. Von Hindenburg went on to be elected president. Ludendorff was too weird even for Hitler and the National Socialists. The German general from the Great War who marched alongside Hitler in the early days was not Ludendorff; it was August von Mackensen.

6   It is easy to tell where the Americans got to: They erected distinctive six-foot obelisks with pointed tops, like dark miniatures of the Washington Monument, each with a red diamond plaque and the

unit indication. In this case, there is marker for the 4th Division posted on D903 right outside the hamlet on Nanteuil, due east of the city of Verdun, and proof positive that the Americans got there.

7   The best discussion of these sorry episodes is in Smythe (*Pershing*, 180–202).

8   The American data is a jumble of confusion. See Leonard P. Ayres, *The War with Germany: A Statistical Summary* (Washington, D.C.: U.S. Government Printing Office, 1919), 120.

9   The journalist was the experienced veteran George Seldes. Held up by the army censors, it was published ten years later in *You Can't Print That! The Truth Behind the News, 1918–1928* (Garden City, New York, 1929), 24–40. The interview was then reprinted in a final collection of his reportage, *Witness to a Century* (New York: Ballantine, 1987), 96–101.

10   This, the key quote, is found both in Seldes, *You Can't Print That*, 34–37, and in *Witness to a Century*, 98–99. Interestingly, Hitler believed American intervention was decisive as well. See Ernst Hanfstangel, *Hitler: The Missing Years* (New York: Arcade, 1957), 40–41. At the end of a lecture I gave on the Second World War, a historian asked me whether I still believed that the Americans had won the First World War. When I replied by quoting von Hindenburg, she retorted dismissively, "Oh, he just said that," thus confirming some of Voltaire's more sarcastic jibes about intellectuals. An interesting approach to writing history: Just ignore whatever you don't like.

12. A Conclusion of Sorts: The Temptations of Myth

1   Johann Peter Eckermann, *Gespräche mit Goethe* (Stuttgart: Philip Reclam, 1998), 311.

2   The famous Viennese literary critic Karl Kraus made this advertisement the subject of one his sarcastic essays, entitled "Promotional Trips to Hell"; it appears (in English) in Karl Kraus, *In These Great Times*, edited Hary Zohn (Manchester: Carcanet, 1984), 89–94. The translators mistranslated the German word *granaten* in the final sentence, rendering it as *grenades*—a common error. I have changed the word accordingly.

3   Transcribed from a personal copy of the letter (in English, but with French capitalization) in my possession. The emphasis is in the original.

4   Michel Huber, *La population de la France pendant la guerre* (New Haven: Yale, 1931), 413. There is no contrary data in the Service Historiques des Armeés, *Inventaire Sommaire des Archives de la Guerre (N24 and N25)* (Troyes: La Renaissance, 1967).

5   In the French original, the words are in capitals, just for emphasis. Yves Buffetaut, *La bataille de Verdun, de l'Argonne à la Woëvre* (Tours: Éditions Heimdale, 1990), 90.

6   Joseph Bedier, *L'effort française* (Paris: Renaissance du livre, 1919), 16.

7   See the extensive discussion, together with the sources referenced in this paragraph, in John Mosier, *The Blitzkrig Myth* (New York: HarperCollins, 2003), 28–42. There are numerous articles now available on the Czech fortifications; unfortunately they are all in that language.

INDEX

Index

Index

Index

Gladstone, William Ewart, 36
Goethe, Johann Wolfgang von, 323
Goiran, François Louis, 77
Gorchakov, Prince, 38
Gouraud, Henri, 110
GQG (Grand Quartier Général), 7, 9,
    11, 98, 117, 122, 128, 131, 140,
    142, 154, 155, 157, 160, 161,
    165, 175, 181, 184, 185, 187,
    189–91, 196, 198, 206, 208, 215,
    218, 220, 234, 236, 238, 255,
    259, 262, 264–66, 269, 274, 280,
    281, 283, 285, 287, 296, 301,
    302, 306, 310, 316
Grant, U. S., 60, 91, 100, 176, 227,
    324
Gravelotte, 39
Graves, Robert, 139
Greece, 24, 124, 153, 154, 157, 161,
    166, 174, 188–89
Grignotage, 146
Guedalla, Phillip, 197–98, 226

Haesler, Marshal von, 203–4
Haguenau, 35
Haig, Sir Douglas, 161, 163, 164,
    197–98, 204, 268, 291, 308, 315,
    316, 318
Halleck, Henry, 324
Hand grenades, 109, 146, 147
Hankey, Maurice, 151–52, 156, 221
Hannibal, 26, 39
Hartmannswillerkopf, 9, 40, 158, 198,
    218, 220
Hastings, Battle of, 331
Hattonchâtel, 113, 143
Haudainville, 268
Haudimont, 316
Haupt, Hauptmann, 261–62, 287
Haute-Chavauchée, 110
Haxo, François-Nicolas, 49
Hedin, Sven, 179
Herbebois, 251, 253
Herbillon, Colonel, 194–96, 214, 236,
    238, 252, 278
Herr, Frederick, 97, 129, 138, 215,
    266
Heym, Captain, 98–99, 101, 114

Hill 213, 149
Hill 304, 267, 273, 274, 277, 280,
    309–10
Hill 344, 253
Hill 378, 254, 260
Hindenburg und Beinecke, Paul von,
    20, 100, 157, 158, 200–4, 284,
    295, 303, 304, 309, 311, 314,
    318, 320–21, 333
Hitler, Adolf, 35, 40, 89
Horne, Alistair, 1, 2, 11, 31
Hötzendorf, Conrad von, 202, 205
Houdainville, 57
Howitzers, 76–77, 81–82, 98, 104,
    106–7, 113–14, 120, 141, 147,
    161, 168, 237, 250, 266
Huber, Michel, 178, 300, 326
Hungary, 166, 303

Indirect fire, 66, 74, 103, 108, 123,
    125, 242
Infanterie coloniale, 47, 48
Intelligence, 29, 111, 159, 160, 165,
    284, 303
Isonzo, Battles of the, 2
Italy, 24, 36, 124, 153, 154, 164, 166,
    174, 184, 188, 194, 202, 203,
    221, 303

Japanese military, 199
Jarny, 137
Joffre, Joseph, 79–81, 101, 107, 114,
    115, 117–22, 128–29, 131, 140,
    146–48, 154, 156, 158, 159, 161–
    68, 174, 175, 187, 189–201, 203,
    204, 206, 208, 213, 216, 217,
    224, 225, 234, 236, 239, 255–57,
    266, 269–71, 279–81, 284–85,
    287, 290, 291, 294–95, 301, 302,
    305, 307, 312, 318, 332
Journalists, 17–22
Jouy, 96
Jünger, Ernst, 139

Kampfgeschwader der Deutsche
    General Stabs Staff (Kagohl),
    247
Kitchener, Lord, 156

379

Index

Moltke the Elder, Helmuth von, 33, 37–40, 45, 55, 100, 201, 230
Moltke the Younger, Helmuth von, 100, 101, 201, 205
Mont Sec, 134, 259
Montalembert, Marc-René de, 49
Montfaucon, 15, 105, 124, 126, 130, 134
Moral, 90–91, 205
Mort Homme, 16, 267, 273, 274, 277, 279, 280, 308
Mortars, 70, 76, 104, 105, 109, 110, 120, 146, 169, 250, 274
Moselle River, 5, 35, 40, 54, 60, 112
Moulainville, 58, 59, 113, 267
Mudra, Karl Bruno Julius von, 104–7, 109–10, 146–50, 203, 207, 208, 210, 213, 214, 278, 290, 319
Mulhouse, 35
Muzzle-loaded rifled muskets, 65, 66

Nachrichtendienst, 284
Namur, 51, 53, 59
Nancy, 4, 14, 51, 95, 96, 112
Napoleon I, 26, 45, 78, 90, 91, 197, 205, 227, 229, 239, 275, 324
Napoleon III, 36–38, 78, 229
Netherlands, 51
New York Times, 17, 19, 21, 155–56, 160, 297
Newton, Sir Isaac, 73
Nice, 49
1984 (Orwell), 296
90-millimeter field gun, 121, 169
95-millimeter field gun, 122, 169
Nivelle, Robert, 285–87, 289, 290, 301–3, 305–8, 310, 311, 333
Nixéville, 94
Normandy, 320
North Africa, 47
North German Federation, 18, 36
Norton Cru, Jean, 22, 64, 139, 254, 283
Notre-Dame de Lorette cemetery, 327

Observation balloons, 132, 210, 245, 286

On the Principles of War (Foch), 191
105-millimeter howitzer, 81–82, 86, 98, 106, 147, 168, 169
120-millimeter gun, 99, 106, 107, 121, 123, 127, 137, 170
155-millimeter Rimailho gun, 81, 82, 87, 106, 107, 121, 137, 168–71, 237, 261
Operation Market Garden, 239
Ornain River, 94
Orwell, George, 296
Ouvrages, 50, 57–59, 331

Paris, 3, 49, 94, 153, 222, 247, 314
Paroches, 97, 99, 113–14
Patton, George, 90
Pau, Paul Marie, 79
Pauli, Wolfgang, 32
Pearl Harbor, 199, 239
Pemberton, John C., 91
Percée, La, 162
Percin, Alexandre, 125
Pershing, John J., 316–17, 319
Pétain, Philippe, 33, 51, 80, 91, 95, 149–50, 220, 229, 236–38, 257, 264–69, 271, 272, 274–81, 285, 290, 301, 303, 305–12, 315–18, 325, 332, 333
Pézard, André, 130, 131, 139
Phenol, 123
Picardy, 5
Pierrefeu, Jean de, 23
Pillon, 55
Pioniere, 104, 105, 109, 112
Poincaré, Raymond, 23, 114–15, 117, 183–84, 189, 190, 194–96, 198, 214, 217, 265, 269–71, 279, 284, 285, 296, 306, 325
Point C, 134, 138
Point X, 16, 134, 137, 138
Poirier, Jules, 5
Polybius, 151
Polygon, 71–72
Pont à Mousson, 35, 316
Poste à Bruyères, 15
Price of Glory, The (Horne), 1, 2
Prisoners, 92, 110, 137, 148, 176, 270, 271, 299, 305, 310

Index

Propaganda, 160, 182, 225, 230–31, 233
Prussian forces, 97, 141

Raffécourt mill, 274, 276
Railroads, 45, 46, 54, 97, 105–6, 108, 112, 114, 117–19, 125, 131, 132, 136, 214, 268, 288, 301–2, 321
Ravin de Dieusson, 110, 148
Ravin de Meurissons, 110
Raynal, Commandant, 289, 301
Recoil phenomenon, 73–74, 86, 99, 173, 242
Redoutes, 50
Regret, 255, 260, 268
Reims, 4, 55, 149
Reinforced concrete, 72
Rembercourt, 94
Renault, Louis, 152
Repington, Charles, 21, 24–25, 156, 174, 184, 219
Revigny, 94–96, 98, 101, 106, 112, 137
Rhine River, 33, 43, 51
Ribot, Alexandre, 195
Richelieu, Cardinal, 45
Rifles, 63–66, 250
Rimailho, Émile, 171
Riviera (Côte d'Azur), 13
Robertson, Sir William, 24–25, 161, 225
"Role of the Forts in the Battle of Verdun, The" (Bichet), 57
Romagne-sur-Montfaucon cemetery, 15–16, 319–20
Romania, 89, 153, 166, 174, 293–95, 303, 304
Romans, 26, 52, 54
Roques, Pierre Auguste, 129–31, 135–37, 139–42, 162, 270
Rotating turret, 88
Rouquerol, General, 139
Royal Air Force, 227
Rozelier, 58, 267
Ruffey, General, 95
Russia, 89, 90, 124, 152–53, 158, 166, 175, 184, 187, 189, 198, 201–4, 213, 221, 228, 287–88, 293, 294, 303, 309, 331

Saint Hubert, 104, 110
Saint Michel, 84, 267
Saint-Mihiel, 13, 20, 51, 53–56, 59, 84, 96–98, 112–14, 117, 118, 134, 140, 142, 143, 195, 198, 206, 207, 213, 314–20
Saint Privat, 39
Saint-Symphorien, 268
Sainte-Claire Deville, General, 171
Salonika, 154, 157
Samogneux, 253
Sarrail, Maurice, 79, 95, 106, 108, 129–31, 133, 135, 136, 147, 148, 162, 189, 199–200, 208, 278, 285, 315
Sarreguemines, 39, 43
Sartelles, 59, 268
Schlieffen, Alfred von, 94
Schmitz, André, 139
Schneider firm, 81, 106
Schneider howitzer, 82
Schoenenbourg, 44
Second World War, 43–44, 90, 91, 183, 199, 227, 239, 247, 329, 331–33
Sedan, 51, 330
Serbia, 184, 188, 189, 198, 202, 204
Séré de Rivières, Adolfe, 6, 48–49, 56, 63, 65, 71, 89, 100, 114
Serrigny, Colonel, 149, 280
7.7-centimeter field gun, 76, 82, 141, 237
17-centimeter mortar, 249
75-millimeter French field gun, 75–76, 80–81, 83, 86–88, 106, 107, 112, 120–22, 127, 168–72, 237, 302
Shells, 66–73, 75, 76, 83–88, 90, 102–3, 104, 122–23, 170–73, 211, 212, 242–45
Shiloh, Battle of, 324
Shrapnel shells, 172, 173
Siege artillery, 68, 70
Singapore, 199
Sivry-la-Perche, 59
65-millimeter mountain gun, 112
Skoda, 67
Smoothbore muskets, 65
Soissons, 14

Index

Somme, Battles of the, 2, 24, 25, 28, 149, 163, 164, 167, 198, 287, 288, 291, 293, 294, 296, 302, 304, 312, 323
Souilly, 94–96, 235, 266, 268
Soupir, 192
Souville, 235, 254, 267, 288
Spicheren, 39
Stalingrad, Battle of, 3
Stenay, 51, 53–55, 235, 302
Stevenson, Robert Louis, 270
Storm troopers (Sturmabteilungen), 249–50
Stralsund, 43
Strantz, Hermann von, 98, 111–13, 140–42, 146
Strasbourg, 35, 40, 89
Strategic bombing, 226–27, 246–48, 328–29
Switzerland, 89
Swope, Herbert Bayard, 313
Swords, 63

Talou, 253
Tanks, 109, 291
Tannenberg, 204
Tavannes, 57, 58, 267, 288, 301–2
Taylor, A. J. P., 1, 36–37, 39, 40, 101, 163–64, 225
10.5 centimeter howitzer, 82, 107, 114, 141
Thayer, William Roscoe, 231
Thiaucourt, 140
Thiaumont, 59, 267, 289
Thiers, Adolphe, 36, 38, 48
Thionville, 89
13-centimeter gun, 170
30.5-centimeter howitzer, 98, 214
38-centimeter gun "Big Max," 210–12, 214
Thirty Years' war, 43
305-centimeter gun, 212
Tittoni, Tomaso, 203
TNP (trinitrophenol), 69, 73, 123, 172
TNT (trinitrotoluene), 69, 70, 172
Tolstoy, Leo, 295
Toul, 51, 54, 56, 59, 96, 192, 193, 258

Tourelle à éclipse (disappearing turret), 85–87, 89
Tranchée de Calonne, 143
Trémeau, General, 77
Trench warfare, 203–4, 210, 242, 243
Trinitrates, 69–70
Troyon, 57, 96–101, 112, 114, 258
Turkey, 24, 124, 153, 161, 174
21-centimeter howitzer, 98, 106, 109, 114, 214, 237, 250
210-millimeter howitzer, 147
220-millimeter mortar, 70, 84, 129, 171
270-millimeter mortar, 84, 129

Vacherauville, 59, 252, 267
Varennes-en-Argonne, 105, 107, 129, 130
Vauban, Marquis de, 49, 63
Vauche forest, 254, 261
Vauquois, 6, 15–16, 106, 107, 118–20, 124–37, 150, 162, 175, 198, 206, 207, 218, 259, 268, 272, 273
Vaux, 57, 113, 211, 255, 267, 279, 288–89, 301, 304
Vaux-Chapitre woods, 289
Velosne, 320
Verdun
    First Battle for, 27–29, 96–101, 124
    Second Battle for, 28–30, 101–15, 124
    Third Battle for, 28, 115, 118–20, 124–37, 218
    Fourth Battle for, 28, 29, 118, 119, 134–45, 218
    Fifth Battle for, 6–8, 11–12, 26, 28, 29, 167, 183, 195, 220, 225, 241–91, 293, 296, 300–1
    Sixth Battle for, 28, 303–6
    Seventh Battle for, 12, 26, 308–10
    Eighth Battle for, 28, 30, 314–18
    Ninth Battle for, 28, 30, 314–16, 319–21
Verne, Jules, 14
Vicksburg, siege of, 3, 91
Vignes Rouges, Jean de, 139
Viviani, René, 189, 195
Vizetelly, Alfred, 18

Index